FOOD & POWER

Thank you for choosing a SAGE product!
If you have any comment, observation or feedback,
I would like to personally hear from you.

Please write to me at **contactceo@sagepub.in**

Vivek Mehra, Managing Director and CEO, SAGE India.

Bulk Sales

SAGE India offers special discounts
for purchase of books in bulk.
We also make available special imprints
and excerpts from our books on demand.

For orders and enquiries, write to us at

Marketing Department
SAGE Publications India Pvt Ltd
B1/I-1, Mohan Cooperative Industrial Area
Mathura Road, Post Bag 7
New Delhi 110044, India

E-mail us at **marketing@sagepub.in**

Subscribe to our mailing list
Write to **marketing@sagepub.in**

This book is also available as an e-book.

FOOD&POWER

Expressions of Food-Politics in South Asia

Edited by

KANCHAN MUKHOPADHYAY

Los Angeles | London | New Delhi
Singapore | Washington DC | Melbourne

First published in 2020 by

SAGE Publications India Pvt Ltd
B1/I-1 Mohan Cooperative Industrial Area
Mathura Road, New Delhi 110 044, India
www.sagepub.in

SAGE Publications Inc
2455 Teller Road
Thousand Oaks, California 91320, USA

SAGE Publications Ltd
1 Oliver's Yard, 55 City Road
London EC1Y 1SP, United Kingdom

SAGE Publications Asia-Pacific Pte Ltd
18 Cross Street #10-10/11/12
China Square Central
Singapore 048423

Published by Vivek Mehra for SAGE Publications India Pvt Ltd and typeset in 10.5/12.5 pt ITC Stone Serif by AG Infographics, Delhi.

Library of Congress Cataloging-in-Publication Data

Names: Mukhopadhyay, Kanchan, editor.
Title: Food and power : expressions of food-politics / [edited by] Kanchan Mukhopadhyay.
Description: Thousand Oaks : SAGE Publications India Pvt Ltd, 2020. | Includes bibliographical references and index. |
Identifiers: LCCN 2020008933 (print) | LCCN 2020008934 (ebook) | ISBN 9789353883768 (hardback) | ISBN 9789353883775 (epub) | ISBN 9789353883782 (ebook)
Subjects: LCSH: Food supply—Political aspects. | Food supply—Social aspects. | Food habits. | Food preferences.
Classification: LCC HD9000.6.F5854 2020 (print) | LCC HD9000.6 (ebook) | DDC 338.1/9—dc23
LC record available at https://lccn.loc.gov/2020008933
LC ebook record available at https://lccn.loc.gov/2020008934

ISBN: 978-93-5388-376-8 (HB)

SAGE Team: Rajesh Dey, Vandana Gupta and Rajinder Kaur

Contents

List of Figures

List of Tables

Introduction

In a plural and hierarchical society, lifeways of component social groups are often influenced by their respective position with respect to that of others. It is obvious that those placed in lower rungs of the hierarchical order would find their condition unsatisfactory and they possibly would aspire to lead a life similar to those in the higher layers. The relatively fortunate ones may not like the idea of sharing resources and privileges with others, but in almost all situations they would want all sections of the society to accept their ideologies that rationalize existing hierarchies and exclusivity of their privileges. Ideas and practices related to food are integral components of varied forms of lifeways that are influenced by dominant ideologies of social and economic inequalities (and sometimes by rebel ideologies favouring equality).

In South Asian societies, preference for or avoidance of certain food items on the basis of caste, class, gender, religion, regional and ecological factors has long been studied by social scientists, especially by anthropologists, almost since the beginning of ethnographic tradition in this part of the world. The other crucial issue dealt with by them in detail was inter-community food relations. Quality and quantity of such transactions (or lack of any transaction at all) have been used to comprehend relative social distance between communities. More critical studies took notice of ritual pollution as an integrating factor (Mayer 1960, 1996; Harper 1964) and matrix analysis to assess caste ranking (Marriot 1964). Theories of universal nature were tested in India and in neighbouring countries by Harris (1966), Yalman (1969), Simon (1970), Hanchett (1975) and Khare (1976) in varied fields like cultural ecology, ceremonial reciprocity, cognition and symbols in food.

Another genre of study that has relevance to the present context focused on politics and political economy of food in India and its neighbourhood. Situations of unequal distribution of food at national and regional levels and even at household level, hunger, malnourishment, acute scarcity of grains affecting large sections of South Asian population were critically studied. Some representative studies of this genre are Boyce and Hartman (1979), Prindle (1979), Sanyal (1979), Alamgir (1980), Chen (1980), Appadurai (1981), Chen et al. (1981), Greenough (1982), Hartman (1983), Abdullah and Wheeler (1985), Nichter (1985), Breckenridge (1986), McAlpin (1987), Chatterjee (1989), Patnaik (1991), Chakrabarty (1996) and Kelleher (1997).

Several studies have examined the use of food, and cookbooks became the identity markers for diasporic communities in different parts of the world as well as back in the home countries (Appadurai 1988a, 1988b; Rao 1986). Essays presented in an edited book (Khare 1992) have dealt with gastronomic ideas and experiences of some Hindu and the Buddhist communities (for a detailed review, see Mukhopadhyay 2011).

The principal argument presented in this book is that food practices of a people is a product of multiple factors. People often eat what they prefer to eat, but it is not so simple always. Sometimes they eat what is available to them or what they are asked to eat. Thus, their natural or cultural preferences are interfered with by hegemonic factors capable of influencing their opinion. In India and its neighbouring countries combination of factors like religion, caste and analogous systems of social ranking of a group of people, and their economic standing often delimit their food practices. The dominant sections of the local or regional society play a major role in affecting their food practices; in addition, the state and market forces too impact food-related behaviour of people by exercising control over production and trade of food and its availability and accessibility to the consumers.

The present volume envisages to understand the nuances of power relation between those who eat and those who decide (or at least try to decide) what others should eat. Gastro-politics, as defined by Appadurai (1981, 495), is 'conflict or competition over specific cultural or economic resources as it emerges in social transactions around food'. In a stratified society where different groups have differential access to either kind of resources, manifestations of power relations are bound to be varied. Chapters presented in this volume have examined food practices as expressions of varied forms of power relations; each study has examined the extent and nuances of cultural hegemony, sometimes loud and at other times subtle, and how those dominated have adjusted to ascendancy and at times how they have resisted hegemony.

Chapters of this book reflect the diversity of food scenario in India and its neighbouring countries in a smaller scale. Different authors are specialized in various subjects including anthropology, geography, history and linguistics, some are social activists. Among the authors there are very senior researchers as well as relatively junior ones, but each one of them has worked for years on the subject they have written upon. Three of the authors belong to the communities they have written about, those auto-ethnographical accounts present views of the insiders with authenticity.

The book can notionally be divided in two parts, the first seven chapters present broader perspectives of the problems identified in the preceding paragraphs; some of those are regional in character and have covered a large part of India, while others have dealt with relatively local issues. While chapters authored by Ziya Us Salam, M Sreenathan and Svetlana Ryzhakova have taken a broad sweep of either Northern or Dravidian-speaking Southern states of India, Sumit Mukherjee has confined his study to the cold desert of Spiti in Himachal Pradesh, India, and Ala Uddin to the Chittagong Hill Tracts, Bangladesh. The second part contains chapters that take closer view at the issues; while Vishvajit Pandya and Madhumita Mazumdar have critically examined interactions between the Jarawas of Andaman Islands and 'others', study of the Chepangs of Nepal by Om Gurung and Uddhav Rai has also followed the tradition of ethnography of small endogamous groups, Urmimala Sarkar Munsi and Chhanda Mukhopadhyay have adopted discrete positions through their work on student community of a university campus and of the occupational group of sex-workers in a metropolitan city respectively. Shibani Roy's reflexive commentary on food practices of two families in Old Delhi presents a further departure in scale and scope.

The studies may initially seem disjointed, but certain issues run through the works and reveal links that bind a large number of communities of South Asia with all their social, cultural, economic and political variations and complexities. As most of the authors have appropriated the bottom-up approach in their study, they reveal how the dominated people adjust to hegemony of different forms and what strategies they adopt to resist domination in different times and space. Ratna Dhar has discussed how the Muslim Manganiyars of Rajasthan try to identify themselves with the culture and food ethos of their Hindu Rajput clients; they take recourse to the past and connect it with their present for the purpose. Saradindu Biswas offers a counterpoint with his narrative of the Chandals, a large section of whom have opposed Brahmanical domination for long not only ideologically, but politically too. A similar phenomenon was observed among the Santals; as noted by Kanchan Mukhopadhyay, the community challenged *diku* hegemony *whenever* they could.

The extent of economic dependence on dominant sections of society is one major reason for the variation. When the people ascribed with lower position can gain independent access to economic resources, as was the case with the Chandals in some parts of Bengal, there would be a higher probability of their challenging the hegemonic orders. Oscillation of the Santals between their traditional religious practices when food was available to them and Vaishnava form of Hinduism in times of food scarcity supports the proposition. However, economic determinism does not hold good in all situations. While discussing gastric ideas and practices among classical musicians of North India, Svetlana Ryzhakova has brought to the fore another form of adjustment. The practitioners share certain common ideologies among themselves irrespective of religious affiliation of the individuals; food and human body are often used as metaphors by them to converse about music. Those ideologies enjoy relative independence from pronouncements of major institutional religions. Ethnic identities get blurred among the marginalized sex workers residing in city brothels, reports Chhanda Mukhopadhyay, which affects their food practices to a large extent.

In her chapter on materiality of Boro food culture, Dharitri Narzary has argued inseparability of tangible and intangible forms of culture and its association with the spiritual world and worldview of the people. She has highlighted the role of socio-political factors to create cultural marginalization and has claimed that such marginalization based on discriminatory evaluation of cultural practices creates the foundation for reinventing traditions.

Relationship between ethnic identity and food has been discussed since long. Chapters by Sumit Mukherjee on Spiti Valley, by Shiba Desor, Manish Chandi, Saw John Aung Thong on the Karens have examined the issue from different angles. Market forces that have made inroads into Spiti Valley have tilted the equilibrium—the food item which was linked to their identity—*tsampa* or roasted barley flour—is losing popularity among younger persons. But the people are apparently happy because cash crop has made them money-rich. The Karens, on the other hand, have shown resilience to cope with the changing situations and keep their identity intact. Both the situations mentioned here negate the primordial view of ethnicity; those can be better explained as 'mediation of social relations and ... negotiation of access to resources, primarily economic and political resources' (Jones 1997), that is in tune with the instrumentalist approach.

Food has been used as a tool to dominate or to counter domination in different ways. Vishvajit Pandya and Madhumita Mazumdar have shown how food, especially rice, has been used to exercise authority over the Jarawas. The student community has used rejection of food as a political tool to challenge the domination, as has been described by Urmimala Sarkar Munsi. B. Francis Kulirani has shown how orthodox and discriminatory caste rules were defied in Kerala more than a century back through *panthibhojanam* or eating together sitting in a row. Moumita Dey has discussed expressions of gender politics related to food among the educated and relatively affluent urban people. She has noted that women are discriminated against and, in most cases, the perpetrators have been women themselves. This brings to the fore the problems of consciousness and false consciousness. Among all items of food, beef undoubtedly is the most politically used tool in India, so much so that cow has been treated as a 'political animal'.[1] The chapter by Ziya Us Salam has shed some light on this much discussed and debated issue.

Despite all debates and protest movements, certain values and preferences related to food are widely shared by many communities in the sub-continent. The millet-eaters admit, rice is a much preferred food, even when they cannot afford to procure it. This is valid in Nepal or among the Santals in Eastern India. Such scheme of ranking edible items is often dictated by dominant views held by the socially, economically and politically powerful ones. While listing principal food items of any region, often the cultivated ones are mentioned first relegating the wild and non-domesticated food items to a less preferred position. Brahmins in Nepal do not eat such food, and as has been noted by Nabakumar Duary, foraged items and their sellers are given peripheral or marginal space in a rural market.

The chapter written by Amitabha Sarkar is particularly relevant for the present times. He has described in detail how the Dandami Maria of Bastar have remained connected with their forested environment for fulfilling their material and spiritual needs, including food requirements. The author has flagged the issue of industrialization and of setting up mines in their habitat; he has tried to assess the impact of such activities on life of a community largely dependent on local eco-system. We feel a shudder to realize; we possibly have entered a road of no return.

The editor of this book sincerely hopes that the topics discussed here will be helpful for researchers and academicians in their scholarly endeavours. He is equally hopeful, those engaged in activism or in action research would find ideas and information presented here relevant for their activities.

Note

1. see https://in.news.yahoo.com/why-is-the-cow-a-political-animal-110119929.html

References

Abdullah, M. and E. F. Wheeler. 1985. 'Seasonal Variations in the Intra-Household Distribution of Food in Bangladeshi Village'. *American Journal of Clinical Nutrition* 41: 1305–1313.

Alamgir, M. 1980. *Famine in South Asia: Political Economy of Mass Starvation*. Cambridge, MA: Gunn and Hain, Oelgeschlager.

Appadurai, A. 1981. 'Gastro Politics in Hindu South Asia'. *American Ethnologist* 8: 494–511.

———. 1988a. 'Cookbooks and Cultural Change: The Indian Case'. *Comparative Studies in Society and History* 30 (1): 3–24.

———. 1988b. 'How to Make a National Cuisine: Cookbooks in Contemporary India'. *Comparative Studies in Society and History* 30 (1): 3–24.

Boyce, J. and B. Hartman. 1979. *Needless Hunger, Voices from a Bangladesh Village*. San Francisco, CA: Institute for Food and Development Policy.

Breckenridge, C. 1986. 'Food, Politics, and Pilgrimage in South India, 1350–1650', in R. S. Khare and M. S. A. Rao (eds), *Food, Society, and Culture: Aspects of South Asian Food Systems*. Durham, NC: Carolina Academic Press.

Chakrabarty, M. 1996. 'Gender Differences in Cereal Intake: Possible Impacts of Social Group Affiliation and Season'. *Anthropologisher Anzeiger* 54 (4).

Chatterjee, M. 1989. 'Socio-Economic and Socio-Cultural Influences on Women's Nutritional Status and Roles', in C. Gopalan and S. Kaur (eds), *Women and Nutrition in India*. Nutritional Foundation of India.

Chen, L. 1980. 'Seasonal Dimensions of Energy Protein Malnutrition in Rural Bangladesh'. *Ecology of Food and Nutrition* 8: 175–187.

Chen, L., E. Huq and S. d'Souza S. 1981. 'Sex Bias in the Family Allocation of Food and Health Care in Rural Bangladesh'. *Population and Development Review* 7: 55–70.

Greenough, P. 1982. *Prosperity and Misery in Modern Bengal*. New York: Oxford University Press.

Hanchett, S. 1975. 'Hindu Potlatches: Ceremonial Reciprocity and Prestige in Karnataka'. In *Competition and Modernization in South Asia*, edited by H. E. Ullrich, 27–59. New Delhi: Abhinav Publications.

Harper, E. 1964. 'Ritual Pollution as an Integrator of Caste and Religion'. In *Religion in South Asia*, edited by E. Harper, 151–196. Seattle: University of Washington Press.

Harris, M. 1966. 'The Cultural Ecology of India's Sacred Cattle'. *Current Anthropology* 7 (1): 51–60.

Hartmann B, J. Boyce. 1983. *A Quiet Violence, View from a Bangladesh Village*. London: Zed Press.

Jones, Sian. 1997. *The Archaeology of Ethnicity: Constructing Identities in the Past and Present*. London; New York, NY: Routledge Press.

Kelleher, M. 1997. *The Feminization of Famine: Representations of Women in Famine Narratives*. Duke University Press.

Khare, R. S. 1976. *The Hindu Hearth and Home*. New Delhi: Vikas Publishing House.

Khare, R. S. ed. 1992. *Eternal Food: Gastronomic Ideas and Experiences of Hindus and Buddhists*. New York, NY: State University of New York Press.

Marriott, M. 1964. 'Caste Ranking and Food Transactions: A Matrix Analysis'. In *Structure and Change in Indian Society*, edited by M. M. Singer and B. Cohn, 133–171. Chicago, IL: Aldine.

Mayer, Adrian. 1960. *Caste and Kinship in Central India*. Berkeley, CA: University of California Press.

———. 1996. 'Caste in an Indian Village: Change and Continuity 1954–1992'. *In Caste Today*, edited by Chris Fuller, 32–65. New Delhi: Oxford University Press.

McAlpin, M., 1987, 'Famine relief policy in India: six lessons for Africa' in M. Glantz (ed.), *Drought and Hunger in Africa: Denying Famine a Future*, Cambridge: Cambridge University Press. pp. 393–413.

Mukhopadhyay, K. 2011. 'Anthropology of Food in India: The Scopes and the Prospects'. *Journal of the Indian Anthropological Society* 46 (2&3): 135–144.

Nichter, M. 1985. 'Cultural Interpretations of the States of Malnutrition among Children: A South Indian Case Study'. *Medical Anthropology* Winter: 25–48.

Patnaik, U. 1991. 'Food Availability and Famine: A Longer View'. *Journal of Peasant Studies* 19 (1).

Prindle, P. 1979. 'Peasant Society and Famine: A Nepalese Example'. *Ethnology* 18 (1): 49–60.

Sanyal, T. 1979. *And Keeping the Flame Alive: A Study on Food Habits and Dietaries with Nutritional Efficiency of West Bengal Tribes*. Cultural Research Institute, Scheduled Castes and Tribes Welfare Department, Government of West Bengal.

Rao, M. S. A. 1986. 'Conservatism and Change in Food Habits among the Migrants in India: A Study in Gastrodynamics'. In *Food, Society and*

Culture, edited by R. Khare and M. Rao, 121–140. Durham, NC: Carolina Academic Press.

Simon, F. J. 1970. 'The Traditional Limits of Milking and Milk Use in Southern Asia'. *Anthropos* 65: 547–593.

Yalman, N. 1969. 'On the Meaning of Food Offerings in Ceylon'. In *Forms of Symbolic Action*, edited by R. Spencer, 81–96. Seattle, WA: University of Washington Press.

Changing Economy and Culture of Food in Spiti

Sumit Mukherjee

Introduction

A group of population's choice of food and its consumption pattern ascertain its 'food culture', which again is primarily linked with the availability of food and the ability to procure it. Availability of food is mostly determined and controlled by geographic conditions, which, in turn, constantly challenge human abilities to produce food of their own choice in a given situation. In other words, the adaptive capacity of humans helps them to cope with the restricted resources and evolve an ecosystem-based model for sustainable living. Thus, food in the words of a field-oriented anthropologist 'is never merely about hunger and nutrition, ingestion and digestion, edibility and sustainability, but about moral categories that embody and embed eating in potentially dangerous relationships of humans to land and water, to plants and other animals, and to each other' (Borneman 2013).

This is much truer in the case of the geographically isolated Trans-Himalayan endogamous ethnic group—the Spitian or the Bodh tribe. Till the late 1980s, they were less exposed to the world beyond the Spiti Valley including the Lahaul Tehsil of the Lahaul-Spiti District. Barring a few exchanges with their Tibetan counterparts, they pursued a typical form of agro-pastoral economy. They are a good example of an environmentally adapted people thriving on ecosystem-based goods and services and living within their own traditional habitat for at least a thousand years. In this long span, these people have developed traditional food processing technologies for preparing food from locally available substances largely governed by ethnic preferences, agro-climatic conditions, socio-cultural ethos and religion (Savitri and Bhalla 2007).

The increasing exposure and gradual acculturation with neighbouring zones like Lahaul Valley, Kullu Valley and Kinnaur after regular public transport and communication systems were initiated in the 1980s, brought in a chain of transformations in the physical and cultural environment of Spiti Valley.

Since the 1960s, the government has been bringing in considerable programmes and funds to improve the livelihood and standard of living of the local population under direct central funded programmes such as the Desert Development Programme (DDP), the Border Area Development Programme (BADP) and the Integrated Tribal Development Programme (ITDP). As a result, almost all villages have been connected by roads, electricity and recently, by mobile or Wireless Local Loop (WLL) phone connectivity. These government programmes have been a major vehicle of change that has provided food through Public Distribution System (PDS) as well as fuel, communication, employment, education and health, mostly at a subsidized rate.

Changes have been cantered fast so that the economy tilts towards the highly profitable green peas and apple orchards; hence, from the traditional subsistence agriculture or a critically balanced subsistence economy, there has been a shift to surplus or profiteering economy. At present, Spitians produce 'cash' in their fields and thrive mostly on supplied staple food items, majority of which are obtained non-local sources.

Thus, it is gradually becoming eminent that the wave of globalization has started reaching such distant corners in terms of agrarian evolution and aspects of food-related economy, thereby complying with the view that 'food has become something bigger than itself. It's about far more than sustenance. It's about commodities trading, globalization, trade, energy, biotechnology and government policy' (Bozzo 2011).

Material and Method

A recent field study by the author in six villages, spread all over the Spiti Tehsil of Lahaul and Spiti District of Himachal Pradesh has revealed a phase of widespread transformation affecting all aspects of economy, society, and culture including food, mainly due to a spurt of changes in the agro-economy of these marginalized population. Field studies were undertaken in two phases during the summer and autumn of 2015 and 2016, respectively, as part of a project, 'Man in Biosphere' undertaken by the Anthropological Survey of India.

Data and information were gathered from all government and non-government institutions, including local bodies like monasteries, which play a vital role in the Spitian society. Discussions with groups and key informants played a vital role in extracting valuable insights. Primary-level investigations were done among the households in a few sample villages.

These sample villages were selected, spreading over lower, middle and upper Spiti, to represent the geographical and eco-cultural variations of the whole valley region (see Table 1.1). Tabo and Poh villages are located in the Sham or (lower region) of Spiti, while Kee and Langja are from the middle zone; Mud is located in Pin Valley and Chichong village lies in the uppermost part of the Spiti Valley near its last village Losar, on the extreme west. On an average 30 per cent of the selected households and several hotels and homestays, shops, etc., were studied in detail to assess the expected changes. The altitude ranges from 10,750 ft in Tabo to 14,200 ft in Langja (see Table 1.1). In brief, all villages are completely dominated by one scheduled tribe—Bodh or Bhot—with very few instances of scheduled caste families residing in the villages of Poh, Langja and Mud. In terms of population size, Chichong and Langja are smaller with 28 and 32 households and Tabo is the largest having 135 households (Table 1.1). In terms of net sown area per household, Langja and Chichong are on top with 0.86 and 0.57 hectare, respectively. Several tehsil-level offices provided important data on land records, land use, crop coverage, etc., at the village level (see Figure 1.1).

Eco-cultural Backdrop

Spiti, the 'middle country', which lies between Tibet and India, is bound on the north by Rubsho (Ladakh), west by Lahaul and Kullu, south by Kinnaur and east by Chinese Tibet. It comprises the valleys of Spiti and Pin rivers. Spanning over an area of 7,101.12 sq. km, it is inhabited by only 12,457 people thereby having a population density of below 2 per sq. km as per Census 2011. Spiti is locally pronounced as Piti and written as Spiti. Historically, various kingdoms of Tibet, Ladakh, Kinnaur, Lahaul and Kullu kept changing hands to rule over the area (Figure 1.1).

The region constitutes a cold desert biome with harsh climatic conditions, which can be attributed to two factors. One is its location on the leeward side of the Himalayas, which makes it a rain-shadow zone inaccessible to the annual south-eastern monsoon winds that sweep the rest of the country, thus creating desert conditions with low levels of

TABLE 1.1 *Primary Census Figures for Studied Villages 2011*

Village Name	Total Geographical Area (in Hect.)	Net Area Sown (in Hect.)	Total Households	Per Household Net Sown Area (Hect.)	Total Population of Village	Total Male Population of Village	Total Female Population of Village	Total Scheduled Castes Population of Village	Total Scheduled Tribes Population of Village
Chichong	491.93	15.96	28	0.57	144	63	81	0	144
Kye	492.72	18.74	69	0.27	367	217	150	0	367
Langja	421.8	27.53	32	0.86	158	82	76	12	144
Mud	77.55	10.97	45	0.24	213	100	113	4	205
Poh	113.26	26.19	68	0.39	313	146	167	23	286
Tabo	230.77	43.22	135	0.32	592	330	262	0	496

Source: PCA and VD tables, Census 2011.

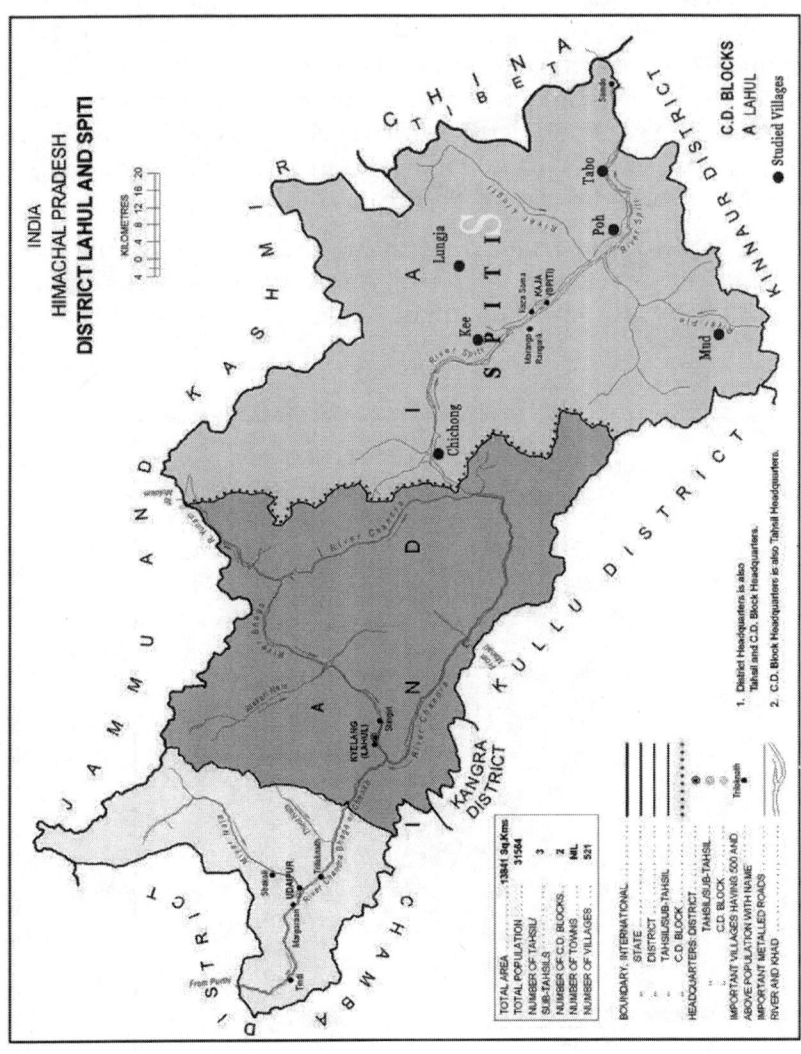

FIGURE 1.1 *Studied Villages in the Map of Lahaul and Spiti District (Census, 2011)*

Source: District Census Handbook (DCHB) Lahaul and Spiti, Census of India 2011.

precipitation. Atmospheric temperature can range over 70 degree Celsius, from –40 in peak winter to 30 degree Celsius in peak summer, with the minimum temperature remaining sub-zero from September to April in most places. Most areas receive much lower snowfall compared to the adjacent Lahaul, Kullu and Kinnaur regions. The average annual precipitation in Kaza is recorded at 170 mm annually. The Pin Valley, as a prominent exception, receives more snow in winter and milder summer. The overall climate in Spiti is thus dry and cold with a long winter extending from mid-November to March. Blizzards, snowstorms and avalanches are common. The soil is not very fertile, and the climatic conditions allow very short growing seasons making it a bare landscape. Water resources are minimal and comprise glacier-fed streams (Figure 1.2).

It is important to understand that the cold desert ecosystem possesses unique and diverse geographical and anthropological conditions controlled by altitude and climate. Human health and all other

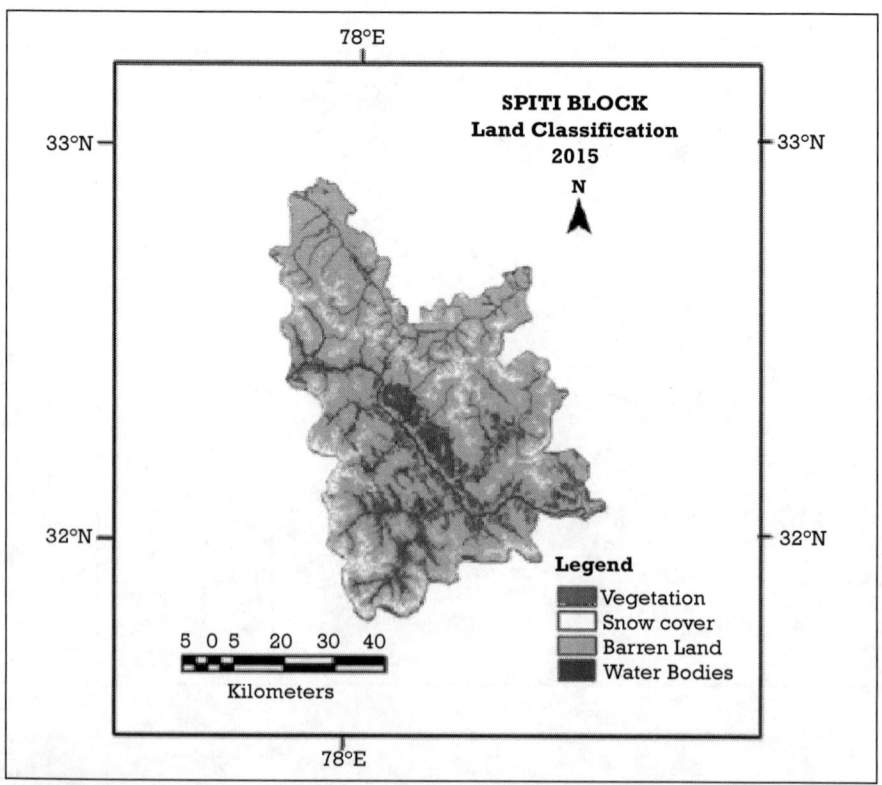

FIGURE 1.2 *Land Classification Map of Spiti Block*

Source: Based on Kumar et al. 2018. *Journal of Mountain Science* 15(8): 1658–1670.

activities here are largely affected by the extreme cold climatic conditions. Human habitation in this region spreads over high to very high altitudes—ranging from just below 10,000 ft at village Sumdo to above 14,850 ft in Komic, the highest inhabited motorable village in the world. There are very few areas with good vegetative cover in the cold desert.

The river Spiti originates at the base of the Kunzam range and flows eastward to join the Sutlej at Khab in Kinnaur. Spiti has its subdivisional headquarters at Kaza, and there are 231 census villages of which only 82 are permanently inhabited as per Census 2011.

This extremely fragile ecosystem exhibits very less but a diversity of highly endemic species. As many rare and special varieties of flora and fauna are found here, several parts have been declared as national parks and wildlife reserves by the government for their protection. Furthermore, the cold desert has been declared as the 16th Biosphere Reserve (Compendium BR 2012) of India in 2009, which includes Pin Valley National Park and its surroundings, Chandratal and Sarchu, and the Kibber Wildlife Sanctuary.

Abiding by the Tibetan Tantrik Buddhism, the custom of sending the surplus able-bodied manpower to the monasteries is still followed by the Spitians religiously. In general, the eldest son inherits the landed property of family and the younger ones are sent to different monasteries to learn Lamaism, and thus the unwanted fragmentation of small land holdings are avoided. In case of larger land holders families, one or two younger sons can stay back in the family and practise polyandry by the marrying elder brother's wife. This tradition, now limited to a few families, helped to restrict the growth of the society in a manner disproportionate to their static and restricted resource base. The eldest daughter inherits all ornaments from the mother and is free to decide upon further distribution among her younger sisters. Even daughters, mainly among poorer families, are also sent to the nunnery and get trained to become a Chomo. Nowadays, most villagers either feel shy or completely avoid mentioning the practise of polyandry. However, the elderly women of Mud village of Pin Valley reported that at least one-fourth of the total households have been practising such a marriage system in the village. In the other five studied villages only few such cases were otherwise indicated.

Instead of very low density of population, there has been a substantial increase in the absolute population from merely 2,272 in 1868 (Harcourt 1871) to 12,457 in 2011, with a decadal growth rate of 16.65 (Table 1.2). Most interesting aspect of the demographic trend of Spiti is that there has been a continuous and increasing rate of decadal growth in contrast with the decreasing trends in other part of the same district. The population is

TABLE 1.2 *Decadal Change in Population of Tehsils by Residence, 2001–2011*

Sl. No.	Tehsil	Population						Percentage Decadal Variation 2001–2011		
		2001			2011					
		Total	Rural	Urban	Total	Rural	Urban	Total	Rural	Urban
1	2	3	4	5	6	7	8	9	10	11
1	Udaipur (S.T)	9,446	9,446	–	8,889	8,889	–	–5.90	–5.90	–
2	Lahul (T)	13,099	13,099	–	10,218	10,218	–	–21.99	–21.99	–
3	Spiti (T)	10,679	10,679	–	12,457	12,457	–	16.65	16.65	–
	District Total:	**33,224**	**33,224**	**–**	**31,564**	**31,564**	**–**	**–5.00**	**–5.00**	**–**

said to have doubled in the period from 1951 to 1981. Higher population growth in recent decades is probably due to better survival, lower death rates and higher number of households as a result of the breakdown of the polyandrous system (NCF 2011).

Owing to higher altitude and ruggedness of terrain, one third of the land having more than 30 degree of slope remains beyond any economic use. Considering the Upper Spiti Landscape. Taking the Upper Spiti Landscape, upstream of Lingti and Spiti River confluence, if we take that the actual habitable land is 900 sq. km of the total 3,944 sq. km, then human density is considerably higher, 11 per sq. km than taking total land of the district (NCF 2011). Spiti has a sex ratio close to hundred and a large proportion of the population consists of minors (<15 years), thereby indicating a growing population. Moreover, the literacy rate has been consistently improving, and is close to cent percent for the school-going age group of 5–18 years.

Agrarian Tradition and Trend

In a landlocked Trans-Himalayan valley with extreme climatic conditions, primary ecological factors determine most of the economic and social aspects of the inhabitants, including food production. In the Hierarchy Theory of Ecological Studies, climate is a first-order determinant of agro-ecosystem, followed by edaphic factors, human intervention and other natural disturbances. The natural quadruplet of physiography, climate, soils and water resources exert recognizable influences on agricultural land use. It can be hypothesized that spatial variations in physical environment impose limits on the distribution of farming system, although the actual distribution depends on human willingness and ability to ameliorate physical conditions through culture and technology (O'Neill et al. 1986).

What makes the most efficient use of environmental resources here is a high degree of ecological perception among the indigenous cultivators, as indicated by the farmers' ability to select those systems and techniques of production and management. The most remarkable feature of farming in Spiti is its snow-fed irrigation system known as the Kuhl. Tapped from the snout of a glacier, Kuhl is a water channel that leads to a circular tank from which water is let out in a trickle through pipes. When water reaches the field, an intricate network of gravitational channels distributes it all over and allows it to flow down to the next field.

Despite such ecological control factors in an area where only 0.26 per cent land is available for cultivation and has a short cropping period of only four dry warmer months devoid of rainfall, the agricultural biodiversity is remarkably rich. It is reported that the West Himalayas, including the Spiti Valley, are one of the few global centres of agricultural biodiversity and form part of the 'Southwest Asiatic Centre' (north-western Indian sub-centre) of Vavilov's eight global 'Centres of Origin' of crop plants. The West Himalayan cold desert regions show high genetic diversity in cold wheat, barley (particularly hull-less types), buckwheat, pros millet, amaranth, chenopods, field peas, lentils, etc. These crops are particularly adapted to cold and drought conditions. It has further been noted that high altitude (10,826 ft) varieties of barley (*Hordeum vulgare L.*) show similarities with local Tibetan barleys and tall varieties of wheat (awned and awnless) from Lahaul and Spiti have shown resistance/tolerance to oxidation. These traditional crops and other newly adopted ones are of high nutrient value and less perishable even without the application of pesticides and preservatives (NCF 2011).

Only one crop of a few kinds of grains grows in a year, though none without irrigation. Prior to the 1990s local crops such as gandam or wheat (Triticumaestivum), neh—the husk-less barley (Hordeum vulgare L.), jau or common barley (Hordeum Himalayans), and a wide range of medicinal plants were grown.

A comparative data of the kind of commodities produced and prices prevailing about a century ago in Lahaul and Spiti is presented in Table 1.3.

Black pea, locally known as sanmah nako, was once the most valued traditional lentil grown in Spiti. This crop is well suited to the region's peculiar geo-climatic conditions since it is drought- and frost-resistant and requires very little irrigation. Being a legume with high nutritive content, it can also be consumed as a pulse (like kidney beans) and it

TABLE 1.3	Available Amount of Grain Crops in Standard Seers per Rupee, 1998	
Grain	**Lahaul**	**Spiti**
Barley (Neh)	25	18
Wheat	20	18
Black peas	15	20
Mustard seed	12	10
Buckwheat	50	18
Cheena	–	24
Potatoes	32	–
Tobacco	8	–

Source: Tobdan (2015).

TABLE 1.4 *Cropping Pattern in Spiti Valley, 2007–2008*

Crops	% Area
Cereal	
Wheat	2.87
Barley	38.99
Pulses	
Rajmash	0.53
Kala matar	0.11
Oilseeds (Sarson)	0.16
Vegetables	
Potato	8.38
Peas	32.62
Cabbage	0
Radish	0.03
Fruits	
Apple	16.15
Apricot	0.11
Other fruits	0.05
	100
Total cropped area in hectare	**1,220.2**

Source: Kumar et al. 2015.

increases soil nutrients. Other than cooking as a pulse, the black pea also makes delicious sprouts and is a good source of cholesterol and blood sugar lowering fibre (Kumar et al. 2015). This pea is still grown in smaller extent for its high nutritional value, merely 0.11 per cent of cropped area was used during 2007–08 in Spiti (Table 1.4). Having no direct market outside the district and with the end of trade with Tibet, the crop has been fast replaced by the highly profitable green pea.

After a span of eight years the cropping pattern in the studied villages (2015–2016) has shown further changes with green pea occupying the top rank followed by barley, but apple advanced a lot. In Table 1.5, green pea occupies first rank in 71 out of 82 villages and barley is the top second rank crop found in 64 villages. In the third rank, potato is dominant with 51 villages but beans appeared in 14 villages as well. In overall ranking wheat is at the fourth position, beans fifth followed by apple, mustard and almond.

Till 2015, during this study Tabo and Poh had apple orchards in 35 and 6 hectare, respectively and the former one showed its diminished

TABLE 1.5 *Ranking of Major Agricultural Produces at the Village Level in Spiti, 2011*

Agricultural Crops	First Rank		Second Rank		Third Rank		Total/Overall	
	No. of Vill.	% of Vill.	No. of Vill.	% of Vill.	No. of Vill.	% of Vill.	No. of Vill.	Rank
Almond	0	0.00	1	1.22	0	0.00	1	8
Apple	4	4.88	0	0.00	2	2.44	6	6
Barley	3	3.66	**64**	**78.05**	2	2.44	**69**	**2**
Beans	0	0.00	0	0.00	14	17.07	14	5
Green pea	**71**	**86.59**	8	9.76	3	3.66	**82**	**1**
Mustard	0	0.00	0	0.00	4	4.88	4	7
Potato	3	3.66	1	1.22	**51**	**62.20**	**55**	**3**
Wheat	1	1.22	8	9.76	6	7.32	15	4
Total	82	100.00	82	100.00	82	100.00		

Source: DCHB Lahaul & Spiti, Census of India 2011.
Note: The different grey shades in boxes denotes higher to lower values and bold figures are highest valued in each rank.

TABLE 1.6 *Village-wise Ranking of Major Agricultural Produce, 2015*

Village Name	Altitude (in ft)	First Rank	Second Rank	Third Rank
Chichong	13,250	Green peas	Barley	Beans
Kee	12,350	Green peas	Barley	Beans
Langja	14,200	Green peas	Barley	Potato
Mud	12,500	Green peas	Barley	Potato
Poh	11,100	Green peas	Wheat	Potato
Tabo	10,750	Apple	Green peas	Wheat

Source: Field study 2016.

interest on green peas (5 hectare) and barley (1 hectare). It was also learnt from the local cultivators that altitude and climate are the two powerful factors for keeping the upper limit of apple at below 12,000 ft (Table 1.6); however, recent trend shows the presence of experimental apple orchards in Kaza and Rongrik villages at above 12,500 ft altitude. But most striking fact is that kala matar is left far behind and except in Mud and Langja there was no mention of the crop in the other villages studied.

Examination of the area under each crop in the villages studied (Table 1.7) shows a clear dominance of green pea cultivation, followed by barley. Wheat was either absent or negligible (less than a hectare) in villages other than Tabo and Poh. In villages at higher altitude, wheat is sometimes rotationally cropped with barley.

Agriculture has made considerable progress in Himachal Pradesh since the early 1970s as is evident from increase in the production of food grains from 9.45 lakh tonne in 1972–1973 to 14.94 lakh tonne in

TABLE 1.7 *Village-wise Area under Major Crops (in Hectare), 2015*

Village	Altitude (in Ft)	Total Cropped Area	Green Peas (Hect.)	Apple (Hect.)	Barley (Hect.)	Wheat (Hect.)	Potato (Hect.)
Chichong	13,250	18	10	0	8	0	0
Kee	12,350	38	23	0	15	0	0
Langja	14,200	21	13	0	8	0	0
Mud	12,500	11	7	0	4	0	0
Poh	11,100	27.0	10	6	4	6	0
Tabo	10,750	43.22	5	35	1	2.22	0

Source: Field study 2016.

TABLE 1.8 *Net Sown Area (in Hectare) Available per Household in Studied Villages, 2011*

Village	Altitude (in ft)	Total Geographical Area	Total Households	Net Area Sown	Per Household Net Sown Area	Per cent Net Sown Area to Total Area
Chichong	13,250	491.93	28	15.96	0.57	3.24
Kee	12,350	492.72	69	18.74	0.27	3.80
Langja	14,200	421.8	32	27.53	0.86	6.53
Mud	12,500	77.55	45	10.97	0.24	14.15
Poh	11,100	113.26	68	26.19	0.39	23.12
Tabo	10,750	230.77	135	43.22	0.32	18.73

Source: Census of India (2011).

2010–2011 (Government of Himachal Pradesh, 2012). Productivity of different crops has also increased, but the most important change has been the diversification of agriculture towards high-value cash crops, including fruits and vegetables, especially in the areas falling in the temperate agro-climatic zones in cold desert conditions.

Minor crops, sown on less than a hectare of land, include varieties of vegetables, little black pea, etc. There is increasing successful experimentation of vegetables grown in artificial green houses in all villages supported by the demonstration and material support of the Agricultural Department of Himachal Pradesh.

Changes in Agro-economy

It all started perhaps after the successful experimentation and introduction of green pea and apple at lower Spiti (Sham) back in the mid-1990s. These two crops had already transformed the agricultural economy in the adjacent Kinnaur District since the last four decades. Agri-horticulture department of the state encouraged experimental plantation of apple extending slowly uphill, which so far has been doing well up to Poh village.

The main crop that farmers grow in their farms is garden pea followed by barley (Table 1.9). Along with this they also grow black pea, which is a traditional crop of Spiti. These crops are well suited to the region's geo-climatic conditions since they require minimum irrigation and are fairly drought-resistant and hardy.

The trend of change in cropping pattern for 24 years, the key period of the prevailing agricultural dynamism in Spiti, tells us the exact time period and relative changes in major crops from traditional to recent ones (Table 1.9). The sudden increase in area under green pea, post the 1990s, was the period of switching from traditional black pea to green pea. With a few ups and downs in the introductory phase, pea crop has shown a steady growth and still remain so. The most interesting temporal trend emerging from the graph is the 'mirror image' relation between the graph lines of barley and pea (Figure 1.3). It seems evident that each year the increase and decrease of area under those two crops are inversely related. An increase in green pea area has resulted in proportionate decrease in the area of barley and vice versa. Hence, within the very limited cropping area, green pea is sown on the same plots previously occupied by barley. It is also clear that farmers have preferred to grow these two crops alternatively either in the same or similar size of plot, though at present, the gap between those two crops is widening at the cost of barley.

TABLE 1.9 Changes in Area under Different Crops in Spiti during 1985–2009

Year	Barley (Ha)	Barley (%)	Peas (Ha)	Peas (%)	Wheat (Ha)	Wheat (%)	Masur (Ha)	Rajma (Ha)	Mustard (Ha)	Potato	Total Area (ha)
1985	573.00	62.62	232.00	25.36	74.00	8.09	0	0	10.00	25.00	915.00
1986	649.00	60.88	255.00	23.92	118.00	11.07	0	0	11.00	33.00	1,066.00
1987	503.00	48.83	341.00	33.11	113.00	10.97	0	19.00	16.00	31.00	1,030.00
1988	624.00	57.09	319.00	29.19	95.00	8.69	0		7.00	42.00	1,093.00
1989	648.71	58.56	334.57	30.20	56.41	5.09	0	1.09	10.29	46.99	1,107.81
1990	570.49	54.66	343.01	32.87	87.68	8.40	1.00	0.13	5.40	33.63	1,043.64
1991	584.17	54.38	362.00	33.70	86.91	8.09	1.38	1.33	8.76	28.12	1,074.30
1992	581.37	55.32	344.42	32.77	86.03	8.19	4.00	1.00	9.28	24.87	1,050.97
1993	571.66	53.83	363.61	34.24	83.26	7.84	2.00	1.00	11.25	27.98	1,062.02
1994	536.00	51.94	362.00	35.08	84.00	8.14	3.00	1.00	16.00	30.00	1,032.00
1995	465.00	42.74	487.00	44.76	91.00	8.36	6.00	1.00	16.00	22.00	1,088.00
1996	535.13	50.02	390.17	36.47	92.00	8.60	2.00	5.00	17.76	27.79	1,069.85
1997	460.00	42.75	468.00	43.49	91.00	8.46	0	9.00	20.00	28.00	1,076.00
1998	552.00	53.49	365.00	35.37	89.00	8.62	0	8.00	18.00	35.00	1,032.00
1999	517.00	48.91	427.00	40.40	81.00	7.66	0	9.00	23.00	31.00	1,057.00
2000	505.00	47.82	463.00	43.84	66.00	6.25	1.00	5.00	16.00	30.00	1,056.00
2001	528.00	49.39	474.00	44.34	55.00	5.14	4.00	5.00	3.00	30.00	1,069.00
2002	528.00	49.21	474.00	44.18	58.00	5.41	8.00	4.00	1.00	20.00	1,073.00

Year											
2003	560.00	52.09	447.00	41.58	57.00	5.30	4.00	5.00	2.00	26.00	1,075.00
2004	459.00	38.90	665.00	56.36	56.00	4.75	0	0	0	0	1,180.00
2005	544.00	50.56	484.00	44.98	48.00	4.46	0	0	0	0	1,076.00
2006	471.00	46.18	549.00	53.82	0	0	0	0	0	13.00	1,020.00
2007	496.00	49.01	516.00	50.99	0	0	0	0	0	14.00	1,012.00
2008	466.00	46.18	543.00	53.82	0	0	0	0	0	13.00	1,009.00
2009	488.00	42.58	585.00	51.05	73.00	6.37	0	0	0	8.00	1,146.00

Source: Revenue Department, Kaza.

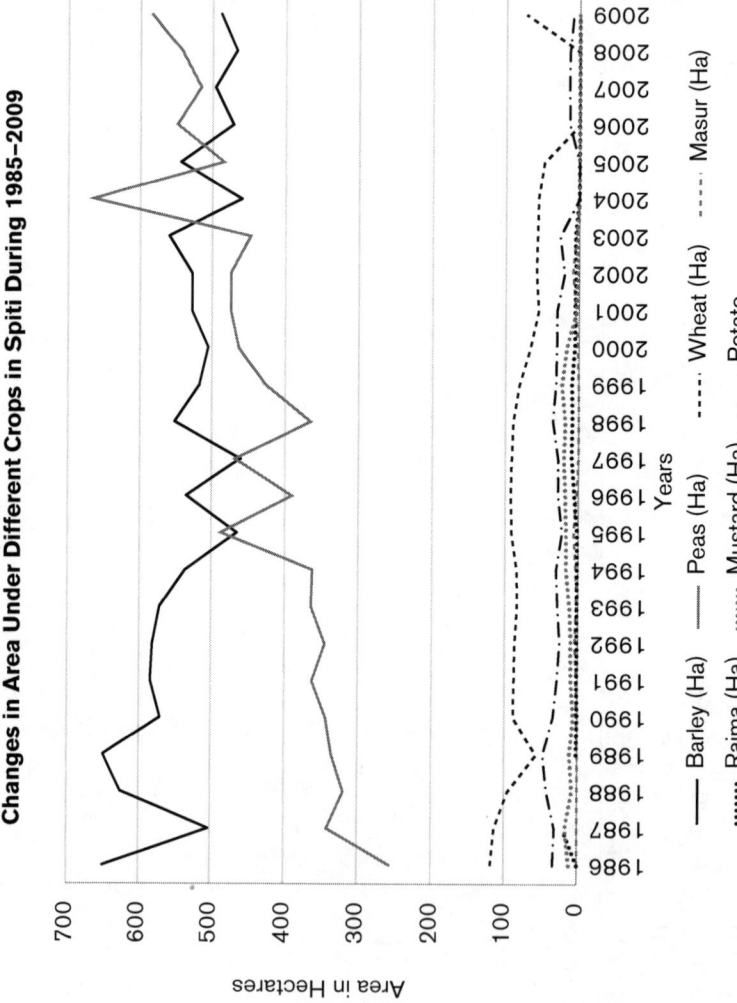

FIGURE 1.3 *Trends of Change in Cropping Pattern of Spiti during 1985–2009*

			Production of and Earnings from Apple in Lower Spiti
TABLE 1.10			(Sham) Area, 2009

Village	No. of Boxes (20 kg/box)	Production (kg)	Earnings (₹)	Earnings per Household (₹)
Tabo	2,431	48,620	2,528,240	50,565
Poh	905	18,100	941,200	21,888
Total	3,336	66,720	3,469,440	37,306

Source: NCF (2011).

Note: A sample of 50 in Tabo and 43 households in Poh in Lower Spiti (Sham) area has been taken for the data presented. Here per HH earning will be the average derived from total earning/total no. of HH. 3,469,440/93=37,306.

Earnings from both the new commercial crops are quantified in Table 1.10 drawing examples from Tabo and Poh villages. During 2009, a single household on an average earned ₹50,565 in case of Tabo and ₹21,888 in Poh from apple crop only. Similar assessment was attempted during 2016 study, and it was found that in 2015, the apple crop brought in an amount of ₹6,660,000 in the village, which amounts to an income of ₹154,884 per household. Though in fact 6 out of 43 households in Poh did not have any apple orchard, they earned a good amount working in others' orchards, who mostly stayed outside Spiti or do not have their own family member to manage and cultivate the crop. Similarly, ₹11,160,000 was the total earning from green peas for the village and a total of ₹414,419 per household on an average (Table 1.11).

Noticeably, five or six personal four wheelers and a dozen two-wheeler vehicles were owned by the residents of Poh Village. There are two medium-sized shops in the village selling various household utility goods, groceries and several fast food and packed food items like branded ready-to-eat noodle, biscuit, soft drink, sweet candy, chocolate, jam, jelly, butter, etc.

			Production and Earnings from Two Main Cash Crops
TABLE 1.11			in Poh Village, 2015

Crops	No. of boxes (20 kg/box)	Production (kg)	Earnings (₹)	Earnings per Household (₹)
Green peas		180,000	11,160,000	259,535
Apple	2,220	44,400	6,660,000	154,884
Total			17,820,000	414,419

Source: Field Study 2016.

Note: A sample of 43 households taken for the data presented.

In Tabo, the new generation rich villagers have started investing huge amounts in the tourism industry and have built eight hotels, guest houses of good standard in the village, where as many overseas tourists are visiting as the Indians. Most of these hotel property owners own expensive vehicles. In both the villages a good proportion of families have purchased their second home outside Spiti and many of their children are staying permanently in other districts or states for higher studies or have joined jobs.

The field survey undertaken during 2015–2016 recorded that around 25–30 per cent households from different villagers migrate, totally or partially, outside Spiti during winter months and have their own houses or apartments in towns and cities such as Manali, Kullu, Mandi, Bilaspur, Rampur, Chandigarh and Delhi. In fact, the number of children studying and living outside Spiti is increasing; this is same with elderly persons who need regular medical supports.

Pastoral Past and Animal Husbandry

In the course of the field study, Lama Shushul Dewa, the Head Lama of Lo-Tsa-Ba-Lha Khang of Pooh Village of Upper Kinnaur, during a meeting at the village in 2015, expressed that the pastoral nomads of Dok Pa community from the Rongcheng-Kham-Uchang region of southern Tibet crossed over to Shipki La in Sutlej Valley of Kinnaur. First the nomads reached Pooh and Namgia villages of Upper Kinnaur. Finding this valley relatively rich in natural pasture in milder summer than their homeland, they settled down permanently and gradually spread all over Spiti Valley.

Animal husbandry is the second mode of economy. But natural condition is a powerful limiting factor; it offers merely 22 per cent pasture and other grazing ground. It was nearly impossible for a household to think of rearing more than one milch cattle (Tobdan 2015).

Some observers have remarked that the inhabitants of Spiti had less preference for commerce and trade. Sherring (1916) found that the wants of the Spiti landholders were few and they did not care much about leaving the valley. He recorded that the Spiti people are not essentially traders, their country affords but little pasturage, and they have seldom more sheep than to meet their own wants.

It is interesting to observe that the system of social formation adopted in Spiti has been much responsible for the type of its economy. They have small family within which they do not have the necessity and possibility of division of labour. Therefore, there is no member in the family attending exclusively to the profession of trade like in Lahaul and Kinnaur, where the social organization is different. However, in summer, after the sowing season and before the harvesting period, when the load of work in the fields is light, the people move out on trading excursions to purchase goods of their urgent need. During harvest time, traders from Bashahar, Tibet and Jangthang come to Spiti to purchase their much-prized produce of neh, ghoont (pony) and other items, and then they dispose off their surplus produce. The Spitians also take their articles to the seasonal fairs (Tobdan, 2015).

Gerard, in 1842, opined that the people of Spiti had a history of trade with their neighbours. They exported wool, borax, salt, and blankets and imported several commodities and a great deal of iron from the plains, that is, their neighbours in the south. He also informed that on his way to Kaza, he met with a large party of people from Pin proceeding towards Lara, on the road to Jangthang, and forming the third *kafila* or caravan, that had gone there within a few days, for items like tea, wool and salt.

Similarly, the Spitians bought sheep of a very fine breed, salt, wool, tea, turquoises and goats, paying in lieu grain, woollen cloth and a few horses from Jangpa of Tibet. From Lhasa came tobacco, tea, sheep wool, turquoises, amber, water pots and other wooden vessels. From Bashahar and Kullu came iron, cooking utensils, brass, coarse cloth, copper, tobacco, rice, dried fruits, teacups, timber, amber, glass beads, etc.

Spiti also purchased sheep from the shepherds of Malana and Manikaran valleys of Kullu, who used to graze their herds along the mountain ridge bordering Spiti. As the men of both the sides did not know the language of each other they had developed a sign language (Tobdan 2015).

Sheep, goats, cattle and yaks are mostly consumed internally and are an important source of protein for people, particularly in the long high-altitude winters. Dzos and yaks are used for draught, and donkeys and horses for thrashing and transportation. Since agricultural mechanization is just beginning to catch up in places, animal power remains critical for agriculture. Dung from cattle, yak and equids is an important source of fuel for people. In fact, dung is so important in rural areas that the community regulates collection of dung from pastures.

Food Culture and Changes

It is rather obvious that the fast transformation from a purely subsistence economy into a market economy, since last two-and-a-half decades, has deep impact on food preference and consumption pattern of the economically empowered Spitians.

Majority of the food items of Spitians were locally grown and procured through limited trade till the end of the 1980s. During his first visit to Kaza in 1983 the present author had only the option for standard urban Indian meals at the PWD Guest House pre-ordered and cooked by a non-Spitian Himachali chowkidar. There was one small Tibetan food stall at the Kaza bus station serving only during short office hours. There was not a single roadside shop or food stall in any of the villages along the bus route. Travellers from other parts of India required special inner-line-permit to enter Spiti Tehsil, and identity proof of the Spitians was checked before allowing them to travel outside Spiti by the only daily bus to Kullu.

Traditional foods prepared from major cereals are common in almost all parts of Lahaul and Spiti districts. Some of them are used as staple, while others are festive foods. A few major popular food items are mentioned here:

1. *Chilra/chilte/iwar* is a popular staple food made from fermented wheat/buckwheat/barley into a slurry consistency. It is still consumed occasionally.
2. *Aet* is a thin *roti* (chapati) made during marriages.
3. *Aktori* is a kind of thick *roti* made of buckwheat flour and buckwheat leaves; once a staple it is less popular now.
4. *Chhura* is made of wheat flour, *chhang*, *lassi*, spices; it is another form of *roti* and is rarely eaten now.
5. *Thuktal* is an occasional food item prepared by steam-cooking *tsampa* (roasted barley flour) and boiled potato.

Few other traditional popular cuisines still consumed almost regularly and particularly during the winter months are *thukpa* and *zara*. One Tibetan food item that remained most popular in the staple dietary habit of Lahaul and Spiti and even in the adjoining districts is thukpa. It is a stew-like preparation where homemade wheat flour noodles along with tsampa, pieces of *sokana* (a local leafy vegetable) and dry mutton, beef or lamb are boiled together for half an hour in water after adding salt. *Chhurpee* (dried local cheese) is added and sometimes garnished with pieces of dried sheep fat. This is revered as the most healthy and wholesome food after a day's hard labour and keeps one warm. During very cold winter months, it is a mandatory item in the daily menu. Several variants of the dish are served in almost all local restaurants of Spiti, though use of raw fat and local chhurpee is rare and various vegetables like cabbage, lettuce, and zucchini are added in place of rarely found sokana leaves.

If thukpa is the common stew, *thenthuk* is the greater version and is consumed as a wholesome meal. Various fresh vegetables are boiled in water and tsampa is added along with salt and turmeric powder to taste. A handful of black peas, pre-soaked in water, is also added to it followed by sautéed onion and tomato. Occasionally, pieces of mutton, lamb, beef or egg are used for a non-vegetarian thenthuk. At the end, small pieces of hand-flattened wheat flour dough are dropped in the boiling soup. Options of chhurpee, ghee, butter or white oil are left to the consumers.

A very popular local dish zara is still consumed in winter. It is a porridge prepared with roasted and powdered black peas mixed with tsampa and served with homemade *ghee*. This item is considered good for pregnant women and lactating mothers.

The salted butter tea called *poh cha* or *cha soma* in Bhoti dialect, used to be the most popular Tibetan beverage still consumed throughout the higher Himalayan region. It is slowly disappearing from Spitian homes and is now consumed only during winter. During 2015–2016 field study, the author was offered this tea only on three occasions, once at the village headman's house at Langja, at a religious gathering in Nako village and by Nima Lama at the Kee monastery.

Another tasty and popular snack item is pakki marku, which the author cherished a lot during his first field studies back in 1983–1984; it has become a rare dish in Spiti and is served on special occasions.

Most popular non-vegetarian item was dry or smoked lamb or mutton, or yak meat made into small pieces and prepared with thukpa. Earlier milk tea, green vegetables were almost unknown, but occasional consumption of potato, both boiled and in curry, was noticed when PDS was not there.

It should be mentioned here that Tibetan Buddhism is practised by almost all Spitians, but that does not stop them from consuming animal products, which is essential for survival in harsh cold desert condition. However, the present Dalai Lama requested the Lamas of Spiti to avoid taking any animal or fish products as far as practicable to avoid unnecessary criticism from tourists and officials visiting Lahaul and Spiti districts. There is no such bar for the common villagers. The same rule is applicable for consumption of chhang and arak, the alcoholic drinks prepared from barley and wheat.

TABLE 1.12 *Traditional Fermented Foods of Lahaul and Spiti*

Product	Chilra	Zuan	Butoru
Raw material used	Buckwheat flour and wheat flour	Barley grains	Wheat flour
Source of the inoculums	Khameer/Malera	Phab	Khameer/Malera
Nature of product	Flat spongy pan cake	Porridge-like preparation	Flat deep-fried dough
Consumed as	Breakfast/staple food	Snack	Snack
Season	Regularly prepared and consumed. Consumption is less during winter due to low temperature and longer fermentation period	Prepared and consumed mainly during winter season	Occasionally prepared

Source: Kanwar et al. (2007).

In traditional food culture of the Spitians it is believed that food items prepared through fermentation of different grains are easy to digest and give them instant energy or strength; they can also be preserved for a longer period after cooking.

In Table 1.12, three fermented food items are listed (Kanwar et al. 2007). These food items are rarely prepared presently, except in certain ceremonies and rituals as important ingredients like buckwheat has almost totally disappeared from the fields of this region.

Impact of PDS Food

With a view to removing the bottlenecks coming in the way of an effective and efficient PDS and to strengthen its base, the Civil Supplies Corporation was established in 1980. All stable food grains and sugar are supplied from the state PDS and are distributed through the network of Fair Price Shops (FPS), spread all over Spiti, at subsidized rates.

Each family in Lahaul–Spiti, being a tribal district, gets specially subsidized ration items through TPDS as shown in Table 1.13. Ration cardholders collect those commodities for the whole year during September–October, just before the winter sets in, from the respective FPS. Though the prices are very low, rice is sold at ₹3 and wheat for ₹2 per kg, the villagers buy half of the entitled rice due to poor quality and because they are not traditionally rice eaters.

It may be noted that sale of various India-made foreign liquor or IMFL (this is the term used in India by governments and general

TABLE 1.13 — *Quantities of Commodity Entitled per Family of Four per Month under Tribal Area PDS*

Commodity	Quantity
Rice	15 kg
Wheat	20 kg
Dal chana	2 kg
Black masur	1 kg
Malka	1 kg
Rajma	1 kg
Mash	1 kg
Moong sabut	1 kg
Iodized salt	1 kg
Sugar	2 kg
Refined oil	1 l
Mustard oil	1 l

Source: ePDS Himachal Pradesh (2018).

people to describe any non-indigenous hard drink manufactured in the country) sold through licensed shops has increased among Spitians with increased economic solvency and growth of tourism. The district authority here has recently imposed restriction on consumption of such liquor during family and community ceremonies; the hosts are supposed to prepare traditional drinks for entertaining their guests. It has been observed that villagers brew local drinks from rice and wheat available through PDS.

On the other hand, they find entitlement of sugar too meagre, usually a family has to purchase 20–30 kg of the sweetener from open market every year.

Compared to the locally grown commodities in pre-PDS period, there is substantial increase in variety of food items in the Spitian menu. Instead of only black pea, they now get five or six types of pulses to choose from. Edible oil was available in small quantity as mustard was grown in some parts of Spiti. But consumption of cooking oil has increased manifold as they are now supplied with two types of oil. Moreover, with import of many varieties of vegetables grown profusely in Lahaul Tehsil, their habit of taking fried, deep fried and sautéed food has increased.

The most widespread impact of subsidized food supply can be seen in the growing habit of taking boiled rice or roti, dal and vegetables regularly for lunch and dinner. The change from 'tsampa-thukpa-chilra-butoru' to 'chawal-dal-sabzi' has partly been necessitated by an urge to place them at par with the 'modern' society they have been exposed to. Another new trend is growing consumption of locally grown green peas, which is cooked with dal, sabzi and even with thukpa. Villagers feel proud to offer freshly harvested peas to the tourists and guests as a welcome gesture with a note *'Bahut mitha hai'*.

Sugar is mostly consumed in milk tea, which they take four to five cups a day and offer to the visitors too. Even while working at the field, they carry one large thermos full of milk tea per group of two to three persons. Packed biscuits are also consumed with tea.

Owing to scarcity of green vegetables in winter, they use more of pulses and potato in their various cuisines and eat with rice or roti for lunch and dinner. They also substitute vegetables with meat of yak, and goat or lamb once or twice in a week.

Impact of Tourism

Spiti is being visited by tourists from India and abroad during summer and sometimes during the winter months too. Political disturbances in neighbouring regions have benefitted the tourism industry of Spiti in recent years. Local people have responded to the opportunities by opening hotels, homestays, shops and restaurants, not only in major tourist places like Tabo, Kaza, Kibber, but also in smaller places like Nako, Poh, Dhankar, Langja, Rongrik and Losar. Many of those visitors prefer food of their own choice, though some ask for local cuisines. As a result, food that was exotic to the Spitians is being cooked and is hitting the taste buds of the hosts. Sale of non-indigenous liquor has gone up as the habit of liquor consumption among the locals has also changed.

Gradual acceptance of chicken in their food habit is a striking feature in and around Kaza, Tabo and Losar. Though it is meant primarily for tourists and immigrant labourers, younger Spitians are slowly developing liking for such meat. But regular supply of chicken to Spiti is difficult due to the harsh climate and high altitude, so frozen chicken is the answer. But hen eggs have gained popularity mainly for relative ease in transporting to any corner of the valley.

On the other hand, tourism has helped to introduce some of the traditional dishes among certain tourists, who prefer to stay in villages as guests of Spitian families. They usually are served with cuisines prepared mainly from locally produced wheat and buckwheat, barley tsampa, black pea and kidney beans, cooked with homemade ghee and butter.

The most visible change in the food habit of the locals has been caused by huge quantities of packed food imported from outside the region, as well as fast food, green vegetables and fruits, so far unknown to the Spitians. Hot beverages like tea and coffee are in high demand among visitors from warmer regions and are now available in most of the village shops. Nima Lama of Kee monastery stated that tea and coffee with milk and sugar has become steadily and ubiquitously popular all over the Spiti Valley with increasing tourism; hence, the traditionally popular salted-butter-tea or Tibetan tea has been pushed aside, and served only as part of rituals and in the monasteries. On the other hand, Amchi Lopzang Gatuk, the popular traditional Tibetan doctor from Poh, believed that the habit of drinking tea and eating junk food is the cause of increase in digestive disorders and gastro-intestinal diseases.

Significance of Neh (Barley)

Barley (*Hordeum vulgare L.*) is one of the founder crops of old-world agriculture and probably the first crop cultivated by humans. Called 'qingke' in Chinese or 'nas' in Tibetan, the six-rowed husk less or naked barley has been used as a major staple food by Tibetans for generations (Zeng et al. 2018).

Continuity of popularity of barley crop, especially the endemic husk-less variety, is the remarkable exception in the region. In fact, its primary product tsampa is omnipresent not only as a staple food item but holds a very significant position in Buddhist religious and socio-political identity. This can be justified in several ways:

1. Tsampa is roasted ground barley and is eaten in a dozen of ways. It is quite easy to prepare; it is known as convenience food and often used by the Sherpas, nomads and other travellers. While traditional tsampa is prepared with tea, yak butter tea is blended with tsampa to make dumplings or porridge, sometimes water or beer is used in its place. In the past, travellers used to depend on it for several months, and had it with ja-thang, salted butter tea. Chhang, the native beer, prepared from the whole grain of neh, is used profusely on all social, religious occasions and all kinds of gatherings.

2. Besides constituting a substantial, arguably predominant part of the Spitian diet, its prominence also derives from the tradition of throwing pinches of tsampa in the air during many Buddhist rituals. Tsampa is the most sacred offering made during prayer to the god at monasteries and at homes of not only the Spitians, but of all Buddhist communities across the Himalayan states of India and Tibet. Small quantities of this flour are sprinkled and placed in rows of small metal bowls at the altar of Buddhist deities at all monasteries and stupas.

3. Tradition of offering tsampa predates Buddhist beliefs in this area; it was originally used as an offering to animistic gods to request their protection. The tradition was consequently incorporated into Buddhism as a 'mark of joy and celebration' used at celebratory occasions like marriage and birthday. Now it is used in New Year celebrations, where the act is accompanied by chanting of verses expressing desire for good luck in the forthcoming year. Tsampa-throwing also occurs at most Buddhist funerals, where the action is intended to release the soul of the deceased.

4. Tsampa is also used as medicine and health drink. Paste of tsampa and cumin is applied to toothaches or other sore spots. Tsampa is also known among Tibetan sportsmen for its ability to provide rapid energy boosts; roasting of the flour breaks it down to an easily digestible state, allowing the calories therein to be quickly incorporated by human body.

5. The phrase 'tsampa-eater' was used to promote a unified Tibetan identity. Whereas Tibetans speak various dialects, worship in different sects and live in different regions, all Tibetans were thought to eat tsampa. In 1957, the India-based magazine *Tibet Mirror* addressed a letter to 'all tsampa-eaters', encouraging them to participate in what would become the 1959 Tibetan Rebellion. Recently, with the rise of Tibetan diaspora, less emphasis has been placed on tsampa and more on Tibetan Buddhism in constructing a unified Tibetan identity.

6. The very importance of tsampa is further strengthened by the fact that the present Dalai Lama, the supreme religious leader of Gelug School of Tibetan Buddhism, with a large following world over, takes it at breakfast, regularly and religiously. He likes it mixed with tea and rich, fermented, sometimes slightly added with cheesy butter from yak's milk. It is interesting to note that tsampa is marketed online worldwide as a ready-to-eat food (Seal 2015).

7. It is also reported that traditionally the people of Spiti paid all revenue in the form of *neh*, which was known as *nethal* or *neh-thal* or

barley-tax. Trebeck, who visited Spiti in 1822 during the reign of Ladakh, reports, 'the whole revenue of Piti is collected in grain, by a measure called khal, equal to eight pakkasers, and of the value of thirteen annas' (Moorcroft and Trebeck 1841). He further explains that some 2,937 *khal* of neh valued at ₹2,386 was being collected annually from 267 houses, leaving aside about one-third of the houses considered as unworthy of levy for having no land. Out of the total collection, a part was used for local expenditure. He further says that trade was being done by barter and money was almost useless.

8. The Spitians, particularly the elderly persons, still consume tsampa every day at breakfast. It is considered a healthy food that must be eaten during four months of severe winter. A family of four members, on an average, consume one quintal of tsampa in four to five months. This whole quantity is produced locally. It is a common practice to offer barley to families who do not have enough land to grow it. Sometimes, villages falling short of barley purchase it from villages with surplus.

9. Growing barley in the village means growing a quality fodder for their livestock at no extra cost, as barley plants are regarded as a good source of nutrition for domestic animals.

10. Reflecting its foundational role in Tibetan culture, tsampa is also the name of a Tibetan typeface.

11. And finally, instead of increasing usage of pesticides in commercial agriculture in the region, crops like black pea and barley are kept free from any chemicals.

12. The other exception of clear discontinuity of locally produced food in Spiti is the animal protein they consume from their own livestock. It is alarming to note that they have started to discontinue the practice of rearing sheep and goats as they receive a better return from green peas; in the case of Poh village, even by 2015, the author had witnessed that all sheep and goats were either sold out or consumed as the villagers found it difficult to graze or feed them—they had decided to convert the village pasture to grow apple and peas. Moreover, they believed that it was impossible to save those crops from the animals by guarding or fencing.

This trend, if spreads further, will certainly put a huge lapse in the security of animal protein food, which is too important diet for the people of this cold-desert region. But still today, the region is self-sufficient in animal food products as yak and other cattle varieties are intricately linked to the religious and cultural traditions of Spiti.

Concluding Remarks

It is evident from the above discussion that a distinct process of trans-formation has been set and is being experienced by the people of Spiti in this era of globalization of market economy. The changing food culture and related economy should be considered as part of the whole process.

Primarily all the government programmes have been major vehicles of change, which have provided better amenities such as food (through PDS), communication, employment, education, health and fuel, mostly at subsidized rates. Apart from these, two other major agents of change have affected the local population—opening up of the green pea cash crop market in the mid-1990s and widening the area to tourism in 1992. Both these agents have further provided cash income that has helped in improving livelihoods in the region.

Paradoxically, the overwhelming change or so to say the rapid 'development' in agriculture economy, in a region having very small arable land and cold dry weather, has not helped them in becoming self-sufficient in food. On the contrary, they have lost a good part of food security with an inflating bank balance. Their expenditure on food is limited to exotic food items, including the fast food sold in the local market, as they have developed the habit and taste of subsidized food from PDS.

The limited land resource is restricting further expansion of cash crop, diminishing the scope of investment of surplus capital in cultivation. Increase in nucleated families, mostly landless, due to decrease in polyandry, is also raising the demand of arable land. Through the welfare schemes of government new plots of land are allocated to the economically weaker families encroaching upon the so far uncultivable waste or from common property.

Nima Lama of Kee monastery has started campaigning against the excessive cultivation of irrigation-intensive green pea in his village with a foresight of acute water crisis in the near future; he claimed to have observed the warming of the Spiti weather. According to him, the average temperature is increasing resulting in increasing rainfall and flash flood and decreasing snowfall, which is not at all suitable for the unstable Spiti landscape and geology. Ms Dechan Angmo, the elected Panchayat Pradhan and owner of a huge orchard of Tabo village, lucidly narrated the impact of present development process as 'more apple, more tourists, more vehicles, more pollution, more warming, then more apple and greenery (sic)' in her typical Hindi accent while interviewing during 2016 field study. She has seen that almost 70 per cent of the crop fields of Tabo has been transferred to apple and apricot orchards within less than a decade. Nono Chhering, the last surviving princess of erstwhile Spiti Kingdom, also expressed genuine concern about the present and next generation of youth, who will completely forget about Spiti food, Spiti dress or Spiti dialect. They will belong to neither Spiti culture nor the culture of the city; they have started living in for their education and jobs.

Nevertheless, from development point of view, the farmers of Spiti Valley are looked at enviously by their counterparts in other districts southwards. Whatever the distant future is, the present generation Spitians and their siblings are really enjoying the fruits of speedy development and the pan-Indian cuisines.

References

Borneman, J. 2013. 'Foreword'. In *Food: Ethnographic Encounters*, edited by Leo Coleman. Oxford: Bloomsbury Publishing.

Bozzo, A. 2011. 'The Economies of Food'. CNBC. Available at https://www.cnbc.com/id/42662144

Census of India. 2011. *Distract Census Handbook, Lahaul and Spiti, Part A&B*. Himachal Pradesh: Government of India.

Gerard, Alexander. 1842. 'Narrative of a Journey from Subathoo to Shipke, in Chinese Territory'. *JASB*, 363–379.

Harcourt, A. F. P. (1871) 1972. *The Himalayan Districts of Kooloo, Lahoul and Spiti*. Delhi: Vivek Publications.

Kanwar, S. S., M. K. Gupta, C. Katoch, R. Kumar, and P. Kanwar. 2007. 'Traditional Fermented Foods of Lahaul and Spiti Area of Himachal Pradesh'. *Indian Journal of Traditional Knowledge* 6 (1): 42–45.

Kumar, N., G. Singh, and D. Kumar. 2015. 'Kala Matar: An Indigenous Legume Crop of Spiti Valley in the Trans-Himalayan Cold Desert of India Facing Threat of Extinction'. *International Journal of Current Research in Life Sciences* 4 (8): 346–348.

Moorcroft, W., and G. Trebeck. (1841) 1971. *Travels in the Himalayan Provinces of Hindustan and the Panjab; Ladakh and Kashmir; in Peshawar, Kabul, Kunduz, and Bokhara*. New Delhi: Cosmo.

NCF. 2011. *Management Plan for the Upper Spiti Landscape Including Kibber Wildlife Sanctuary*. Prepared by Nature Conservation Foundation, Mysore and Snow Leopard Trust-India.

O'Neill, R. V., D. L. Deangelis, J. B. Waide, and T. F. H. Allen. 1986. *A Hierarchical Concept of Ecosystems*. Princeton, NJ: Princeton University Press.

Savitri, B. T., and C. Bhalla. 2007. 'Traditional Foods and Beverages of Himachal Pradesh'. *Indian Journal of Traditional Knowledge* 6 (1): 17–24.

Seal, R. 2015. 'Breakfast of Champians: Dalai Lama's Tsampa'. *The Guardian*. Available at www.theguardian.com/lifeandstyle/2015/jan/10/dalai-lama-breakfast-tsampa-recipe

Sherring, C. A. (1916) 1974. *Western Tibet and the Indian Borderland*. Delhi: Cosmo.

Tobdan. 2015. *Spiti: A Study in Socio-cultural Traditions*. Mysore: Kaveri Books.

Zeng, Xingquan, Yu Gao, Qijun Xu, and Martin Mascher. 2018. 'Origin and Evolution of Qingke Barley in Tibet'. *Nature Communications* 9 (1). https://www.researchgate.net/publication/329726696_Origin_and_evolution_of_qingke_barley_in_Tibet

2

Tracing the Beef Politics of North India

Ziya Us Salam

It is the summer of 2013. Business is brisk in Noida's Murga Mandi near Sector 55. Watermelons and musk melons are in high demand here, mangoes follow closely behind. Fruit carts line up one side of the road with almost every vendor screaming his lungs out to attract customers. Women buyers are variously addressed as *Mataji, Behenji* and *Baji.* Only an occasional girl is called *Didi.* These words say it all about the composition of the crowd, ranging from senior women to middle-aged ones, from Muslim Bajis to Hindu Didis. For fruit sellers in Noida they all come alike. Business transcends faith and generations.

Behind a row of push carts of fruits, vegetable vendors sit on the pavement, their stuff neatly spread out on sheets made by stitching jute sacks, their weighing scales rusty, and often dodgy. The shouts are repeated; men are addressed as well. Again, depending on the age and perceived faith of the buyer, men are called out as 'Uncle' or *Chacha, Bhai* or *Bhaiya.* An occasional seller even addresses some men as 'Sir'. For the vegetable vendors what matters is their business, the age and religion of the buyer is immaterial. Of course, in between calls for buyers, vendors talk of politics too. The government is often the butt of jokes, the rising prices an all-season subject. For a couple of hours after sunset the business is brisk. Then as buyers begin to head home to catch up with their evening serials on television, the business begins to slow down, and the vendors start chatting with each other more animatedly. Many support the Bharatiya Janata Party, others stand by the Samajwadi Party and believe Akhilesh Yadav, the Uttar Pradesh Chief Minister, is a better leader than Rahul Gandhi, perceived as a reluctant politician. They swear by their respective political parties and leaders, but at the end of the day, help each other load the leftover vegetables into sacks, pull them inside the shops, fold their sheets of jute sacks and head home together. By the time they do so, the muezzin from the mosque, just behind their shops, would have made his last call for prayer for the day.

A few yards away from the vegetable sellers one finds neatly lined shops of meat. Most sell chicken, a handful trade in fish. Only a couple of shops offer mutton. None sells beef. From Wednesday to Monday, the business is good, particularly high on Sunday when no shopkeeper has the time to chop and clean the meat pieces properly as there is invariably a queue of buyers. On Tuesdays, the business is dull. On this day, most regular customers stay away. Only a handful of Muslims or Christians step in. They can expect to take home neatly chopped and perfectly cleaned meat as the shopkeepers have time in their hands. In the absence of constant business, one often finds the meat sellers sauntering across to fruit sellers in the vicinity and indulging in small talk. Occasionally, they have to be called back when a customer arrives. Life goes on. Peaceful. Harmonious. There is camaraderie.

Cut to summer of 2017. The fruit sellers are all there in the same market. It is early summer, and the carts are teeming with watermelons and musk melons. Only select varieties of mangoes have hit the market yet. Like other days, they still call out to prospective buyers. There are *salwar-kameez*-clad women; there are a few in saris. Only a rare one is seen in a burqa. Business is still good.

A few yards behind the fruit carts are spread vegetables. Yet again, there is noise in the market. Except this time, there are more calls for buying *singada*, the vegetable used during Navratra fasting days. It is indeed Navratra time, and demand for onion, garlic, etc., has been impacted. The downfall in business is handsomely compensated in Ramzan when more buyers pick up onions for fritters at *Iftar* (evening meal with which Muslims end their daily Ramadan fast at sunset) time. Again, men and women pick up their stuff and move on. On their way back, many stop by at a temporary market barely a few yards away from the fruit sellers. The shops sell stuff for *pooja* (prayer), including *mata ki chunri*. There are coconuts too, a few conch shells as well. *Dhoop* is in high demand. In fact, such is the demand for Navratra pooja and food items that many fruit sellers double their earnings by setting up a small shop of pooja material near their pushcart selling fruits. Not all sellers are Hindu; some are Muslims. All is fair and fine. But something is amiss. The hustle-and-bustle is missing from the meat shops. The path leading to the meat section is covered by huge curtains of blue cloth attached to slim bamboo sticks. The shops are all closed. Only occasionaly dog barks there at a stray customer, promptly driving them away. It is Navratra time, one is told. 'But the shops used to open in the past. What has changed this year?' one reasons with a shopkeeper sitting outside his shop, shutter down, a pack of cards in hand.

'Nothing. *Sarkar ka aadesh hai*,' (government's order) he says, clearly unwilling to get into a conversation.

'But there is no order not to eat meat during Navratras. Those who believe in Navratras do not eat but others do, largely Muslims, Christians, etc.,' one adds.

'*Hume nahin maloom* (I do not know),' he says, then inching closer, he reveals the reason: 'Hindu Yuva Vahini *wale aaye thhe. Bole dukaan band kar do nahi toh dekh lena. Sach bataun*, nowadays, you cannot even buy eggs in many sectors of Noida. *Aur phir yahan ki hi kya baat.* You cannot buy meat in Ghaziabad, no beef, no mutton, no chicken, no fish. Even in Gurgaon, I am told, the shopkeepers have been asked to keep their shops shut during Navratras. *Hamari toh saal mein do baar chhutti ho gayi.*'

(The workers of Hindu Yuva Vahini came here. They said, shut your shop, else you will see the consequences. To tell you the truth, nowadays you cannot even buy eggs in many sectors of Noida. Then why to talk of this place only? You cannot buy meat in Ghaziabad, no beef, no mutton, no chicken, no fish.... We have got two times vacation in a year.)

'But why? We have always bought eggs and meat right through the year...,' one says, not ready to give up.

'*Pehle jo khao, so apki marzi.* (Earlier, what you ate was your wish) So many brahmins, kshatriyas come to my shop. They do not eat non-veg on Tuesdays. That is why the business is down on Tuesday. But now we have this Yogi government. The government does not want any-body to eat meat during Navratra time. You must remember, it is the government that showered rose petals on pilgrims coming with *Ganga jal* during Shivratri, and cut the Hajj subsidy. So, people compromise on these nine days. Nobody would like to be killed for selling fish or chicken. People remember the fate of Akhlaq,' the shopkeeper says with a finality as he tucks his cards into his pocket and moves away.

Incidentally, Akhlaq was a Dadri resident in western Uttar Pradesh, about 50 km from where we stand. He was dragged out of his bedroom, lynched on suspicion of storing beef in his fridge in September 2015. The police raided Akhlaq's fridge before trying to lay their hands on the possible killers, as if storing beef was a bigger crime than killing a man! Meanwhile, Bharatiya Janata Party legislator Sangeet Som claimed the party was capable of giving a befitting reply in case any innocent was arrested. The incident sent shock waves across the country with many questioning this imposition of dietary habits on everybody. It seemed people's dietary habits were to be decided by the majority community. In a nation of more than a billion people, there seemed only one way of eating. Beef was a no-no. It mattered little to attackers that people in South and North-East India, including Hindus, happily ate beef. In fact, soon after Akhlaq's killing, Kerala House canteen in New Delhi was raided by Delhi Police following a complaint from a Hindutva outfit that the canteen was serving beef curry, and it hurt their sentiments. Suddenly, it seemed a crime to eat the food one had been eating since birth. The canteen management succumbed. The curry was removed from the menu, though it came back within 24 hours. It, however, required the intervention of Kerala Chief Minister Oommen Chandy who wrote to the prime minister for a simple beef curry to sail through to diners' table all over again! Mr Chandy objected to the entry of the police in the canteen and lodged a formal complaint with the Delhi Police Commissioner about the raid. Significantly, he pointed out that the canteen served Kerala cuisine, both vegetarian and non-vegetarian, and stayed completely 'within the confines of the existing law'.

'Beef has long been the king of the table in Kerala, and for the simple reason that it is appetizing. It accounts for more than 40 per cent of all meat consumed in the state. Around 80 per cent people here regularly eat meat, and not just in Christian and Muslim homes, and not just the rich either. There are no precise figures, but there is enough anecdotal evidence to suggest that more Hindus could be eating it regularly than Christian and Muslims put together,' reported the *Times of India* (Nair, 2015).

The guests at Kerala House canteen in New Delhi were lucky. The Kerala chief minister heard their woes and intervened. No such luck visited the more humble eaters of beef biryani in Gurgaon (now Gurugram) in September 2016. The biryani carts selling the stuff by the roadside in Gurgaon and Mewat were all raided and their stuff confiscated by the police following a complaint from a Hindutva outfit which alleged they were selling beef biryani. The police virtually destroyed the shops, breaking their utensils too. Alleged, Irshad Muhammad, who made about ₹300 a day from his biryani cart, 'I only use buffalo meat and chicken and even keep the skins as proof. The police said they'll check the meat,' he told NDTV. 'The police came and destroyed all our pots and pans. What do we do if we can't earn?' said Wasim, another biryani seller. Men and women, young and old, may have been eating road-side biryani for years in Haryana. Suddenly, their right was infringed upon with the state government clearly favouring those who attacked the shops and later lodged a formal complaint with the police. In an upsurge of Hindutva, biryani became an expression of indignity to be hurled at the minorities.

The biryani sellers in Haryana got no relief whatsoever. Their liveli-hood was badly impacted. Some took to selling chicken biryani which found only a few takers. Others turned to vegetarian biryani which attracted even fewer customers. For many years they had worked in Mewat-Alwar region without disturbance and sold their biryani to largely Muslim clientele. On every Eid, the business was brisk with more people ready to spend a few extra rupees on the festive occasion. It stopped in 2016. The humble biryani sellers paid for the imposition of the dietary habits of the majority community in the state. Incidentally, selling, slaughtering and the consumption of beef in any form was banned in Haryana under the Gau Raksha and Gau Samvardhan schemes started by the state government. It was made a punishable offence. That it gave a free run to hooligans to impose their food prefer-ences on the innocent did not matter. Incidents were reported where the biryani sellers alleged that various Hindutva outfit members robbed them of their livelihood by turning their loaded pans and cauldrons upside down though they sold only chicken biryani. The idea was to harass the sellers and force them to take to vegetarianism. Cow, it was alleged, was held sacred by Hindus, and considered the repository of all 33 crore deities, according to an interpretation, slaughtering the animal hurt the sentiments of the Hindus, they alleged. What they never added was, only some North Indian Hindus considered the animal as sacred, for others it was a part of their dietary tradition. It resulted in a hilarious situation where the ruling Bharatiya Janata Party clamoured for a ban on all beef sale, purchase, slaughter, etc., in North India, but promised the locals in North-East India that it would not bring a law to stop the sale and purchase of meat, as almost all locals ate meat there. 'No beef ban if we come to power in poll-bound north-east states,' it sought to reassure the voters in March 2017. The assurance came at almost the same time as its government in Uttar Pradesh went crack-ing at abattoirs, closing them down following mere allegations of the abattoirs being illegal. Within weeks there were reports of unquiet and rising unemployment in the state. Hundreds of meat shops and slaughterhouses, including government-run abattoirs, were sealed by the Adityanath Government, leading to severe shortage of meat. It affected the livelihood of thousands of people who made a living by using common government abattoirs for a small fee.

Incidentally, the BJP went one step further in Kerala Vidhan Sabha elections with one of its candidates promising to make arrangements for the sale of the best beef in the state! It prompted Majlis Ittehadul Muslimeen chief Asaduddin Owaisi to quip, 'The BJP's hypocrisy is that the cow is mummy in Uttar Pradesh and yummy in Northeast and Kerala.'

The tragic and reprehensible killing of Akhlaq killing, unfortunately, proved to be merely the first such killing in the name of the cow. It set a template which claimed many more innocent lives. Muslim men going about their usual business were waylaid on the highways, at town squares, in agricultural fields and mercilessly lynched. While the women were left unharmed, the men paid the price, the idea being to instil fear in the community. For the first time in the history of independent India, one witnessed crimes being glorified online. In the past, criminals attempted to move away from the sight of crime, trying their best not to leave any evidence behind. Not so with lynching cases. The attackers not only lynched the victims, they also made videos of their actions and uploaded them online. Their temerity stemmed from a belief that their political masters will not only bail them out, but even reward them. Their confidence was not misplaced. Two years after Akhlaq's killing, the accused, out on bail, were provided contractual jobs with National Thermal Power Corporation, allegedly because of the good offices of the local BJP MP, Mahesh Sharma, a Union minister too. 'Fifteen of the youths accused of lynching Mohammad Akhlaq in Bishahra village of Dadri in September 2015 over suspicion of storing beef in his house have landed contractual jobs with NTPC Limited. Tejpal Nagar, the local BJP MLA, facilitated their recruitment in a meeting with senior NTPC officials on October 9 2017),' *The Hindu* reported (Ali, 2017). One of them even sought to contest elections from the constituency in 2019! When one of the accused, Ravin Sisodia, perished in police custody, Mahesh Sharma went to his village to console. In doing so, he wrapped the body of the accused in the Tricolour before it was sent for last rites. Killing a Muslim on allegations of cow slaughter was akin to a soldier laying down his life at the border!

Following Akhlaq's gruesome murder, shared widely through videos online and WhatsApp, casualties were reported from places like Jammu, Delhi, Alwar, Saharanpur, Hapur, Raigarh, Giridih, Udaipur, etc. Some were killed merely because they were Muslims and transporting cattle, others only because they were Muslims, neither were they transporting cattle nor eating them. They were not even seen with a cow skin. Just the fact that the mob wanted to kill a Muslim seemed sufficient reason. For instance, in western Uttar Pradesh's Hapur, a middle-aged gentleman Qasim was lynched by people. He had no animal with him when he was attacked by a mob who beat him mercilessly until he almost died. Then he was pulled by hands and feet as the mob threw him into a pit to die. The policemen were not just bystanders. In a picture which went viral, they were actually seen clearing the path for Qasim to be disposed of by the mob. Another man, a 60-plus man Samiuddin who tried to rescue him, was badly mauled, abused, his beard pulled at. He spent 20 days in various hospitals under treatment. The day he was discharged, Yudhisthir Sisodia, the principal accused in the Hapur lynching case, was given bail by a session court and came out of the jail to a hero's welcome.

The Hapur case, however, paled in comparison to the political ramifications of the lynching of Alimuddin in Jharkhand's Raigarh. A coal merchant was also accused of transporting beef in his van. He was waylaid in the market in the town and beaten mercilessly in full view of shopkeepers and others. A video was made of his lynching and promptly shared by the attackers. Among the recipients was the teenage son of Alimuddin who rushed out to help his father. Too late, it turned out. Alimuddin breathed his last before the son could meet him in the hospital where he was taken by the police a few hours after the assault. Eleven men were arrested by the police and convicted of the crime by the Jharkhand High Court. Later, eight of them were given bail by the state High Court. The men came out to a rousing reception with Union Minister Jayant Sinha greeting them with garlands and sweets like they had just won a trophy for the country. Clearly, the stakes in beef politics of North India went beyond matters of justice and fair play. It was not just acceptable to kill a Muslim for the most frivolous reason related to the cow; it was in fact to be appreciated.

In some cases, men were lynched because a dead animal was found near their house. In other instances because sweepers were seen removing a dead animal. In still others, because the mob just decided that a coal merchant was actually a beef merchant! Or, as in the first noted case of Akhlaq, that the deceased had somehow managed to kill a cow in a congested locality, stored the beef of the entire animal in the freezer of his medium-sized fridge and went to sleep! That the allegations bordered on the credulous and challenged common sense, mattered little. What mattered was rallying the Hindus against the perceived challenge of Muslims. The Hindu religion was in danger was the underlying message. And the Muslims cared not for their sentiments was drummed into their conscious and subconscious mind. Beef became an easy glue in North India. The masses asked no uneasy questions. They, in fact, proved happy recipients of lies, prejudices and oddities. The politicians supplied them enough fuel to keep the fire burning till the next elections. Then they reaped a rich harvest: the BJP formed a government with a thumping majority in Uttar Pradesh less than two years after Akhlaq's lynching. The BJP's government in Jharkhand, formed with allies' support, suddenly became stable and strong. So much so, in the 2019 Lok Sabha elections, the party, with the ally All Jharkhand Students Union, romped home on all but two of the 14 seats in the state. The victory came on the heels of allegations of Jharkhand becoming the lynching capital of the country with more instances reported of lynching from the state than any other state. Not just Muslims, even Christians and Dalits were lynched in the state. Cow was no longer just an animal believed to be sacred by millions. Cow was now a political animal whose worth went much beyond a temple. Talking of a temple, for all the fuss about cow slaughter and consumption of meat by Muslims, Christians and Dalits—four men were publicly thrashed in Una, Gujarat, for skinning a dead cow while three Christians were assaulted in Jharkhand's Khunti District for allegedly selling cow meat—there is not a single cow temple in the country, nor does the cow feature among the animals held sacred by pious Hindus in ancient India. In fact, the sacred texts of ancient India, including the Vedas, Upanishads and the Puranas, talk in detail of what kind of food to serve to propitiate a deity. And, cow meat was never regarded as a taboo. In fact, it was a delicacy in ancient India with beef being served to the most honoured guests by the rich. The people with lesser resources served mutton! Noted historian, D. N. Jha, whose work, *The Myth of the Holy Cow* has become a benchmark for tracing the evolution of the cow from a dietary preference to a sacred sacrificial offering and to a political animal, minced no words in stating,

> The cow was never used for spiritual elevation. In the 20th century everybody used the cow as a political weapon. In the late 19th century and early 20th century, Dayanand Saraswati used it for the mobilization of the Hindus. This even resulted in many Hindu–Muslim riots. Since 1925, the RSS (Rashtriya Swayamsevak Sangh) has used it in

the same way. It has been used for politics, not just simple politics, but communal politics. It is an attempt at polarization. The cow has nothing to do with the sacred or the spiritual. It is just a political animal. (Jha 2002 as cited in Salam 2019)

In ancient India, much before the Muslims set foot in India, cow was consumed by the upper castes. As Prof Jha put it,

The RSS does not know what is happening in this country. They say only Muslims and Dalits eat beef. It is all nonsense. If you go back in history, there is so much mention of cattle sacrifice and of cows being killed to propitiate deities. There is no doubt that the cows were killed and the Brahmins ate meat. The practice continued even after the Vedic period. It existed during the Buddhist period and also during the times of the Mauryas. The Manu Smriti also mentions it. These fellows (Hindutva proponents) do not realize that the historical evidence is totally against their viewpoint. Everybody knows that cows were killed on such occasions as marriage, the sacred thread ceremony, the arrival of the guest, the time of death, at the time of house-warming. There are many instances listed in scriptures. If there was an honourable guest, he would be served cow meat. In agrarian societies, it was very common. It took Brahmins a long time to change their outlook towards the cow. Later, much later, they gave up eating its meat. If you look at the Vedas or the Dharma Sutras, cow killing was fine. After the Mauryan period, references (to cow slaughter) become fewer and fewer in texts. Towards the beginning of the first millennium AD this change was taking place, mainly in northern India. (Jha 2002)

In ancient India, Hindu deities were known to favour meat. For instance, the main food of Agni comprised meat of barren cow and ox. Similarly, sterile cows were sacrificed for Maruts. The Mahabharata too refers to the well-respected king, Rantideva. He is described as a man 'in whose kitchen two thousand cows were butchered each day, their flesh, along with grain, being distributed among the Brahmans' (ibid.).

Jha is not the only historian to point towards cow being a utility item, even one of dietary preference. He has had support for long. For instance, a scholar like P. V. Kane (2006) in his book *History of Dharmashastra* referred to Vedic passages which talk of cow killing and beef eating. Similarly, H. H. Wilson, the first Chair of Sanskrit at Oxford, wrote, 'The sacrifice of the horse or of the cow, the gomedha or ashvamedha, appears to have been common in the earlier periods of the Hindu ritual.'

In modern India, however, things have been spectacularly, and often, tragically different. The cow has become an instrument for mobilization of the ignorant. It started soon after the failed First War of Independence in 1857. Though initially it was an anti-British movement, with Muslims very much part of Gau Rakshini Sabhas and Samitis that were formed in Punjab, Awadh and Gujarat, the British slowly turned the focus of the movement from the colonial masters to the local people. And, a movement that began with protests against the cow being a part of the British kitchen every day, soon turned into a divisive campaign against Muslims. Noted scholars Dharampal and T.M. Mukundan highlighted the colonial game of divide and rule with much clarity in *British Origin of Cow Slaughter in India*. They stated:

The enormity of the movement and the threat it posed to the British may be gauged by the statement of Viceroy Lansdowne when he said: 'I doubt whether, since the Mutiny, any movement containing in it a greater amount of potential mischief has engaged the attention of the Government of India'. The fact that the movement was directed against the British and not against the Muslims, as commonly believed, was clear to Queen Victoria and her officers. Queen Victoria said in a letter to Viceroy Lord Lansdowne, 'Though the Muhammadan's cow killing is made the pretext for the agitation, it is, in fact, directed against us, who kill far more cows for our army, etc., than the Muhammadans'. Faced with a challenge, the British did what they were best at: divide and rule. They soon spread the rumour that the Muslims were cow-eaters, and ably turned what was a political movement against the British into a communal issue between the two leading communities (Dharampal and Mukundan 2002).

The movement for cow protection developed animosity towards perceived cow eaters: the Muslims. Writing in *Gita Press and the Making of Hindu India*, Akshaya Mukul said:

The later decades of the nineteenth century and the early ones of the twentieth were a time of rising religious antagonism between Hindus and Muslims, marked by frequent riots and competitive communalism. Besides the battle for supremacy between Hindi and Urdu, incidents of cow slaughter and music before mosques were becoming flashpoints between the two communities—from the major riot of 1893 in Azamgarh, Mau and adjoining areas on the issue of cow slaughter during Bakra-Id, to the resurgence of widespread violence in 1917 in Bihar's Shahabad, Gaya and Patna. (Mukul 2015)

The fire spread gradually but incessantly. Noted Hindu reformer Dayanand Saraswati worked actively for cow protection, setting up Gau Rakshini Sabhas across North India. Predictably, his politics was exclusionary, not inclusive. Early in the 20th century, as the newly formed Hindu Mahasabha joined hands with Saraswati's Arya Samaj, the cow was well and truly adopted by reactionary forces. They were given a cloak of dignity through their association with leaders like Madan Mohan Malviya, Lala Lajpat Rai and Babu Rajendra Prasad. With widely popular leaders lending their name to the movement, the leading party of the time, the Congress, too was compelled to take up the issue of cow protection in a big way. However, due to the involvement of the Mahasabha and others, the cow protection movement continued to be truly an anti-Muslim movement, the assumption that Muslims ate cow as part of their daily meal became widely accepted. That the Dalits ate too, and the people in South India, in general, ate the cow as well was off the radar. In the perception battle, Muslims were the villains. The lingering image was one of a Muslim as a person indulging in cow slaughter for a living or a meal. It did not change much post Independence. Of course, the Constitution of India neither gave the cow the status of a national animal nor made cow protection a part of fundamental rights. However, through Article 48, it became part of the Constitution's Directive Principles of State Policy. It read, 'The State shall endeavour to organize agriculture and animal husbandry on modern and scientific lines and shall, in particular, take steps for preserving and improving the breeds, and prohibiting the slaughter, of cows and calves and other milch and draught cattle.' The Article nudged the future governments towards a policy of cow protection, in a way encouraging the establishment of a blueprint for a ban on slaughter. It summed up the deliberations at the Constituent Assembly where some members spoke animatedly in favour of cow protection.

As recalled by Seema Chishti in *The Indian Express*, R. V. Dhulekar said:

And our Hindu society, or our Indian society, has included the cow in our fold. It is just like our mother. In fact, it is more than our mother. I can declare from this platform that there are thousands of persons who will not run at a man to kill that man for their mother or wife or children, but they will run at a man if that man does not want to protect the cow or wants to kill her.

The proponents of Hindutva, however, were not about to give up after Independence. Nearly two decades after the end of the British rule, a Member of Parliament, Swami Rameshwaranand of the Bharatiya Jana

Sangh, led a march of sadhus to the Parliament on 7 November 1966. He sought a nationwide ban on cow slaughter. The march of the sadhus led to police firing which took a toll of seven lives. The then Prime Minister Indira Gandhi sacked her Home Minister Gulzarilal Nanda. A year later, Mrs Gandhi constituted a committee to look into the proposal for a national law to ban cow slaughter. The committee was headed by Justice A. K. Sarkar and counted the RSS chief M.S. Golwalkar among its members. The members were granted six months to deliberate and submit their recommendations. However, for the next decade or so, it failed to come up with recommendations for a nationwide ban on cow slaughter. It was finally wound up in 1979.

The issue of cow slaughter too ceded space from main politics, replaced as it was with the demand for construction of a temple in Ayodhya to replace the Babri Masjid, which was claimed by Hindtuva votaries to have been built over the birthplace of Shri Ram. Liberating the Ramjanmabhoomi had a better ring for the common man in the late 1980s and 1990s. The issue of cow slaughter, however, was never abandoned. It was merely put on the backburner ready at a moment's notice to be revived. Narendra Modi's landslide victory in 2014 meant the issues which had been allowed to gather mothballs were freshly dusted and presented anew in front of polity and society. After stray voices in support of cow slaughter, Akhlaq's lynching announced loud and clear that cow slaughter and beef will occupy prime space in Hindutva politics in the coming years. As it turned out, Modi's lieutenants had well imbibed Dhulekar's words, and pressed on to capitalize on the issue. For them too, Hindu society was akin to Indian society. Though the BJP never made a law banning cow slaughter across the country, probably keeping mind its voters' dietary habits in the North-East and South India, it has already reaped electoral dividends. With around 45 reported instances of lynching between 2014 and 2019, the party, despite the Supreme Court direction, pressed not for a law against lynching but moved ahead to ban the sale and purchase of cattle anywhere except authorized markets with a lengthy procedure of documentation. It effectively meant a ban on the purchase, sale or slaughter of the animal, gravely impacting the leather industry. Incidentally, according to official figures, the period post 2014 has accounted for around 97 per cent of lynching cases since Independence. The party laughed all the way to Parliament, increasing both its seats and vote share in the new Lok Sabha constituted after the 2019 General Elections. Enjoying a thumping majority of its own, the party set the terms for political discourse. Playing catch up, Opposition parties too started talking in terms of *gaushalas*! Beef politics was very much on the platter and nobody could decline. In the winter of 2019, Uttar Pradesh's chief minister, BJP's Adityanath Yogi announced protection of cows with blankets. He had earlier talked of the cows being given an Adhaar-like number. Earlier in 2019, he had set up a corpus for funding the management and running of shelter homes for stray cattle. 'The corpus will be raised through 0.5 percent of the total excise revenue, 2 per cent from 'mandi' cess and 0.5 percent of the annual toll tax,' the state health minister Siddharth Nath Singh stated soon after the Lok Sabha elections in 2019.

Yogi's Madhya Pradesh counterpart, Kamal Nath of the Congress party, promptly released an elaborate scheme for cow protection, establishment of cow sanctuaries, etc. In competitive cow politics, Nath did not want to lose. The Gwalior district collector went a step further. He announced that anybody desirous of procuring a gun licence had to donate 10 blankets to gaushalas!

In neighbouring Rajasthan, President Ram Nath Kovind gave 'previous sanction' to the Ashok Gehlot-led Congress government for the introduction of Rajasthan Bovine Animals (Prohibition of Slaughter and Regulation of Temporary Migration or Export) Bill in June 2019.

The peaceful, gentle cow had well and truly become a political weapon, and beef, the new ammunition for parties to strike. Whether the Hindutva votaries won the elections or not, it was the common man who invariably lost. From the farmers who suffered due to stray or aged cattle which they were no longer allowed to sell or slaughter, to the biryani sellers of Mewat to the meat merchants of Noida, the loss was entirely that of the faceless masses. The politicians sowed hate, reaped the dividends. In beef politics of North India, it was the common man who was deprived of both affordable meat and a sustainable livelihood.

References

Ali, Mohammad. 2017. 'Dadri Accused Get Contractual Jobs at NTPC'. *The Hindu*, 14 October. Available at https://www.thehindu.com/news/national/dadri-accused-get-contractual-jobs-at-ntpc/article19859696.ece (accessed on 13 February 2020).

Chisti, Seema. 2017. 'Directive Principle, Not Right: How Cow Protection Became Part of Constitution'. *The Indian Express*, 1 June. Available at https://indianexpress.com/article/explained/directive-principle-not-right-how-cow-protection-became-part-of-constitution-4683383/ (accessed on 13 February 2020).

Dharampal, and T. M. Mukundan. 2002. *The British Origin of Cow-slaughter in India—With Some British Documents on the Anti-Kine-Killing Movement 1980–1894*. Kempty, Dawla: Society for Integrated Development of Himalayas.

Kane, P. V. 2006. *History of Dharmashastras*. Vol. 8. Pune: Bhandarkar Oriental Research Institute.

Mukul, Akshaya. 2015. *Gita Press and the Making of Hindu India*. Noida: HarperCollins.

Nair, Anil. 2015. 'Why Kerala Has No Beef with Beef'. *The Times of India*, 8 March. Available at https://timesofindia.indiatimes.com/home/sunday-times/deep-focus/Why-Kerala-has-no-beef-with-beef/articleshow/46489828.cms (accessed on 13 February 2020).

Salam, Ziya Us. 2019. *Lynch Files: The Forgotten Saga of the Victims of Hate Crime*. New Delhi: SAGE Publications.

3

Dravidian Food Culture
Discourse on Identity and Diffusion

Sreenathan M.

Introduction

Food has emerged as a promising enterprise of localizing culinary experiences of the global others. It became a mediating cultural item for negotiating otherness. Globalization has opened a new food landscape of global culinary cultures across the world. It can be viewed as a palate colonization of the West. Such a classic view on colonization as a metaphor of exploitation does not sustain in the global narrative frame. Exchanges and mobility of cultures do not suit any more in the exclusive frame of exploitation and dominance in the emerging web-cultural context. Experiencing the other has emerged as a web-induced metaphor, which emphatically necessitates the avenues of experiences of global humanity. In this context, it has projected food tourism as a way of experiencing the other. Globalization from the West to the East has brought the international taste to the local tongue. The classical view generated against the West confirms it as nothing but the cultivation of the taste of the West in the East. Hence, as per the so-called 'ideological interpretation', it is nothing more than the colonization of tastes within the frame of globalization. The necessity of arguing in line with the classical dichotomy between the West and the East created by the print can be questioned. To the netizens, global experiences can be more humane than that. As per the channels offered by globalization, there can be an equal possibility of the reverse, that is, the framing of the idea of localizing food culture from the East to the West. If the reverse process has not succeeded to that extent, it cannot simply be blamed as globalization-induced colonization. On the other hand, the failures of not attaining the reverse localization must be verified, as those might have happened due to economic and cultural reasons. However, the debate needs to be settled before arguing against a process of exchanges. The trend of arguments continues with the believed background of print legitimacy by ignoring the web context of digital emancipation. It is expected in this context, discussion on any cultural package would frame the subject more overtly in lieu of digital humanity. The digital humanity is conceived more as a process of emancipation than print-inculcated compassion. The theme focused here is on a specific cultural package of Dravidian food culture.

Landscaping of Dravidian Food Culture

In the Indian context, food is conceived more as an identity marker and understood in terms of one being holy or forbidden (Siddique Mohamad Asim 2011, Utsa Ray 2015). While understanding the dietary practices in India diachronically, different trajectories of conflict and negotiation emerge. Food culture of India stands against the imagination of Eurocentric nation state ideology, which is heavily rooted in the singularity of representation. Cuisine in India is pluralistic from its very representation, which reflects the lineages of sub-regional, regional, caste, class, religious and cosmopolitan converged paradigms. Ever growing inclusion, exclusion, diffusion and enforced expulsion of food made India a culinary hotspot. The country bears culinary strands derived from hunting-gathering communities to globalized cosmopolitan societies. Tracing the dietary ideas and practices along the line of linguistic lineages, food cultures of India suggest both diverse and converged patterns. As a linguistic area, South Asia is a well-acknowledged model of convergence. A review on food cultures of India shares the realm of convergence and mutually exclusive cultural traits as in linguistic lineages. Keeping the evolutionary nature of the consumption tradition and associated social practices, it cannot be expected that any cultural package as that of food culture would remain in isolation. With this proposition, this chapter has its focus on Dravidian food cultures. This embodied reasoning necessitates defining Dravidian food cultures at the outset. Primarily, the word Dravidian is reflected here as a linguistic family, which otherwise comprises various speech communities representing

30 or more languages. Looking at it ethnologically, they are represented diachronically by groups of almost all economic practices. It includes small and relatively isolated communities with low development indices, identified by the Government of India as Particularly Vulnerable Tribal Groups (PVTGs), to representatives of knowledge economy, thus covering a very wide ethnic sphere of the Dravidian language speakers. It is important to recognize that Dravidian is not a single social category and thus they cannot be expected to have a single culinary culture. Hence, the postulation is on food cultures of the Dravidian.

Food and Language

Edward Sapir's (1949) insight serves as the underlying framework of this cultural analysis on food culture. In his words, 'vocabulary is a very sensitive index of the culture of a people'. No doubt, there is a strong relation between food culture and the food lexicon of respective languages. Food lexicon can tell us a lot about the eating or drinking habits of the people. Dravidian ensemble covers the simpler PVTGs to complex cosmopolitan communities, cutting across the wide spectrum of social-cultural variations. Thus, the Dravidian languages provide objective evidences in the form of domain-specific words. Culture-specific words are conceptual tools that reflect a society's past and current experiences of food culture. There cannot be a linear culinary tradition traceable to any speech group without fractured punctuations. Vestiges of multiple representations of food culture practices are expressed by all linguistic lineages. As the society changes, some of the habits may gradually be modified or discarded, while some new ones may be enjoined. Outlook of a society is assessed from its stock of food cultural lexicon, which offers insight into the cognitive taxonomy of food and associated cultural practices.

Like language, food also is a cultural product (Blench R. M. 2004). It is a marker of humanness between nature and culture. Levi-Strauss (1969) has highlighted the distinction between nature and culture in order to define humanness, while the raw represents nature, cooked signifies culture. It is the cultural process of cooking that transformed some animals into humans. In other words, it is through culinary practices that humanity distinguishes itself from the natural world. Selected natural materials are culturally structured into food and the transformation also is engineered by culture. Procurement and consumption are always governed by ecological and economic conditions within the cultural milieu. Ecology delineates the cognitive categorization of the edible and non-edible among natural items. The idea of edibleness does not propose what is good to eat, rather it conforms to the semantic value of edibleness. All edible items listed in an ecological niche cannot be equally tasty and healthy to all who consume; there is a choice involved in it at individual or social level. Such dietary preferences and its cultural reasoning among social groups are subjects of detailed enquiry. Food culture of any group holds the food package trajectories embedded in different economic practices. Along with ecological, the social and cultural reasoning, and the economic factors also delimit the choice of edibility. Further, the physiological state of individuals plays a significant role in the making of choice. What is healthy to eat is a concern of nutrition and health sciences; those disciplines are sometimes insensitive or even opposed to the Levi-Strausssean concept of transformation of food as a cultural product. Modern dietary specialists often suggest raw or just heated food rather than cooked one.

Semiotics of Dravidian Food Sphere

Anthropologically food is a primary need (Doglas 2004). This need is highly structured when we look at it from the perspective of structuralism. It involves raw substances, culinary practices, habitual patterns, recipes and politics of consumption. As a system it covers the topic of semiotics, nutrition, social structure and cultural ethos and to related discourses and associated images. As it is a sign system, its signification can be interpreted. It can be conceived as a language expressing social structures and cultural systems (Levi-Strauss 1969).

This study has traced the line of enquiry made on choice (Caplan et al. 1998); a culinary package choice is basically a socially loaded representation. One may ask, to what extent food culture can be valued as altruistic in its praxis. There lies the narrative turn, as food culture has a myriad of ideological underpinnings and it is positioned against altruistic imagination. The cultural construct of culinary can be understood by recognizing the importance of each node, those represent different trajectories of palate adaptation. It is a continuous process of addition, omission, admixture and innovation. Hence it would share plurality in identity construct. Dravidian food culture represents the very plurality of tastes of varied times and choices. The word Dravidian in 'Dravidian food culture' does not qualify 'food culture' as a uniform food choice or culinary practice. On the contrary, it pluralizes the food cultures practised by different speech communities. This way of understanding redefines the premise as 'food: culture'. However, the term 'Dravidian' itself stands with a plural representation and justifies the terminology, Dravidian food spheres.

As it is mentioned earlier, Dravidian as a linguistic family represents a gamut of diverse speech groups. Each speech group has both shared and exclusive traits in language and culinary culture. Also, continuous co-existence with other families of languages helped diffusion of linguistic and cultural traits at inter-linguistic family level. Thus, Dravidian food cultures represent different levels of sharing, innovation and conservation of food traits in diachronic and synchronic contexts.

Dravidian Culinary Mapping

The boundary of a language and its dialect diversity is pertinent in drawing the food map of a speech community. A language is an ensemble of dialects. Dialects can be differentiated geographically as rural or regional, coastal, urban and marked with social variables like class, caste and religion. Food culture of a speech community can also be marked with the same line of differentiation. Unlike dialect continuum, food mapping shows different isoglosses coexisting in the food atlas and isolexic lines can be crossed between different isoglosses. Within the family, demarcation between different dialects of a language and between different languages is not absolutely discrete. The same can be observed in case of food culture as well. Raw materials used may be common, the cooking process may be shared, but not always the recipes. Other ingredients used may or may not be common and the end product may be different as per the taste of each group. Both shared and exclusive paradigms are evident and thus it is diverse in representation. The culinary practices indicate differences like languages and these differences become markers of identity. Beyond such differences at certain levels, sharing of features is seen between languages of a family. Similarly, certain commonalities in food culture can also be present inherently. Apparently, differences of identity sustain. Thus, to say, different food atlas can be drawn at family, subfamily and individual language levels. Mapping of unique and common food traits within Dravidian diversity and across other language families of India is typologically possible. The cultural reason for existence of all traits is not diffusion, and that is an issue which needs further probing. Why selective features are accommodated and others are not preferred has not been convincingly explained by typologists in case of linguistic convergence. Like languages, cultural diffusion also remains selective. Diffusion of culinary practices shows a pattern of borrowing and integration. But it is not to the extent of culinary replacement that is not allowed by receptive cultures in order to maintain their respective identity. It can be argued that reduction in heritage food repertoire is not encouraged by cultures within India.

Dravidian Food Study—Synthetic Paradigm

Tracing of food culture of Dravidians touches archaeological, histori-cal, ethnological and linguistic discourses. However, placing all such discourses and their conflicting views would not suffice to continue the study of the subject. Notwithstanding the inadequacy, framing some of the discourses becomes necessary. Elaborate accounts on prehistory and linguistic archaeology need to be touched through references in order to build the background setting of this discussion.

Dravidian Food Archaeology

In recent times, much attention has been directed towards the linguistic archaeology of India. Franklin Southworth (2005) has reconstructed the prehistoric linguistic map of South Asia. The presence of the Dravidian family of languages in India has been elaborately discussed and their antiquity was traced to Neolithic and later to the Mesolithic (Fuller, 2003a) Dravidian culinary practices, including food items, methods of preparation and consumption practices. This opens a framework comprising economic activities and associated food culture practices. Southworth (2005) also traced the historical and etymological back-ground of South Asian crops and crop names. He has discussed in detail diffusion of crops and crop names across linguistic boundaries and migration of crops from Africa and other continents to India. Crops and associated linguistic groups and direction of borrowing of terms and inclusion of crops have also been discussed. By assessing the sharing pattern of crop vocabulary, it can be assumed that cultural con-vergence is more common than exclusively associated packages. This in turn leads to two kinds of inferences—either common borrowing from an extinct language or deep-level interaction between Dravidian and Indo-Aryan languages in prehistoric times. Southworth (2005) has undertaken an analysis of Dravidian etymological data (Burrow and Emeneaue 1984), in terms of subsistence reconstructions with generally convincing results. It has shown that the earliest phase of Dravidian expansion records no sign of agriculture but (lexically) reflects animal herding and wild food processing. This is associated with the split of Brahui language from the remainder. The next phase, including Kurux and Malto, shows clear signs of agriculture (taro production but not cereals) and herding, while South and Central Dravidian had a wide range of agricultural production (Southworth, 2005).

Dorrain Fuller has widely studied the Dravidian crop vocabulary (2001, 2002, 2003a), Indus and non-Indus tradition of agriculture (2003b), African crops in prehistoric South Asia (2003c), culinary changes in

TABLE 3.1 *Four Modes of Diffusion/Evolution of Cuisine in Terms of Food Items and Associated Cultural Practices*

Cultural Process	Archaeological Expectation	South Indian Examples
Food item already used, evolution/elaboration of existing cooking practices	Crops already present in earlier period	Horse gram, moong bean, native small millets
Food item(s) borrowed with practices of preparation	One or more food items introduced together with introduced artefacts for preparation	Crops and ceramic forms from North Deccan, including wheat and barley, possibly use of milk, and new jar forms
New food items added to existing culinary practices	New food item appears without other associated changes	African crops, e.g., pearl millet and hyacinth bean, in the second millennium BC. These foods, including pigeon pea, fit the existing summer millet/pulse category.
New food item with newly created culinary role	New food item associated with new, but not introduced, changes	

Source: Fullet et al. (2004).

prehistoric India (2005) and jointly on southern Neolithic cultivation system (Fuller et al. 2001). He has illustrated the following four modes of diffusion/evolution of cuisine in terms of food items and associated cultural practices of food preparation (Fuller et al. 2004; see Table 3.1).

Fuller also established linguistic models for different modes in the evolution and diffusion of words in a given language in relation to foodstuffs. These included: name evolving from earlier linguistic roots; name borrowed with food item; pointing to a semantic shift whereby existing name was re-applied to new species and compound name created from existing words. To conclude, Fuller (2003a) believed that Proto Dravidians (PD) have been part of the pre-agricultural complex following wild grain using Mesolithic representatives.

Current perceptions on Dravidian agricultural heritage (Fuller 2001, 2002, 2003, McAlpin 1981, Southworth 1976, 1988, 1992, 2005) vary widely and the debate over Dravidian antiquity reflects conflicting views. The linguists could not yet conclude unanimously whether the Dravidians were originally pastoral people from the mountainous areas of Central Asia (Zvelebil 1990) or of South Asia (Krishnamurti 2003). In deciding this question, the agricultural loan word links of Dravidians with Sumerians can be of importance (Blazk and Boisson 1997, Blazek 1999). Southworth (1979), however, thinks they participated in the Indus civilization, from which they acquired agriculture and the accompanying vocabulary. The PD reconstruction reflects a southern package of food production (millet/cattle). This early form differs considerably from the data of the later iron-age stage of the Dravidian languages with developed millet/rice agriculture. Historical depth for PD is estimated to be 2500–2000 BCE but could be older; Proto-South Dravidian (PSD) is estimated to be between 2000 and 1500 BCE, and PSD1 between 1500 and 1000 BCE (Southworth 2005).

Review of discourses on crop names and archaeological packages suggest some trajectories of culinary practices. Fuller et al. (2004) have emphasized diffusion of culinary culture in prehistoric India. What was exclusive to the Dravidian could only be connected with the southern Neolithic ash-mound culture, and inference can be drawn in favour of millet consumption. A study conducted among the Particularly Vulnerable Tribal Groups (PVTGS) of Kerala attests the fact that millet consumption has been their heritage. Grain husking and crushing technology have been commonly used by them; they also consume tubers, fruits, leaves, pulses, freshwater fishes, crabs, some birds and small animals. Roasting, boiling and steaming are popular culinary technologies practised by those communities. Cholanaikan, Kadar, Kattunaikan, Kurumba and Koraga are the five PVTGS of Kerala (Sreenathan, 2012). Among them, only Kurumba practice little agriculture in slash and burn mode. These days, the Kadars are adapted to practice agriculture, but there is not much trace of tradition among them. In brief, the above studies endorse millet and pulse as primordial items of food among the Dravidian 'heritage' communities. Not only has the linguistic archaeology affected Dravidian prehistory, it has also promoted multidisciplinary research on Dravidian studies. This in turn produced a rich body of critical discourses on Dravidian prehistory.

Dravidian Farming Societies

Keeping the conflicted discourses on pre-historic agricultural traditions of the Dravidians aside, the evolution of scriptural evidences of culinary tradition among the Dravidians can also be traced. Like the Rigveda for the Indo-Aryan tradition, Sangam literature was the ancient written source for the Dravidians.

Accordingly, the land of Tamilakam was divided into five *tinais* (recourse zones): *neytal* (coastal area), *mullai* (plains or grassland), *marutam* (paddy fields and riverbed), *kurinci* (uplands and hill) and *palai* (desert). Each tinai is marked with its geographical characters and associated economic practices. Neytal represents the coastal area and was inhabited by fishermen, sailors and salt manufacturers. Abundance of seafood defined the food culture of this zone. Sangam poems of this region also mentioned that the women folk of this area used to drink a special intoxicating brew called *munneer*. The next region that is close to the coast is the grassy plain land with pastoral settlements, where inhabitants made their livelihood out of pastoral practices. Mullai inhabitants' food culture was marked with dairy products. The fertile marutam was inhabited by agriculturalists and paddy and sugarcane were cultivated largely. The poems confirm that the people of marutam tinai were fond of toddy and *ooncor* (mutton-rice, a preparation similar to biryani of present times). The inhabitants of the upland or hilly forest area, called the kurinji, were engaged in hunting, gathering and cultivated millets through the punam mode of slash and burn system. They also grew fruit plants and vegetables. Though they hunted small animals, a large part of their food came from gathered fruits, tubers and honey. People inhabiting the distant desert or barren land of the border area, the palai, robbed the traders of their money and merchandize.

Sangam literature reflects well-marked stages of transformation from hunting and gathering economy to agriculture and pastoralism. The emergence of trading centres and urban centric behaviour are also portrayed along with the capital themes of love and marriage, war and worship. It had outlined the culinary diversity very well that prevailed among the Dravidians. Each of the above zones had its own deities, flora, fauna, ethnic groups and their economic and cultural practices, including culinary culture. Different varieties of grains, millets, pulses, tubers and vegetables were domesticated. Different fruits, sugarcane and coconut were consumed. Cock and some other birds, fish, crab, turtle, rabbit, deer, goat, cattle, wild boar and porcupine were also eaten. Milk, *ghee*, curd, and butter were used in large quantities. Varieties of rice preparations, vegetable and meat curries were prepared and consumed. Use of oil, ghee, spices and salt was common. Methods of boiling, roasting, frying and steaming were followed and the use of cooking vessels of different sizes was in vogue. The crop items identified by Southworth (2005) and Fuller (2003a) and grown and consumed by the Dravidians have been also endorsed by Sangam literature. Consumption of beverage was considered aristocratic and was socially accepted; the habit of alcohol consumption was considered a mark of affluence and vigour.

Varieties of brews were in use. Despite differences in the geography of habitat and of economic practice, Dravidians developed a habit of consumption of certain common varieties of food crops and edible fauna. Culinary practices among hunter-gatherers and shifting cultivators were simple in comparison to pastoral communities and those who were largely dependent on agriculture. Both agricultural and pastoral communities had rich and elaborate culinary culture. The fisherfolk had slightly different culinary practice, which was dominated by fish consumption. The frequency of consumption was varied as was the choice of eating. Otherwise, every stratum of society used to exchange and was familiar with the foodstuffs and culinary techniques of others. Dravidian food culture in those days was not vertically divided based on the intake of meat. Depending on availability and affordability, everyone consumed dishes made with meat. Inter-tinai exchange and egalitarian trends existed in Dravidian food culture. Deep cultural bipolarization started due to contact with the non-Dravidians, which started during the Sangam period. Jain and Buddhist vestiges found in Sangam literature supposedly accept the contact and its influence (Champakalakshmi 1996; Joseph 1997). This influence was more spatially structured, agriculturists and pastoralists were heavily influenced by those contacts than the rest of the occupational groups. Later, the agriculturist and pastoralist groups became the Dravidian mainstream and the rest remained as forest and coastal outliers. At the initial phase of Jain and Buddhist contacts, the Dravidian food map was redrawn on the basis of preference for meat eating and its abstinence.

The post-Sangam era had a different socio-cultural arrangement centred on institutions like temples and new movements like Bhakti cult of the Nayanars and Alwars. The large-scale migration of Brahmin fortune hunters in search of royal patronage and cultivable land in the river valleys led to intense interaction between the Aryan immigrants and the local Dravidian population, marked by conflict and co-operation (Champakalakshmi 1996).

With this contact interphase, the concept of pollution became socially rooted and eventually a new sense of food crystalized based on the concept. Tracing the notion of pure–impure dichotomy to Dravidian etymological base, it becomes clear that the notion of impurity was initially associated with death rituals and menstruation, but it was not practised at the level of social discrimination and unsociability. Under the Aryan influence, a sense of discrimination infiltrated into the Dravidian society, leading to the emergence of untouchability. The community of Pulaya, who got marginalized and discriminated in the post Sangam period, present one of the clear examples. Occupational purity became a concern in the text of Tirukkural and Manimeghalai, which in turn marked the diffusion of Aryan traits within the Dravidian cognitive space. Eventually, untouchability became a rule and purity gained a central space in all cultural frames. This led to the notion of purity in food among the Dravidians.

Bipolarity in Eating Habits

Traditional Dravidian eating habit changed due to their contact with the Middle Indo-Aryan population. During the Sangam era, there was a marked influence of Jainism and Buddhism in Dravidian areas. *Tholkaappiyam*, the Tamil grammar of Sangam era, and the ethical treatise *Tirukkural*, were written by Jain sannyasins. *Chlapthikaram*, another Sangam work, is also credited to a Jain follower. There are enough evidences of Jain presence in South India and many remnants are still preserved (Joseph 1997).

Due to Jain and Buddhist influences, mainly of the Jains, Dravidian culinary culture became polarized and vegetarianism came to be the preferred dietary habit. They also promoted changes in agriculture by providing better seeds and agriculture calendar.

During the Sangam period Buddhist practices were very popular in the Dravidian area. *Manimeghalai*, the Sangam text, is believed to be authored by a Buddhist. Introduction of agriculture among the pastoral communities is credited to the Buddhists. Spread of education, introduction of literacy centres near Buddhist temples and popularization of the Ayurveda system of medicine are credited to them. The heritage of non-violence is also rooted in Buddhism. The last phase of Buddhism was dominated by tantric beliefs; the practitioners were less interested in social service but more in earthly pleasures. Seeking affluence and eroticism became the order of the day. In this situation, Shaivism and Vaishnavism emerged as alternative paths for the people, their simpler lifestyle attracted majority of them. Emphasizing upon the purity of food and following the sanctity of culinary culture, Brahmins practised the Jain model of vegetarianism. Such food practices encouraged the production of certain agricultural goods in abundance. Abstinence from eating meat and some selected vegetables was strictly followed. In sequel to this, the Vaishnava and Shaiva traditions too recommended the selection of religiously sanctioned food items, abstinence from certain other items and fasting. Religious protagonists imposed new trends in the culinary culture by introducing the idea of purity on it. Socially practised concept of purity was extended to choose food and its making. Community-specific food culture was redefined and Brahmin-centric culinary practices got acceptance. Gender divide in the habit of eating together was introduced allowing certain preferences towards men. The husband was to eat his meal first; after all male members of the family finished eating, the remaining food was to be shared among the females of the family. Having major meals twice a day was prevalent during that period. Eating with the right hand became a rule imposed by the Aryans. A vertical division in culinary practices emerged when certain food items were earmarked for certain groups. It was in consonance with the Brahmanical dominance in food culture. These changes in culinary culture were evident in rudimentary conditions earlier, but the same became absolute reality during the post-Sangam period.

To sum it up, the social organizational pattern of the Sangam period was characterized by diverse food culture of different ethnicities based on ecology, climate, custom, region, caste, class and religion. Choice of food, cooking procedures, consumption style and sharing of food had multiple identity structures. Aryan contacts redefined the social organization and eventually changed the culinary culture, though a broad uniformity could be seen in culinary practices. Sharing, however, reflected social inclusion and exclusion. Rule of eating together was brahmin-centric and was determined hierarchically. Thus, food became a symbol of hierarchy and prestige. Such social order penetrated other caste groups as well, and borders of co-eating emerged along the line of elite castes. The downtrodden untouchable castes were not allowed to eat the food taken by the elites.

For all traditional societies, including the Vedic society, the basic culinary patternwas meat eating and so was the case with the Dravidians. This universal paradigm of culinary tradition was fractured and vegetarianism got rooted in the Dravidian context under the influence of Jainism, Buddhism and Brahmanism. The practice widened further and included abstinence of onion, garlic, cloves, tomatoes, in addition to meat and poultry items. This made all sections of the society to follow specific patterns in the selection of food items. Despite following practices recommended by their respective religions, the communities continued to eat what they were eating traditionally. Brahmins, however, were the exceptions. The divide was negotiated by the non-Brahmin groups by strictly following vegetarianism during religious festivals or at the time of worship. Rest of the time, they remained as Dravidians as they were in pre-contact days. Social structure influenced the culinary practices to such an extent that a sharp line between 'our food' and 'their food' was drawn. This divide could be seen at the community, regional, caste, class and religious levels.

To the mosaic of culinary culture of the Dravidians, Christian faith has also contributed with their biblical food traits and dining practices; eating three times a day was their contribution. The colonial strand of localization of taste for cake and biscuit to the local tongue can be mapped. Though a significant stress on meat and poultry consumption can be seen in comparison to vegetarian practices, individual preferences were well accommodated. Islamic religion also contributed with their culinary practices and showed preference for meat and poultry. The fasting practice was also followed according to their religious doctrine. Some of the local food items were absorbed as part of religious practices, which reflects a syncretic tradition in the process of localization.

Diffusion of Culinary Culture

The food lexicon of the Dravidian reflects on the borrowing of items from all cultures that came in contact (Witzel 2006). Many items were borrowed from Middle Indo-Aryan languages like Prakrit and Pali. Words for rice gruel, boiled rice, jaggery, ghee, curd, toddy, feast are borrowed from the above languages. Similarly, vestiges from Sanskrit language and other modern Indo-Aryan and foreign languages are also visible in the Dravidian food lexicon. The loan words of Dravidian food lexicon suggest diffusion of food traits from a very early period of history.

Despite keeping the identity in culinary culture alive at the regional, sub-regional, caste, class and religious levels, there is a syncretic pattern of food traits across boundaries. It is mainly because of the development of urban centres, mobility of people and growth of open markets. Restaurants have allowed people to taste the cuisine of others, thus blurring the boundary between 'our' and 'their' food, rather encouraging the cultivation of innovative tastes. New experiences enforced people to accommodate each other's taste, which propelled a diffusion of food traits. Other than the Brahmins, it was accommodated by all as a process of assimilation of the otherness, which has been localized and connected with food heritage. The openness induced cosmopolitanism of culinary culture among the Dravidians. Being part of India culturally, the North Indian dishes introduced in South India have been well accommodated; this is evident from the popularity of North Indian restaurants in the South. North too has accommodated the Southern cuisine. Chinese, Arab and Italian food items too have been well received by the Dravidians. It all renders a narration of accommodating otherness by declaring that though food identity is rigid, it is negotiable. Rigidness here may not be equated with religiosity, rather as heritage of taste and of ecological adaptation, and not by deserting the other. Like a *sprachbund* (linguistic area) marked with linguistic convergence, Dravidian food culture from the very beginning had shown commonness due to proximity and contact of cultures. Hence, it may be inferred that Dravidian food culture has not entirely descended from a proto Dravidian base, food traits have been shared and integrated. A substratum analysis will clearly reveal the process of borrowing of traits from different sources in different periods and their eventual localization. To identify what is Dravidian, one must move beyond the heritage package and identify it as a strategy of integrating the otherness. As has been mentioned, Dravidian food culture is not singular in nature but plural by existence. Limits of tolerance and intolerance are viably negotiated not by imposing authoritative identity, but by tolerantly imbibing the differences. This kind of inclusiveness by negotiation is the crux of a non-violence philosophy promulgated through vegetarianism. Against such singular paths of religious faith, Dravidian food culture stands apart with its inclusive plurality of people's faiths. That defines its identity of syncretic culinary web. It shares the narrative that choice cannot be imposed, it has to be based on the historical allegiance through which one would make one's selection. The philosophy behind Dravidian food culture is of tolerance, non-violence and negotiation; the way it asserts identity of Indianness is the taste of convergence.

Conclusion

The evidences gathered so far point to an ecology of multiplicity in Dravidian food culture. The practices developed along the line of its history suggest heterogeneity. Each linguistic group practise their food culture differently based on the embedded socio-political bearing. It still symbolizes the caste hierarchal order in sharing consumption practices in states other than Kerala. It is evident that feudalistic tradition of culinary practices is maintained among some of the speech communities. Accommodating the other remains a xenophobic experience. Kerala stands comparatively liberal in accommodating the others mainly due to continuous political practice and urbanization. Urban sphere has brought an amount of cosmopolitanism in eating habits dominated with non-vegetarianism. Religious underpinnings of food politics had long been negotiated with their consumption choice. The history of South India is not unique in experiencing others, and thus politics of choice, consumption and co-eating habits vary across linguistic divides. Otherwise, Dravidian food cultures reflect the identities and diffusion of food traits. Roland Barthes' (1964) concern on food as a system of communication bears a body of images, a protocol of usages, contexts and behaviours. Following Barthes, it can be concluded that the grammar of Dravidian food culture evidently reflects linguistic identity and the pattern of convergence.

References

Barthes. R. 1964. *Elements of Semiology*. London: Jonathan Cape.

———. 1967. 'Toward a Psychosociology of Contemporary Food Consumption'. In *Food and Culture: A Reader*, edited by C. Counihan and P. Van Esteric, 20–27. New York, NY; London: Routledge.

Blazek, V. 1999. 'Elam: A Bridge between Ancient Near East and Dravidian India?' In *Archaeology and Language IV*, edited by R. Blench and M. Spriggs, 48–78. London: Routledge.

Blazek, V., and C. Boisson. 1992. 'The Diffusion of Agricultural Terms from Mesopotamia'. *Archiv Orientalni* 60: 16–37.

Blench, R. M. 2004. 'Archaeology and Language: Methods and Issues'. In *Blackwell's Companion to Archaeology*, edited by J. Bintliff, 52–74. Oxford: Blackwell.

Burrow, T., and M. B. Emeneau. 1984. *A Dravidian Etymological Dictionary*. Oxford: Clarendon Press.

Caplan, P., A. Keane, A. Willets, and J. Williams. 1998. 'Studying Food Choice in Its Social and Historical Contexts: Approaches from a Social and Anthropological Perspective'. In *The Nations Diet: Social Science of Food Choice*, edited by A. Murcott, 168–182. Harlow: Longman.

Champakalakshmi, P. 1996. *Trade, Ideology and Urbanization South India 300BC to AD1300*. New Delhi: Oxford University Press.

Doglas, M. 1975. *Implicit Meanings Essays in Anthropology*. London: Routledge.

Fuller, D. Q. 2001. 'Ashmounds and Hilltop Villages: the Search for Early Agriculture in Southern India'. *Archaeology International* 4 (2000/2001): 43–46.

———. 2002. 'Fifty Years of Archaeobotanical Studies in India: Laying a Solid Foundation'. In *Indian Archaeology in Retrospect*, edited by S. Settar and R. Korisettar, 247–363. Vol. 3: *Archaeology and Interactive Disciplines*. Delhi: Manohar.

———. 2003a. 'An Agricultural Perspective on Dravidian Historical Linguistics: Archaeological Crop Packages, Livestock and Dravidian Crop Vocabulary'. In *Examining the Farming/Language Dispersal Hypothesis, McDonald Institute Monographs*, edited by P. Bellwood and C. Renfrew, 191–214. Cambridge: McDonald Institute for Archaeological Research.

———. 2003b. 'Indus and Non-Indus Agricultural Traditions: Local Developments and Crop Adoptions on the Indian Peninsula'. In *Indus

Ethnobiology: New Perspectives from the Field, edited by S. A. Weber and W. R. Belcher, 343–396. Lanham: Lexington.

Fuller, D. Q. 2003c. 'African Crops in Prehistoric South Asia: A Critical Review'. In *Food, Fuel and Fields: Progress in African Archaeobotany, Africa Praehistorica*, edited by K. Neumann, A. Butler and S. Kahlheber, 239–271. Vol. 15. K¨oln: Heinrich-Barth Institut.

———. 2005. 'Ceramics, Seeds and Culinary Change in Prehistoric India'. *Antiquity*, December. doi:10.1017/S0003598X00114917.

Fuller, D. Q., R. Korisettar, and P. C. Venkatasubbaiah. 2001. 'Southern Neolithic Cultivation Systems: A Reconstruction Based on Archaeobotanical Evidence'. *South Asian Studies* 17 (1): 171–187.

Fuller, D. Q., R. Korisettar, P. C. Venkatasubbaiah, and M. K. Jones. 2004. 'Early Plant Domestications in Southern India: Some Preliminary Archaeobotanical Results'. *Vegetation History and Archaeobotany* 13 (2): 115–129.

Joseph, P. M. 1997. *Jainism in South India*. Thiruvananthapuram: The International School of Dravidian Linguistics.

Krishnamurti, B. 2003. *Dravidian Languages*. New Delhi: Cambridge University Press.

Levi-Strauss, C. 1969. *The Raw and Cooked*. Chicago, IL: University of Chicago Press.

McAlpin, D. W. 1981. *Proto-Elamo-Dravidian: The Evidence and Its Implications*. Philadelphia, PA: American Philosophical Society.

Sapir, Edward. 1949. *Culture, Language and Personality*, David Goodmanmanden Baum (ed.). Los Angels, Berkely, London: University of California Press.

Siddiqui, Mohammad Asim. 2011. 'Vegetarian or Non-vegetarian, Traditional or Modern Food as a Marker of Identity'. In *The Writers Feast Food and the Cultures of Representation*, edited by Supriya Chaudhuri and Rimi B. Chatterjee. New Delhi: Orient BlackSwan.

Southworth, F. C. 1976. 'Cereals in South Asian Prehistory: The Linguistic Evidence'. In *Ecological Backgrounds of South Asian Prehistory*, edited by K. A. R. Kennedy and G. L. Possehl, 52–75. Cornell University, Ithaca, New York: South Asia Program.

———. 1979. 'Lexical Evidence for Early Contacts between Indo-Aryan and Dravidian'. In *Aryan and Non-Aryan in India*, edited by M. M. Deshpande and P. E. Hook, 191–233. Ann Arbor, MI: Center for South and Southeast Asian Studies, University of Michigan.

———. 1988. 'Ancient Economic Plants of South Asia: Linguistic Archaeology and Early Agriculture'. In *Languages and Cultures: Studies in Honor of Edgar C. Polome*, edited by M. A. Jazayery and W. Winter, 649–688. Amsterdam: Mouton de Gruyter.

———. 1992. 'Linguistics and Archaeology: Prehistoric Implications of Some South Asian Plant Names'. In *South Asian Archaeology Studies*, edited by G. L. Possehl, 81–85. New Delhi: Oxford and IBH.

———. 2005. *The Linguistic Archaeology of South Asia*. London: Routledge.

Sapir, Edward. 1949. *Culture, Language and Personality*, David Goodmanmanden Baum (ed.). Los Angels, Berkely, London: University of California Press.

Sreenathan, M. 2012. 'Agricultural Logos in Dravidian Languages (with Special Reference to Primitive Tribal Groups of Kerala)'. UGC Major Research Project (2009–2011).

Ray, U. 2015. *Culinary Culture in Colonial India: A Cosmopolitan Platter and Middle Class*. New Delhi: Cambridge University Press.

Witzel, M., 2006. 'South Asian Agricultural Terms in Indo-Aryan'. In *Ethnogenesis in South and Central Asia*, edited by T. Osada, Y. I. Sato and M. Witzel, 96–120. Harvard-Kyoto Roundtable (7th ESCA). Kyoto: Research Institute for Humanities and Nature.

Zvelebil, K. 1990. *Dravidian Linguistics: An Introduction*. Pondicherry: Pondicherry Institute of Language and Culture.

4

Food for Musicians
Gastric Ideas and Practices among North Indian Artistic Communities*

Svetlana Ryzhakova

Khana to hai, khanewale chahiye!

('The food is there, only eaters are needed!' It means the 'great ocean of art' lies right in front of us, only devoted disciples are needed, who are able to 'absorb' and 'digest' the knowledge.)

'I have never met a single musician in North India, for whom cooking good food and feeding guests would not be extremely important' (Dhar 2005).

Many famous singers, as rumoured, began their career with the addiction to green chilly. The cultural links between music and food, theatre and food, dance and food are plenty and diverse in Indian culture. The well-known Latin saying about the need and sufficiency of 'bread

* The article is written in frames of Dr Svetlana Ryzhakova's project 'Possession, Devotion, Performance: Borders and Interconnections of Personal Self-possession, Worship and Artistic Experience in Indian Artistic Traditions' with the support of the Russian Foundation for Fundamental Research (RFBR), No 18–09-00389.

and circuses' connects the physical with the emotional incarnations of 'food'. This principle is also highly applicable to the characteristics of the culture of the entire Indian society.

Food and spectacles are constantly featured in a myriad metaphorical comparisons, constituting a significant overall cultural thesaurus—starting with the category of *rasa*[1]—'taste'—known in the theory of theatre, culinary art and traditional medicine. It is believed that all entities, both physical and psychical, which 'penetrate' the body of a living being have certain pharmacological qualities and transform the body.

The material used in this chapter is derived from the tradition of Indian classical music, which is widespread in the northern parts of the country. India is the home of a vast number of musical traditions, small and large, divided in various genres and styles. Sometimes it is difficult to make a distinction between 'music', 'dance', 'drama' and 'ritual'; many forms have multiple functions, combining religious dedication, ritualistic purpose with entertainment. Some traditions are strongly related to particular ethnic, caste or religious communities, just like the Kalbelia dance, a recent and highly successful invention. But mostly, the genres and the communities are loosely related to each other; for instance, the tradition of Ghumar musical tune and dance of Rajasthan are known to almost all members of the local social strata, and is practised by women of various ethnic and social groups, from the royal Rajputs to semi-tribal Naths, with different flavours and nuances. Garba of Gujarat has the same importance; however, it has a Hindu ritualistic meaning and relates to a goddess, manifested in the form of a vessel at the centre of the dancing and music-making people; there are even Garbas practised by local Muslim and Parsi communities.

Ethnographic classification of musical traditions of India is not the aim of this chapter; it is a huge and ambitious task, which I cannot undertake in the frame of one article. But what I feel according to my humble experience, music really has a high status in the daily lives and in the social and religious ceremonies of all people of South Asia.

Most probably, the general outcomes of this chapter will be valid if one undertakes similar investigation of other traditions, such as the Karnatic (Carnatic) of South India, or some more local and specific styles.

Music has different set-ups in different social groups and strata of India; sometimes it is totally incorporated in daily routine, in peasant and artisans' work, and sometimes it is separated from any other activity, creating another, divine reality. India is home of one of the oldest sophisticated musical theories of the world. Here I shall address to this pan-Indian, elite, professional, highly developed music, which has not often become a subject of ethnographic and anthropological studies so far, but has full of interesting aspects and possibilities.

Certain food can serve a certain kind of 'master-narrative', describing different technologies of craft and art, and the performing arts here, perhaps, occupies an exceptional place. But what about the situation with real gastric traditions and habits among the professional Indian artistic communities? The mythological patrons of art, *gandharvas* and *yakshas,* are responsible respectively for sound and taste. The study of Indian artistic communities can provide a large material for understanding how ideal and real diets are formed, as different gastric habits are 'attached' to each other.

Artistic communities are sometimes heterogeneous. For example, in the case of Yakshagana of coastal Karnataka, the Hindus, Jains, Sikhs, and sometimes even Christians and Muslims not only perform together but also remain in a much more intimate relationship with each other as members of the troupe. In a similar manner, many groups of performers of Kathak constitute Muslims and Hindus. Custodians of the great musical heritage of Dhrupad, traditionally linked to the sacred tradition of Samaveda, are predominantly Muslims. The question is: Does the general profession lead to the unity of worldview and the rapprochement of everyday habits, norms and customs? Do they eat the same food?

This chapter is written on the basis of memoir literature and my personal experience; it does not cover this curious topic fully, but I suppose, it can bring some light to it. For many years I have kept close contact with musicians and dancers of India, for some of them practice of the art has been hereditary and across generations—*khandani, gharana ka log.* Their families have been already engaged in the profession for a few generations. I used to stay in *gurukulas* (schools of direct transmission of knowledge from teacher to pupils) of different theatrical and musical traditions; I met Dhrupadiyas and Khayaliyas, as well as dancers of various styles, and interviewed them. We enjoyed food and discussed food in both direct and metaphorical meanings (Ramanujan 1992, 10).

In the relationship to food, as well as in the theatrical art, there had been many spontaneous, accidental and unforeseen issues. This is expressed in the Hindi proverb: '*Rāg, rasoi, pagree, kabhi ban jaye',* which means, it's not always possible to achieve perfection in musical performance (unfolding of a raga), food preparation and tying a turban. A significant role here is played by chance, that is, good (or bad) luck.

Memoir literature, describing the life of artists and musicians, is a valuable source. These include Sheila Dhar's *Raga-n-Josh* (2005), Kumar Prasad Mukherji's *The Lost World of Hindustani Music* (2006) and Namita Devidayal's *The Music Room* (2013), with great attention to details describing the 'cultural margins' of classical music in India. Food—both real and imagined—occupies a significant place in these works. My friends and acquaintances, including Russians who have lived in India for a long time, always share their observations and life experiences. Their stories are very interesting for future reflection, and some remain in my memory forever.

One of my good friends, a musician, at the beginning of her life in India, decided to treat her hospitable Indian hosts with a typical Russian dish—the 'vinaigrette'. She visited the bazaar, bought everything she needed, finely chopped the vegetables, cooked it for a long time and spread the excellent contents in an impressive vessel. She poured some herbal oil, sprinkled a little salt and peppered slightly, and to check if the seasoning was right, took a little salad at the tip of the spoon and tried it. Noticing this last gesture, the hosts—to the indescribable surprise of my friend—did not touch the food![2] So, through this untouched bowl of 'vinaigrette', an important lesson of Indian cuisine was learned, as it turned out that in Hindu rituals and performing arts, the author, the master or the cook does not try or 'eat the dish', before it is fully ready, presented and divided between the participants of the meal, guests, listeners, spectators. Often, the first share is received by the gods, and then the remaining food becomes *prasadam*—consecrated 'scraps'.

In any musical or theatrical action, it turns out, as in food, that it is possible to detect the aroma, the first sensation of taste, feeling of 'absorption', aftertaste and nutritional characteristics. It is also possible to distinguish *vipaka*—something that comes after digestion of food. So, from sweet and salty it turns out sweet taste, from sour only sour, and from bitter, sharp and astringent, sharp. Similarly, for dramatic works each of the emotional states leads to some other. Besides, every food has a certain *guna*—quality, described as 'heavy', 'sluggish', 'cold', 'wet', 'smooth', 'hard', 'soft', 'mobile', etc.; *virya*—strength, hot ('solar') or cold ('lunar') and *prabhava*—effect, for example, one acting as a laxative.

Many rules are known in the art of use of spices; even in India, the ritual of 'the feeding of Agni' is practised which refers to the science of energy balance and connection, since fire has the important characteristic of the ability to unite. But questions arise about what kind of saturation does food or performance bring? What is the quality of the submitted 'product'? What impact will it have on the consumer?

The artist and spectator, the cook and the tastes are inextricably linked, and exist only in interaction. Once, after a long musical programme in Kolkata, where a wonderful singer Shubha Mudgal performed, one of the listeners, walking along the dark Chowringhee Avenue to the metro, told me: 'I admired how you tasted music! Thank you, for listening, for coming, for this feast, and for eating!' It turns out that not only the 'cook', but also the 'person who eats' contributes towards making the whole event of the 'feast' a success, and thus should be thanked and praised.

Pre-taste. *Pakka Gana*: To Cook and To Consume Music

Within all the diversity of Indian performing genres and their classifications, the conventions and difficulties of unambiguous translation into the language of such concepts as 'folk', 'classical', 'religious', etc., there is one classifying principle that one should pay attention to when speaking about art and cooking.

Classical music in India in everyday speech is often called *pakka gana*—referring to vocal music,[3] which is formed as a result of *pakna*—'to become ripe' or 'to be cooked'. The word pakka means here something 'strong', 'powerful', 'solid', 'real', 'not ephemeral'. The opposition is the category of *kachha*—the 'immature', 'weak', 'green', 'ephemeral'. In terms of musical and in general artistic craft, these concepts are not just metaphors.

In the case of pakka, we are talking about a long and difficult way of mastering a path in which everything that is casual disappear. The 'raw' and 'green'—in all senses of these words—do not exist for long; so, raw vegetables get spoiled quickly, but they can be preserved and pickled in the form of *achar*. The fresh, 'raw' taste of the artist's personality is necessary at the beginning, but it must be sacrificed for the future and development. This is the result of a long and rigid discipline, constantly compared in a figurative speech with 'fire', heating and brewing the contents of the body.

The body of an outstanding musician, playing and singing, is a body that was borne of years of discipline: *riaz* (Urdu) or *sadhana* (Sanskrit), by combining work with asceticism. Such masters are called sometimes *tapasvis*—'devotees', 'ascetics'. Their physical body disappears in everyday life, but flickers and manifests itself at the moment of fulfilment and transformation. However, the higher personality of the performer is achieved only with the help of a special blessing coming from outside, from above—*ashirvad* (meaning 'blessing' in Hindi) or *talim* ('education' and 'blessing' in Arab, Persian and Urdu). A person not having talim is a humiliating characteristic of the musician, it means almost that all his efforts and works had been futile.

What exactly is ashirvad or talim is often not easy to say, but its presence or absence is quite obvious for fellow musicians, and for many sophisticated listeners. In some cases, it is a question of the educational process lasting for years, in others it is about an almost instantaneous insight. However, this is always the result of a physical contact, usually fixed on shared food, the transfer of objects and in the establishment of a symbolic connection between the teacher and the pupil.

In the ceremony of *ganda-bandha*, establishing the intimate connection between the teacher and the student, a certain type of food is necessary. These can be—and almost always are—sweets. It can be a reciprocal feeding or the disciple eats the food blessed by a teacher. Teachers conduct this ritual in many ways: one might arrange a long ceremony, others might undertake minimal actions. Maya Rao, a famous Kathak dancer, told me her case of becoming a pupil. Her teacher, Sunder Prasad, appreciated her dance talent and decided to take her as a student; he gave her a one rupee coin, someone was sent to buy fresh milk, which was poured to a glass and mixed with a pinch of sugar and spice. Maya was given this drink with the teacher's blessing (Maya Rao_03 PF Bengaluru 2014). With the help of a coin, the 'condensed' energy of the teacher was transformed into a liquid substance, that is, milk, which was blessed, drunk by the girl and digested by her body at a time when she sat off on a long path of being introduced to a discipline over the same body. So milk turned out to be a 'foretaste' of acceptance and the mastering of an art form.

If the body of discipline (the body as a result of *riaz*) can be compared with the basic substance of the prepared dish (like rice), then the ashirvad can be compared to salt and spices that make the food special, tasty, personified and manifested.

Music, religion, medicine and food are interrelated. Sheila Dhar notes that the pakka gana or classical music is inaccessible to external observers, but 'people who are involved in music are pleased to realize that they know what *gharana*, *gayaki*, *samvadi* and *abhog* are; it is roughly the same as the knowledge of the ancient Greek language—inaccessible to ordinary people. The esoteric aura coupled with raucous, uninhibited singing voices of majority of masters, sometimes these sounds are not even very pleasant, not instantly enjoyable, but, apparently, are useful, like religion or medicine' (Dhar 2005, 238).

Pakka, in the case of art, means its thoroughness, thoughtfulness, refinement and foundation with a complex theoretical system. With the patterns of ritual and medicine, the musical art in India brings together the disciplinary knowledge, a theory supported by many years of practice and its verification in performance. 'Hardness' of classical music is combined with its 'fluidity' and elusiveness. So, 'to drink' some music instrument, for example, sitar, as a characteristic of a person refers to his knowledge and musical skill (Jan_03 PF New Delhi 2005). It turns out that the instrument itself is something like a 'top' or 'bunch' around which the musical ocean extends. The instrument and music are made from one substance, which is described as a kind of 'liquid' so that a person, a student, can 'drink', if only he has sufficient 'capacity' 'inside', an internal space capable of perceiving its greatness. Then he can become a master himself, a 'cook'. So, even the very presence of spices in the house carries a smell, the very presence of soaked rice before it is cooked creates anticipation. The presence of food transforms the space into a *rasoighar*, a kitchen, a sacred place in the house of Hindus, with respect to which many customs, habits and taboo are observed. Similarly, the very presence of musical instruments in the house requires a special attitude towards them: They are understood as the embodiment of the Goddess Saraswati, and the place where they are being kept is transformed into a kind of shrine, a music room. Both generate anticipation—an important part of both the meal and the concert.

Colours, Emotions, Smells and Aroma: Interconnections and Associations

One of the most interesting features of Indian culture is its synergy, that is, the habit of looking for a correspondence between realities that refer to different cultural codes. Thus, Indian musical melodies have artistic imagery and are expressed in *ragamalas* (miniatures), where sounds correspond to planets, etc. The most obvious explanations for the similarity and difference between complex musical realities are made through gastronomic language. Thus, Kumar Prasad Mukherji writes about the difference between the heavy vocal styles of Gwalior and lighter Marathi Natya Sangit: 'the difference is not between attar and incense, the fragrance of both of which is rich and overpowering. It is difference between a dish of *biryani* with the flavour of garlic, onion and saffron, and a dish of bland vegetable *curry*' (Mukherji 2006, 80).

The famous Kathak dancer and musician, Birju Maharaj, tapping on the intricate rhythmic drawings, resorts to their verbal coding, emphasizing long and short vowels: '*Sab-jee-puu-ri-or-ka-chori*' (literally 'vegetables, puri and kachori').

Certain dishes, even the very common ones, have been traditionally associated with specific places, and accordingly, have been rooted in their cultural context. Thus, K. P. Mukherji notes:

> Lucknow cuisine was also different. Biryani, it was generally thought, was not fit for discerning palette. It was eating by Delhiwalas. The Lucknowites favored pulao, thirty-six kinds of which were in existence then. The kebabs, especially kakori kebabs, used to melt in the mouth. The poultry for the mussallam and a memorable dish called chicken handi would be fed small balls made of kesar (saffron), and the milk for the sheermal bread would be from a cow that had devoured tons of rose petals. But the cuisine, which the affluent Muslims and the Hindu Kayasth of old Lucknow favored, was singularly unimaginative when it came to desserts. What I occasionally ate at garden parties of the minor potentates to accompaniment of chaitis, kajris and ghazals by lesser-known Lucknow tawayefs were balai, shahi tukra, kheer and mangoes, preceded of course by glorious kebabs. Right from the days if the first Mughal emperor Babar, Muslims were fascinated by the mango and cultivated numerous varieties. (2006, 36)

A close connection can be discovered between cultural codes of food and sex, sex and music. In many parts of India, prostitutes call the client the phrase: 'has the gentleman eaten?' or 'have you already had tea, or not?' (PF Calcutta 2003). In Andhra Pradesh and many other states, a woman cannot be asked to eat if she is alone at home: this can be misunderstood. It is not for nothing that the proverb says that 'a woman has two breasts, one gives to her child, the other to a husband'. Penis in the slang of hijra is often called *paneer*, cheese.

On the other hand, the connection of *tala* (musical rhythms) and *raga* (melodies) is regularly described as their 'love affair', where rhythms act as a 'feminine' beginning, creating regularity, the foundation of being, and melodies as 'masculine', developing, flying, but always returning to the landscape of their tala, to the structure laid down by the rhythm. Sexual connotations in subtle, sublimated forms are also an indispensable component of musical performance: the performance of one or another raga is often modelled as a personification of the melody, its 'walk', 'courtship', for certain sounds, the disclosure of its nature and essence, the discovery of hidden, secret places and also its development.

The important task of the musician is the creation of life; incorporeal melodies seem to take bodies, first of all, bodies filled with 'food' and 'love-attraction', and make their earthly way. It is no accident that the great Indian Muslim musician, Alauddin Khan, father of Ali Akbar Khan and teacher of Ravi Shankar, named his daughter Annapurna Devi, a Hindu name, literally meaning 'full of food', especially common in the sacred city of Varanasi and is associated with the goddesses Lakshmi and Durga. Annapurna Devi was a brilliant musician, perfectly played the sitar, but led a solitary way of life and was known only to a narrow circle of real connoisseurs: her music was never intended for sale.

The connection of emotions with the taste of food has been noticed for a long time, primarily in fiction and folklore, although it does not find unequivocal scientific confirmation. Lewis Carroll in *Alice's Adventures in Wonderland* noticed through his heroine:

> I won't have any pepper in my kitchen at all. Soup does very well without. Maybe it's always pepper that makes people hot-tempered,' she went on, very much pleased at having found out a new kind of rule, 'and vinegar that makes them sour—and chamomile that makes them bitter—and—and barley-sugar and such things that make children sweet-tempered. I only wish people knew *that*: then they wouldn't be so stingy about it, you know.

A fighting, active character, or a piercing look of a person in India is called *pirchi-mirchi* (sharp, peppery).

Pandit Pran Nath said that true music exists only for those who can mentally replace the flavour of kebab with each musical note (Dhar 2005, 58). So comprehensive development and involvement in a variety of emotionally coloured spheres of being, especially bodily sensual and gastronomic, is expected from a real musician and artist. However, we are talking about the cultural baggage; at the moment of direct performance, as we have already said, the artist departs from his own experiences, just as the Indian cook never tries food during cooking.

The influence of a product's quality on the body, whether it has a heating or cooling effect, is a significant factor. Singers, as a rule, avoid cooling products and food (for example, bananas, as will be discussed below). However, there are exceptions. K. P. Mukherji remembers how once right before her performance, Begum Akhtar, the famous singer, who was called the 'queen of ghazals', was sitting in the dressing room, smoking and eating ice cream. To the question of one of the admirers, if her throat hurts, she had smiled and replied: *'Gale se thhode hi gana gaya jata hai?'* (Do you really think that sounds are produced with one throat?) (2006, 97), thereby hinting on the involvement of a much more complicated process of sound production and stage work than it appears to the uninitiated viewers (Rahaim 2012).

To Cook and To Consume, To Consume and To Enjoy

Food preparation and feeding is intertwined in India with a multitude of norms, traditions, customs, prohibitions and regulations. Who can feed whom, as is well known, is determined, first of all, by the varna and caste systems. In practice, of course, the strictness of these rules varies, and people almost always adjust to the real circumstances.

Since it is believed that food carries the properties of the person who prepared it, in theory, not everyone should take it. *Ashtanga Sangraha*, a treatise on Ayurveda, does not recommend accepting food for quite a number of persons, such as those

> dying, poorly thinking, hunter, prostitute, breeding bird, crazy, atheist, non-Aryan man, worshiping lingam, winemaker, acrobat and actor, fisherman, jeweler, musician, gunsmith, people who are cruel, laundresses, women who have a second husband, as well as food prepared by a person who is not drunk, in a state of anger, patients who have been touched by a foot or given without due respect. (Vidyanath 2006, 35)

Thus, musicians and actors were in the category of low-status groups, and the food they cooked was not suitable for being eaten by representatives of high castes. Until the early 20th century, musicians—even highly respected performers of serious music—invited to the houses of wealthy patrons were fed in the servants' room before or after the performance. Their art was highly enjoyed, they were appreciated as masters, but they were never perceived as equals, and the eating habits manifested it in the most vivid way.

Many musicians earned their living by training, and music teachers were considered as servants or vegetable sellers; however, their craft itself had a high cultural status. Thus, it is not accidental that while describing the ideals and education of girls from her caste, Sheila Dhar, who belongs to the Mathur Kayastha caste, constantly refers to the correspondences between 'the world of music' and 'the world of food';

the presence of a home music teacher is thus regarded as necessary and regular, as the daily purchase of milk and fresh vegetables from sellers-peddlers.

> Because most Mathur Kayastha families were such staunch believers in entertainment, the first qualification they looked for in a prospective daughter-in-law was her ability to sing and dance. If she could also make conversation in English, it was an added and almost equally valuable asset. The ideal for girls therefore was to attend English-medium schools and learn Indian music at home. Most families were of the view that cooking and housekeeping were not as important because there were always servants to attend to all that. Accordingly, our household provided itself with a music teacher who constituted a regular and continuing service, just like the milkman or a vegetable hawker. (Dhar 2005, 38)

The rise of the social status of musicians began to occur in the first half of the 20th century, together with the formation of a broad public space and the raising of the status and recognition of music itself. But earlier to that period and even after, those musicians, artists and dancers, professional and amateur, who were interested in their art and wanted to master their crafts, Just as well as those friends and admirers who wanted to spend time in their company for a relatively longer time of their lives, formed their own space. But even here there were various interesting incidents. Namita Devidayal mentions the curious case of a common meal that the royal children used to have with the children of musicians.

> Maharaja [of Kolhapur] grew very fond of Alladiya Khan and his family and wanted them around him all the time. The Khansahib's three sons, Nasiruddin, Badruddin and Shamsuddin, who were better known as Badeji, Manji and Bhurji (literary, meaning the big one, the middle one and the one with curly hair!) spent most of their time in the royal palaces. They played with the young princes and ate with them even though they were commoners. They were treated not as subjects but as the princes' companions and were dearly loved by the king. The king even ordered his children's tutor to teach the three boys Sanskrit scriptures, especially the ones that were relevant to music. The Brahmin teacher would say, 'Yes, sire' to his face, but he could not bring himself to commit such a monumental act of blasphemy—teaching Muslim infidels sacred Hindu text—and he would find some excuse or the other not to tutor them. One day, after listening to a particularly moving concert by Alladiya Khan in

the palace courtyard, the prime minister pulled the king aside and said, 'Sire, I have something important to discuss with you. It is very well that you are bringing up those young boys as if they were your own. But do you think this way they will be able to learn any music from their father? Who do you think will carry on this tradition of those boys turn into decadent prince-like creatures?' The king was stunned into silence. He was unwittingly finishing off a musical legacy. If these little boys weren't trained from the time they were young, the music would die with their best musical secrets only to their own blood. This musical lineage had to be preserved. 'But how can I possibly ask them to leave? I don't think I can bring myself to say it,'—the king said, looking troubled. 'There is only one way,' the prime minister suggested. 'You know how proud these boys are. You will have to insult them so that they themselves leave in a fit of anger.' 'Hmm. A good idea. See! This is why I need a minister like you to advice me,' the maharaja smiled. A few days later, a small-time prince from a neighbouring kingdom came to visit Kolhapur. That evening, Shahu Maharaj sent a message to the Khansahib's three boys that they could not eat with the royal guest. This had never been said to them before. They were outraged, particularly the young Manji Khan, who was known for his temper. They went up to the king and Manji huffed, 'We don't need to eat with you. With our music, we can buy 56 kings like you.' They stormed off and never returned. The king's courtiers were horrified at the boys' insolent outburst. No one spoke to the maharaja like that. But Shahu Maharaj merely smiled. He had achieved exactly what he wanted. And, sure enough, each of the boys went on to become great singers'. (Devidayal 2013, 133–135)

Indeed, well known and good musicians (as well as courtesans) were the pride of the courts of the maharajas; they were bought, exchanged, enticed; they were both objects and property, but also possessed freedom of behaviour and action unprecedented for other subjects. Nevertheless, in their relations with others, including their patrons, even the royalty, the musicians, apparently, often behaved like ascetics; this is evident from numerous stories.[4]

There are many stories revealing the close and constant ties between kings and musicians. On the one hand, the artists, of course, depended on their patrons, on the other hand, they lived in a parallel world, where they moved and trained themselves in the spiritual world of music.

Practitioners in India considered their audience—the inner circle and the wider circle of listeners—as concentric circles who were treated with art and food, thereby applying a similar principle as in 'cooking technology'.

What a musician does in Indian classical music is similar to what a cook does. The dish should be prepared according to an old, well-proven recipe. The dish must be creatively prepared, the 'signature' of the master must be evident. Each of the ingredients should be well established, all spices should 'work' together, in a single bouquet, and should be combined. But listeners should also have the experience of the consumer, the experience of the enjoyer and be able to evaluate the whole meal. The everyday life at home of many musicians of North India, who teach at home and/or often perform among very small groups of selected listeners, necessarily includes real cuisine and hand-made cooking. The regularity, routine of daily cooking, combined with musical work, is considered to develop a taste—both gastronomic and artistic.

Sheila Dhar writes:

When Zia Moinuddin Dagar travelled to New York to stay with an ardent American disciple, the first thing he did was to take charge of the kitchen and start operations on the lamb korma so that it would be ready by the time the first day's music session ended. Only then did he settle down to tune his rudra veena. The lesson progressed while the dish slowly cooked. Throughout the day, he would periodically rise from his instrument to peer into the pot intently and stir it a bit. The ardent disciple ended up learning at least as much about Mughlai cooking as about raga and playing technique. Within 20 days the resident smells of Italian sausage, spaghetti sauce, and oregano in the old Manhattan apartment yielded unconditionally to the more authoritative odours of coriander, cumin and garam masala. The ustad confirmed that the tone and pitch of the pupil had simultaneously become so much more satisfactory that it was time to have a combined food and music feast for all friend and acquaintances. (Dhar 2005, 241)

Such outstanding musicians as Himmath Nivas, Munnavar Ali Khan from Bombay, Siddheshvari Devi from Varanasi, Begum Akhtar always served their frequent guests with food and music, and they all cooked with their own hands. Sheila Dhar writes that Fayyaz Ahmet Khan liked to talk simultaneously about the ragas and the culinary talents of his wife; every visit to his house was a feast. Food, combined with art, as Sheila Dhar remarked shrewdly, is an extremely important thing, not only and not so much pragmatic, it is a kind of cultural gesture, a sign of *mahadaulat*, royal generosity (Dhar 2005, 241).

I have repeatedly witnessed and participated in art classes, alternating with meals. The musician, dancer and researcher of the ancient Indian theatre culture, Piyal Bhattacharya from Kolkata, begins his day of a long class with a careful cooking of several dishes, and in the middle of classes comes the time of the meal. What and how musicians and dancers should cook and eat—Piyal generously shares this knowledge with his students. A small circle, especially of close and devoted disciples, spend a long time with him in a small house, where regular classes are taken and where everyday life takes place. Together they go to the bazaar, prepare food, students perform a variety of daily work. Piyal believes that along with musical, dramatic and dance skills, he must teach his students to be independent, in everyday life, competent and good cooks. Their diet—rice, dal, stewed vegetables, fish in sauce, sweet-sour tomato chutneys—is always freshly prepared. Seven years Piyal spent in Kerala, studying the dance and drama art of Kathakali at the Kerala Kalamandalam Institute, and often in the mornings for breakfast he prepared a small portion of upma with a moderate amount of spices. The wonderful sitar player Rajiv Janardan begins his teaching day with cooking and music classes alternate with food and conversation; because the transfer of skill occurs in a variety of ways, many details are shown casually, and knowledge and skills are layered gradually.

This practice is rooted in the philosophy of food, in the presentation of the *Annamaya jagat*—'the whole world is food', all bodies are forms, the manifestation of food, food is the content of every being. The main property and nature of food is that it needs to be distributed: not to share it with others means to destroy its essence. The distribution of food to living beings is an integral part of the daily Hindu ritual of *panchajana*, a person begins his day by feeding those who need—animals and birds, wandering ascetics and people who have rejected worldly existence, etc.

Since the Vedic texts, one can speak of a special attitude too food (*anna*), combining phenomenology and ritual. So, Baudahayana Dharma sutra says:

He who does not give me to the gods, the divine souls of the deceased, his servants and guests, eats me—in his madness swallows the poison, that I eat, I am his death. But for the one who commits an *agnihotra*, performs a *vaishvadeva*, and then eats—in contentment, in purity and in faith—what remains after he fed those whom he needs to feed, for that I become ambrosia, and he enjoys me. (Baudahayana Dharma Sutra, II, 6, 18: see Olivelle 2000, 18)

And here we come to an important point—pleasure, enjoyment—most closely associated with food and aesthetic sphere including music. Here it is necessary to recall the closest relationship of food as a cultural category with the Hindu goddess Lakshmi, whose main feature is the bestowal of happiness, good luck and material prosperity. Lakshmi is associated with sensual pleasure (the God of Love Kama is the son of Lakshmi), the harvest and the food. In Odisha, the Kaumudi-purnima festival is considered the seed of a new crop; people retell a story about Lakshmi and the disappearance of food (Becher 1970, 91–105). The worship of Lakshmi is widespread throughout India, but rarely it is the only and independent object of worship. Lakshmi more often is worshiped in conjunction with Vishnu (as a legitimization of royal power, or as an ideal married couple) and with Ganesha (then this is the blessing of the house, happiness, good luck, well-being). But the famous saying 'where Lakshmi dwells, there Saraswati has nothing to do' related two goddesses to different estates or lifestyles. Lakshmi is the personification of money and material prosperity, that is, the goddess of merchants, and families who are living with material concerns and interests, and Saraswati is the patroness of scientists, teachers and students, musicians, and people of creative professions.

Nevertheless, there is an area that unites Lakshmi and Saraswati, namely, pleasure. Caused by different reasons, it, nevertheless, has a common nature, and here food, erotica and performing arts are as close as possible to each other. 'Mazaa hain, na?'—could be told about the pleasure of a different kind—it might refer to tasty food, interesting conversation, admiration for beautiful objects, musical performance. Maza (Urdu, Hindi), that is, 'pleasure', seems to be a variant of the concept of rasa, which relates to an aesthetic feeling, emotion, impression associated with the notions of communication and involvement. Here, the corporeal closely approaches the apparently sensible, audible, tangible, smell—all of the senses that comes together to form taste. Any object to which pleasure is directed could be observed, heard, touched, smelled and tasted. The practice of eating food with fingers emphasizes on the desire to remove any mediation in obtaining pleasure from food.

To Be Full. Veg vs Non-veg: Clash of Diets

The variety of diets in India is really impressive. There is an extremely wide range of diets—from egg- and fish-eaters (regarding the Bengalis who are ardent fish lovers, it is joked that for them fish appears to be a certain kind of plant) to strict vegetarianism, and even avoidance of any red foods, onions and garlic. A particular product can be excluded from the food of an individual for various reasons, both medical and ideological. A particular caste and family tradition might also prescribe a certain diet.

Most musicians, actors, dancers, like other artists, often move around a lot, touring, travelling in different areas, and inevitably encountering people of different ways of life, having different diets. As a rule, like all sorts of people in travel, they do not strictly observe the food norms attributed to the caste, and almost always make various compromises. Thus, Hindu dancers, agreeing to perform at the courts of Muslim rulers, could even place a garland of tulsi (basil), the symbol of Vishnu, on the stage to designate a sacred presence.

Namita Devidayal retold the remarkable story of Bhaskarbua Bakhle and Nathan Khan. This story is about how an artist can overcome a border that is insurmountable for others. From these musicians there were no records left—both lived in the pre-recording era. The case took place at the beginning of the 20th century. The famous singer Nathan Khan was invited to sing at many princely courts throughout India. Bhaskarbua longed for learning music from him, and chanced to meet Nathan Khan, at times, for very short periods when he happened to visit his village, Dharwad. Bhaskarbua lived in the house of his uncle, an orthodox brahmin, who prevented him from approaching the low-caste and Muslims. The uncle treated the lower castes haughtily and had the habit of purifying his surroundings with consecrated water to cleanse himself from slightest defilement. Bhaskarbua managed to get acquainted with Nathan and began to learn from him slowly. One evening, Nathan Khan came to visit his pupil at his uncle's house. Soon Nathan Khan felt hungry and demanded on a rich mutton preparation for dinner. Khan drank and smoked as he taught his student through-out the night. Bhaskarbua was confused as such practices were strictly forbidden by his uncle, but on the other hand, he could not refuse his teacher. The teacher and student slept on the floor, amidst the mess of empty plates and decanters. When Bhaskarbua woke up it was still dark; he realized that his uncle would soon be entering the house after completing his bath at the river. He peered into the distance and spotted the familiar figure, in a dhoti and holding on to a bronze vessel, approaching the house. Trembling with fear, he woke up the teacher and pleaded, 'I beg you, go away. I'll try to clean up everything quickly, or I'll be expelled from the village!' 'What happened, son?' Nathan asked. 'My uncle is coming! He will kill me!' cried the poor young man. Unperturbed, the teacher said, 'Give me the tanpura'. After a moment, Nathan Khan tuned the instrument and began singing the hymn to

Shiva in the raga of Bhairavi. Bhaskarbua was delighted and surrendered to the will of fate and the gods of music.

Through his half-closed eyelids, he saw his uncle entering the house and standing quietly for a long time at the door. Finally, he went in, touched the Nathan Khan's feet and said with tears in his eyes: 'I have been praying to Shiva for the last sixty years. And only now I feel—I truly saw it! Thank you, Khan-sahib!' (Devidayal 2013, 114–115).

Many famous musicians of India preferred abundant and high-calorie food; this is vividly recorded by Kumar Prasad Mukherji. The routine of the famous musician Haddu Khan was as follows: in the morning he did a 100 squats, poured cold water from the well and drank a litre of milk, in which 40 sweet jalebis were soaked. Then he began his *riaz* (practice) and practised for four hours. In the afternoon he ate oily meat dish with roti. Evening meal was also plentiful, as a rule, consisting of *dahi* (curd) and *khichri* (dish made of rice and lentils). At the age of 60 he suffered a stroke and was paralysed. On the other hand, Krishnarao Shankar Pandit, who always ate ghee, lived to be 97 years old. Allauddin Khan, the teacher of Ali Akbar and Ravi Shankar, lived till 100. Ustad Badal Khan, who played the sarangi, lived 110 years. Ustad Rajab Ali Khan, who used to eat heavy meal and drink local wine, died at 90, like Alladiya Khan, the founder of Jaipur gharana. Ustad Ahmed Jan Thirakwa, a well-known tabla player, used to have biryani and kebabs, even at midnight, and all this, apparently, helped him live up to a very respectable age. K. P. Mukherji, however, remarks:

The doctors, of course, would no doubt tell us that with a more balanced diet, free from cholesterol, and with regular exercise, he would not have died an untimely death at a mere 93. Be that as it may, Muslim ustads I have known – with the sole exception of the diabetic Faiyaz Khan – in old age were all hearty eaters of rich food, kept highly irregular hours and were none the worse for it. Also, most of them would have been able to drink modern-day musicians under the table, Bhimsen Joshi excepted. The medal, however, goes to Ustad Keramatulla Khan, the famous dhrupad singer. (2006, 59–60)

He then gives a wonderful story about how he was once invited from Baroda to Bombay for a concert, and for a long time there was no information from him about whether he accepted the invitation and whether he would appear. Arriving, he looked very old and decrepit, but on stage, he arranged a sort of musical 'war' with the table accompanist, displaying his skills before the audience. For supper, he demanded a whole one of the bališt (the distance from the elongated little finger to the extended thumb when the other fingers are clenched in the fist) of rotis, lamenting what else he had eaten in one evening and two. The old man briskly digested the fat as well as the *gajar-ka-halva* (dessert 'carrot halva', consisting of finely grated carrots, stewed in condensed sweet milk for a long time with melted butter, sugar, cinnamon and dried fruits). It turned out that the musician ate breakfast with warm milk, *jalebi* soaked in it (Mukherji 2006, 59–60).

On the other hand, there are musicians who believed in a minimalist diet and the proverb that applause is the true food for musicians. Such musicians had vegetarian dishes or 'raw food', something that has been taken directly from nature (e.g., bananas also come under this category). Interestingly, in India this food does not belong to the category of 'food', anna.

The inclination of most Muslim families, including musicians, has been towards fatty food and meat, and those from Gujarat and Kashmir on sweets. This is evident in Sheila Dhar's story of an outstanding singer, Bade Ghulam Ali Khan. In her book, he is placed in a chapter titled 'When Music Is Love for Food'. This story occurred in 1945 in Delhi, when Sheila, a teenage girl, was to meet the singer and his accompanying disciples from the Punjab, bring them to the home of Nirmala Joshi, where they were to be received, and after some rest and supper were to attend the scheduled concert.

> When the cook came in with freshly fried pooris, Bade Ghulam Ali Khan could not help saying witheringly in his native Punjabi, 'So you decided to cook every tree and every bush you could lay hands on!' Fortunately, the poor man could not understand a word that was being said to him. I got the general drift and was appalled at the terrible blunder that had resulted in such a glaring mismatch between guest and host.
>
> I was the person in charge, so the maestro turned to me, pushing the thali roughly away. 'Such music as mine, and this food?' he thundered in a shocked tone. 'The truth is I can't manage with this at all. I'm going to cook my own dinner. I'll make a list of what I need. It's impossible for me to sing without proper nourishment. Even when we sit down to practice at home, a big pot of good food is always at hand, and we dig into it regularly to keep up our strength. Somebody told me that every note I sing has the aroma of kababs. Do you think I can sing the way I do if I have to feed on grasses swimming in fluids of various kinds?'

I was sure my father would think I had made some horrible mistake when we did not arrive even six hours after we were expected. The disciples had set off with a long shopping list that features six broiler chickens, a kilogram of khoya or solidified whole milk, a kilogram of almonds, a tin of clarified butter, fifteen different spices, and a stack of tandoori rotis. A charcoal fire was lit and a portable stove set up in the open courtyard because no meat of any kind was allowed in the family kitchen. Full-scale cooking operations started at around nine with great enthusiasm and expertise and a delicious, one-dish meal was triumphantly produced within two hours. The maestro heaped vast quantities on to a china plate since the metal thalis were not available for this kind of depraved eating. Nor was any space inside the house, so the dinner took place outdoors and was all the more enjoyable for that. Three or four hearty belches announced the end of this phase of the proceedings and we finally set off for the site of the concerts. Hearing him was pure and instant intoxication. My father was totally overcome. (Dhar 2005, 44–46)

K. P. Mukherji, in turn, recalls the story of the journey of Bade Ghulam Ali Khan. In December 1951, he gave a concert at the Madras Academy, where he made a sensation. The president of the Academy, a wonderful singer with a degree in English literature, G. N. Balasubramaniam fell before him and said: 'You are the greatest!' Orthodox Tamil brahmins were shocked and tried to blacken the Muslim singer. But Balasubramaniam said to them: 'There is no caste system among musicians. He may not be a Hindu, but I bowed to Devi Saraswati, the goddess of the learning and art who reside in his throat!', and invited Ghulam Ali Khan to settle in his house. However, his wife bluntly stated that if meat and fish trampled their way into their house, then she would hang herself. In the end, the singer was removed to a separate dwelling, and Khan Sahib, who loved to cook his own food also, was much relieved. He lived in Madras for several months and conquered the entire South with his music (Mukherji 2006, 124–125).

'Intoxication' by music or food is a topic that links musical and culinary codes. Musicians believe that the nature of alcoholic beverages, honey, musical and theatrical art is one (PF New Delhi 2005). Their action unfolds in a different world, somewhere nearby, somewhere between the ordinary reality and the world of the gods. This is the space in which the gandharvas, *apsaras*, yaksas, *vidyadhara*—the 'semi-divine' mythological beings who possess a dual nature—dwell. Their common characteristic is a constant movement, transformation, transition of the boundaries between worlds. Musicians feel a certain connection with them.

Symphony of Eating: Traditions and Cases

Indian food, like music, is a result of an amalgamation of various masalas/ragas. Apparently, the fine cuisines and musical genres were formed in those places where the cultural mixture has been particularly high and clear, for example, in Lucknow. Mutual adaptation of melodies and rhythms (as had been the case of the import of chilli to India by the Portuguese), modulation of tones in the Western sense of the word, changing of the musical keys (Mukherji 2006, 51)—all of this gave rise to the modern musical system, as well as a variety of ingredients and techniques that enriched food.

The very process of eating is somehow similar to listening to music. Collective feast in India is not a part of a daily routine at home (collective feeding more common at weddings and other mass events), in fact, food is rather an individual affair. Wife feeds her husband and then eats the food herself; food is served to guests, and children eat separately. The principle of thali is noteworthy when, unlike the European consecutive and fixed serving of dishes, everything is served immediately, giving the consumer maximum freedom of choice and variation. Indian traditional dishes represent a visual display of the 'grammar' of food. Metal plates or *thalis*, often contain cells, stamped in such a way that the rice is placed in the middle, and around it there are rows of spicy dishes. Nearby in separate bowls there are various semi-separate dishes with hot, sour-sweet and other tastes. When eating, a person combines food, as one independently composes 'chords' from combinations of given elements. So, in some ways it is akin to a poetic game with words or musical sounds.

Consumption of food can take very little time (and the main meal of the day is often arranged late in the evening, from eight to ten or eleven hours, just before departure for rest), but its preparation can stretch almost for most of the day. Once I stayed for several days in a Bengali house; the food was served non-stop in small portions from morning till late evening, with small breaks. Morning tea with biscuits was followed by a breakfast consisting of payes (sweet porridge of rice or thin noodles with sugar, cardamom and raisins, probably the influence of South Indian cuisine). A little later fruit was served, mostly papaya, sometimes with the addition of pineapple, *chiku* (persimmon) and guava. The afternoon meal began with a bitter dish, toasted in oil with sesame and *karela* (bitter Chinese pumpkin), followed with stewed fish in hot-sauce with chapati, and some rice with stewed vegetables, fried eggplants, hard-boiled eggs in a sauce, and fish curry. This dinner was married to a sweet-condensed sweet yogurt or *dahi*, sweet balls in syrup, a *rasgulla* and milk sweets, *sandesh*. The midday meal consisted of tea (without sweets, although sometimes with dry biscuits), small sweets with water, and also fruits. Dinner was arranged at about eight or nine o'clock in the evening, and it consisted of rice, *daal*, stewed vegetables and fish dishes, accompanied with chutney and achar (spicy pickled vegetables and green mangoes), and sometimes finished with kheer, a dessert. Before going to bed, warm milk with saffron was served. Such lavish spread was not, however, a daily rule: it was a weekend, and I was the guest of honour. Interestingly, however, there was a division of tastes, which was interpreted as an emphasis on certain qualities. It was similar to the slow beginning of the development of a raga, the *alap*, during which each *svara* (note) was shown separately, most clearly and the sounds were nuanced.

Dependence, Wishes and Prejudices

There might be individual dietary preferences: one might love *bhindi* (ladyfinger), another karela, one might choose sweet the other a sour preparation. Certain flavour combinations characteristic of a particular region of India, for example, garlic with raisins, sweets and fruits with pepper, might seem horrible to others. In the musical world of India, however, with all its diversity, there are some common ideas and practices—attachment to certain dishes, fruits, foods, spices.

Apparently, a common place for singers is their prejudice against bananas. While this fruit is considered the most 'pure' diet for Buddhist monks, singers consider it to have a 'cooling' effect, and even capable of leading to colds, nasal congestion and loss of voice. Mango is also considered dangerous: it can awaken yakshas—spirits or some kind of 'demons', which can master the artist, especially during his performance.

However, the most interesting in Indian culinary representations and practices is a kind of 'alchemy' of spices. It can be said with all certainty that it was the use of spices in the process of cooking that distinguished food prepared by humans from animal food. Spices can be called 'diamonds of the Indian cuisine'.[5] Not being an independent dish (their nutritional value is small), they are a necessary 'tool' for its creation.

Their use appears as a special science, having a philosophical basis, similar to the art of theatre, music, literature, dance. Spices contain alkaloids—complex nitrogenous compounds of plant origin—which exert a strong influence on the human body; for example, piperine in black pepper, caffeine in tea and coffee, theobromine in cocoa and chocolate. There are glucosides and essential oils (alcohol, menthol, camphene, camphor) in the spices. They have a bactericidal, therefore, a preserving property. Spices add an aroma and a special flavour to a dish that is fully attained when heated. In most spices, the aftertaste is dusky, dense, bitter with a burning sensation.

Addition of spices to food can be compared with the addition of rare metals to steel. It is the spices that add taste to the Indian food.[6] In order for the taste of the spice to be manifested, some neutral base is needed, which usually are two substances—water and rice. This is similar to the science of sound, namely, the way music and speech are created. To make the sound different, pauses are necessary. Musical tones and sounds of speech, like spices in cooking, are emotionally, 'tasted' and put on a neutral base called silence. The long background sound of the tanpura accompanying the Indian vocal and instrumental music, is a symbolic substitute in music, just as water and rice adds the base to spices while cooking. The sanctity of any art form is expressed as being the unmanifested, imperceptible, invisible, inaudible, and that forms the basis of the world of the Brahman. Sounds, movements, colours, tastes are interpreted as 'garments', 'vestments' of the Brahman, and as they adhere to him, they are considered sacred (PF New Delhi 2004; Kolkata 2011).

A connoisseur of spices when preparing a dish, like a doctor, takes into account the mental and physical state of a person. This is based on the idea of the prevailing gunas of the source material, their thera-peutic and energetic effects, as they are associated with legends and mythology. The most 'pure' enlightening guna is *sattvik*—produced by cardamom, cinnamon, cumin, ginger, mint, saffron, basil. The 'fire' qualities of the *rajasik* guna are possessed by peppers and cloves; and the 'dark' and soothing properties of *tamasik* guna are related to asafoetida, garlic and nutmeg.

People of different professions had knowledge of the spices necessary for maintaining certain parts of the body, giving tone and activating the work of the brain, muscles, ligaments and vessels. So it is believed that the work of the head is improved by nutmeg; frontal lobes with the use of basil and sandalwood; throat with clove and tamarind; heart with cardamom, lotus seeds, rose and saffron; abdomen with black and cayenne pepper and cumin; sexual activities with coriander; and the legs with lotus roots and *haritaki*. One of my acquaintances noticed that just like some Russian men hide vodka, Indians too hide the jar, of pickled vegetables if doctors forbade them to eat spicy food. Alcohol and spices are 'alchemical' and form attachments. A wonderful story about how a famous singer Pran Nath extorted saffron from her husband, a Kashmiri, and with whom he was strongly attached, has been narrated by Dhar (2006, 75).

As for musicians, in their environment, there is an attachment to certain spices. So, for example, Indians love chilli; it is believed that chilli is able to open the 'breath' of a person. Many famous singers claimed that they were addicted to green peppers. The reason, as it is believed, lies in its warming abilities, and the toning effect it has on the whole body. But the main love, especially among singers, is for clove, tamarind, cardamom and saffron.

Each of these spices has its own traditions of cooking. Clove (Syzygium aromaticum) is placed almost in all dishes, from meat to spicy tea masala, is part of the famous mixture of garam masala, it is added to paan or simply chewed separately. It is believed that clove favorably affects the throat and improves the voice. Tamarindus indica, which has a pronounced sweet-sour taste, has many medicinal qualities. It is rich in iron and vitamins, and used for healing rheumatism and cough; it is a strong antioxidant. Cardamom (Elettaria cardamomum) and saffron (Crocus sativus, dried stigmas of saffron flower) is added mainly to drinks—milk and tea, in small quantities, boiled and drunk in mornings or evenings, separately from food. These spices are believed to facilitate the quality of voice. A hot basil (Ocimum sanctum) drink, clears the throat and purifies the mind. Thus, the directed ennobling of food through spices turns out to be an instrument of influence on the body of the consumer, which in turn, in the course of practice and representation, must itself become an instrument, a conductor of sound and music.

With a variety of diets for different musicians, there is often a conscious attitude towards their food, whether it is strictly vegetarian, or rich, plentiful or dominated by meat dishes.

'Aftertaste'

Coming back to where we began our talk about food and spectacles, let us recall: food exists in a wide cultural context—in physical and psycho-emotional spaces. Not only absorption itself, but also anticipation, and aftertaste, which lasts for a long time, and that can be fixed in cultural memory, in different cultural codes and symbols, pertain to the meal.

Unlike the Western high musical culture, breeding 'material' and 'spiritual', and where music, food and bodily sensuality seem incompatible, the Indian deeply connects with these spheres of being. Partially metaphorical, here the metaphors come so close to actual reality that they almost begin to turn each other, like the fire caused by the singing of the great Tansen. Good music as if is about a good kebab!

In Indian musical technique, whether it is vocal, instrumental or dance, the performer strives for what can be called the materialization of sound, idea and fantasy. Any representation, whether a concert before a large audience or a daily practice of a musician or an artist in seclusion, is aimed at the incarnation of the invisible into the visible, the inaudible into the audible. Food does the opposite way, it dematerializes—the solid becomes liquid, digested becomes energy.

But both food and music have transforming abilities. They are neighbours who support each other in the maintenance and transformation of the human body, its right attitude and development. Polishing, grinding of the taste, its development and refinement constitute the essence of the art that is now called classical, like cuisines that are embedded in certain traditions (Udupi, Bengali, Mughlai, etc.).

But even the simplest food and the mastery of performing art are needed to be shared, and this inseparably unites both music and food in any of their manifestation. As the Mahabharata says, 'The secret of luck, happiness is to give, not to store, not to achieve success, but to let it go so that it returns by itself'(Mahabharata, Anushasanaparva, Kn. 13, Ch. 163). Sacrificing yourself, purchasing to give out just to give is the law of nature, the source of profit. Everyone can make his life meaningful and fruitful, giving out food.

Notes

1. In the Vedic texts, rasa probably means 'the taste of Soma juice'—the sacred drink used by the gods and priests at the sacrifice. Later the rasa acquires a number of additional meanings: 'essence', 'pleasure, aesthetic sense, embracing the person in perception'. In the food code there are six basic tastes: *madhura* (sweet), *amla* (sour), *lavana* (salty), *kata* (burning), *ticta* (bitter) and *kashaia* (astringent). Tastes—rasas—are accompanied with 'minor tastes' or 'flavours' *anurasa*. *Rasasastra* in traditional Indian medicine is a kind of 'alchemy', working with metals and plants. Every rasa affects life's breath, *prana*. There are also rasas

for 'emotions, mental states'. In theatrical art, according to the tract of Natyasastra, eight rasas are singled out, and according to *Abhinaya darpana*, there are nine.

2. In the Indian theatrical theory of aesthetic perception, the source and subject of impression, 'representing' and 'perceiving', actors and spectators are clearly defined and separated, see (Ghosh 1992: 7–90); in metaphorical gastronomic language they are designated as 'those who cook' and 'those who eat'. In theatrical performance, the audience and/or customers should 'taste' and 'forget', while actors/masters/artisans should not 'taste' those emotions, experience those states that they represent, that is, they should not at the moment, experience the feelings that they depict. It can be said that with the unity of action, be it a ritual or a theatre, the functions of controlling perception and perception itself, right up to the trance, are divided among its participants.

3. In the hierarchy of Indian arts, vocal music has absolute authority and takes precedence over all other types of music (which includes instrumental music and dance, and some types of dramatic play). The word itself which is usually translated into the European term 'music' or *sangit*, which in Hindi literally means 'singing', or 'united singing'.

4. One of the most touching legendary stories is associated with singer Mantol Khan, the ancestor of the famous musician Alladia Khan. He lived in Atrauli, known by dozens of good singers, a small town, not far from Aligarh. Maharaja Alvar, a small Rajput princedom, heard about him and wanted to invite him to his court. But Mantol, according to stories, led a reclusive life, did not leave the house, wore saffron or black clothes, and like a fakir did not have shoes and hats. The embassy was sent for the singer, but he did not accept it, because his music was not intended for sale. He continued to study at home with his students, and did not go outside for three years. One day in the spring, the son of Mantol, Karim Baksh, persuaded his father to go and see the flowers. The astonished singer saw a tent camp in the courtyard of his house: these were the messengers of Maharaja Alvar, who were still waiting for him and hoping for his favour. Mantol repeated his refusal, and even said, 'You can arrest me, but I myself will not go, as if not knowing that the power of the Maharaja does not extend to Atrauli located on British territory of India.' However, he was persuaded, and he and his son finally went to Alwar.

   They arranged a magnificent reception and an evening performance, which was supposed to be performed only by his son. However, at the request of the raja, deliberately he began to get confused, and the father who was present there could not stand it and began to sing himself, showing how it should be presented. Gradually, he forgot about himself, and the night passed away. All spectators present and the maharaja wept, shocked by the impression. Raja offered Mantol Khan any reward, which he replied: 'If you are really happy with my music, and want to reward me, kindly, do not call me to come again' (Mukherji 2006, 47–48).

5. Once spices played a significant role in geographical discoveries (the search for routes to India and other overseas countries) of Europeans: their value in medieval Europe was equated with gold. They were revered as jewels both literally and figuratively. In 408, Alaric, after his army captured Rome, demanded, along with gold and precious stones, 40 kg black pepper as an indemnity. In search of spices, Venetian, Spanish, Portuguese, Dutch travellers and seafarers travelled to the East. Christopher Columbus' diary entry reads: 'I'm doing everything possible to get to India, where I will be able to find gold and spices.'
6. The subject of 'curry' as a special ethnographic problem, as a kind of common place in the colonial cuisine (Master trope of colonial cuisine), by analogy with the 'Hungarian goulash' and 'English muffin' is discussed in detail by Cecilia Leong-Salobir, in connection with colonialism (Leong-Salobir 2011). The author explains that the curry, which is dissolved and produced with sauce, appeared as a result of transporting 'Indian taste' to the West, and contradicts the basics of Indian cuisine. In Indian cuisine, each dish should have its own seasoning; masala is made during cooking and the sauce is obtained as a result of cooking and not made separately.

References

PF—personal field notes of the author.
Devidayal, Namita. 2013. *The Music Room*. 6th ed. Noida: Random House India.
Dhar, Sheila. 2005. *Raga'n Josh. Stories from a Musical Life*. Ranikhet: Permanent Black.
Ghosh M. 1992. *Nandikeshvara's Abhinayadarpanam. A Manual of Gesture and Posture Used in Ancient Indian Dance and Drama*. Calcutta: Manisha.
Lakshmi, Stutley M., and J. Stutley. 1977. *A Dictionary of Hinduism*, 160–161. London.
Leong-Salobir, Cecilia. 2011. *Food Culture in Colonial Asia: A Taste of Empire*. London: Routledge.
Mukherji, K. P. 2006. *The Lost World of Hindustani Music*. Gurgaon: Penguin Books.
Olivelle, P., trans. 2000. *Dharmasutras: The Law Codes of Apastamba, Gautama, Baudhayana and Vasistha*. Delhi: Motilal Banarsidass.
Rahaim, Matthew. 2012. *Musicking Bodies: Gesture and Voice in Hindustani Music*. Middletown, CT: Wesleyan University Press.
Ramanujan, A. K. 1992. 'Food for Thought'. In *The Eternal Food. Gastronomic Ideas and Experience of Hindus and Buddhists*, edited by R. S. Khare. New York, NY: New York Press.
Vidyanath, R. 2006. *A Handbook of Ashtanga Samgraha (Sutra-sthana)*. Varanasi: Chaukhamba Surbharati Prakashan.

5

Transaction of Food, Beverage and Ranking of Space

Nabakumar Duary

Introduction

Humans exist and act in space; there cannot be any human existence or action in a void that has no dimension. Whenever and wherever humans survive and perform, they add some cultural context and assign certain meanings and values to the space of occurrence. Thus, a given space bears both tangible and intangible qualities and sometimes is presented as an extension of the social webs.

It has been noted, in recent years, that anthropological discourses consider space as an integral part of culture, this is a departure from the earlier works where it used to be mere backdrop for human society and culture; location of a study used to be described in a few opening paragraphs. Though Low and Zuniga identified six thematic categories in the study of space (2003, 1–47), the present study has been confined to a narrower arena; it deals with one specific category of public space.

A private space is often built physically as well as a cognitive construct to represent characters of individuals or collectives occupying and using it, but imprint of all persons active in that space is not evenly distributed. While some of the occupiers exert principal influence on the nature of the space, others may leave lesser impact. A public space can be as complex as the society itself. Despite it being *public* in nature, it should not be taken for granted that all members of a country or of a community will have free access to occupy and use it. Even those who can enter such a space and utilize it, their access can be very different on the basis of their ascribed and achieved attributes. All citizens of a country cannot walk into high offices of that land; there are religious places which are exclusively accessible for followers of a single faith.

This chapter has discussed the space of a marketplace; such places have their own set of norms and rules related to the use of space. Those usually involve people who use the space as sellers or buyers, different categories of commodities and services that they transact, and the ways and methods of transaction between them. In a stratified society, all members cannot have equal access either to status or to space; they operate from locations that are not equal with one another while performing their roles. This observation can be extended to the commodities and services that are exchanged, sold and bought in a marketplace; those are almost always ranked in relation to the status of the producer, service provider and consumer. This chapter has tried to understand how food and beverage items sold and bought in a weekly rural market are ranked and how that scheme of ranking is expressed spatially.

Majority of Indian population inhabit villages, which are known for their complex caste-based organizations. Since ages, people have practised traditional caste-specific occupations for their livelihood. They sell the commodities produced or goods purchased from other producers, while a few sell their services too following their age-old traditional occupations. The haat or weekly market is an ancient institution; it has remained to be the major channel for redistribution of goods in local areas through barter, ceremonial exchange, or in terms of money and credit. Earlier, such markets were usually situated on the riverbank to make use of water transport as well as to ensure availability of sufficient water for people and animals present at the market. Weekly markets are found in almost all corners of India, but their characters differ from one region to another due to diverse environmental factors and socio-economic and cultural variation among the local people. Weekly village markets are not only venues for trading activities, but are also the meeting place for people of the area where they exchange information and opinion. Different agencies like government tax collectors and private moneylenders have used rural markets for their respective business. Thus, haat remained an integral part of village life and associated with economic, social, cultural, and political life of the society; it reflects the range of local culture and spectrum of economic pursuits of the area within a limited space.

Rural weekly markets have also contributed a lot in shaping Indian lore and literature in innumerable ways. The space, transactions, performances and enactments have found place in proverbs, puzzles, folktales, myths, traditional beliefs and practices, and in mantras of the traditional medicine men.

Each market has a distinct name prefixed to it, which can be the place name, or personal name of some famous person of the locality, who can be founder of the market. Such a person can be a landlord or even a 'benevolent' robber. It can carry name of some local deity too. Though most of the weekly markets are general in nature, those deal with anything that has demand in the local area. But then there are specialized weekly markets that deal with certain commodities or livestock; it can be vegetable, flower, cattle, paddy, betel-leaf, handwoven cloth, mat, or some food items. Some weekly markets are private properties, the owners collect rent from shopkeepers on each market day. In recent times, some changes have taken place in weekly markets, like means of transport, infrastructure, commodities dealt with, measurement of commodities like *bhaga* or portion to weight and volume, mode of payment like barter to cash, change of container like leaf packets to plastic pouch and so on.

As weekly markets play such significant role in life of rural people, such markets have received critical attention in social science research. Studies on economic transaction eventually focused on appraisal of markets. Rural markets have been studied in India by S. C. Sinha et al. (1961), D. P. Sinha (1968), J. K. Sarkar (2002), Nabakumar Duary (2016) and many others. Those studies have discussed economic institutions, socio-cultural ramifications of economic activities, exchange of gifts, ceremonial distribution of goods, mechanisms of barter system and significance of social, ritualistic and political spheres of life including traditional relationship between tribal and peasant communities, development and culture change and other aspects. However, none has dealt with the ranking of social groups in a local area and space distribution of what they sell or buy in weekly village markets.

The present study was carried out at Fekohaat in Gopiballabpur Block-II of Jhargram District in West Bengal in 2016. This place is in Jangalmahal area, which is primarily a forested area located on south-western part of West Bengal and is spread over four districts, Paschim Medinipur, Jhargram, Bankura and Purulia. There are around 102 weekly markets in the area (Duary 2016,146).

This study has discussed distribution of space among different kinds of shops, specifically those selling food and beverage items. The weekly market of Fekohaat was selected for the study because it is one of the largest weekly markets of the area and is located at a juncture of three states—West Bengal, Jharkhand and Odisha. Several small rivers flow through this area and it has a sizeable forest cover influencing the availability of natural resources. The villages here are inhabited by different ethnic groups; among them there are several scheduled caste and scheduled tribe communities, who are adept in making use of the natural resources. It is these people who visit the weekly market as sellers and buyers.

Land and the People

Jungalmahal, literally 'forested country', has an identity of its own based on its geophysical setting, language and culture. The name finds its mention as early as in 1770 in a letter written by Warren Hastings, the first governor of the British colony in Bengal. The forest-clad area has a high concentration of scheduled tribe communities in the state of West Bengal and was known for its natural beauty and tranquil public life. The studied market Fekohaat is located within a newly formed district Jhargram of this area. Most parts of Jhargram are formed of lateritic rocks and soil. The tropical forest in the district is spread over 620 sq. km, thanks to the presence of the forest annual average rainfall in the forest division is about 1,400 mm. Major rivers of the area are Kangsabati or Kasai, Tarafeni, Subarnarekha and Dulong; there are several rivulets like Deb, Palpara, Rangium and Kupon.

The common flora of this area include *sal* (Shorea robusta), *piyal* (Buchanania cochinchinensis), *shimul* (Bombax ceiba), *segun* (Tectona grandis), *mahua* (Madhuka indica), *arjuna* (Terminalia arjuna), *gamar* (Gmelina arborea), neem (Azadirachta indica), *babul* (Acacia arabica), *amla* (Emblica officinalis), *kend* (Diospyros melanoxylon), each of which is used by the people for various purposes. There are many domestic birds and animals like cow, buffalo, goat, sheep and poultry birds. Wild animals include different types of birds, fish and other aquatic animals, rats, wild cat, hare, squirrel, jackal, mongoose, parrot, frog, cobra and snail. Non-domesticated flora and fauna provide a sizeable portion of food, especially to the rural poor.

Archaeological findings from the area show presence of human habitation for millennia. In this district, rural population constitute 96.52 per cent of the total population; while 20.11 per cent of them belonged to scheduled caste communities and 29.37 per cent were from scheduled tribe communities (Census of India 2011).

Economic practices of different caste groups are diverse in nature. Most of the caste groups are engaged in cultivation either as landowning cultivators or as agricultural wage workers. Some caste groups still practise the traditional calling of their respective communities; there are artisanal groups like smiths, potters, weavers and hide workers while some provide services as priest, barber or washer. Many of them have embraced non-traditional economic activities too. The poor tribals and the caste-ridden people in forest areas partially depend on forest resources for their food, material for constructing shelter and for medicine. They collect a few minor forest products in different seasons for their own consumption, a part of the collection is sold at weekly markets for earning some cash.

The Hindu caste communities are placed in three distinct social ranks in the local society. In the upper rank they place Brahmin, Kayastha, Mahishya, Kudmi and Mahato; in the middle rank lie the Goala, Karanga, Chutor, Tanti, Napit, Jale, Sadgope, Swarnakar, Shankhari, Kansari, Bania, Vaidya, Teli, Raju, Kamar, Moyra, Barujibi and Dandamanjhis; and in the lower rank are placed the Mochi, Dom and Kadmas. This scheme of dividing the local society into three tiers is not always accepted unanimously; the middle and low-ranking communities often question its sanctity. A more complicated issue in hand is to decide the relative position of communities placed within one tier; almost every segment claims superiority over some others and in few cases, they have actively tried to augment their rank.

Economic activities of the Scheduled Tribe communities also demonstrate wide variation. There are the Lodhas/Savars, who once used to depend on hunting and gathering, now they are partly dependent on it. The Koras are a community of earth workers, the Mahalis are bamboo artisans. Then there are Bhumijs, Santals, Mundas and Oraons, who are settled agriculturists. Among all scheduled tribe communities, the Santals are economically and educationally stronger in comparison to others.

To justify why the Scheduled Tribe communities are being discussed as a separate category from the Hindu caste, the example of religion the former group profess would suffice. It has been noted that such communities from the Jangalmahal area in West Bengal and its adjoining areas falling in the states of Jharkhand and Odisha profess Sarna religion. Dalton (1872, 56–57) and Dehon (1906, 124) stated that Sarna religion was of composite nature, where Roy (1918, 1) has defined Sarna religion as an organized system of spiritualism set on a background of vague animatism, which institutionally recognize deities, nature and ancestors' spirits (Duary 2000, 183). Ramdayal Munda, a prominent educationist and a scheduled tribe himself, appealed to the Register General of India that the Adivasi religion of greater Jharkhand should be mentioned as Adidharam in the Census of India (2000).

It may also be added that there are followers of Muslim and Christian faith in the area, in addition to some tribal communities who have embraced Vaishnavism and other religious schools within the Hindu fold.

While assessing the economic standing of the entire population of the Jhargram District, measuring the landholdings can be an effective scale in this largely rural population dependent on agricultural activities. In that case, the Mahatos would be placed on top for holding the highest amount of land. In many cases, the middle and lower-ranking communities work as sharecropper of wage workers for Mahatos.

Produce from land includes different types of paddy, green and leafy vegetables like potato, sweet potato, pumpkin, snake gourd, brinjal, lady's finger, cabbage, radish, cauliflower, arum, bitter gourd, ginger, sweet gourd, carrot, tomato, green chilli, bean, spinach, celery, parsnip and several other varieties.

The artisan communities comprising Mahalis and Doms make bamboo craft items like winnowing fan, fish container, strainer for *handia* or rice beer, baskets of different sizes and cages for keeping birds. Some of the scheduled tribe communities grow *sabai* grass to make rope and make broom of date palm leaves. Such produces are usually sold at weekly markets. Some local artisan communities produce and sell earthen, iron, brass, silver, gold metal items and handloom products.

Traders visit weekly markets of this area to purchase vegetables, bamboo items, broom, rope and other craft items in bulk. Commodities that are brought from outside are mass-produced household articles, spices, edible oils, pulses, wheat, sugar, molasses, medicine for cattle and poultry, chemical fertilizer, insecticide, pesticide, spectacles and sunglass, cosmetics, washing soap, readymade garments, footwear, umbrella and cheap electronics goods.

As has been mentioned, people of the Jungalmahal profess differ-ent religious faiths. There are Hindus, Sarnas, Muslims and Christians among them; the Hindus again are divided into several religious groups. Each of those groups has their own preference of festive food and drinks. They also have certain restrictions related to intake of food and drinks in daily life, on social occasions and in special situations. Such prescriptions for food sometimes have gender divisions—what is good for the men may not be good for women and vice versa. There are rules about proper ways of inter-dining during social occasions, especially among the Hindus who value hierarchy among caste groups. Even outside the caste boundary, Hindus are not supposed to accept cooked food from the tribal communities. Caste-like inequalities exist when there is no caste; the Santal do not eat food cooked by the Lodha, sit-ting together to eat food is also not allowed. Rules regarding acceptance and non-acceptance of food and beverage from others have in-built contradictions. High-ranking Hindu people, known to the Santals as *diku*, do not accept cooked food from the Santals. But they take handia a beverage made from cooked rice and *mahua*, a distilled beverage from Santal sellers at the marketplace. The Christians among the tribal com-munities can freely eat beef and pork, but most of the Hindus eat none. The Vaishnava people do not eat egg, chicken, pork, beef and crab, but some of them eat fish. Some Vaishnavas are so orthodox that they do not accept cooked food from any non-Vaishnava. Hindu caste groups, especially the higher-ranking ones, do not eat food sitting together with Muslims, Christians and Sarnas.

So, items of food and beverage are also ranked on the basis of reli-gious affiliation and caste ranking of the producers and consumers. Such scheme of ranking is evident from the space allocation of those items at the market; this is reflective of the social ranking of the people in the local society.

Location

Fekohaat is located in the village Fekoghat (J.L. No. 159) in Chingramoza in Sardiha Gram Panchayat in Gopiballabpur Block-II of Jhargram District, West Bengal, India. The nearest railway station is at Jhargram town, 16 km away. This market is well connected to Jhargram, Medinipur, Kharagpur towns and some places of the states of Odisha and Jharkhand by road. From Fekohaat, the borders of Odisha and Jharkhand are 15 km and 5 km away, respectively. This market is located close to Feko Chowk, a crossing of three roads, on

Mumbai–Kolkata Highway. The approach road to the market is made of *muram* or laterite sand. Dulung, a branch of Subarnarekha River flows near the haat. Earlier people coming to this weekly market carrying with commodities used the stream for water transport. Now people come to this place by road using different means of transportation like trucks—small and large, motorized cart, motorbike, bicycle, bullock cart and rickshaw.

Ownership and Management

Total area of this haat is around 12 acre. It is the largest haat in terms of area and in the number of buyers and shops in Jhargram and adjacent districts as well as in the entire Jangalmahal area of West Bengal. The market is located on a level land where some banyan, peepal, sal, neem, tamarind and *kadam* trees are present; there is a bamboo bush too. Location of the haat has shifted twice, once from the village Chorchita to Kuthighat on the bank of Subarnarekha in 1968 due to insufficient space and conflict with local politicians, and then finally to its present location in 1972. The land of this haat is a private property.

Present owners of the haat are Md Anwar Khan and Md Gaffar Khan, who reside in Medinipur town. They are owners of several other haats at Binpur, Sonakonia and other places. Their father Late Md Nasir Ali Khan took Binpur haat, one of the oldest weekly markets of the area, on lease from the then government in 1940. He was a resident of Kolkata city, who later shifted to Kharagpur to look after the weekly markets and other landed properties in different parts of Medinipur District. On market days, the owners remain present at the haat from morning till evening and supervise more than two hundred employees and mitigate disputes between the staff, shopkeepers and buyers. Principal job of the staff of the haat is the collection of *tola* or rent from all shops and for each cattle and poultry bird sold at the market.

Infrastructural Facilities

There are four separate single-storied pucca buildings, each one having a single room with open veranda on all sides. These are located on one side of the haat which is earmarked for the sale of bovine animals. One building is used as market office, where some staff prepare the *chharpatra* or clearance papers required for the movement of purchased animals. Another building is used as rest house for traders visiting the haat, especially the *garu byapari*, who often stay there overnight. There are 225–230 permanent low height two- or four-slope thatched hutments called *chalaghar*,[1] arranged in rows in certain parts of the market. In addition, there are numerous low-height mud platforms for the shopkeepers to sell their merchandize. Moreover, there is a small pond, five tube wells, three dug wells, one pump-set for drawing underground water and a water reservoir. There is no electricity, lavatory, bathroom, garbage container or pit and no drainage system in the entire market area.

Sellers and Buyers

The Bengali word *haature* denotes one who attends the haat and include both sellers and buyers. Then there are two separate terms—*bikreta* or seller and *kreta* or buyer. They come to the haat from villages in Jhargram District, both far and near, and from many villages of the neighbouring districts of Bankura and Paschim Medinipur. A few petty businessmen come from two relatively distant districts of Nadia and North 24 Parganas to sell *tabij* (talisman) and *grahashanti angti* (metal finger ring to pacify planetary bodies). Some *byaparis* or businessmen come to this weekly market from the states of Jharkhand, Odisha and Araria districts of Bihar; they trade in animals like cow, buffalo, goat and sheep.

Local producers come to the haat with their saleable items, some sell their services too. There are some caste-specific products and services that are sold at the haat. Some Brahmin priest worships at Hindu shops; Kudmi Mahato and Mahishya—the communities of Chasha or cultivators—bring vegetables; Barujibi comes with betel leaves; Tanti or weaver brings handloom products; Teli sells grocery items; Kamar or blacksmith sells iron implements; Kumor or potter brings earthen pots and other clay products; Chhutor or carpenter sells wooden items; Swarnakar or goldsmith comes with gold and silver ornaments; Jugi sells bedding material; Sankhari sells sea-conch bangles; Kanshari brings brass metal objects; Goala or milkmen brings curd, ghee, *ghol*; Moyra or confectioner brings sweetmeat items, Jele or fisherman brings fish; Moochi or cobbler sells and repairs shoes and slippers; Napit or barber opens his hair dressing shop; and the Dom comes with palm-leaf brooms.

However, traders do not always sell products that their traditional calling expects them to produce. Many people come to the haat from local areas as well as distant places with their commodities like *madur* or handwoven mat, rope, garments, electrical goods and many other items. Some people sell their skill of repairing umbrella, electric flashlight, kerosene oil lamp, iron bucket, while some others work as menial not-so-skilled workers and earn wage by cleaning and plastering floor of the chala shops, as water-carrier, daily-rent collector from shops, collecting dung from part of the market where animals are sold and sell the same in dry form as fuel to tea stalls and food shops. Some work as mediators in trading cow, buffalo, vegetable, onion and other items, some as Khalasi and carry out unloading and loading of living and non-living items from trucks, or as *kanchua* who ties the sharp iron knife on the leg of a cock with a string before cock fight.

Men and women of tribal communities like Santal, Munda, Bhumij, Kora, Mahali and Lodha and of low-ranking Hindu caste groups, who often are from poorer section of the local society, visit the haat in large numbers. Sometimes they carry with them saleable items like small quantity of kitchen garden products or edible items collected from the wild. It was estimated that 90 per cent of them were male and 10 per cent female. Out of females about 80–85 per cent was from the scheduled tribe and the rest from scheduled caste communities (Duary 2016, 170).

It is difficult to distinguish between buyers, sellers and traders as all the three categories can be found in a single person. Villagers who come to Fekohaat with some goods to sell would purchase some essential commodities for the family. The traders, hawkers, petty businessmen, drivers of vehicles and the service caste people like barber or cobbler would focus on the job they are supposed to perform at the haat. Still, they often would purchase certain items during their stay in the haat at their convenience.

Those who come to the haat do not always carry out economic transaction, for many of them the haat offers opportunity to meet kin and acquaintances for different purposes. This is a venue for social mixing and entertainment for many; they spend long hours drinking local beverages. A few come here with cock and participate in the cockfight, or just to watch cockfight and sometimes gamble over it.

Markets within the Market

There are some fixed places in different parts of the market for sale of certain commodities, including livestock and food and beverage. Those places are known after the items that are sold there. So, there is *sabjir haat* for vegetables, *mashlar haat* for spices and condiments, *alu-peanjer haat* for potato, onion, garlic, ginger and other items with longer self-life, *charar haat* for saplings, *chal-atar haat* for rice and wheat, *jamakaparer haat* for clothes, *masharir-gamchar haat* for mosquito net and napkin, *bene haat* for votive offerings, *phaler haat* for fruits, *jharur haat* for brooms, *pital-kansar basaner haat* for brass and bell-metal utensils, *lohashal*—temporary workshop of ironsmith, *lohar haat* for iron items, *banser haat* for bamboo items, *chhatar haat* for sale and repair of umbrella, *juto-chappaler haat* for shoes and slippers, *mahua o bakharer haat* for dry mahua flower and herbal yeast, *babui darir haat* for rope made from *babui* grass, *sal patar haat* for *sal*-leaf plates and bowls, *gorur haat* for cow and buffalo, *chagaler haat* for goat, *hans-murgir haat* for poultry birds, *macher haat* for fish, *sutkimacher haat* for dry fish, *mangsher haat* for chicken, mutton and pork, *handia haat* for locally made rice beer. In addition, there are places earmarked for sale of fodder, mostly paddy straw and green leaves, different kinds of rope for cattle, and some place for cock fight. There are several small spots in the periphery of the haat where edible items collected from the wild are sold. Those include small creatures like *jalkencho* or *barua* (*Tubifex sp.*), these are sludge worms collected from local waterbodies; *katkam* or freshwater crab (*Ozeotelfusa*); *gujigenra* or small freshwater snails (*Limnaea sp.*); *chung* or dwarf snakehead fish (*Channa gachua*); and different types of wild tubers, flowers, leaves, roots, and fruits.

Fekohaat Dry Fish Vendor

Fekohaat—Women Selling Leaf Plates

Santal Woman Selling Handia

Then there are places for keeping different types of vehicles; such a place is called stand and is used to park motorbikes, bicycles, motorized and animal-driven carts, car, and trucks.

Different types of shops and saleable items have been listed and classified in Table 5.1. The list is suggestive and not exhaustive.

Table 5.1 shows varieties of merchandize, which is related to the daily consumption pattern of the local people in their households for economic activities and for recreation. Supply and demand of local produces vary seasonally, overall consumption pattern of the people differ during festivities.

TABLE 5.1 *Classification of Shops and Saleable Items*

S. No.	Saleable Items	Type of Shops		Name of the Items
1.	Food and beverage	Raw food	Plant products	Grocery goods, vegetables, mushroom, yeast, spices, grains, fruit, wild tubers, sugar, gram flour, edible oil, betel leaf, betel nut
			Animal products	Fish, dry-fish, chicken, mutton, pork, egg, worms, snails
		Dry and ready-to-eat food		Nuts, biscuits, cake, chocolate, bread
		Fried and puffed food		Fried salty food grains, groundnut, *muri* or puffed rice, popcorn, potato chips, *chura* or pounded rice
		Cooked food		Boiled rice, vegetable curry, fish, chicken, sweetmeat, different types of fried and fast food
		Drink		Tea, cold drinks, handia, mahua
		Fruits		Ripe kend, apple, banana, guava, pineapple, berries
2.	Non-food Items	General		Different household and outdoor items made of plastic, fibre, iron, steel, tin, brass, silver, gold, glass, wood, terracotta and clay utensils, amulet, sea-conch bangle, glass bangle, sal leaf plate and bowl, broom, bamboo baskets, strainer, bird cage, plastic rope and rope items, stationary items, kerosene oil, tobacco, coconut,

(Table 5.1 Continued)

(Table 5.1 Continued)

S. No.	Saleable Items	Type of Shops		Name of the Items
				items for religious rites, dress materials, readymade dress, mosquito net, umbrella, sunglass, lock and key, gunny bag, plastic bag, incense stick, seeds and saplings of vegetable and fruit plants, fertilizer, pesticide, insecticide, medicine for plants, common allopathic medicine, herbal medicine, aphrodisiac and medicines for skin diseases, lottery tickets, tailoring items, data storage discs, cell phone chargers and battery
	Implements	Agriculture		Iron and wooden agricultural implements
		Fishing		Fishing implements – net, bamboo traps, hook and loop
		Distillation		Wooden articles used for mahua preparation
		Musical		*Madal* and *ghungur*
3.	Livestock, fodder and hide			Livestock – goat, sheep, cow, buffalo, duck, hen, pigeon
				Fodder – paddy straw and green leaves
				Goat hide
4.	Repairing shops			Shoe, metal container, gas lighter, flashlight, kerosene lantern, umbrella, tailoring for old and new clothes

As the space allotted to different kinds of merchandize is more or less fixed, it is possible to calculate how much space is given to any one category of commodities. Table 5.2 presents a comparative picture of space use for the major categories of products and services.

Table 5.2 depicts more than half of the total area is used for livestock and fodder. On the other hand, less than a quarter of the space is used for all kinds of food and beverage items. This space division has a relation with the functional requirement of space for different kinds of trade. A cattle market cannot be the size of a vegetable market. A notable point that can be seen here is that space allotted for sale of non-vegetarian items is very little in comparison to that for grains,

S. No.	Space Use for the Purpose	Share of the Total Area (%)
	TABLE 5.2 *Space Use in the Market for Different Kinds of Commodities*	
1.	Raw and cooked food and locally produced beverage	20
2.	Non-vegetarian items: fish, chicken, mutton, pork, egg	2
3.	Livestock and fodder	52
4.	Repairing shops	1
5.	Other items	25

pulses and vegetables. This can be due to discriminatory attitude on part of the management of the haat; this can also be due to the economic condition of the area, generally people might not be able to afford to buy much of meat or fish regularly.

Location and Distribution of Shops

An aerial view of the haat shows that most chalas are located in the central part of the haat and are arranged in rows aligned in different directions. Frontage of those shops is often covered with multi-coloured plastic sheets and cloth shades to protect the shops and customers from sun and rain. Rest of the haat, especially the peripheral areas, is uncovered.

All the chalaghars together cover a combined area of below 10 per cent of the total space. These chalas are allotted to fixed shopkeepers to trade with a specific variety of item, which can be readymade garment, brass, silver or gold items, or grocery. The second tier of space is characterized by shops standing on low-height earthen platform or on ground and are open to sky. Such space is allotted to shopkeepers for trading in a certain type of commodity, including cooked food items. Both categories of shop owners open their shops on each market day; some of them are in occupation of that given space for generations. In the third tier, there are allocated space for shops to deal with certain specific items, some of the shopkeepers have the right to use a specific space for long.

As has been mentioned, there are permanent structures in the western part of the haat, which are used for official purpose by the management. Then there is open space for loading and unloading livestock and food stuff for parking vehicles. Figure 5.1 locates stalls dealing with food and beverage.

Figure 5.1 shows that while cooked food stalls are in central part of the *haat* (marked as Zone I), it is not so for all other food items. The shops in the centre sale fried snacks, *paan*, cooked rice served with

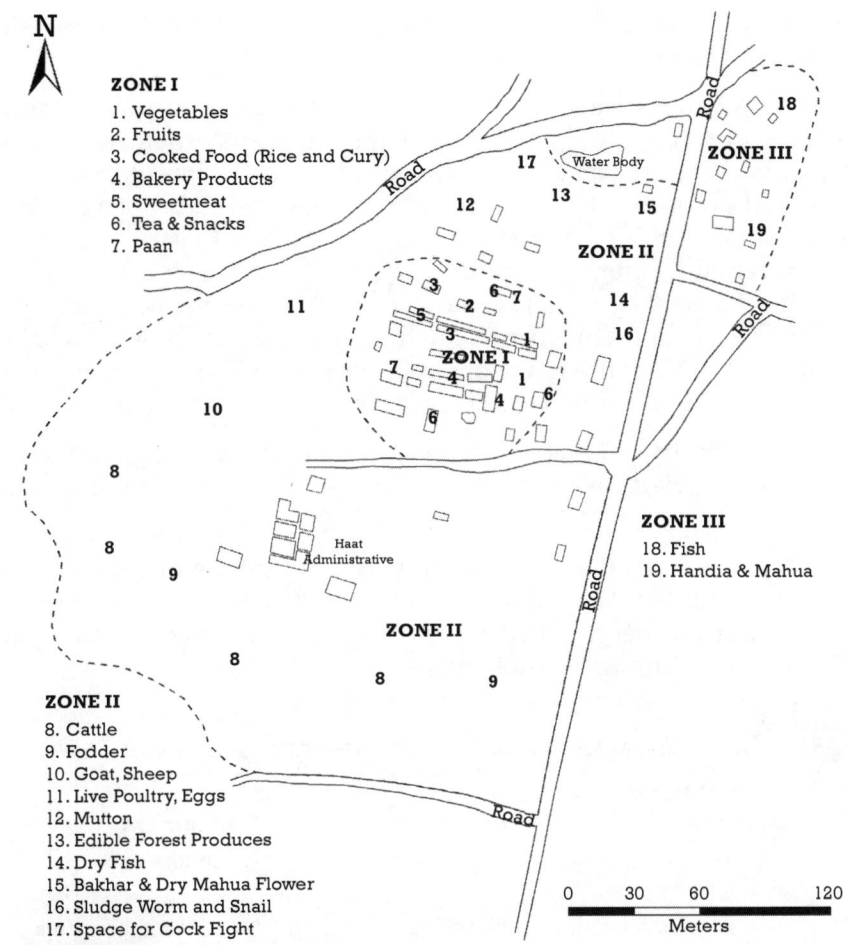

ZONE I
1. Vegetables
2. Fruits
3. Cooked Food (Rice and Cury)
4. Bakery Products
5. Sweetmeat
6. Tea & Snacks
7. Paan

ZONE III
18. Fish
19. Handia & Mahua

ZONE II
8. Cattle
9. Fodder
10. Goat, Sheep
11. Live Poultry, Eggs
12. Mutton
13. Edible Forest Produces
14. Dry Fish
15. Bakhar & Dry Mahua Flower
16. Sludge Worm and Snail
17. Space for Cock Fight

FIGURE 5.1 *Layout Map of Distribution of Food and Beverage Items in FECO Weekly Market*

vegetable or fish or meat curry, and non-alcoholic beverages like tea. Space allotted for sale of raw non-vegetarian items like fish, dry fish, chicken, mutton, pork, or egg are located beyond the centre of the *haat* (marked as Zone II). Live cattle and poultry, non-cultivated food of animal and plant origin, raw material for making local brews like dry *mahua* flower to make mahua and *bakhar* used for fermenting rice to make handia, and various non-cultivated plant and animal products are sold in Zone II. Stalls selling alcoholic beverages like *handia* and *mohua* are not accommodated even in the second zone; there is a space outside the *haat* but adjacent to it (marked as Zone III) for such stuff.

The distance and the location of Zone III ensure that only those who are interested to have a drink will visit those stalls.

Observation of Fekohaat confirms that there is a close relation between the economic position of consumers with their food habit; people with lesser means cannot afford to buy such items of food which they find expensive. On the other hand, the social status of a community is linked with what members of that group will eat. Members of a high-ranking caste, especially the vegetarians among them, cannot buy or eat a meat item that is relatively cheap, however poor they may be. The santal or members of a low-ranking caste group will have less of such inhibition; the range of choice of food will be much wider for them who are positioned lower in the local social hierarchy.

Social identity of sellers and consumers of different food and beverage items at Fekohaat reveals the extension of the scheme of ranking to those items.

Table 5.3 shows the relationship between ranking of communities and food and beverage produced, processed, sold and consumed by those groups of people. This relationship is represented by the space allotted to trading with edible items.

TABLE 5.3 *Social Identity of Food and Beverage Sellers and Consumers*

S. No.	Type of Food and Beverage	Sellers	Consumers
1.	Cooked food and non-alcoholic beverage	High-ranking castes	All people
2.	Non-vegetarian items: fish, chicken, mutton, pork, egg	Fishermen of fishing castes, other low-ranking castes and tribal communities	Most of the items are purchased by almost all excepting those who are vegetarians. Pork is mostly purchased by tribal communities
3.	Handia and mahua	Tribal communities	Tribal communities and low-ranking castes
4.	Dry fish, sweet-water and sea fish	Fishing castes	Tribal communities and low-ranking castes
5.	*Jalkencho* (sludge worm) and *gujigenra* (freshwater snails)	Fishing castes and tribal communities	Tribal communities and low-ranking castes
7.	Tubers, flowers, leaves, roots, fruits and seeds collected from the wild	Tribal communities and low-ranking castes	Tribal communities and low-ranking castes

Discussion and Conclusion

Food and beverage practices of people of a specific area depend on the availability of resources, both local and imported, usually sourced from local eco-system or elsewhere. This general statement has to be understood against the backdrop of social, cultural and economic variation within the local and larger society. Cultural practices related to food and beverage in rural Indian societies have never remained uniform even within a small area; often the socially, economically and politically powerful groups and especially the men among them, have presented their preferences as universal and ideal. This has happened notwithstanding the fact that food beyond the foodscape of the dominant can act as identity markers for some of the low-ranking less powerful groups. Handia is one such item; as it is consumed by the 'marginal' groups, the beverage has also been marginalized in mainstream food discourses. It has been observed that while some Hindu men from middle or low-ranking caste groups drink handia or mahua at market or some other public place along with people from tribal communities, they do not eat pork during their drinking sessions. Members of several tribal communities, on the other hand, cannot think of a better combination than spicy pork curry and strong mahua. The wealthy land-rich and often high-caste diku men would not even consider drinking those beverages in public, and that too at a marketplace. For the Vaishnavas and Muslims, drinking alcoholic beverages is a taboo and they would not break it at least in public space.

That some edible items are sold at the centre of the market, some in the periphery and few are not even provided any space within the haat is a physical assertion of food-related preferences of the dominant ones. Higher-caste traders occupy the central space and run their business from better-built structures; that arrangement indicates the rank of the merchandize they deal with. What they sell can be consumed by everybody coming to the market, because those are the 'normative' food items. Those trading in the periphery or outside the premises of the haat squatting on ground under open sky not only sell meat and alcohol, but also often collect, sell and eat plant food that include various types of leafy vegetables, roots, tubers, flowers, fruits, and seeds that grow in the wild. Such items also are excluded from the central space; foraged non-cultivated food is frequently equated with lowly life.

The peripheral or marginal people, on the other hand, continue to eat and drink what they like to; sometimes those items are preferred for cultural reasons too. By selecting edible items that the local environment and resource bases offer, they remain autonomous in matters of food and drinks to a large extent. While they have been excluded from the central space and placed in the periphery or margin, they have not withdrawn from transacting edible items of their choice but have continued to do so largely in their own terms. Creating a niche for their own food and beverages, they use the space for other kinds of transaction as well. Going beyond exclusive economic transaction, they utilize the space and time for social and cultural transactions too.

Note

1. These are low-height one/two/four-slopped sheds made of bamboo and wooden poles and are thatched with paddy-straw or palm-leaf. The structure of chalaghar, often referred to as *chala*, and the earthen platform on which the chala stands are maintained by the owner of the shops.

References

Dehon, P. 1906. 'Religion and Customs of the Uraons'. *Memoirs of the Asiatic Society of Bengal* 1 (9)" 121–181.

Duary, Nabakumar. 2000. 'Change and Continuity in Ho Religion—An Impact Study in South Bihar'. In *Tribal Religion: Change and Continuity*, edited by M. C. Behera, 179–195. New Delhi: Commonwealth Publishers.

Duary, Nabakumar. 2016. '*Hater Chitra o Baichitra*'. In *Jangalmahal Katha*, edited by Tapas Maity, 143–178. Medinipur: Upatyaka.

Low, Setha M., and Denise Lawrence-Zuniga. 2003. 'Locating Culture'. In *The Anthropology of Space and Place: Locating Culture*, edited by Setha M. Low and Denise Lawrence-Zuniga, 1–47. Hoboken, NJ: Blackwell Publishing Ltd.

Munda, Ramdayal. 2000. *Adi-Dhram: Religious Beliefs of the Adivasi of India*. Coimbatore: Sarini and Birsa, Chaibasa.

Roy, S. C. 1918. *Oraon Religion and Customs*. Calcutta: The Industry Press.

Sarkar, J. K. 2002. *Bhagdiriya Haat* (in Bengali). Special Issue on Weekly Market in Different States, in Pranab Sarkar, ed., *Lok*, 205–208. Kolkata: Geeta Printers.

Sinha, D. P. 1968. *Culture Change in an Intertribal Market*. Bombay: Asia Publishing House.

Sinha, Surajit Chandra, Biman Kumar Dasgupta, and Hemendra Nath Banerjee. 1961. 'Agriculture, Crafts and Weekly Markets of South Manbhum'. *Bulletin of the Anthropological Survey of India* 10 (1): 1–163.

6

Man, Medicine and Foods in Chittagong Hill Tracts, Bangladesh

Ala Uddin

Introduction

Food is basic for human survival. None can survive without food; it is essential for maintenance and building of body tissues and muscles. While food is many-splendored thing (Counihan 1999), it has social, cultural, biological, nutritional, ritual and many more aspects. Food does not simply fulfil the biological needs of human body; it has mental and healing effects as well. In many cultures rural people consume about half the food as medicines. Although food cannot replace medication entirely, it is the basis of sound health; a healthy diet eventually contributes towards lowering health risks. In fact, a healthy diet has been evidenced to reduce the risk of obesity, cardiovascular illnesses, and even certain types of incurable diseases including cancer. However, understanding which food to eat for specific benefits can sometimes be difficult, especially in traditional societies, like that in the Chittagong Hill Tracts (CHT) of Bangladesh. Like the CHT, people in many societies do not specifically know the medical benefits of food, but they believe certain foods contain some good element needed for better health. Traditional practice and folk wisdom lead them to follow healthy diets that eventually keep them well.

However, as a result of development and population growth, traditional diets and accompanying physical activities have been replaced with patterns of consumption that conversely increase the risk of developing several diseases among the people. The increasing burden of diseases worldwide is associated with changing dietary and lifestyle practices, including a decline in physical activity and an increase in high-fat, energy-dense diets (WHO 2002). To understand the transition, this chapter explores food as medicine at the biosocial aspects of healing, what may be called, social determinants of health. It attempts an insight into the medicinal power of traditional foods among the indigenous people of CHT. Thus, this chapter explores the medicinal power of traditional 'hill foods', consumed by the indigenous people, which eventually protect their lives as 'inherent medicine' as well.

At the community level, traditional foods have been closely associated with their foodways for long. Apart from providing basic consumption, foods contribute to health through other socio-economic means such as forming the basis of non-cash economies (Wein, Freeman and Makus 1996; Willows 2005). Additionally, the activities related to traditional food systems also confer health benefits through increased physical activity.

This chapter explores the dynamics of 'hill foods' referring to food and medicine among the indigenous people of the CHT. Proceeding in several steps, I first offer a short note on the living conditions of the indigenous people and then analyse the traditional means of livelihood as well as food habits. The traditional food habits of the indigenous people and the changing pattern of diets are important for an understanding of the determinants of food and health, which I examine at length, conceptually and empirically, in the third section of this chapter, before concluding with some general observations toward promotion of the traditional foods that eventually contribute as preventive medicine to the indigenous people living in the CHT in particular.

Study Methods and Analytical Framework

This chapter draws upon an ethnographic study conducted in 2018 among different ages (e.g., aged and adult from both sexes) of indigenous people (e.g., Chakma, Marma, Pangkhoa and Mro) living in the CHT—mainly in Rangamati and Bandarban districts. In order to understand the health and medicinal benefits and nutritional values of foods, I also talked with some medical doctors and traditional healers in both districts.

Indigenous knowledge system has been the major analytical framework of the study. The term 'indigenous knowledge' is used to describe the knowledge systems developed in a community, which is the basis for local-level decision-making in areas pertaining to food practices, health and nutrition, natural resource management and other socio-economic issues. The study incorporates both emic and etic perspectives—emic perspectives on what/why the indigenous people consume particular foods (from the locals) and etic perspective on the medical benefit of the foods (from the physicians). However, the findings have been analysed from meso level, incorporating both micro and macro levels of understanding.

Lifeworld of the Diverse People of CHT

The CHT is a unique part of Bangladesh, with a mountainous ecosystem rich in biological and cultural diversity. The socio-economic and cultural life of its indigenous people is closely associated with hills and forests. The lifeways and life experiences of its indigenous people are governed by the ethnoecology of the region. Their religious, cultural and economic activities depend on forests and natural resources. The region hosts 11 distinct indigenous groups who differ significantly with the majority Bengali in terms of ethnicity, culture, language, religion, dress and other socio-political aspects, while physiologically and socio-culturally, 'there is a great affinity and kinship with the people of northern India, Nepal, Sikkim, Bhutan, Burma and Thailand' (Roy 2003, 16). The indigenous people of the region speak a number of different languages, and there are wide differences in lifestyles among its inhabitants. They have never developed a particular sense of collective unity, 'none of them appear to have any general term for all hill dwellers' (Lewin 1869, 28). Each group refers to itself by its own distinct identity (for example, Chakma, Pangkhoa, or Marma). Comprehending the dynamics of different ethnic groups, one of the earliest British administrator-cum-ethnographer, Captain Lewin (1869, 28) classified them into two groups: (a) Khyoungtha or children of the river (Arakanese origin)—people who reside in the river valleys, and (b) Toungtha or children of the hills (mixed origin)—people who reside on the mountain ridges. Among the indigenous groups, the Chakma, Marma, Tripura, Tanchangya, Kheyang and Chak who reside mainly in river valleys are referred to as Khyoungsa (valley-dwelling people). While the Pangkhoa, Mro, Bawm, Lushai and Khumi who reside mainly on mountain-ridges are referred to as Toungsa (mountain-dwelling people). The Khyoungsa–Toungsa dichotomy is not a classification based merely on their type of habitat; rather, it forms the basis for food preference and availability of foods. This dichotomy reveals the distinct socio-cultural and politico-economic lifeworlds of the indigenous people, including perceptions on displacement, fear, relations with insiders and outsiders and food habits. Even then, for the purpose of this chapter, the generic term 'indigenous people' refers to both Khyoungsa and Toungsa.

Traditional Foods

The CHT characteristically represents a traditional society with regard to health condition and disease. It possesses a rich heritage of indigenous knowledge, though much has been lost in the process and course of 'modernization' across the sectors. In general, they eat whatever they find in the hills. The ordinary food of the indigenous people consists of rice, fish, oil, salt and chillies (Hunter 1973). Rice is the staple food; most of them eat rice thrice a day as breakfast, lunch and dinner. With rice they usually eat boiled vegetables and fish. Usually they use less oil and *moshla* (masala), which are also expensive to them. Lunch and dinner are two major meals, while in breakfast they eat the leftover rice with chilli and traditional smashed foods. They also eat various types of insects and small creatures like ant, crab, cricket, beetle and snail (Ahsan 1993). They all are fond of pork, which is forbidden in the plains of Bangladesh, as it is strictly forbidden to the Muslims; the Hindus too preferably do not eat pork.

Traditional indigenous foods are those that originate from local plant or animal resources and obtained by gathering or harvesting, and thereby possess cultural meaning as a traditional food (Willows 2005). For long, the cherished food practices within the traditional lifeways have protected them from illness and helped them to heal as well. Below we present a short description of foods available in the hills and consumed by the indigenous people, and accounts from the physicians working in medical centres or hospitals about health benefits.[1]

Foods	Health Benefits
Honagulo ton (*Kanai dingya*) 	• The bark, roots, green leaves and fruits are good food to the indigenous people. • It is used for relief from several diseases such as jaundice, tumour, prostate pain, diarrhoea, constipation, rheumatic fever and dog bite.

Foods	Health Benefits
Bnashkoroil (Bamboo shoots) 	• Bamboo shoot is the edible part of bamboo that the indigenous people eat, especially in the rainy season. • The main nutrients in bamboo shoots are protein, carbohydrates, amino acids, minerals, fat, sugar, fibre and inorganic salts. • According to the locals, it helps to reduce cholesterol and urinary infection and problems with skin, and prevents diabetes, cancer, heart disease and helps in building strong bones.
Kadol (Jackfruit) 	• It provides a moderate number of calories in addition to lot of fibre, vitamins, minerals and antioxidants. • Indigenous people eat seeds of jackfruits as vegetables. • It boosts the immune system; improves energy levels; and, promotes bone health. • It is also beneficial for the cardiovascular system. • It prevents colon cancer. It also increases sperm count.
Mishali mach (Small fish) 	• It is cooked in bamboo tube. • As it is prepared through bamboo firing, a different taste is infused in it. • It is a good source for protein.
Shamuk (Snails) 	• It provides protein, iron, Vitamin B12, magnesium, selenium and omega-3. • It is especially good for brain development and memory of children.
Kakra (Crabs) 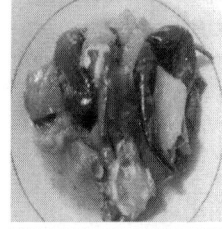	• Indigenous people eat crabs, especially in the rainy season, with pumpkin. • Crab is a good source of key vitamins and minerals such as Vitamin B12, selenium, zinc and iodine, and contains variable levels of cadmium.

Foods	Health Benefits
Hangor Shutki (Dried Shark) 	• Shark is distinctively popular in the hills. • Since larger sharks are not available, small sharks are dried for special taste. • Shark meat has one of the highest levels of mercury of any fish. • Shark has the benefits of omega-3 which is known to improve brain health, heart health, and reducing diabetes.
Jhi-jhi poka (Crickets) 	• Associated food with local wine (rice beer, *dochuyani*). • Crickets are a complete protein source; they contain all the essential amino acids; also have omega-3 and six fatty acids and are high in calcium and Vitamin B12.
Nappi/Chidal 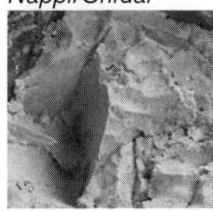	• Nappi is a very popular food among the indigenous people. It is made by fermenting small sweet water fish with rice husk and yeast. The resulting gooey mess is then dried and formed into soft cakes. • They literally stay forever. • Contains vitamins, phosphorus, magnesium, selenium and iodine.

Traditional Foods and Sound Health

Unhealthy diet and physical inactivity are the two major modifiable risk factors responsible for the development of several diseases. While the indigenous people are largely jum cultivators and live in remote hills, their physical movement and activities eventually help them with sound physique.

Although some indigenous people told that they eat whatever they find in the nature, but those are not really 'good/rich food'. Many others stated, 'Nature is our life. Whatever we find in nature is nutritious and medicinal to us. Because of the benefits of these foods, we usually do not need to visit doctors. When we feel ill, we use some plants, also from nature, that really help us. Such as *akand* (shallowwort), *tulsi* (holy basil), *pudina* (mint).' A 68-year old Chakma man, in this regard, said, 'Hill is our mother; nature our god. We do not know which is good for what but believe the foods that we have in the hills are good for our health and mind.'

Although the indigenous people do not know much about the medicinal benefits of the foods, they consume traditional food available in the hills. As observed elsewhere, traditional foods and nutrient intakes vary as per local geography (Johnson et al. 2009), seasonality (Delormier and Kuhnlein 1999) and cultural group (Kuhnlein et al. 2004). The energy spent in obtaining traditional foods was significant given the very physical demands of hunting, fishing, trapping, growing and gathering (Samson and Pretty 2006). As observed in CHT, physical activities required for jum cultivation make the indigenous people physically fit and energetic.

BOX 6.1 Jum Cultivation: Traditions, Transformations and Consequences

The main form of livelihood in the indigenous communities of CHT is *jum* cultivation (swidden)—a peculiar kind of cultivation on the hill tops and slopes without cattle or plough. For long, it is the major means of livelihood of the indigenous people. The term 'jum' came from the local Chakma word for swidden cultivation. The Tanchangya also use the same word to mean their traditional swidden cultivation. Rest of the indigenous communities call swidden cultivation in their distinct languages; for instance, in Pangkhoa language swidden cultivation is *lo*, in Marma language *yah*, in Tripura language *hug*, in Mro language it is *ua*.

Until the mid–19th century it was the main distinguishing criterion as Lewin (1869) asserted: 'hillmen were exclusively swidden cultivators, locally known as Jhumia (Jumma)'. In this regard, Lewin's observation is pertinent: 'Throughout the whole of the Hill Tracts I know of no single instance of a Hillman cultivating the plough' (1870, 39). In the early days agricultural production from jum for a single year was higher than that of conventional wet-rice cultivation on plain land. This is because, in addition to rice, many other crops are obtained from the same plot, including oilseed, cotton, chilli, cowpea, cucumber, gourd, paddy, melon, pumpkin, maize, yams, sweet potatoes, fruits, winter vegetables and the like without involving any extra effort or costs (Adnan 2004, 96–97). Thus, jum has been the primary source of food, shelter and clothing of the indigenous people.

However, the above scenario has been changed by the early 20th century with the English introduced plough cultivation, which inevitably brought the Bengali peasants into the hills. The English perceived, revenue in the Hills was not enough compared to their expectation and expenditure for militarization and administration in this region (Mohsin 2002[1997]; Roy 2000; van

---

Schendel et al. 2000). Accordingly, to get more revenue, they introduced and encouraged plough cultivation in place of traditional jum, because plough cultivation was more profitable to the English than jum cultivation, as a fallow period of 7–10 years is required for the later one.

Given that the indigenous people had no familiarity about plough cultivation, the English rulers and Chakma Raja invited the Bengali neighbours to teach the ways of plough cultivation in the plain lands which were scarcely available in the hills. Hence, the Bengali peasants taught plough cultivation to the indigenous people; some Bengalis worked as day labourers in the paddy land and some others began trade on temporary basis. Subsequently, by the 1890s, about 3,000 hectare (11.58 sq. mile) had been put to the plough where over half the plots were being worked by the Bengali settlers, their in-migration was encouraged by the British (Ali 1993). Accordingly, some Bengali people settled in the river-valleys, who later engaged with plough cultivation, trade and acted as intermediaries of the colonial rulers. By the 1890s more than half of the 3,000 hectare reclaimed lands were occupied by Bengali settlers (Mey 1984). By 1960, most of the valley lands had been converted into plough cultivated wet-rice fields by the Bengali and Khyoungs (for example, Chakma, Marma and Tripura) (Adnan 2004).

Another dimension of the regulations in the CHT by successive governments (since colonial times) is the forestry laws, which have had a massive impact on the lives of the people. Classifying the areas of hill as 'forest', successive rulers displaced and deprived the locals of the forest in the name of afforestation under the 'Reserve Forest Act'. In 1871, the colonial administration declared 5,670 sq. mile out of 6,882 as Government Reserve Forests (Cowan 1923, 14). Further restrictions were imposed creating two types of forests: (a) Reserve Forests; (b) District Forests (now known as Unclassed State Forest), while the Reserve Forests were put entirely under the management of the Forest Department. Jum cultivation and any other use of forest resources were totally prohibited in the Reserve Forests.

Although displacement of the indigenous people began in the colonial period, the most devastating displacement was caused by construction of the Kaptai hydroelectric dam—a 'national development and integration' programme of postcolonial Pakistan in the 1960s. It transformed the total environment of the hills, which immediately submerged best cultivable lands (about 54,000 acre) previously occupied by the Chakma, Marma and Tripura in the river banks of the Karnaphuli River and its tributaries. The submergence displaced hundred thousand people, who were mostly Chakma. The valley-dwelling Khyoungsa had been directly affected by the displacement as Kaptai dam submerged the vast riverbanks. Although the mountain-dwelling Toungsa were not directly displaced by the dam, the displaced Khyongsa people moved to settle into the steep hills. Hence, the fallow period of jum in both valleys and hills decreased due to the pressure on limited lands.

Therefore, the areas suitable for jum cultivation were reduced by two-thirds. Additionally, the fallow cycle for jum was reduced from 15–20 years to 8–10 years. While jum was harmonious to maintenance of the hill ecology avoiding soil erosion, the restrictions led to soil degradation, poor yield and marginalization of the indigenous people (Ahamed 2012; Dewan 1991; Gain 2013; Mohsin 1997). As a result, the return from jum became inadequate for the subsistence of its cultivators.

From the very beginning of their settlement in this region, it has been observed that the Khyoungsa settled in river valleys (near river or stream or water bodies), while the Toungsa settled in the mountain ridges (Hutchinson 1906; Lewin 1869; Sopher 1964). In the pre-colonial period, jum and collection of forest resources were their principal livelihood means. After the introduction of plough cultivation, the Khyoungsa combined this new method of cultivation with traditional jum, while the Toungsa have predominantly been practicing jum as the certain means of their livelihood along with forest-related activities. They continued to manage their livelihood without having to turn to wet-rice peasant economy (Sopher 1964). However, dislodged from the cultivable land due to the Kaptai Hydroelectric Dam in the 1960s and government-sponsored population transfer programme from 1979 onwards (Bengali in-migration to CHT),[2] the Khyoungsa were forced to move away from plough cultivation due to the scarce cultivable land. As a result, like the Toungsa, the Khyoungsa become dependent mainly on jum. But with increasing land scarcity, they now depend also on forest-related activities such as firewood collection, forest extraction, bamboo and tree plantation, fruit garden and day labouring for their subsistence.

In course of time, the indigenous people saw the arrival of several non-local foods and fruits in the CHT; tea, coffee and orange plantations began in the late 19th century; commercial teak, rubber and tobacco plantations were established soon thereafter. However, jum still remains the most prevalent form of cultivation, though the outcome from jum is steadily decreasing under the stated circumstances.

Traditional Diets and Health Benefits

Traditional diets of CHT can supply healthier fat and a greater amount of vitamins and minerals. Often foods eaten by the indigenous communities are rich sources of omega-3 fatty acids. They are also associated with lesser omega-6: omega-3 fatty acid ratio, which may also be important for cardiovascular health. As explained by some physicians, higher proportions of omega-3 fatty acids have been associated with less advanced atherosclerosis in indigenous people compared to the plainsmen. Traditional foods are also rich in micronutrients, the consumers get higher portion of riboflavin, iron, zinc, copper, magnesium, manganese, phosphorus, potassium, selenium and vitamins A, D, E and B–6, as compared to the days when traditional foods are not consumed due to scarcity of those items in the lean season (Miah, Alam and Mohabbatullah 2015). Good sources of vitamin C have also been documented in largely animal-based diets of the indigenous people. This suggests that the dietary risks and benefits of omega-3-rich traditional foods as related to cardiovascular disease must be viewed within a broader context of cultural ecology.

Importance of traditionally consumed wild plants worldwide in contributing essential micronutrients to diets is well described, although a systematic understanding of nutritional composition of those plants is yet to emerge. However, the indigenous people believe they get good quantity of nutrients from traditional foods, '… they are not only of good taste, they have rich micronutrients'. Traditional plants are often used in both food and medicine, potentially offering pharmacologic and therapeutic benefits through diet. For example, dried shark, consumed by many indigenous peoples in a variety of medicinal and food preparations, are high in omega-3, and improve brain health, heart health and reduces diabetes (Samantha, Papastamatiou and German 2017).

However, it is impossible or even undesirable to define the complex nutritional benefits of traditional foods separately from the health benefits of traditional food systems. Apart from just nutritional value, indigenous diets and consumption patterns arose from complex and holistic food systems that provide both health benefits and cultural unity. Among the Chakma and Marma, traditional food consumption is associated with other measures of culture such as speaking in own language, using traditional medicine and participating in traditional events. According to local physicians, it has been estimated that Pangkhoa and Mro people engaged in traditional activities related to hunting, gathering and trapping expend more megajoules (MJ) of energy per day compared to those staying in the village.

Food consumption patterns among the Chakma and Marma children living in the river-valleys are fairly similar to the Bengali school-aged children in both Rangamati and Bandarban districts with traditional foods being consumed infrequently. The Bengali settlers buy food from local markets from the indigenous people—thus the Bengalis consume hill foods and indigenous people consume foods produced outside the hills. Risks of specific dietary deficiencies were identified in some indigenous populations. Low intakes of zinc, calcium and Vitamin D have been reported among the school children, and low intake of magnesium, folate and vitamins A, C, and E among Pangkhoa and Mro women, who live in the remote parts of high hills, where they face food scarcity more than the river-valley people.

Data obtained from medical centres and doctors suggest that the dietary intake of indigenous people with diabetes does not differ significantly from the general diabetic population. In contrast, some groups are more likely to consume traditional or country foods. Elders and older indigenous people consume more traditional foods than younger people. In CHT, approximately 10–40 per cent energy is obtained from traditional sources and for a third of the Pangkhoa and Mro, hunting and trapping remains a way of life. Those who live in the high hills are still 'healthy' as they have to work hard for their survival.

Major Source of Food

As mentioned above, the main form of livelihood for the indigenous people of CHT is jum, which is a peculiar kind of cultivation on the hill tops and slopes without cattle or ploughs. Apart from juming, plough cultivation is also practised on a small scale. This method was introduced in CHT in late 18th century by the Bengalis who were invited by Circle Chiefs to settle on lower parts of the hills where irrigation was possible. It has implications on foods and diets that I will discuss after a while.

Today, one divides the region into 'jum-land' and 'plough-land'. From quantitative point of view, however, the former is still of more importance in the economy than the latter. On jum-land the main crop is paddy; it has several varieties. Other crops grown with paddy in the jum are millet, several varieties of maize, sesame, cotton, pumpkin, melon, cucumber, potato, chilli, fruits, bean, onion, turmeric, etc. All those crops are sown on a common piece of land but are harvested at different points of time. The agricultural activities thus depend on successive seasonal changes between dry and rainy periods, on temporal distribution of the jum-land and plough-land cultivation, and on alternation of the crops—paddy or otherwise as well (Lewin 1869). Since most indigenous people are *jumma* (jum cultivators) who have no flat land to till, the jum-land crops are major sources for their subsistence. Hence, jum cultivation is the only significant source of food for the indigenous people. Except for the deep jungles, hunting is practically non-existent in the valley. Fishing, though practised, does not provide much food. It is done with 'traps' or by draining a portion of a stream with a dam (Bessaignet 1958). In addition to crops of jum, they also collect vegetables and fruits grown in nearby forests and gather plenty of vegetables like *borboti* (yard-long bean) from their gardens, catch fish (such as *mishali*) from the rivers/hilly-streams.

The distinction between Khyoungsa and Toungsa is inferred to be in part a product of long contact with civilization based on wet-rice culture. The Khyoungsa have long been carrying on jum in juxtaposition to wet-rice cultivation until they were displaced and lost cultivable lands owing to the Kaptai dam in the 1960s and the Bengali exodus in CHT since the late 1970s, who settled in the river-valleys dislocating mainly the Chakma, Marma and Tripura. On the other hand, until recently, the Toungsa have acquired the character of jum cultivators, without having turned to a wet-rice peasant economy (see Sopher 1964).

Determinants of Food and Health

Over time, the amount of traditional food consumed has declined in the CHT, coincident with food system changes including the introduction of modern/western foods, loss of sustaining natural resources, and growing dependence on market-based foods. In the past, local 'hill foods' were sufficient to provide meals to the indigenous people; those were sufficient to fulfil their nutritional as well as medicinal needs. In effect, they were physically strong and occasionally visited the traditional healers who treated ailments mainly with medicinal plants available in the hills.

However, since the 1970s the scenario has been changed in the CHT. A well-recognized transition has occurred, with historic consumption patterns replaced by mixed diets (local and imported). In effect, traditional diets and associated physical activities have been replaced with patterns of consumption that increase the risk of developing several diseases in the indigenous communities. The degree to which market-based diets are relied upon by indigenous peoples varies considerably, with intake of nutrients, market and traditional foods affected by regional and socio-demographic factors. To understand the transition, we need to look back to the changing pattern of economic activities as well as population transmigration in the CHT.

Change in Traditional Economic Behaviour

Economy of the indigenous people is fundamentally a subsistence one as they produce to satisfy their own needs. However, development of a commercial economy that has taken place in the area has helped to introduce certain elements of exchange. However, these are not yet the main factors instrumental in commercializing the area. The process of commercialization emerged primarily from two factors. One is the necessity to provide small hill towns and their Bengali population with food. Since independence, a number of Bengali traders have increased greatly, and the indigenous people supplied them with vegetable products. In exchange for this, they earn money which they use for purchasing manufactured goods available at the local bazaar. Each hill town has in fact a bazaar at which weekly, and sometimes more frequently, the indigenous people come as sellers and buyers (Lewin 1869; Sopher 1964). The second factor responsible for gradual penetration of an exchange economy in place of subsistence economy is the development of the Chittagong Port. With expansion of the city, production and supply of more food from the surrounding area became necessary. Here lies one of the directions towards which the economy of the Hills is going to move in future. In fact, many plainsmen purchase vegetable products at the hill town bazaars for supplying those to the port city of Chittagong city (Bessaignet 1958; Lewin 1869; Sopher 1964). The hill economy is therefore moving towards a town–village relationship, a major feature of capitalistic exchange. As an inevitable effect, the indigenous people have been economically entangled with the plainsmen, which eventually brought a significant shift in their lifeways, including food habits.

Transmigration, Land Encroachment and Development

The current ethnic composition in CHT is strikingly different from what it had been a century earlier. In 1872, the population had been almost entirely indigenous, 98.26 per cent. In comparison, the Bengali accounted for a microscopic minority 1.74 per cent, which rose to the level of around 9.09 per cent over eight decades (in 1951), and then doubled in the next two decades (19.41 per cent in 1974). Until the Partition of 1947, the Bengalis in the CHT constituted less than 9 per cent of the population, and thereafter, until the CHT became a part of Bangladesh in 1971, the Bengali population was about 12 per cent. Soon after the independence of Bangladesh, the population of Bengalis began to increase. The most rapid increase in Bengali population occurred during 1974–1981 (38.93 per cent) as an effect of the state-sponsored transmigration programme (1979 onwards). In the next decade, there was about 10 per cent increase in the Bengali population. Clearly, the indigenous people have been outnumbered by the Bengalis in the last three-and-a-half decades (see Mohsin 2003; Roy 2000). More than 60 per cent Bengalis living in rural CHT have been there for less than 30 years, and around two-thirds of those are recent immigrants (Barkat et al. 2009, iii). Demographic composition, ethnic conflict, security problems, deprivation and displacement are all interrelated issues in the hills including food security.

Due to increased population and occupation of land by the government in name of development projects, now jum has become restricted, thus unable to meet the demands of the indigenous people. Timber, rubber and coffee plantation and tobacco cultivation have been introduced in the hills, though tobacco has been identified as a harmful cultivation for both land and people.

Prior to the recent large-scale transmigration, relatively moderate migration of the Bengalis started during British colonial period. In the changed circumstances, the indigenous people not only depend on 'imported/plain land's foods', but they also cultivate alien foods as they grow huge and faster in small lands. As a result of the above changes, they feel that they were very strong and healthy in the past, but nowadays, they do not possess sound health. They also believe, with the introduction of 'imported' foods like rice from plain districts, potato, sugar and fruits, they are now facing various kinds of diseases such as liver infection and tuberculosis. Although they are aware of it, they have no other option but to rely heavily on bazaar foods. During my fieldwork in a village in Bilaichhari Upazaila in Rangamti district, I observed people were buying painkillers and medicines for gastritis themselves from a local grocery store. They take painkillers on days they go to the jum land to work. Earlier, they never took or knew about such medicines. According to them, their body is not that strong as it used to be in the past. Now they cannot withstand hard work. The situation is not only applicable for the valley-dwelling Khyoungsa people; such phenomenon was observed among the hill-dwelling Toungsa people too.

Current dietary surveys among the indigenous groups as well as the Bengali settlers reveal that often diets are poor and do not meet dietary recommendations for saturated fat, fibre, sodium, fruits and vegetables. Poor dietary patterns were also observed among indigenous children who reside in urban areas and consume fast food and packed food frequently. They were found to consume less than the recommended servings of milk, fruits and vegetables. Availability of food is also determined by poverty and rurality for indigenous people living in river-valley, while factors such as remoteness and hill-dwelling may affect food patterns in other regions.

Promoting Traditional Foods

A healthy diet helps the human body to become more resilient that eventually helps to prevent chronic inflammation and diseases. However, without knowing this science, indigenous people have been practising their traditional food habits for long. The traditional foods they consume not only meet the demands as foods, but also help prevent diseases and keep them strong. Access to traditional food has been limited by changing demographic and social situations that preclude the traditional sharing of labour or value associated with traditional livelihoods.

Given the benefits associated with traditional diets, a return to traditional dietary practices seems worthwhile. While traditional foods and food knowledge support health system, a community health promotion intervention needs to be promoted in the CHT. However, there are challenges in implementing such an idea. Access to traditional foods has been altered through the loss of traditional lands and legislative restrictions on the use of land and forest resources. Willingness to consume traditional foods is also affected by concerns over contaminants in the food chain/market chain—production for profit (Earle 2013). In order to support and promote documentation of traditional food knowledge, the use of indigenous educational stories and grocery store initiatives may be employed in a culturally congruent manner.

Conclusion

The indigenous people of the CHT are highly vulnerable in the issue of food security due to their limited access to and availability of food. Their food habit includes rice as staple supplemented by meat, fish and vegetables. In addition, they forage food from the jungle and hills in forms of wildly grown tubers, vegetables, snake, frog and many other items. They regularly consume *nappi*, a semi-dried fish-paste with a strong flavour and supposedly having high protein content (Das 2008). Low yield of jum crops, damage due to drought and attack of wild animals, water stagnation as well as flash flood are the other major causes of food insecurity in the CHT. Average calorie intake was found to be higher in Khagrachhari (2,173 kcal per capita daily) followed by Bandarban (1,964 kcal) for the indigenous people. Among the ethnic groups, the Chakma were found to have higher intake of calories (2,102 kcal), followed by the Marma (2,081 kcal), while the lowest calorie intake was among the Tanchangya (1,901 kcal), which was significantly lower than the national average (*News Today* 2012).

Empirics of the ethnography conducted in CHT shows that 'hill foods' are both diet and medicine to the indigenous people. Without knowing the biological aspects of healing, they are practising such a food habit for long. Here, food and medicine synchronize well both culturally and ecologically. However, the traditional diets and associated physical activities of indigenous peoples have been replaced with patterns of consumption that increase the risk of developing several ailments including cardiovascular disease, diabetes and cancer. Still, traditional foods remain important from both cultural and nutritional perspectives and are particularly associated with beneficial fat, carbohydrate and nutrient profiles. Despite challenges such as food insecurity and biological contamination, traditional foods remain important for chronic disease prevention and their use can be successfully promoted in the indigenous communities.

The preceding discussion highlights how traditional foods offer cultural, social and nutritional benefits that in turn contribute to the health of indigenous communities through a variety of complex pathways. This must be conceptualized in a systematic and holistic manner. This author urges that the government of the country needs to support and promote local foods with medicinal benefits and ensure traditional right to their lands and forests that they had in the past.

Notes

1. Here I got information from the indigenous people of the CHT, while I depended on several sources for understanding the medicinal benefits of the foods: Duna Wang et al., 2004; Eneji et al., 2008; Nongdam and Leimapokpam, 2014; Samatha, Papastamatiou and German, 2017; Ranasinghe, Maduwanthi and Marapana, 2019. Also, I am grateful to my indigenous friend, Nuku Chakma, who provided me pictures of those foods along with essential information.
2. One of the major upheavals the indigenous people had to face was a government plan to settle hundreds of thousands of landless Bengali families from plains to hills between 1979 and 1984. As a result the indigenous people have become landless and been displaced from their lands.

References

Adnan, S. 2004. *Migration, Land Alienation and Ethnic Conflict: Causes of Poverty in the Chittagong Hill Tracts of Bangladesh*. Dhaka: Research & Advisory Services.

Ahamed, F. U. 2012. 'Negotiating Boundaries: Dynamics of Identity Formation in the Chittagong Hill Tracts (CHT), Bangladesh'. In *Alternative Voices of Anthropology*, edited by A. K. Danda and A. R. Das, 233–259. Kolkata: Indian Anthropological Society.

Ahsan, S. 1993. *The Marmas of Bangladesh*. Dhaka: Ahsan Publishers.

Ali, S. M. 1993. *The Fearful State: Power, People and Internal War in South Asia*. London: Zed Books.

Counihan, C. 1999. *The Anthropology of Food and Body: Gender, Meaning and Power*. London; New York, NY: Routledge.

Cowan, J. M. 1923. *Working Plan for the Forests of Chittagong Hill Tracts Division*. Calcutta: Government of Bengal Press.

Das, A. K. 2008. *Food Security Assessment Report, Chittagong Hill Tracts*. Available at http://www.nri.org/projects/bandicoot/docs/MSFApr08.pdf (accessed on 1 April 2020).

Food as Medicine: The Power of Diet for Employee. Available at https://meetz-ipongo.com/food-as-medicine-the-power-of-diet/Wellness (accessed on 1 April 2020).

Delormier, T., and H. V. Kuhnlein. 1999. 'Dietary Characteristics of Eastern James Bay Cree Women'. *Arctic* 52 (2): 182–187.

Dewan, A. K. 1991. *Class and Ethnicity in the Chittagong Hill Tracts of Bangladesh* (PhD dissertation). Canada: McGill University.

Dun Wang, Yao-yu Bai, Jiang-hong, Li, and Chuan-xi, Zhang. 2004. 'Nutritional Value of the Field Cricket (Gryllus Testaceus Walker)'. *Entomologia Sinica* 11 (4): 275–283.

Earle, Lynda. 2013. *Traditional Aboriginal Diets and Health (National Collaborating Centre for Aboriginal Health (NCCAH)*. Available at https://www.ccnsa-nccah.ca/docs/emerging/FS-TraditionalDietsHealth-Earle-EN.pdf (accessed on 1 April 2020).

Eneji, C. A., A. U. Ogogo, C. A. Emmanuel-Ikpeme, and O. E. Okon. 2008. 'Nutritional Assessment of Some Nigerian Land and Water Snail Species'. *Ethiopian Journal of Environmental Studies and Management* 1 (2): 56–60.

Gain, P. 2013. 'The Chittagong Hill Tracts: An Ecological Disaster'. In *The Chittagong Hill Tracts: Man-nature Torn*, edited by P. Gain, 15–63. Dhaka: SEHD.

Hunter, W. W. (1876) 1973. *A Statistical Account of Bengal*. Delhi: D K Publishing House.

Johnson, J. S., E. D., Nobman, E. Asay, and A. P. Lanier. 2009. Dietary Intake of Alaska Native People in Two Regions and Implications for Health: The Alaska Native Dietary and Subsistence Food Assessment Project. *International Journal of Circumpolar Health* 68 (2): 109–122.

Kuhnlein, H. V., O. Receveur, R. Soueida, and G. Egeland. 2004. 'Arctic Indigenous Peoples Experience the Nutrition Transition with Changing Dietary Patterns and Obesity'. *The Journal of Nutrition* 134: 1447–1453.

Lewin, T. H. 1869. *The Hill Tracts of Chittagong and the Dwellers Therein, with Comparative Vocabularies of the Hill Dialects*. Calcutta: Bengal Printing Company.

Miah, M. A., M. Alam, and M. Mohabbatullah. 2015. 'Household Food Security among indigenous Hill People in Khargachari Hill District of Bangladesh'. *Bangladesh Journal of Agricultural Economics* 37 (1&2): 69–88.

Mohsin, A. 1997. *The Politics of Nationalism: The Case of the Chittagong Hill Tracts*. Dhaka: The University Press.

Nongdam, P., and T. Leimapokpam. 2014. 'The Nutritional Facts of Bamboo Shoots and Their Usage as Important Traditional Foods of Northeast India'. *International Scholarly Research Notices* 2014 (1): 1–17.

Ranasinghe, S., S. D. T. Maduwanthi, and R. A. U. J. Marapana. 2019. 'Nutritional and Health Benefits of Jackfruit (Artocarpus heterophyllus Lam.): A Review'. *International Journal of Food Science* 2019 (6): 1–12.

Roy, R. C. 2000. 'Land Rights of the Indigenous Peoples of the Chittagong Hill Tracts, Bangladesh' (IWGIA Document No. 99). Copenhagen: IWGIA.

Samson, C., and J. Pretty. 2006. 'Environmental and Health Benefits of Hunting Lifestyles and Diets for the Innu of Labrador'. *Food Policy* 31 (6): 528–553.

Samantha C. Leigh, Yannis Papastamatio, and. Donovan P. German. 2017. 'The Nutritional Physiology of Sharks'. *Reviews in Fish Biology and Fisheries* 27 (3): 561–585.

The News Today. 2012. 'Food Security in CHT at Risk'. *The News Today*, 3 July. Available at http://www.newstoday.com.bd/index.php?option=details&news_id=21737&date=20 (accessed on 1 April 2020).

Wein, E. E., M. M. R. Freeman, and J. C. Makus. 1996. 'Use of and Preference for Traditional Foods among the Belcher Island Inuit'. *Arctic* 49 (3): 256–264.

WHO. 2002. *Diet, Nutrition and the Prevention of Chronic Diseases: Report of a Joint Who/Fao Expert Consultation*. Geneva: WHO.

Willows, N. D. 2005. 'Determinants of Healthy Eating in Aboriginal Peoples in Canada'. *Canadian Journal of Public Health* 96 (Supplement 3): 532–536.

7

The Role of *Panthibhojanam* in the *Navodhana* Movement of Kerala

B. Francis Kulirani

Introduction

The southern Indian state of Kerala is much acclaimed for pioneering some of the revolutionary social reforms in inter-caste and inner-caste relations during the late 19th century and early 20th century. The period marked the beginning of Kerala Navodhana Prasthanam (renaissance or reformation movement). Momentum for the movement was provided by the tyrannical rule of the *savarnar*. The term savarnar though has a connotation of the Varna system of Hindu social categories elsewhere in India, the savarnar cluster in Kerala did not have a balanced distribution of all the four Varna categories. The cluster was dominated by the Nambuthiri Brahmins, who were priests, custodians of learning and trustees of large tracts of temple properties, along with the Ambalavasi (temple-servant castes). Next in rank were the Samantha Kshatriya rulers and their vassals, who controlled land and other resources. The Vaishya component of the savarnar cluster in Kerala had a very negligible representation of communities; they had their origin outside the state. The scene was dominated by the Nairs (Shudra by Varna ranking), as the management and proprietorship of land resources were vested with them. In addition, they maintained large militia in their capacity as Naduvazhis and Deshavazhis (territorial chieftains) and provided military assistance to the rulers. Thus, the savarnar cluster was dominated by the Nambuthiris and the Nairs; they imposed an oppressive *janmi* (feudal) system of economic relationship on others. A unique aspect of the savarnar category in Kerala was that the Jews, Christians and Muslims also were co-opted into the cluster, as they were traditionally involved in maritime trade and were bestowed with trade rights and grants.

Victims of the prevailing system were the *avarnar* or *panchamar* communities, as they were not part of the Varna system. The avarnar cluster of communities comprised the Izhava/Ezhava/Thiya tenant cultivators or tillers and toddy tappers, Kaniyan or traditional physicians and astrologers, Vishwakarmajar including the smiths, carpenters, casters and craftsmen, the artisans and weavers, the services castes, the fisherfolk and agrarian serfs and rest of the communities.

The social order described above had manifested during the medieval period (AD1100–AD1800) in Kerala and was marked by the rise of *naduvazhi* or territorial chieftains after the fall of the Second Chera or Kulasekara Empire. This phase in the history of Kerala is associated with the legend of the last of Chera ruler Ramakulasekara Perumal, who embraced Islam. Before proceeding on his pilgrimage to Mecca, he had parcelled out his kingdom among his descendants and territorial chieftains, marking the end of unified territoriality (see sarvavijankosam.com). The territorial chieftains of the Cheras in Venad, ErandValluvanad and many other minor principalities parcelled out the territories and land resources among them and enforced an oppressive feudal *janmi* system (Menon 1979, 51). Breakdown of the political authority of the king and resultant decline in social, religious and cultural life paved way for the emergence of the priestly caste of Nambuthiri brahmins with the patronage of the local rulers and Nair militia. A social order based on Varna system was codified and enforced. The economic oppression was further aggravated by triple social evils, which were 'untouchability', 'unapproachability' and 'unseeability'. Those were observed by the people of Hindu society at all levels (Menon 1979, 66). As these discriminatory principles operated from top to bottom of the caste society, it became a clever tool in the hands of the Nambuthiris to keep the lower castes from uniting against them. Each caste considered the one lower to them as polluting by touch, those farther away in rank from top had to maintain specific distances while approaching a higher caste member. Communities who were placed outside the *kizhalar* had to hide in bushes when there was chance encounter with the upper-caste people; in order to avoid such a scare, the entourage of the upper castes shooed away through the village paths. The feudal regime was so oppressive that it imposed disabilities and debarred the avarnar categories of people from public utilities such as use of tanks and roads. Religious disabilities debarred them from the use of temples, burning ghats, etc. (Iyer 1970, 46).

Graded hierarchies were created among all Varna groups to form caste clusters. The Brahmin cluster consisted of the Nambuthiri, Paradeshi Brahmin and Brahma Kshatriya; the Ambalavasi or temple servant cluster consisted of Antharalar-Pushpapakan, Nambishan, Thiyattunni, Chakkiyar, Nambiyar, Pisharadi, Variyar and some others. The Kshatriya cluster had in it the descendants of Chera, Chola, Pandya, Aya, Mooshika dynasties and the Samanthas, while the Vaishya cluster comprised mainly Moothan, Tharakan, Tamil and Konkani Vaniks. The Shudra comprised 18 Nair sub-castes that were graded internally into high (the first 14 among them) and low (last 4 service groups). The Jews, Syrian Christians and Muslims constituted the last cluster among the savarnars. The avarnar base of the caste pyramid was quite wide but was internally graded. The Vishwakarma groups and the Kaniyan or astrologers, who were attached to the *janmis* were ranked high, followed by the tenant cultivators like the Ezhava/Izhava/Thiya, Dheevarar, Saliyan, Vishwakarmajar, Kushavan, Ambittan, Veerashivar, Uppara, Panan, Velan, Kumbaran, Cheramar, Sambavar, Sidhanar, Kuravar and some others.

The gradations of caste clusters determined the degree of social interaction that was permissible among castes at all levels. The custom of such observances came to be locally known as *ayitham*. The concept and practice of ayitham permeated all aspects of social life in the medieval period. The word has its origin in the dualistic concept of *shutham* and *ashutham* (pure and impure) and the term ayitham is a crude form of ashutham or impurity. The word also has a connotation of hypogyny practised by the savarnar against the avarnar, as well as within both categories. The customs and practices comprised *theendal* (contamination), *pula* (pollution), *thodeel* (touch pollution), *panthibhojanam* (exclusivity of castes in dining together while seated in rows during feasts); separate sets of plates and cups in food shops as well as segregation of avarnar/savarnar in food shops and schools (both traditional educational institutions and institutions established after the introduction of colonial education system); negation of temple entry, denial of entry into houses for the avarnar as well as from the use of public roads; denial of right to use foot wear, umbrella, gold ornaments and to hold rites and rituals of the Hindu tradition. Burial places were also segregated.

Caste system in Kerala during the medieval period had several weird paradoxes; restrictions on inter-marriage and inter-dining were applied not only between different castes but also between different sub-castes of a caste too (Menon 1979, 70). This produced a bewildering system in which certain sub-castes among the lowly ranked castes were treated as untouchables by the superior sub-castes among them. Status of non-Hindu groups of Jews, Christians and Muslims were higher than that of the Hindu avarnar groups. A Nambuthiri Brahmin was required to take fewer number of dips in water to purify himself after touching a Christian than the number of dips he had to take after being defiled by touch of a lower-caste Hindu. Number of dips required to purify a Brahmin depended on the polluting individual's caste affiliation. Eventually, endogenous and exogenous influences brought in the much-needed social change.

Kerala Navodhana Prasthanam

Towards the end of medieval period Kerala came under the influence of *prachinakavithrayan* (ancient poet trio) comprising Cheruseri Namboothiripad (15th century), Thunchath Ezhuthachan (15th century) and Kunjan Nambiar (18th century). With their contributions and efforts, modern Malayalam language could become independent breaking the monopoly of savarna authority over learning the language and created an awareness about the oppressive nature of the caste system. Their task was carried forward by *adhunikakavithrayam* (modern poet trio) of Malayalam, namely Ulloor S. ParameshwaraIyer (1877–1949), Kumaranashan (1873–1924) and Vallathol Narayana Menon (1878–1958).

The colonial period in Kerala (1505–1947), starting with the Portuguese, the French, the Dutch and British governance in that order, introduced colonial modernity, western values and philosophies and formal education. North Malabar Region came under the centralized rule of the Islamic Arakkal Kingdom (16th and 17th centuries to 1819) and Mysore invasion (1766–1792), which weakened *janmi* rule and caste hierarchy.

The combined influence of all the above socio-political and cultural factors contributed to the reformation and renaissance in Kerala. K. N. Panikkar (2017) in a popular article gives an overview of the renaissance movement in India and distinguished certain features specific to the movement in Kerala and Tamil Nadu.

> In both these areas, the renaissance was a slow starter possibly because the emergence of a middle class was relatively late in the region. In the 19th century, Kerala (Travancore, Cochin, Malabar) was educationally and socially backward. What distinguished the Kerala and Tamil Nadu experience was its lower-caste orientation. Most of the reform movements in this region emerged from the lower castes, unlike the North Indian renaissance which was mainly upper cast preserve. (Panikkar 2017)

According to Panikkar the three phases had varying objectives; the first phase was 'predominantly engaged with social and cultural matters, and relative neglect of political; the second phase was an attempt to the bring together anti-colonial politics and the social quest for modernity; the third phase begins with the end of colonial rule and represented by radical cultural activism with a left orientation' (Panikkar 2017). There are others (like M. G. S. Narayanan) who hold the view that Kerala witnessed a century of social reformation during 1850–1950.

The Reformists and Their Movements

The first of the social revolutionaries was Vaikunta Swami (1809–1851), wrote Bhaskar (2009). Social reformation works carried out by Swami in the old Travancore region of Kanyakumari came to be known as Vaikunta Swami Munnettom. In 1836, he established Samathwasamaj, meaning egalitarian society, and organized movements to stop caste atrocities that were being committed against the Nadar. He also worked for the prevention of *uzhiyavela* or forced agrarian labour without payment of wage. Members of the Channar, Pulayar, Parayar and Kuravar communities, who constituted the Kizhalar, were exploited through this system by feudal lords. Ayya Vaikuntar devised novel ways to challenge such caste discrimination. It is interesting to note that the protest movement used feast as a means for reform and to challenge the inequality, and this came to be popularly known as Saha-panthibhojanam.

The custom of panthibhojanam, as prescribed by caste rules set by the Nambuthiris, prevailed for long. It stipulated, while partaking food in any feast, the *panthi* (rows of seated people) should comprise persons of the same caste. It demanded members of upper and lower castes should form separate rows according to their rank. Mixing of eaters belonging to different castes amounted to ayitham, equalling to mixing of one's saliva in another's food. Anyone who deliberately violated the norm faced ostracism from his or her own caste; if it was done accidentally, the person who committed ayitham had to perform *prayachista* (penance) as prescribed by the caste council.

Saha-panthibhojanam was a reform movement that challenged the norm of panthibhojanamand deliberately encouraged members of higher and lower castes to sit together and partake their food during a feast; this was a symbolic gesture to encourage violating barriers between castes. The teachings and philosophy of Ayya Vaikuntar attained the form of Ayyavazhi religion; it is symbolized by a lotus with 1,008 petals and temples where the followers pray are called pathi.

But it was Subraya Paniker alias Shivaraj Yogi Thycaud Ayya Swami (1814–1909), who took panthibhojanam to the level of a protest movement against casteism and one of the main programmes of Navodhana or renaissance movement. Most historians agree that his caste affiliation was Shiva Vellala, though some others think he was a Brahmin. In his capacity as the Residency Superintendent of Thycaud (1873–1909) under the Ayilliyam Thirunal Maharaja of Travancore, Ayya Swami in 1875, on the occasion of Thaypooja night at Thycaud temple, organized a joint *Savarna-avarnapanthibhojanam*. It was participated by Brahmins and one of his famous disciples Ayyankali, hailing from the Pulaya community, later became a prominent leader of the Navodhana movement and founded the Pulaya Mahasabha. The Savarna-avarnapanthibhojanam event organized in 1875 can be flagged as the first ever occasion in known history wherein feast became a means of protest. Ayyaswami was ridiculed for this act by the savarnar of Thiruvananthapuram by the epithet *Pandiparayan* (Tamil Sambavan—implying 'low caste affiliation'), upon which he came out with his worldview and philosophy—'*intha ulakathile ore jathithan, ore mathamthan, ore kadavulthan*' (in this world there is only one caste, one religion and one God). Ayyaswami also encouraged the lower-caste men to wear elaborate headgear as a mark of protest and challenge against the authority and domination of the savarnars.

The conducive factors in early periods of the Navodhana movement, as described above, produced a series of elites among the lower-caste groups, who led the revolt against upper-caste domination. Some members of the upper castes who were inspired by the humanistic message initiated reform movements for change in the attitude and world view of the orthodoxy. The prime movers of the reform in the later period belonged to Ezhava/Izhava caste. Aarattupuzha Velayudhan Panicker (1825–1874), who is also known as Kallusery Velayudha Chekavar, is credited to be the first Ezhava 'strongman' to challenge the mighty savarna and led many famous revolts by building temple (1852), demanding *achipudava samara* or right to wear lengthy lower garment extending below the knees for Ezhava ladies and *mookkuthi samara* or right to wear nose stud, organizing *karsha thozhilali samara*—the first ever strike by agrarian workers—as a part of *achipudava samara* and staging Ezhavas, for the first time, to perform Kathakali classical dance drama. Arattupuzha Velayudha Panicker became the first martyr of Kerala renaissance. Chattampi Swamikal (1853–1924) and Sri Narayana Guru (1855–1928) carried forward Thycaud Ayya Swami's movement into early 20th century.

Chattampi Swamikal provided the intellectual foundation for the Kerala Navodhana Prasthanam. Born to a poverty-stricken mother of a Nair *tharavad* (ancestral house used by extended families) of Kollur, Thiruvananthapuram, and a Nambuthiri priest of a small temple, his parents united under *sambandam* (hypogamy) mode of marriage. His childhood was deprived of father's affection and care. This denial made Ayyapanalias Kunjan full of disdain for caste discrimination and for poverty that prevailed in the society. Kunjan could not afford school, had his early learning from childhood friends and benevolent teachers. At the age of 15, Kunjan Pilla was enrolled in the *pathshala* (school) run by Raman Pilla Ashan of Petta, where he was appointed the *chattampi* (monitor of rules), a title that stuck to him for rest of his life. The transition of Kunjan Pilla Chatampi to Chatampi Swamikal was earned through his interpretative skills and ascetic life. Chattampi Swamikal pioneered literary contributions in Malayalam. His works *Prachina Malayalam* (Ancient Malayalam), *Vedadhikaranirupanam* (Critique of Vedadhikara), *Christumathasaram* (Essence of Christian religion), *Jeevakaruniya Nirupanam, Advaithachinthapathathi*, etc., gave directions to Kerala Navodhana Prasthanam.

Sri Narayana Guru became the prime mover of Kerala Navodhana Prasthanam. He was born in the village of Chempazhanty in Travancore into the peasant caste of Ezhava. He had his early education in gurukula system. He started his career as a teacher in his village, earning him the nickname Nanu Ashan. Due to his quest for learning he came in contact with Thycaud Ayya Swamikal, who eventually became his mentor. Guru's message of *Oru jathi* (one caste), *Oru matham* (one religion), *Oru Daivam* (One God), *manushenu* (for humans) 'was an advocacy of universalism inspired by humanism for the victims of feudal oppression' (Panikkar 2017). This postulation of Sri Narayana Guru echoes the teachings of Thycaud Ayya Swamikal. In an era when avarnars were denied right to worship in the Hindu temples, Guru established a series of temples for members of his own Ezhava caste and those below it, starting with the Arivipuram Shiva Temple in 1888. When the upper castes objected to, he justified that the installation (stone lifted from river) was Ezhava Shiva. Elsewhere in the temples established by Guru he used mirror, stone or abolished idol altogether. He promoted education, healthcare and industries for the development of the lower castes. The efforts of Narayana Guru were directed towards the eradication of the caste system. Establishment of 'Sri Narayana Dharma Paripalana Yogam', a caste association for the Ezhavas in 1903, also marked an effort to spread the reforms initiated by the Guru.

Another prominent personality of the movement was Ayankali (1863–1941). He was member of Pulaya/Cheramar community, who were held under slavery as agrarian labourers by the *janmis* along with similarly placed Paraya/Sambavar community. Ayankali worked for the amelioration of both the castes. Major revolts led by Ayankali were *villuvandi samarm* in 1893 asking for right for all to travel in bullock-carts through public roads, *karshakathozhilali samara* in 1905, which was agricultural workers' strike, and *kallumalasamaram* in 1915, which claimed the right to discard stone bead neck chain and iron earrings that the Pulaya women were mandated to wear as a symbol of slavery, and the right to education (1907–1914). He and his followers were physically attacked on many occasions and Ayankali was compelled to resist in equal terms.

The clarion call for reform and renaissance by Sri Narayana Guru had many spirited followers from his own community. Among them the prominent leaders are Mulur S. Padmanapha (1869–1931), Pandit Karuppan (1885–1938), K. Ayappan (Sahodaran Ayappan 1889–1968), Advocate C. Krishnan (1867–1938) and Dr Palpu (1863–1950).

Mulur's contributions were in the literary field as a poet. Pandit Karuppan belonged to the Araya-Vala (fisher folk) community. Apart from contributions to Malayalam literature through his poem *Jathi Kummi*, he established 'All Kerala Araya Mahasabha'. Dr Padmanabhan Palpu was a physician and bacteriologist. He was denied opportunity to practise as a physician in Travancore because of his caste affiliation, which was ezhava. He was ridiculed by the dominant castes, who stigmatized him as *Chovonuchethumathi*—being a Chovan, that is, the local term for Ezhava. According to them, he should rather be engaged in toddy tapping, the traditional occupation of his caste. Dr Palpu was compelled to migrate to Mysore for career opportunity. Later, he led an agitation in Travancore from 1890 onwards for right to employment for the local youth in Travancore in place of Tamil Brahmins and was instrumental in forming Sri Narayana Dharma Paripalanayogam

(SNDP). Dr Palpu shared his personal experience of ill treatment by the savarnars of Travancore with Swami Vivekananda during a meeting in Bangalore in 1892. Swami Vivekananda decided to have a first-hand experience of the situation and toured Kerala as part of his pan-India travel. While on a visit to Bhagavathy Temple, Kodungallur, Swami Vivekananda was denied permission to enter the temple and venerate the deity because his caste was not known to the priests. This exasperation made Vivekananda to exclaim that 'Kerala is a lunatic asylum'. He urged Dr Palpu to double his efforts to fight caste system in Kerala.

Advocate C. Krishnan from Kozhikode was the initiator for rationalism and was known as *Midavadi* (centrist) as he ran a newspaper by the same name. But the reformist disciple of Sri Narayana Guru who rose to the stature to match with Guru's ideology was Kumbalathuparambu Ayyappan (1889–1968). Ayyappan took Guru's message of 'one religion, one god for humans' and 'do not ask, speak and think about jati' to a higher level to negate caste through the slogan 'No Caste, No Religion', No God' for mankind 'Need Dharma' (equity/justice). His revolutionary deeds earned him alias like 'Sahodaran Ayyppan' and 'Pulayan Ayyappan' to ridicule his friendship with the low ranked Pulaya caste. Ayyappan confronted the notions and concepts of ayitham head on through programmes that were ethical and interventional. He was appalled by the practice of ayitham by both savarnars and avarnars and the means he chose to fight the socially degrading practices perpetuated by the orthodoxy earned him a place among the social reformers of the time.

The spirit of renaissance movement was carried forward to early 20th century and Ayyappan shifted the focus to the observation of ayitham within the avarnar sections. Panthibhojanam movement had evolved from saha-panthibhojanam to imply inter dining of savarnars and avarnars by early 20th century. But observation of panthibhojana-ayitham by the emergent Ezhava community of Travancore-Cochin continued to haunt leaders like Ayyappan. Being a keen ethical interventionist (Sekhar 2017) and a believer in the organic and biological unity of human body (Ilayidom 2017), Shodaran Ayyappan took Saha-panthibhojanam and panthibhojanam as practised by Ayya Vaikundahar and Thycaud Ayya, Narayana Guru and Chattanbi Swamikal to break this caste custom in public with a proclaimed propaganda (Sekhar 2017). On 29 May 1917 at Cherai, Ernakulam organized a publicized *misrabhojanam* (inter-dining with mixed seating arrangement) for Izhava and Pulaya castes after holding a public meeting. Rice along with curry made of jackfruit seeds and chickpeas was served. As scheduled, a person named Ayyar from Pallipuram and who belonged to Pulayar, a lowly-ranked caste, served the food. The gathering was large and beyond the expectation of the organizers. Ayyar's son was made to sit in the middle of the crowd; he mixed the rice and curry and everyone in the gathering tasted a mouthful from his leaf-plate. Impact of this event was felt all over Kerala. The orthodoxy within his community was infuriated and earned him the epithet 'Pulayan Appayppan'. He followed up by holding similar feasts at Shringapuram, Moothukunnam and Chendamangalam, notwithstanding the opposition and social boycott by the Ezhava orthodoxy.

> The small but significant act by Sahodaran and his Dalit friends paved the way for greater movements in Kerala like Fraternity Movement (Sahodaraprasthanam), Inter-marriage movement (Misravivaham), Labour Movement, Civil Right Movement and Universal Adult Franchise Movement by democratising and modernising society at grass roots. (Sekhar 2017)

The centenary of this revolutionary event was commemorated in 2017 with many public events and symbolic gestures to pay tribute to Panthibhojana Samara under the aegis of the Government of Kerala. In an event organized on 30 May 2017 to celebrate the 100th year anniversary of Panthibhojanam, Kerala Chief Minister Pinarayi Vijayan, opposition leader Ramesh Chennithala, several members of the state legislative assembly including Hibi Eden, V. D. Satheesan, S. Sarma and many other dignitaries gathered at Thundidaparambu to have a community lunch together. Sahodaran Ayyappan's daughter Aisha Gopalakrishnan was also a guest at the event.

'We should think about where our state has come in 100 years after the Misrabhojanam,' observed the Chief Minister of Kerala on the occasion. He noted,

> still our girls have to take extreme steps to be safe from certain godmen, still women are killed and attacked, still people adopt certain superstitious practices to get rich, still girls' marriage don't take place due to *chovvadosham* (astrological issues), people rush to jewelleries on the day of Akshaya Tritiya, sexual abuses happen in religious centres. In this 21st century is our state going back to barbaric ages. These malpractices are still present in many communities. (*The News Minute* 2017)

The Chief Minister added,

> in this time when Dalits, women and children are attacked and assaulted, it is very relevant to think about misrabhojanam. The event was an announcement of equality on behalf of a group that was

enslaved for centuries. Through the event the suppressed were given dignity. It was Sahodaran Ayyappan who sowed the seeds of forward and logical thinking in Kerala. (*The News Minute* 2017)

The news reports of the centenary event noted that the ruling party and the opposition have agreed that successive governments in Kerala have failed to break the caste walls (*The News Minute* 2017).

Elsewhere it was observed,

This is all the more relevant in the present when we face alarming totalitarian impositions on our basic rights and liberties. The state itself comes up with undemocratic and medieval restrictions on food rights and cultural diversities among the people. As Sahodaran did, it is imperative to proclaim our organic human fraternity, uphold basic human rights and our freedom of choice in matters of food, attire and other cultural ways of living. A brave new struggle has become imminent to defend our myriad persuasions based on our chosen lives, a legacy of achievements of the likes of Sahodaran, who upheld pluralism and modernity in society. (Sekhar 2017)

Latent Forms of Ayitham in Kerala Society

Kerala has succeeded in its effort for *ayitochatanam* or eradication of the practice of ayitham through reformation and enactments to a large extent. Vaikom Sathyagraha in 1924–1925, Temple Entry Proclamation in 1936, Untouchability Act 1956, Scheduled Caste and Scheduled Tribe Prevention of Atrocities Act 1989 have gone a long way to prevent the practice of ayitham. However, the practice continued to survive in subtle ways, especially in the area of commensal relations in central and southern Kerala.

The region continued to be under the grip of restrictive commensal relations even in the 1960s. Members of caste groups who continued to work as agricultural labours for the erstwhile feudal families were served food in pits dug in the ground and covered with banana leaves, which later gave way to areca nut spathes and then to earthen plates and pans. Such plates and pans were segregated from other household vessels; after eating their meals the labourers were expected to clean their dishes. When they were invited to social events organized by the landlords, food was served to them in temporary sheds erected outside the courtyard of the house. Strategies that were adopted to implement the practice of segregating commensal relations were by extending caste exclusive invitation during festive occasions, and by engaging

Brahmin cooks to prepare and serve food to both the savarnar and avarnar groups. While invitations were extended to both avarnar and savarnar, the latter usually partook only fruits, tea and coffee or confectionaries. The above practice of avoiding meal from lower-caste hosts continued well into the later half of the 20th century. The Christians of Kerala were no exception to the practice of caste discrimination (Tharamangalam 1996). The author can recall instances in which people of lower castes collected food remnants from discarded leaves at the feast pandals of upper castes and Syrian Christians during 1960–1970s out of sheer poverty and food scarcity that prevailed then.

When the upper castes were invited to ceremonies in the household of Christians and Muslims, the women folks of those caste groups either avoided participation or paid visit to the latters' houses during evening and accepted fruits and vegetarian snacks. The menfolk generally participated but maintained their food preferences. However, there is a marked change in the area of food preferences, as reflected in the percentage of non-vegetarians in Kerala (97 per cent in 2016, Indian's Express Survey), which indicates that there is change in the food choice of the upper-caste Hindu communities as well. Food preferences of communities are always kept in mind in public functions either by segregating the vegetarian and non-vegetarian sections or by shifting non-vegetarian dishes to separate tables. There is no attention paid to the caste of the co-dinners in any community-feast anywhere in Kerala in the present times.

Conclusion

The observance of ayitham as a part of caste relations in Kerala had deep roots and found expression in the commensal relations maintained by the traditionally polarized savarnar–avarnar sections of society. The reformation and renaissance movement in Kerala, popularly known as Navodhana Prasathanam, had its beginning in late 19th century. The prime movers of the renaissance were persons and collectives from the lower castes, whose major objective was removal of the caste system to establish a casteless egalitarian society. The principle of panthibhojanam had prescribed the rule that there should be caste exclusivity in the panthi or rows while serving food. Any breach in the norm was a serious violation and was dealt with firmly.

An analysis of how panthibhojanam became a revolt against caste system reveals that the movement evolved through three phases. In the first phase, it was manifested as saha-panthibhojanam meaning eating together with the aim to promote inter-caste amity as promoted by Vaikunta Swamy and Thycaud Swamy. In the second phase, panthibhojanam mainly referred to inter-dining of savarnar and avarnar groups of castes. The chief propagators of the movement at this stage were Chattampi Swamikal and Sri Narayana Guru; it was an act of defiance. In the third phase, Sahodaran Ayyappan attempted to transform the movement to achieve egalitarianism by exposing the hypocrisy of the avarnar. In this phase, panthibhojanam came to be truly misrabhojanam or inter-dining.

A variety of methods were used by the reformers to eradicate inequalities in the caste system. Their efforts have set in motion reforms among the upper castes as well. Evidences of such efforts are initiatives of V. T. Bhattathiripad promoting widow remarriage movement in his own community of Nambuthiri Brahmins and exposure of the abusive nature of social practices like *smarthavicharam* (proceedings of a trial by court of law of community elders in which a Nambuthiri lady alleged of sexual misconduct, the accused found guilty were declared as *bhrasht* or outcaste). Reforms among the Nairs, as led by Mannath Padmanaphan, and the formation of the Nair Service Society paved the way for a systemic change in the community from *marumakkathayam* or a matrilineal system of inheritance to a bilineal inheritance as per the Travancore Nair Regulation Act (1924–1925).

At this historical juncture, after celebrating the centenary of Kerala Navodhana Prasthanam, it is pertinent to ask, has Kerala succeeded in eradicating inequalities embedded in the caste system? Formation of caste, community and religious organizations and political formations had continued to gain momentum driven by the spirit of reform movement in Kerala. It is also true, while Kerala has achieved a high degree of social development, the state has failed to break the caste and communal boundaries as evidenced in the electoral politics of the state. So, the current ruling dispensation of Left Democratic Front has felt that Kerala requires a relaunch of the Renaissance movement—Navodhana 2—especially in the context of the contested right of entry for women of child-bearing age (10–50 years) to the Sabarimala Ayyappa Swamy Temple. The controversy has been triggered by the pronouncement of the Honourable Supreme Court's Judgement (Writ Petition Civil No. 373 of 2006, 28.10.2018) striking down provisions of 'The Kerala Hindu Places of Public Worship (Authorization of Entry) Rules, 1965'. Public opinion was divided into the lines of the right of the religious faithful versus the progressive and women's right activists. Entry of two women below 50 years of age at *sannidaham* (sacred premises) on 19 October 2018 added to the prevailing tension. At stake was the much-acclaimed communal harmony of Kerala. The section of the Hindu Achara Samrakshana Samiti and Sabarimala Achara Samrakshana Samiti organized *Ayappa jyothis* (lighted lamps) on 26 December 2018 in favour of upholding the tradition banning entry to women of reproductive age at sannidaham. The ruling front responded by holding a *Vanitha Mathil* (Women's Wall, a 620 km-long stretch of women holding hands along the national highway from north to south of the state on 1 January 2019 and pledge to uphold gender equality on the platform of Navodhanamoollya Samrakshana Samiti (Renaissance-values Protection Committee constituted on 1 November 2018) with participation of about 100 caste and religious organizations. The reverberations of the core issues of compliance with *acharam* (custom) and *vishvasam* (faith) (as debated in the context of the Sabarimala issue and upheld by the erstwhile savarna sections) and Renaissance tradition of Kerala are played out in contemporary Kerala society. This is notwithstanding the hidden political mileage at stake for all players. The incident has amply proven that caste and the associated concepts of ayitham are 'encrypted' in the collective psyche of the Kerala society.

References

Bhaskar, B. R. P. 2009. 'Renaissance from Bottom'. *The Hindu*, 29 August.
Ilayidom, Sunil P. 2017. 'Kerala Renaissance and Sahodaraon Ayyappan', talk delivered on the occasion of centenary celebration of 'Misrabhojanam' at Cherai, Vyipinkara, Cochin, 29 May 2017. https://www.youtube.com/watch?v=lpW9tgtbeF4&t=138s
Iyer, A. Krishna. 1970. *Social History of Kerala Vol II–The Dravidians*. Madras: The Book Centre Publication.
Menon, S. Sreedhara. 1979. *Social and Cultural History of Kerala*. New Delhi: Sterling Publishers Pvt. Ltd.
Panikkar, K. N. 2017. 'Three Phases of Indian Renaissance'. *Front Line*, 3 March.
Sekhar, Ajay S. 2017. 'A Feast that Changed Kerala'. *Deccan Chronicle*, 31 March.
Tharamangalam, J. 1996. 'Caste among Christians in India'. In *Caste Its Twentieth Century Avatar*, edited by M. N. Srinivas, 263–291. New Delhi: Penguin books.
The News Minute. 2017. '100 Years after Historic Anti-caste Panthibhojanam, Kerala Leaders Come Together to Recreate Event'. 31 May. Available at https://www.thenewsminute.com/article/100-years-after-historic-anti-caste-panthibhojanam-kerala-leaders-come-together-recreate (accessed on 25 February 2020).

Online Resources

https://www.outlookindia.com/magazine/story/renaissance-from-the-bottom/299149
http://ml.m.wikipedia.org

8

Feeding the Jarawas

Vishvajit Pandya and
Madhumita Mazumdar

Our ancestor had no stomach. One day in the forest, he found a huge potato that said, 'Take me along with you in the basket hanging on your back.' Our ancestor took the potato and gave him a ride. Further down the path a piece of smouldering resinous wood shouted at our ancestor and insisted that he should also be taken along with the potato. As our ancestor reached the mangrove, he found crabs that were also eager that they should be given place with fire and potato. In the basket potato, crabs and smouldering fire were uncomfortable. Heat caused expansion of the potatoes and crabs. The heat of the smouldering resinous wood released the moisture from the crabs and potato. Ultimately, they all expanded and exploded. Our ancestor was ashamed of what he had unknowingly done. He quickly and secretly put the potato and crabs into his mouth. The potato and crab pleaded him to not gobble them up together and that too without sharing with others. They were angry and told our ancestor, 'We are different, found under the soil and the other under water ... Now that you have mixed us and messed us up, we would always like to sit inside and over you.' The basket on back became stomach and it constantly demanded to be filled in different seasons with different things. Since then our ancestors have had to move from place to place for getting things to fill the stomach, not just for self but also to share. This makes sure that baskets and stomachs all way have something! (Jarawa legend narrated by Bakhol. Porlob Jig camp 2014).

Introduction

One of the abiding themes of hunter-gatherer studies all over the world is about food-sharing practices. To share food is regarded as a social virtue and is seen as one of the essential characteristics of such communities (Boehm 2001; Kishigami 2004; Lee 1992, 73–94; Sahlins 1965, 1972; Service 1966; Woodburn 1982, 1988). In studies that have focused on these practices and documented the changing practices, the larger point made is that with the evolution of hunters and gatherers into settled cultivators comes the possibility of state formation and the politics of giving or denying excess food (Terray 1972; Cf. Meillassoux 1974, 1981; Scott 2017). This chapter draws on some insights obtained from such studies to focus on the hunter–gatherer communities of the Andaman Islands that are recognized as Particularly Vulnerable Tribal Groups (PVTG) by the Indian state. The categorization of these communities was a response to the historical impacts of colonization and settlement of the Islands from the mid-19th century. The hunter–gatherer aboriginals of the Andaman Islands as they were known in administrative records were surrounded by increasing settler population and needed state protection to survive. The Angs or Jarawas, as outsiders call them, are one of the hunter–gatherer communities residing in south and middle Andamans, and it is their story of food and eating that we address within a larger history of colonization, settlement and tribal welfare in the Andaman Islands.[1]

Away from the Islands in the context of the settled communities of South Asian subcontinent, anthropological studies of food have been informed by a range of theoretical frameworks. One of these looks at food within systems of communication where specific messages are communicated by means of foods, as well as about foods. Frequently, communication through food or foodways is concerned with cultural presuppositions used in communication at large (Miller 1995; Pandya and Mazumdar 2012; Sidney and Du Bois 2001). Sharing food or exchanging food through acts of transaction forms a particular web of social relations and is fundamental to the sustenance of caste structures and identity (Marriott 1968). Ideas associated with notions like 'pure' and 'impure' (Dumont 1966) or 'pukka' and 'kuccha' food (Khare 1976, 1986) are central to a social organization. In other words, social contexts are indexed by 'boiled and fried' food and also indicate auspicious and inauspicious occasion in South Asian culture (Das 1977; Srinivas 1952).

Giving or offering food is a way to set up a relationship with divinity too. Consequently, what is offered to divinity as *bhog* retains its purity and is distributed to devotees not as leftovers but as the sacred *prasad*.

So, food is studied not only in its substantive, ritual and symbolic aspects but also in its relational aspects that focus on who gives what food to whom and what types of relationship are set up in the process. As something critical to human sustenance and community life—its meaning, order and values—the act of giving food to the hungry is seen as an act of virtue. Yet the act of feeding the 'hungry' while embodying an act of humanity can also be implicated in relations of power. This chapter aims to focus on 'acts of feeding the Jarawa' both by the state as an aspect of welfare and by 'settlers' as acts of pacification and tries to tease out the tangle of relationships that are set in motion between the Jarawa and the outsider. By doing so it seeks to develop an idea counter to the popular notion in the study of anthropology of food that suggests, 'you are what you eat'.[2] In other words, this chapter tries to understand how cultural negotiations around food between Jarawas, the state and settlers push us to revise the proposition about food and identity in slightly different terms. While official welfare and anthropological discourse retain an interest in conventional questions of hunter-gatherer resource basis and nutrition, what remains less explored are the ways in which such questions are complicated by specific acts of outsider interventions. In the context of such interventions and acts of feeding the Jarawa, the chapter tries to explore a revised proposition 'are you really what you eat?' or 'are you what you are fed?' This chapter in other words seeks to complicate our understanding of food, identity, social relationships and power in a contemporary hunter-gatherer community where the state intervenes in the life of the community through policies of protecting and provisioning and settlers through acts of exploitative exchange.

Feeding the PVTG—Colonial Legacies and Contemporary Dilemmas

Much like Mauss' logic of *Sacrifice,* (Mauss 1981) and *Gift* (Mauss 2001), in the Andaman Islands, food offered by the tribal welfare agency called Andaman Adim Janjati Sevak Samiti (AAJVS), and/or settlers is a sort of 'sacrificial' gift offered to the Islands' PVTGs to set up a relationship with them whereby something is given in expectation to get something at some point of time. In case of the administering of tribal reserves for the PVTGs in the Andaman Islands, food has played a critical role in the configuration of the state's relationships with its tribal communities.

The critical dilemma in this was the state's fundamental commitment to the physical sustenance of the communities by providing food, on the one hand, as well as facilitating or encouraging communities to develop their own capacities for self-reliance on the other. Such dilemmas are evident in the founding document of the AAJVS, titled the 'Retrieval from the Precipice'. The AAJVS believed it was undertaking the momentous task of 'infusing new life into the dying primitive people of the Islands.' In this context, the subtitle of the pamphlet was telling. The AAJVS was to initiate 'A unique experiment to prevent the extinction of the remaining Negrito primitive tribes in the Andaman Islands'. In his comments on this novel experiment in 'tribal demography', the Chief Commissioner S. M. Krishnaratry wrote 'history was made when the AAJVS with its precise objectives to protect the primitive tribes from extinction was registered. A greater history would be made if these efforts being made now succeeded in reversing the tide among the primitive groups' (1977, 28).

As an elaboration of this unique experiment it worked out specific areas of operation. With respect to the Great Andamanese, it stated, 'these remaining specimens of bygone races have to be looked after as closely, watchfully and carefully in their small population if their survival is to be ensured' (Krishnaratry 1977, 30–31). Their future could only be nurtured 'in a sort of controlled demographic laboratory till they have been regenerated to come to their own' (p. 31). Removing them from their 'wretched homes in abandoned Japanese bunkers' and relocating them in Strait Island purportedly accomplished the task of infusing new 'life' into the dying race of the Great Andamanese. Here a new life was to be scripted for them in a settlement with civic amenities and organized economic activities. The Ongees too were to be consolidated from their disparate locations in South Bay and Jackson Creek and provided with new living conditions in a self-contained settlement at Dugong Creek in Little Andaman Island. Finally, the report concluded by suggesting that the emerging bonds with the Jarawas needed to be strengthened and consolidated in the interests of the settlement. In accordance with this policy, the focus of tribal welfare policy was physically sustaining the existing population, protect their resource base in the reserve territory and provide food and rations whenever there was a perceived need for such inputs. In the particular case of food, welfare policies were rooted more in local contingencies rather on the basis of any well-thought-out policy. The contingencies of food rations, in other words, were dependent on the ways in which the lives of the communities played out in the Tribal Reserves. The demands for specific kinds of food and the regularity with which these were demanded often reflected the nature or frequency of contact with outsiders.

The Great Andamanese, who were much earlier acculturated than all the other PVTGs through employment in the administration and changes in their living quarters on Strait Island, displayed the first major shifts in the state's patterns of food provisioning. By the 1980s the small group of 36 Great Andamanese became completely dependent on rice provided by the state. They gave up what was deemed to be the 'laborious' task of hunting and gathering and accepted a more or less sedentary life.

Sedantarization, in turn, triggered new habits of consumption that the state could scarcely reverse. The tribal welfare administration made them kitchen gardens and experimented with coconut plantations, but these proved to be non-starters. Similarly, poultry farming projects yielded little result. The Great Andamanese were keen to seek jobs that took them away from Strait Island to Port Blair. Their integration into Port Blair's urban life and cash economy catalysed demands for new consumables beyond the basics that were provided by the AAJVS. A complex modality of negotiation was put in place whereby several men in the community sought to tweak the rations for regular provisions to procure liquor. Once the administration imposed control on supplies of liquor, an alternative demand for cough syrup emerged along with regular complaints of chronic cough.[3] It was clear that the alcohol and other addictive substances had entered the lives of the Great Andamanese and a hapless welfare administration could do little to prevent it. From rice to cough syrup the disruptive shifts in welfare provisioning often followed an old colonial pattern. Providing food or other items of desire was often deemed an easy way of pacifying and containing the Andamanese in the larger interests of the settlement.

For the British colonizers, tribal islanders were undisciplined childlike savages who had to be civilized and won over by providing items of the world outside of forests (Man 1932; Portman 1896, 1899). So the 'Andaman Homes' were to become places where groups of young Andamanese men, women and children would be brought and held in captivity for a few days of weeks and offered treats as rewards either for compliance or for being obedient retrievers of escaped convicts. The beneficiaries were groups who later on became the conglomerate group known now as the Great Andamanese. The Burmese and Ranchi labourers in their interaction with the Great Andamanese also exposed them to new techniques of trapping pigs and deploying dogs for hunting. Such interactions allowed the entry intoxicants like opium and rum in the forests. If the contingencies of taming and pacifying the Andamanese for purposes of the expansion of the settlement became points of entry for new kinds of food into the forest, there were other more purposive projects too. These were part of a series of moves to 'civilize the savage' by weaning them out of their disorderly 'hunting gathering ways' and make them into ordered and disciplined horticulturalists. Colonial administrators like E. H. Man (1878) attempted to go to different tribal territories and plant fruit trees with the expectation that someday in future native islanders will settle down to horticulture. Although such projects met with limited success the belief that the reconfiguration of Andamanese tastes for food was a useful modality of social interaction and disciplining.

The colonial legacies of 'sedentarizing, feeding and disciplining' the hunter-gatherer communities of the Islands were also evident in the independent Indian administration's policies towards the Ogees settled at Dugong Creek on Little Andaman Island. In 1952, a coconut plantation was set up and registered as Ongee Cooperative Society. Money earned from nearly 50 acres of coconut plantation was to run and manage a cooperative for the hundred odd Ongees and profits were deposited in a bank under each family name. The administration believed that this would enable the Ongees to discipline themselves into new forms of labour and evolve as self-reliant communities in the long run. More than half a decade later we find that the plantation project developed a series of unexpected consequences.

Today, the Ongee population has increased to 125, but the plantation is no more run by Ongees. Instead it is tendered out to a third party and the Ongee are provided free rice, flour, spices, tea, sugar, oil, milk powder, potatoes and onions. There is little in archived reports of the AAJVS that can tell us how, when and why such items were introduced as 'rations' to the Ongees.

Ongees claim that nothing much is left to hunt or gather and they have forgotten how to depend on forest and sea. What they regarded as work in the coconut plantation is now perceived as a job for non-tribal settlers. The provision store in the settlement is the ultimate source of food rations, stocked up by AAJVS. Now, of course, the administration feels that Ongees have become 'lazy and obese'. To revive the sluggish population of Ongees, in 2017, the administration started to distribute bicycles in order to get them to exercise.[4] From these discrete acts of intervention in the reserve emerges a story of tribal welfare discourse and practice entangled in a series of conflicting objectives and views on the sustenance of the PVTGs. Projects of disciplining have often led to problems of health and nutrition and anxieties about nutrition have led to worries about population growth and morbidity. At some point or the other, projects of contacting, disciplining, containing and sustaining the PVTGs begin to collide and yield completely contradictory consequences.

In the case of the more recently contacted and acculturated Jarawas, such contradictions have surfaced with even more startling consequences. The close proximity of the Jarawa Reserve to the non-tribal settlements and to the Andaman Trunk Road that cuts through a large segment of the territory and allows regular and frequent opportunities of contact with the 'outsider' makes the problem of the Jarawas a particularly intractable one.[5] There is a peculiar cultural logic by which state decides what to feed and when not to feed the Jarawas who gave up self-imposed isolation and hostility towards outsiders in 1999. How rapidly the giving and taking of food has transformed the gastro politics (Cf. Appadurai 1981) of Jarawas is a subject that demands attention. It poses a contradiction to the welfare paradigm of feeding and protecting Jarawas. While the administrators continue to control contact and restrict the entry of 'outside food' or consumables, Jarawas seem to have created their own cultural practice of a food-based relation of exchange with the world of the *enen* (outsiders). Unlike the Ongees who are less visible to the outsider, the conditions of the Jarawas, and more importantly their articulations of it, have acquired far greater attention from scholars, administrators, tourists and activists. Yet, what seems to elude most of these accounts is a larger and more long-term understanding of the entwinements of food in the complex and ever-evolving relations between the Jarawas, the state, the settlers and the outsider. It is to these entwinements that we now turn.

Feeding the Jarawa: The Conundrum of 'Hunger' and 'Desire'

The administration's worries about population stagnation over long periods of time have often been combined with anxieties regarding health, nutrition and availability of resources in the Jarawa Tribal Reserve.

In 1999, Ms Shyamali Ganguly, an advocate of Port Blair, filed a Public Interest Litigation, W.P. No. 48 of 1999, in the High Court of Kolkata. Her plea demanded a response from administration as to why Jarawas were seen to be begging for food at the side of the Andaman Trunk Road. Ms Ganguly felt that the Jarawas were accepting the clothes, eatables and medicines because of a shortage of food in the reserve. In her PIL, she sought a court order directing the local Andaman administration to provide immediate relief to the Jarawas with the provision of all sorts of facilities, food, and rehabilitating them as it was done for the Ongees and the Great Andamanese. A bench of the Kolkata High Court that took up the matter ordered the constitution of a six-member committee[6] to look into various reasons for the Jarawas to be on roadside. In simple terms the brief of the committee was to find out what was driving hungry Jarawas to roadside? Could it be a shrinking resource base in the reserve?

The state's understanding reinforced by the Expert Committee looking into the context and various dimensions of Jarawa habitat was that perhaps the growing pressure of settlement around the reserve tribal forest had impacted on the availability of *jungleey khaana* (natural food) that included fish, wild pig, tubers, honey and some marine animals. As language remained a problem for the expert team, the committee could not provide a convincing cause-and-effect relationship to the phenomenon of Jarawas coming out on the ATR seeking food. Moreover, majority of the team members were predominantly oriented to quantitative data as opposed to qualitative data and could formulate no consensus in their report submitted in 2003. It was felt that the impact of the illegal extraction of game meat was not really a major concern and there were no overt indications of a resource crunch in the forest. Yet, Ms Ganguly's evidence regarding the presence of young Jarawa men and women was incontrovertible.

There were more reports that corroborated the fact that with increasing traffic on the ATR, groups of Jarawa men and women made regular visits to the ATR, demanding food from tourists and commuters who sought to photograph them. This food for photograph exchange acquired an added dimension with the mushrooming of small shops on all along the ATR particularly around the place where vehicles stopped for the ferry transfer. Until 2002, there were shops that sold small fried items, but soon packaged food such as biscuits or wafers or wrapped sweets were sold. Often small groups of enterprising Jarawa men or women would gently take tourists or commuters to the nearest shop and gesture at small packs of 'Parle-G glucose biscuits', indicating what they desired in lieu of photographs. This was frequently interpreted as the sign of the 'hungry Jarawa' demanding food out of desperation. Yet, what was observed by both police, welfare staff and others on the roadside was that as soon as the traffic convoy left the area, the accumulated biscuit packs would be brought back by the Jarawa and returned to the shopkeepers. So, the same packet of biscuits would be sold again and again, purchased by the outsiders for Ang and then returned back to the shopkeeper. The Jarawa themselves would seldom consume it. The shopkeepers made profit by selling and reselling the same packets of biscuits. But what did the Jarawas get if they really were not consuming the biscuits or the 'dabo-dabo' as they called these? At the end of all the commotion and with the departure of the last convoy, Jarawas would go up to the shops again and demand items they really 'desired'. These would be chewing tobacco, betel nuts or leaves, or trinkets like strings of plastic beads. In terms of monetary value what Jarawas really got from the shopkeeper was never more than one-tenth of the profit made by the shopkeeper who sold and resold the packs of biscuits that the Jarawas collected on the roadside. In a way, Jarawas' 'desired consumption' provided profit for the shopkeeper.

Ms Shyamali Ganguly's observations as those of the Expert Committee clearly missed this point. Their concerns remained focused on the question of hunger and the duty of the state to address it.[7] This was similar to the responses of tourists and commuters too who felt morally obliged to buy food for the hungry Jarawa. It was hard for anyone to imagine or be convinced by the argument that what Jarawas wanted were items of 'desire'—intoxicating substances, cheap cosmetics or trinkets. The shopkeepers and Jarawas together had transformed what was perceived as providing for 'want' into what really was gratification of 'desire'. This, of course, met with state disapproval and, by 2010, the roadside shops were largely removed.

Yet, when seen in longer term perspective, this form of exchange involving food had its own history of structured practice since colonial times. In spite of political change what remained constant was a structured practice of asymmetrical exchange between the Andamanese and the outsider. In the years after independence, Jarawas had remained hostile to the outsiders for several decades. Though anthropological interest in the Jarawas was high, there was circumspection among both the British administration as well as the Indian political leadership about the best way to approach them because of their overt hostility to any attempts to approach or contact them.[8] Several years after, however, contact expeditions began afresh. One of the ways in which the Indian administration sought to fortify these expeditions was through food. The display of food on an approaching contact boat was meant to signify the friendly intent of the visitation. Most often such items of food would include plantains/bananas, coconut and, occasionally, puffed rice or boiled rice.[9] The choice of these items of food was based on reports that groups of Jarawas were often seen ransacking small settlements in the vicinity of the Reserve and picking up pots of rice, coconut and bananas. There was thus reason to believe that these items of food would be ideal gifts for friendly contact.[10]

There was also the other thought that if the state provided food items 'alien' but 'acceptable' to Jarawas their attitude to outsiders would inevitably change. The acceptance of the 'outsiders' food' could be the first stage to 'acceptance' of the outsider and the final route to the end of hostilities.

These so-called 'friendly contacts expeditions' at the coastline dropping food items in an organized regular manner started around 1960. With increasing number of settlers inhabiting the villages around the Jarawa reserve forest, it was seen that 'feeding' and pacifying the Jarawas was the only way to avoid conflict in these areas and allowing settlers continue with their lives without fears of Jarawa 'attacks'. These contact expeditions, however, (Mukhopadhyay 2002; Sarkar 1990) remained unsystematic in nature and more in the nature of obligatory visits by the governmental excursion without any real outcome in mind. It was only after Ms Shyamali Ganguly's PIL of 1999 that the administration began to address the question of food through the frames of tribal welfare.

In what ways was the state responsible to 'feed' the hunter-gatherer in the forest? A prevailing view was that why should Jarawas who had remained self-sufficient for hundreds of years suddenly need to be fed for their survival? Was the idea of the 'hungry Jarawa' a cultural construct imposed by settlers, tourists and generally outsiders?

The paternalistic impulses of the tribal welfare administration, however, took over, and it decided that henceforth it had to ensure that 'hungry' Jarawas were not to be seen on the ATR begging for food. To provide food to the Jarawa was a social, political and moral obligation that resided in the state alone. No other person or agency could dispose this responsibility. Commuters and passersby on the ATR or villagers from the nearby settlements were strictly prohibited to give food or any other substance or even interact with Jarawas. Signboards were put up along the road and uniformed AAJVS workers were posted along the road and in nearby villages to keep a watch. With the imposition of these new rules and the vigilance on the ATR it was found that by about 2010, the Jarawa's fascination for biscuits or chewing tobacco procured from the shops on the ATR was on the wane.

On the specific question of 'hunger' our later studies have shown Jarawas have no phrase that matches with our own idea of 'I am hungry'.

The general practice to denote 'hunger' is to say 'I wish to take something for myself' or 'give something' to another. This practice to acquire or share something is expressed as *Whey-me Monatandunamey* meaning my portion of the seasons (monatandunamey). Monatandunamey literally means all the seasons with specific food items forming a complete cycle of four distinct durations. So, in seeking food what is invoked or expected is a season and place-specific item to consume. Often after a long day of walk, the person returning quietly takes whatever is around at the camp site. Across age and gender, Jarawas rarely would articulate, 'I would like to take something!'

The understanding of all these issues, however, has varied over time and among studies by experts. Our own findings of these questions were based on fieldwork carried out in the year 2015. The main focus of this study was to understand Jarawa movements in relation to seasons and food resources. We found out that Jarawas have a planned schedule of moving between forest and sea to acquire specific food items of the season. Movements pertaining to food are not random but planned and are based on an elaborate knowledge base into which Jarawa children are socialized. It is wrong to assume that Jarawas move and live temporarily where the food is available depending on situation and season. Just like we do not live in the market as we get food from it but do prefer to stay near the place of work, Jarawas are also very careful and efficiently organize labour to create degrees of proximity to food resources.

Lehey (honey) and *huwey* (pig) are significant items in Jarawa culture as they are seen to be most satisfying and have the greatest cultural and social significance. Both these items generate sociability among the Jarawas. They require a seasonal planning to prepare to get ready for its hunting and gathering. Nearly 60 per cent of the Jarawas in the selected focus groups (particularly middle age upwards) feel that visiting the settlement is one thing but continuously living there is detrimental for them as their options become limited. This is an important clue to what Jarawas think as 'future' and related policy implications for them. This needs to be further explicated and developed. Their food-based relationship with the settlers is prearranged and conducted discreetly and they have learned to keep the matter away from being noticed by other outsiders, in order to protect the 'Jarawa food supplier' and ensure future supply. This has strong political and power relation implications.

The Jarawas' capacity to incorporate outsider's food is a historically old notion that was present since British colonial times. However, the history of post-independence India's 'friendly contact' has made the Jarawas oriented to the fact that the 'outsider' will always give them something to eat. This acquired expectation has made possible the contact, growth of welfare activity, provision of medical facility and presence at ATR. This should not be equated with the fact that Jarawas come to us seeking food but it has been the outsider's notion that give them some food and get closer.[11] This asymmetrical relationship should not be misinterpreted towards food scarcity, or preference for outside food, as it would have long-term negative implications through asymmetrical dependence. Elder Jarawas have expressed opinions that there was a phase (2004–2009) when younger generations were using the ATR as an easy acquisition or foraging site to establish and assert their individual accomplishments in relation to the Jarawa community at large. Sustained observations confirm that Jarawas do encourage younger Jarawas to demonstrate their capacity to acquire resources to sustain interdependence within the community. In fact, it forms the foundation for the young Jarawa boy's initiation ceremony. Jarawa (elders) who have remained somewhat detached from the fall out of the contacts with outsiders since 1998 are very content with all that they gather from the place they have along the western coast. Yet years of contact, visitation on the ATR and the settlements and, finally, the intervention of the state in the provision of certain items of food have generated a different politics around food in the reserve. It is to this that we now turn.

The Gastro-Politics of Rice in the Reserve

Though seldom recorded in the archives, it is well known that it was the tribal welfare administration that created a certain politics of taste and feeding the Jarawas since 1999 when the Jarawas came out at Baratang Jetty without any explicit signs of hostility. This first group was welcomed outside the forest with a treat of a traditional rice pudding made of rice, sugar and milk powder. This was of course preceded by Enmey the young Jarawa man who was found with compound fracture on the ATR and brought over to G.B. Pant Hospital, at Port Blair for treatment in 1998.

In course of the three-month-long treatment accorded to Enmey, the administration saw an opportunity to convert Enmey into an emissary of peace who would persuade his community to end all hostilities with the outsider. Apart from regular medicines and food, the hospital administration introduced him to the wonders of modern technology through novel means and mesmerized him with the charms of the world outside the forest. A radio and tape-recorder was played to him at various times in the day, a television shown in the evening, and planes and helicopters were shown at the local airport or in the skies when these flew by. But what seemed to have had the most enduring impact on his life at the hospital was the taste he acquired for boiled rice, eggs and fish along with domesticated potato.[12] After Enmey's discharge from hospital with items of gifts and food, the hospital witnessed a steady inflow of Jarawa patients (cf. Pandya 2002, 2009). Often the discharged patients were given to take along medicines and rice supply as a goodwill gesture.

There was a slow turnaround from the first week of contact when Jarawas who came out with friendly intent in 1999 at Baratang Jetty were served boiled rice cooked in milk and sugar, as this was seen by the local police outpost as auspicious, welcoming and rejuvenating food, something sweet to welcome. Within a few years rice came to acquire a peculiar salience in Jarawa food habits. What was given as a temporary diet for a patient entered quickly into a diet now more adaptable to new tastes and modes of cooking.

For many, both within the administration and outside, the state's welfare policies for the PVTGs have been a subject of debate and criticism. Food and medicine have often been at the centre of such discussion. Food, as we know, was provided initially to help the community in moments of perceived 'need' but, over period of time, the dependence that this created on specific provisions such as rice has been severely criticized. Rice has often been seen to have played a particularly disruptive role in practices of hunting and gathering among the PVTGs of the Andaman and Nicobar Islands.

Apart from the Shompens of Great Nicobar Island who do not really depend on rice rations and who continue to practise foraging, traditional gardening groups such as the Onges and Great Andamanese have almost given up hunting and gathering resources. By the late 1970s, the impact of the administration's provision of rice and wheat flour rations to Onges of Dugong Creek in Little Andaman was so great that children were often fondly named *Roti* (wheat flour flat bread) and Dalda (poly-saturated vegetable fat for cooking).[13]

These concerns of rice dependency have led to an unstated policy of not encouraging distribution of rice among Jarawas who are relatively new entrants in the state's welfare net. Rice is now regarded as a particularly addictive item that also generates dependency and avoidance of traditional food items acquired through hunting and gathering. Despite such misgivings about rice, it is an item of food that has made its way into the Jarawa reserve as a ready food resource. This rice comes from settlers and poachers as either forms of payment or given out of goodwill gesture or as a token of future reciprocity from Jarawa to the providing enen. This often secret and collusive exchange of rice for other resources in the forest has transformed both the material and symbolic value of rice in the forest.[14]

Rice is regarded by Jarawas as something that can be easily made, much like 'fast food', and procured and is available without much effort. Rice has also taken the position of something like a currency, a medium of exchange for promissory note between things from the outside industrial world. Rice is often given to Angs as a promissory note whereby Jarawas would pay natural forest resource at a time of its availability. With the increase in such interactions between Jarawas and enens, a structure of practice has set in and disrupted the more ordered relations between the state welfare system and the Jarawas. Over a period of time, Jarawas have acquired an ever-transforming taste for *gheeye* (rice). What they would have earlier consumed as soaked rice is now boiled into gruel often to be consumed with something like a fish soup or curry. Developing upon Claude Levi-Strauss's Culinary Triangle (1966) soaked rice (hard/raw/dryish) has now transformed into an over-(cooked) mushy mass (something culturally overcooked akin to rotten in nature that is overripe). In the 'Jarawa 'culinary triangle' raw grains (nature) is to boiled grains (culture), mediated not really by any strictly known cooking procedure but by re-hydrating the grains (neither cooked nor raw no heat only water).[15] In other words, rice that was within the domain of nature was in itself food but now it is transformed in texture and taste by the mediations of cultural contact to food of a particular social value.

Photographs

Jarawa with rice is taken to relatives and gift items. On receiving gifts they are often displayed in the campsite.

Back in the summer of 2006, Annamolai, a young Jarawa man from Tirrur in South Andaman, had just returned to his forest home after two weeks of stay at the G. B. Pant Hospital in Port Blair. We had a chance to talk to him once his stitches on his left-hand shoulder had been removed.[16] He said something interesting about the peculiar quality of rice:

Enen (outsiders) are quite strange! I see them standing in ankle-high mud in the rain holding an umbrella on their heads and putting in *tahayee* (grass) on the ground and then when it all gets dry over time, they cut this gheyee (rice) away. I see the water gets into the grains and then sun dries it up and then again when the enen want to eat it they just put water in the rice, and it all swells up!

Now when the Jarawa patients are brought to the medical facilities, extended family members insist on accompanying the patient mainly to enjoy the medical hospitality and prescribed menu of boiled rice.[17] The need to have a support group in the alien hospital environment is not unreasonable, but one of the main reasons why there is much excitement about a hospital stay is the comfort of getting food without having to 'running or dig in the forest'. In cases of prolonged hospital stay Jarawas insist on visiting the patient with some 'food' from the forest in the belief that, 'hospital food can only remove pain, but forest food makes one take brisk steps to return home!'

Evidently the Jarawa relationship with rice retains a degree of ambivalence. While they regard rice as something that can be quickly made and eaten to quell a bout of hunger it does not offer the long-term sustenance of meat or honey. 'Rice does not sit inside like pig meat or honey does. We run around much to fill stomach but once we have consumed pig or honey, we can rest well for a long duration' (Sai. Potattang Camp March 2016).

Much like Indian urban middle class that has embraced instant noodles and lost its practice of traditional slow cooking, or labour-intensive food, Jarawas regard rice as a quick comfort food. One has often seen Jarawas moving from place to place, carrying rice in discarded water bottles from the roadside. Half the bottle is filled with grains and the other half with water. As the bottled grain absorbs water it sits in the water and then somewhat tough re-hydrated rice grain is consumed. Nonetheless, Jarawas and even young children now know how to make rice in a pot of boiling water, but only when they are going to stay put in a camp. In the company of poachers and fishermen living illegally inside the forest Jarawas have learnt to make fried fish into a *shurba* (curried broth) and to have it with rice. This is a standardized imitation of Indian rice and curry combination with pre-packaged spice blend sold in markets. Frequently these spice packages are provided to Angs to introduce them to new flavours. As a consequence, Jarawas have often collected or stolen from villages *thalis* or deep-ridged plates or bowls to eat rice and broth mixed together. Spice packets too have become a regular item for collection along with edible oil and onions to make food much like that of the poachers camping with them in their camp sites.

Realizing that much of the rice that enters the Jarawa reserve is through outsiders who have succeeded in using it as a bribe to lure young Jarawa men in their practices of illegal exploitation of reserve forest or engaging in illicit sexual relations with Jarawa women (see Barry and Kumar 2016; Pandya and Mazumdar 2019), the welfare administration has had to concede that rice had indeed acquired a salience in Jarawa diet and that they were not dependent solely on their natural or seasonal food cycle. It was a reality that increasing expansion and density of settler populations around the Jarawa reserve territory, the decline or degradation in quality of forest had also made hunting a difficult and often uncertain task. Topo, a Jarawa man in his early thirties, said:

> My father used to go to forest early in the morning (before the first convoy was passing on ATR about 7 a.m.) and would return by the time last convoy had gone by (5 p.m.) He, at a gap of three to four days, would return with a pig that was enough to feed the campmates (about 18 individuals who still belong to Topo's patrilineal band) Now, I am married my father is gone I have my own children and siblings, others have also married and have children; we are more individuals but even if we spend two or three days away in deep forest we may not find pigs or honey combs, even the ripe jack fruit that feeds the pigs are eaten up by deer that have increased. Perhaps enen should kill more deer! Look inside our campsite the old *goteerangey* (skulls) of the hunted pigs are large with tusks and so many of them. The recent skulls hanging on the rafters of the thatch are lighter in colour (due to exposure to smoke) but are much smaller and have no tusks! We have to often hunt what small pig comes by and is never enough meat to go around.

For individuals like Topo, frequent returns from the forest without success in a hunt have encouraged the practice of bringing back trapped dear and exchanging it with poachers secretly after sunset. This has not only facilitated an extraction of food resources from the Jarawa reserve forest but also acted as a license for the illegal entry of industrially produced food items and substances into the forest. Poachers have systematically organized scheduled visits into the forest interiors and leaving behind supplies of rice, liquor, chewing tobacco, spices, oils cooking utensils, along with items of clothing and cosmetics. These were then apportioned and shared by the Jarawas among themselves within a location-specific group as a sort of remuneration for their help in the collection operations. Here it may be noted that poachers who frequented the Jarawa territory to extract resources with cooperation from the Jarawas often stayed in the forest over a period of time and like 'labour recruiters' or *sardars* organize Jarawa groups to collect crabs, trap venison or hunt pig on a time-bound schedule. These groups of Jarawa men and sometimes women too would gather the bush meat and hand over the collection to these poachers who would in return pay for their services with rice, liquor, chewing tobacco or other items of 'desire' such as cosmetics, clothes or trinkets.

This import of 'industrially' produced food and items like cosmetics and clothes has led to not only displacement of traditional Jarawa food items but also the reinforcement of a deep dependency on rice. So deep

has been this gastronomic colonialism that Jarawas now have given up their earlier consumption of large varieties of shells, clams and bivalves. The above figure shells that Jarawas now avoid, as it would make them appear inferior, 'will not make us look good!'

The explanation given by a group of women at Porlob Jig camp was:

We used to eat these as a last resort, particularly on not finding pig or fish! Shells are always around to gather without much effort but once enen started giving rice in large quantity, we took to rice as it could be stocked up and used whenever we needed it. Now we rarely gather shells! If someone sees us eating these they will think we are inferior!

The AAJVS knows this well but has found out that rice does add some sort of value to Jarawa life in the forest and cannot be forcibly withdrawn until the community itself ceases to demand it. In the medical facilities under its watch the AAJVS formally endorsed the policy of providing boiled rice, fish, eggs and potatoes to Jarawa patients and family members accompanying them. What appeared as a sudden and somewhat intriguing change in policy, however, was the introduction of huge pots and pans as part of the dole items for the Jarawas ignoring the fact that Jarawas either grilled or pit-roast most of their food. Some of them did use pans that in the olden days were picked up from the settlements. These were used to boil tubers, crabs, and meat. By the mid-2000s, however, the process of boiling food quickly took over the predominance of grilling on open fire.

It was this observation that drove the AAJVS to provide aluminium pots of different sizes to Jarawas as items of dole to some groups only, but soon it became a much-demanded item by each household. This also has fostered a new habit of Jarawas accumulating dry wood or bringing it back to campsite whenever possible to set a pot to boil. Traditionally, Andamanese did make clay pots by the coiling method but the advent of the colonial settlement in the Islands and the later the Indian administration's policy of expanding the settlement with refugees and migrants from the mainland, metal pots made their way into the forest and soon came to be adopted by the Jarawas as a ready tool to process their newly acquired resource, rice.

In the summer of 2015, administration started an informal school project 'Ang Katha' in different parts of the reserve forest. This bi-cultural and bi-lingual school initiative was started with the intent of keeping younger Jarawas connected to their own language, traditions and knowledge along with acquiring an informed orientation to their growing and inevitable contact with outside world. As part of its community-driven and formulated curriculum, the school has reinforced the value of traditional food items through stories told by elders to the younger generations about the various kinds shells and tubers that were once part of the Jarawa diet and now disappeared. Some of the older varieties of tubers have also been brought over from the interior forest and transplanted around the school spots. At the same time, the planting of banana has also been taken up. As the texts and curriculum revolve around seasons, resources and hunting and foraging practices related to these, there is a conscious attempt to impart in Jarawa children the values of self-sustainability and the dangers of dependency on food provided by the outsiders. The demand for rice, however, continues to pose a challenge to the welfare administration. The only recourse they've had is to limit the supplies of rice provided by poachers. AAJVS workers with the help of community elders now distribute a limited amount of rice to the family of each child that attends the school. The amount of rice provided by the administration is limited to only 4 kg rice per month. They know that this quantity of rice is not enough. But this has been done consciously so that the child and her family do not become solely dependent on the rice provided by the state and can also resist the exploitative networks of exchange that poachers have built around supplies of rice to the Jarawas. This indeed is a tricky trade-off between the objectives of protecting the Jarawa from exploitation by the outsider and while unwittingly mainstreaming them into the foodways of the outsider.

Concluding Remarks

In the process of feeding the Jarawas what became clear was that new tastes could be introduced to make relations of dependence and exploitation (cf. Appadurai 1981, 1988). Much about the ways we produce, distribute, prepare and consume food is always subject to changes. The technological revolution, capitalism, advertising and the rapid pace of our lives, among other things, have strongly influenced what, where, when, how, and sometimes even why we eat. In short, our behaviours and our worldviews have adapted to, as well as created, new conditions and situations in which food is produced, distributed and consumed, along with new means, symbols and values associated with these activities. Change in foodways (Khare 1986; Sidney et al. 2002) reflects and influences change in other aspects of culture. Jarawas are no exception to this idea about changes in foodways. Paradoxically, the state has created the politics of taste and feeding of Jarawas since 1999 when Jarawas came out at Baratang Jetty without any explicit sign of hostility. In the years that followed and with the widespread decline in the Jarawa hostility towards outsiders and their increased interaction the 'outsiders' on the ATR have given rise to a concern and a cultural construct that Jarawas were starving in the forest and needed to be 'fed'. It is this imperative of 'feeding the Jarawa' that has unfolded in complex ways to unsettle any easy understanding of both the politics of food and culture among the Jarawas as well as the shifting relations between them and the state, settler and the outsider.

As Jarawa culture experiences, new politics of feeding and new forms of consumption of their history are rapidly transforming their foodways. The problem for them as they articulate is that,

> our forest will soon be all flat, just land not trees no plants no pigs, no honey; our children's children will then have to go to Port Blair seeking more rice. But the enen will keep on telling us to go back to jungle and get pigs, fish and shells for them. They don't understand that the pigs and honey are all disappearing rapidly. What are we to do? That is why we want to learn about outsiders in the school! (Conversation with elder, Tahapahad at Tirrur Chowkee June, 2018)

Will the changing perceptions of the forest, its resources and more significantly of rice ever converge into a commonly known and understood meaning between tribal, the administrator and outsider? Will changing meanings of rice stabilize into commonly known and understood meanings between tribal, administrator and outsider? This meaning-making in Jarawa culture is profoundly mediated by food.

Notes

1. Jarawas is a term given by the non-tribals to the community that calls itself as Ang.
2. Originally, this statement in 1826 came from a French physician/dietician Anthrlme Brillant-Savarin.
3. Based on ethnographic field notes, 1993.
4. This was perhaps much inspired by the LG then in office who himself from an armed forces background was into cycling.
5. Unlike other PVTGs villages and traffic passing through the reserve forest on ATR, surrounded living on a separate island Angs spread over a reserve territory of 525 sq. km across South and Middle Andaman Island (Sekhsaria and Pandya 2010).
6. In pursuance of the order of the Honorable High Court, Kolkata, dated 9–4–2001, the Ministry of Home Affairs, Govt. of India, constituted an Experts Committee (vide Notification No. U-14040/24/99-ANL dt. 21–7–2001).
7. In 2002, many villagers in the vicinity of the reserve forest complained that since 2000 when 'friendly contacts with Jarawas' were established, administration should also step up food distribution among the Angs and keep them placated and passive. This would ensure that no disturbance and problems would be created by the Jarawas. The assumption was that the Jarawas had food shortage, so they had allowed the administration's contact party to drop food at the coastline since the 1980s.
8. In 1945, N. K. Paterson, who was in-charge of the Islands, was called to Delhi to meet up with Prime Minister Nehru who categorically and emphatically denied the development and involvement of 'Bombay Burma Trading Corporation' in the forestry operations on the Islands. Nehru had made clear that: 'No, No British participation. It must be Indian'. What is striking is that Paterson while respecting Nehru's 'intellectual capacities and emotions' also notes in his brief encounter with then the Home Minister Sardar Vallabhbhai Patel.

> He wanted to see me and when I met him, he said there has been a revival of anthropological interest in the Jarawas, the aboriginal tribes, with which we had been unable to make contact. He wanted an expedition of anthropologists to be put in to make contact with them. I said the Jarawas had been considerably hostile and unapproachable. Patel said that of course was due to our colonial approach. I was a little nettled by this and said that since it appeared sending in an expedition with an armed guard,

would be colonial approach, I was quite prepared to put a party of anthropologist ashore at a point where they would be sure to meet the Jarawas, but I wanted it on record that I would accept no responsibility for their fate. That oddly enough was the last I heard of that one (Peterson, Memoir, IOR London: MSS Eur F 180/1, pp. 31).

9. Much like the contact with Jarawas and dropping coconuts and bananas the state had earlier imposed item of banana and coconut among the Ongees for contact set up till 1950s. This practice of 'dropping for contact' has continued to present for Sentinelese. In fact, live pig all tied up was dropped at seashore for Sentinelese who just ignored it (Pandit 1990). The states assumption is that these are islanders so Bananas and Coconut should be a natural category of acceptance and something to convert the translocating hunter-gatherer into obedient settled gardeners. Both the items have been implicit tools and substance to hegemonies with. Never has it been noticed that they do not grow naturally on any of the islands unless introduced by outsiders (non-tribal). Nicobar Islands that had a long history of sustained outside trade and contact that encouraged raising plantations has become the model for welfare and the future vision of the hunter-gatherer of the Andaman Islands. Needless to say, this plan of hop-skip and jump to make a hunting gathering community into settled gardeners (*Bageecha wala*) has been a failure in welfare implementation among Ongees and Great Andamanese. It may be appropriate to draw a colonial parallel of how food is used as a tool of hegemony. British through Andaman Homes (Man 1882; Portman 1899) used biscuits, rum, and tobacco and later the convicts at the penal settlement did not hesitate to introduce opium (sometimes for sexual favors) among the Andaman Islanders.

10. Jarawas seldom planned to come to settlement for gathering food items. Food items from the settlement are an incidental food resource procured. If something is seen, it is gathered replicating the structure of early contact by administration. If Jarawas were seen at the coastline, administration would go towards them and drop fruits for them.

11. Similar assumption has been made and acted upon in case of North Sentinel Islanders, who have resisted outsiders, sometimes violently.

12. M. V. Portman (1899) mentions that in colonial records there is a mention of hope the islanders would be taken to Calcutta and the natives were stunned at sights like horse carriage. But the most impressive was visiting piggery farm at Barackpore.

13. Ongees are an exception in relation to other PVTGs as they had in past many of the senior social workers sent in the area that were North-Indians and they because of their own food preference imposed the idea of making Roti. Interestingly import of wheat flour to the Ongee settlement was a problem due to moisture and isolation. But because the social worker and his family preferred wheat to rice wheat flour in spite of heavy damage was shipped to Dugong Creek (1983–88).

Similarly, the chewing tobacco became a part of ration supplied because the senior social worker was addicted so the paperwork in 1983 was set up seeking chewing Tabaco as a demand of Ongee. In the same way in 1983 because the senior social worker had a new infant in the family, he suggested regular supply but arguing that Ongee health condition requires a steady supply of milk powder vehemently stating that Ongee women are not capable of breast feeding. So intense was the projection of personal interest in name of welfare of the Ongees that even cattle was brought in the settlement and after a decade or so they went feral and in Christmas of 1998 administration gave special permits to local Nicobarese community to slaughter four of the cattle.

14. Jarawa families try to stock up rice and take it along with them as items of gift while visiting relatives in other campsites. This is particularly true for parents visiting married daughters or married son's visiting classificatory parents.

15. Jarawas who have seen the cultivation and cooking of rice and justify there 're-hydration method of cooking' as that is what cultivators do 'they plant grass in mud and water then when the ground is dry it is all cut and the grain of rice is infused with water to eat! So cooking is not transformation by fire of raw to cooked but cooking for Jarawas is dehydration by sun and rehydration by heat (Cf. Levi-Strauss 1966)

16. Annamolai had taken a small group of settlers in the reserve forest to hunt spotted deer, something that Jarawas do not consume. The deal was that settlers would provide Annamolai a large bag of rice and a bottle of liquor provided three or four healthy deer were hunted. Somehow the deal went sour after two days when deer hunt was gainful, but the rice given in return was way less then expected or negotiated. Also, no liquor was left after two days of deer hunt. The argument escalated to drawing of arrow and the poachers attacked Annamolai with an axe to escape quickly beyond Tirrur settlement in the early hours of morning. Annamolai was upset that the deal went wrong and he did not get the rice and liquor as promised but had worked hard to track down dear.

17. It has been observed at the tribal ward of the G. B. Pant hospital on occasions there are patients from Great Andamanese as well as Onges in the alongside wad for the Angs. Great Andamanese who have the longest and sustained degree of acculturation insist upon 'flavored rice Biriyani to be served to the medical visitors. Often Great Andamanese looking down on the other tribal patients comment, 'Ongees do not know how to ask foe anything more than rice and boiled lentils and are delighted with a piece of fried fish. But the Jarawas are delighted at just boiled rice as they were wild and Junglee till very recently!' Within the Ang community also there is a hierarchy of the settlers and what they would offer to Jarawas. Dada's house (Bengali settlers) is known as consumers of fine rice but the Ranchee walahs are regarded as consumers of thick rice that is boiled and inferior from Jarawa perspective.

Similarly, the south Indians are regarded as making food acrid, spicy and with coconut. In this ethnic stereotyping of food and community by the Angs what still remains a very desired food ingredient from the outsiders' world is onion, and cooking oil. Perhaps the Jarawas are no exception to creating an. India culinary triangle (Cf. Khare 1976; Ramanujan 1999) where roasting and boiling is sort of 'endo cuisine' but frying is marker of high cuisine and exo-cusine. Onions and deep-fried food are generally associated with the food made and served by the poachers in the forest and often shared as a treat with Jarawas.

Bibliography

Appadurai, A. 1981. 'Gastro-Politics in Hindu South Asia'. *American Ethnologist* 18 (3): 494–511.

———. 1988. 'How to Make a National Cuisine'. *Comparative Studies in Society and History* 30 (1): 3–24.

Barry, Ellen, and Kumar Hari. 2016. 'Baby's Killing Tests India's Protection of an Aboriginal Culture'. *New York Times*, 13 March.

Boehm, Christopher. 2001. *Hierarchy in the Forest. The Evolution of Egalitarian Behavior*. Cambridge, MA: Harvard University Press.

Das, V. 1977. *Structure and Cognition: Aspects of Hindu Caste and Ritual*. New Delhi: Oxford University Press.

Dowling J. H. 1968. 'Individuals, Ownership and the Sharing of Game in Hunting Societies'. *American Anthropologist* 70 (3): 502–507.

Dumont, L. 1981. *Homo Hierarchies: The Caste System and Its Implications*. Chicago, IL: University of Chicago Press.

Khare, R. S. 1976. *The Hindu Hearth and Home*. Delhi: Vikas Publishing House.

———. 1986. *Food Society and Culture: Aspects in Asian Food System*. Durham: Carolina Academic Press.

Kishigami. 2004. 'A New Typology of Food Sharing Practices among Hunter–Gatherers with a Special Focus on Inuit'. *Journal of Anthropological Research* 60 (3): 341–358.

Krishnaratry, S. M. 1977. 'Survival of Weakest: An Exercise in Tribal Demography'. *Retrieval from the Precipice*, AAJVS, Port Blair.

Lee, R. 1992. 'Demystifying Primitive Communism'. In *Dialectical Anthropology: Essays in Honor of Stanley Diamond*. Vol. 1, edited by Christine W. Gailey, 73–94. Gainesville: University of Florida Press.

Levi-Strauss. 1966. 'The Culinary Triangle'. *The Partisan Review* 33 (Autumn): 586–596.

Man, E. H. 1878. 'The Andaman Isles'. *Journal of the Royal Anthropological Institute* 7: 105–112.

———. 1882 (1932). *On the Aboriginal Inhabitants of the Andaman Islands*. London: Royal Anthropological Institute Publication.

Majumdar, R. C. 1975. *Penal Settlement in Andamans*. Delhi: Department of Culture, Education and Social Welfare Publications.

Malinowski, B. 1935. *Coral Gardens and Their Magic*. London: Routledge.

Mukhopadhyay, K., ed. 2002. *Jarawa Contact: Ours with Them and Their with Us*. Kolkata: Anthropological Survey of India.

Myka, F. 1991. *Decline of Indigenous Populations: The Case of the Andaman Islanders*. Jaipur: Rawat Publications.

Marriott, McKim. 1968. 'Caste Ranking and Food Transaction: A Matrix Analysis'. In *Structure and Change in Indian Society*, edited by Milton Singer and B. Cohn, 133–171. Chicago, IL: Aldine.

Mauss, H. 1981. *Sacrifice*. Chicago, IL: University of Chicago Press.

———. 2001. *The Gift*. London: Routledge.

Meillassoux, C. 1974. 'From Reproduction to Production: A Marxist Approach to "Economic Anthropology"'. *Economy and Society* 1 (I): 93–98.

———. 1981. *Maidens, Meals and Money: Capitalism and the Domestic Community*. Cambridge: Cambridge University Press.

Miller, D. 1995. 'Consumption and Commodities'. *Annual Review of Anthropology* 24: 141–161.

Pandit, T. N. 1990. *The Sentinelese*. Calcutta: Anthropological Survey of India.

Pandya, V. 2000. 'Making of the Other: Vignettes of Violence in Andamanese Culture'. *Critique of Anthropology* 20 (4): 359–391.

———. 2002. 'Contact, Images and Imagination: The Impact of Roads in Jarawa Reserve Forest of Andaman Islands'. *Bijdragen tot de Taal-, Land- en Volkenkunde/Journal of the Humanities and Social Sciences of Southeast Asia and Oceania* 158 (4): 799–820.

———. 2009. *In the Forest: Visual and Material Worlds of Andamanese History (1858–2003)*. Lanham, MD: University Press of America.

———. 2012. 'Making Sense of the Andaman Islanders—Reflections on a New Conjuncture, (with Madhumita Mazumdar)'. *Economic & Political Weekly* 47 (44): 51–58.

———. 2014. 'Being "Primitive" in a Modern World: The Andaman Islanders'. In *Knowing Differently: The Cognitive Challenge of the Indigenous*, edited by G. Devy, G. Davis and K. K. Chakravarty, 13–44. New Delhi: Routledge.

———. 2014a. 'Events, Incidents and Accidents: Re-thinking Indigenous Resistance in the Andaman Islands'. In *In Savage Attack: Tribal Insurgency in India*, edited by C. Bates and A. Shah, 167–199. New Delhi: Social Science Press.

———. 2019. 'Disruptive Transactions: The Complex Configurations of Sharing and the Vulnerability of Life in the Jarawa Reserve forest in the Andaman Isands', (with Madhumita Mazumdar), *Hunter Gatherer Research* 3.3: 537–556

Pandya, V and M. Mazumdar. 2012. 'Making Sense of the Andaman Islanders' reflections on a new conjuncture'. *Economic and Political Weekly* XLVII, No. 44, 3 November, 51–58.

Peterson, N. K. *Memoir*, pp.31. IOR London: MSS Eur F 180/1.

Portman, M. V. 1896. 'Notes on the Andamanese', *Journal of the Royal Anthropological Institute*, 25: 362–371.

———. 1899. *A History of our Relations with Andamanese*. Calcutta: Superintendent of Government. Printing Press.

Radcliffe-Brown. A. R, 1964 (1922) *The Andaman Islanders*. New York: Free Press.

Ramanujan, A K. 1999. *Collected Essays of A.K. Ramanujan*. Edited by V. Dharwarkar. New Delhi: Oxford University Press.

Sahlins, M. 1965. 'On the Sociology of Primitive Exchange', in Michael Banton (ed.) *The Relevance of Models in Social Anthropology*, pp. 139–159. London: Routledge.

———. 1972. *Stone Age Economics*. Chicago: Aldine-Atherton.

Sarkar, J. 1990. *The Jarawa*. Calcutta: Seagull Books and Anthropological Survey of India.

Scott, J. C. 2017. *Against the Grain: A Deep History of the Earliest States*. New Haven: Yale University Press.

Sekhsaria, P. and V. Pandya. 2010. *Jarawa Reserve Territory*. Paris: UNESCO Publication.

Service, E. R. 1966. *The Hunters*. Englewood Cliffs: Prentice Hall.

Sidney, M. and C, Du Bois. 2002. 'Anthropology of Food and Eating', *Annual Review of Anthropology* 31: 99–119.

Srinivas, M. N. 1952. Religion and Society among the Coorgs of South India. Calcutta: Calcutta Press Pvt. Ltd.

Terray, E. 1972. *Marxism and 'Primitive Societies' Two Socities*. New York: Monthly Review Press.

Woodburn, J. 1982. 'Egalitarian Societies', *Man* (n.s.) 17: 431–451.

———. 1988. 'African Hunter-Gatherer Social Organization: Is It Best Understood as a Product of Encapsulation?' in Tim Ingold, David Riches et al. (eds), *Hunters and Gatherers 1: History, Evolution, and Social Change*, pp. 31–64. Oxford: Berg Press.

9

Asserting 'Freedom'

Building Resistance in Student Communities through Consumption Strategies

Urmimala Sarkar Munsi

Everyday practices around food habits and the passion with table which humans engage in making and asserting food choices tell us a range of stories about happy times of celebration and sharing on one hand and fractious times of strife and resistance on the other. The polarities between belonging and un-belonging, in-group and out-group, beliefs and prejudices around food have always been a source of strife around the world as food continues to remain in the centre of the patterns of identity assertion, turning the otherwise repetitive everyday practice of consumption for survival into the battleground for asserting personal freedom and community identity. By actively performing resistive acts through and with food, often with the help of spectacular displays creating specific focus of attention on the resistive acts such as pubic preparation of food or displays of starvation, often in unauthorized spaces, small communities have continued to gain attention. In her essay, 'You are What You (Don't) Eat? Food, Identity and Resistance', Leda Cooks (2009) points to the symbolic power of food because of its necessity for survival. As an ethnographer interested in identities and their performances among communities, I build on this conceptual frame of creating a performative space around consumption strategies to strengthen the essay's grounding in performance studies as well as critical ethnography.

The reference to partaking in or going without food, the vital life-generating material, is always associated with its performance possibilities. This chapter takes as its core acts of indirect friction such as the setting up of a midnight tea stall to performatively take over the responsibility of women's safety, or acts of direct resistance such as hunger strikes by students against university administration to look at everyday life within the university and its creative and resistive extensions outlined through strategic performances around food.

The women students of Jawaharlal Nehru University (JNU) set up the Guerilla Dhaba, a tea stall, in late September 2017 at the famous T-point of JNU Ring Road. They argued that the act of congregating around that late-night tea stall would continue to secure the participation of women in JNU's public spaces. The tea stall was set up principally in protest against the University administration's decision to force all the public eateries to shut their business at 11 p.m., and also their act of replacing its powerful and famous Gender Sensitization Committee Against Sexual Harassment (GSCASH). GSCASH, an exemplary institution that has been referred to by the Supreme Court as the ideal framework for gender sensitization, has been one of the principle ways of keeping the extensive campus space of the University largely safe for all constituents of the University community in general, and for women in particular. This essay looks at the role played by acts such as these vis-à-vis the more common food-related strategies such as hunger strikes as resistance mechanisms of student communities within university spaces.

The more commonly utilized protest strategy used in the past by university students, in JNU and many other universities, has been the strategy of sitting on a hunger strike. A hunger strike, as clearly indicated by the very name itself, is an act of political and non-violent mode of building pressure or showing disagreement by refusing to take any form of solid food. Hunger/or 'going hungry' is meant to push the agenda through the spectre and image of the reference to the possibility of an extreme outcome (death) in case the demands are not met. It also banks on being able to provoke reactions such as feeling of guilt in others to achieve the desired goals. Going one step further, one may say that a hunger strike banks on the message of appeals for evoking empathy to the human qualities of the other—who is at the receiving end of these protests from a group of people—large or small. The hunger strikers set their own do's and don'ts, such as the length of the strike, the ways of resisting food, the possible intakes, or the precautionary measures that needed to be taken to ensure the safety of the venue of the strike. Like the strike itself, the breaking of the strike by the protesters is also usually performative, making a point to publicize the demands that have been met by the entity against whom the strike was aimed. This entity usually being the state—many such strikes end up in a failure, forcibly concluded by the mechanisms of the state, through arrest or force-feeding protesters.

Guerrilla Dhaba

After some aborted attempts of past years, the JNU administration finalized the closing down of all eateries at 11 p.m. on JNU campus in June 2017. The Campus Development Committee finalized the decision to issue notices to the numerous canteens, dhabas, small tea shops to close shop at the stipulated time. Most of these shops and eateries kept the campus alive and populated, largely by students and sometimes even faculty on campus, till the early hours of the morning. This decision was opposed by students from all schools and many students' organizations appealed to the administration to reconsider this decision as they considered this move to be detrimental to the safety of students who move freely around campus late in the night. The university's night environment has always been considered exemplary, and rather surprisingly completely safe in the city of Delhi, which is considered to be very unsafe for women. The JNU community considered this decision to have been motivated to stop the vibrant culture of academic engagement, whereby the residential students from all subject specializations move freely to their departments, laboratories and the libraries in different parts of the campus and also have access and right to work through the nights in science laboratories. The eateries and the tea stalls provided spaces for the students to gather and relax late through the night and this was considered part of the inherent night culture.

As a show of resistance to this move, the opening of the Guerrilla Dhaba was welcomed as a space created largely to convey a few points to the university. Firstly, the organizers felt that because the eateries would shut down early, the campus would have less reasons for students to remain outside their rooms. This would make it inherently emptier and more dangerous for students who have to remain outside for work or study, or have to travel within the campus late in the night for any other reason, such as working late at the laboratories or the libraries. Secondly, it would take away spaces for debate, discussion and exchanges that have always been a part of the campus culture. Thirdly, this order seemed to assume that the campus is a naturally unsafe space, lacking security (especially since it gave 'security' as the main reason for this curfew), which immediately points towards a differential security requirement for female students. It also assumes that the standards of 'security' need to be upgraded keeping in mind that the women students need to be given the so-called 'secure' space by the imposition of regulatory principles on female students as subjects vulnerable to security lapses, and on male students because they are assumed to be products of the patriarchal misogynistic society.

In the context of the Guerrilla Dhaba, it is important to clarify that more than the context being related to consumption or abstinence of food, it was the use of food or edible material in the resistance strategies that becomes central to my argument. The vision and strategy utilized in the setting up of a tea stall was for the reclamation of the freedom to be out in the campus space late in the night. This was to clarify the right to move freely, to have a safe campus, and also to experience life on campus in an ungendered manner. It was highlighted by many interviewees that they chose to seek to accomplish this by identifying with the problems as the stated reasons for shutting down of the dhabas by the administration of the University, and giving as reason, the necessity to make the campus a safer space.

What becomes essential to argue here is the fact that the reasoning and the highlighting of the issue of 'safety', singles out the women as vulnerable subjects, in the context of campus safety. Here, Haslanger's analysis of the construction of femininity becomes important where she describes the most successful discourses within patriarchy that promote oppressive messages that reinforce and reiterate gender differences/norms (2012, 11). These gender norms are in most cases put forward as the inevitable, in a world that is assumed to be unchangeably patriarchal.

My intent here has been to see these enforcements by the administration of a curfew on dhabas functioning late in the night, as not reinforcement, but introduction of the patriarchal subject positions of women that the JNU community has always fought against. It is also important to understand that such gender norms are presented by the very people who are responsible for making the campus a safe space. Hence, the idea seems also to iterate the unspoken threat that the women students should take care of themselves inside campus, late in the nights. By removing the threats of 'outsiders' who may be coming into the campus at night, the JNU authority was actually referring to a set of behaviours and rules to which all students must conform. The imposition of such a curfew on the dhabas also was to redefine ways of being a student or a campus inhabitant, with an imposed sense of discipline that presupposes and prescribes the nature of femininity in the predominant patterns of existing masculinity that exists within campus.

In her essay, 'On Being Objective and Being Objectified', Haslanger writes:

> Norms are not gendered simply by being associated with men or women; they are gendered by providing ideals that are appropriate to the roles constituting gender .... If we simply extend masculine norms to everyone and take the masculine conception of self and world to apply generally, we would seem to be committed to the view that everyone should occupy the social role (and so take up the perspective on social life) that was once granted only to men. In effect, this move assumes that what was a model for life within one social category among others can (and should) become a model for all of us. (2012, 48–49)

The unconventional tea stall, named affectionately as Guerrilla Dhaba, continued to function from September 2017 till the beginning of 2018.[2] The idea may have had as its root in a Tea Protest organized by the then president of the students' union, but it took on a life of its own as soon as it opened. First situated at the well-known 'T'-point near the Central School, it had to shift location several times as the administration made it difficult for them continue in the same space for more than a few days. It ended up near the main library finally, after being shifted a number of times. It was run by dedicated student volunteers. The stall had no permanent structure. It left no debris at all, and also no remnant except a few posters and directions. It appeared at around 11 p.m. and vanished after 2 p.m., leaving minimum evidence. Tea was served for ₹5 only, but people (especially teachers) could of course donate for the cause. The crowd of enthusiasts lingered around, conversing long after the cup of tea that they drank. Tea was served in proper transparent glasses or cups, which had to be washed by the consumers themselves after they finished their tea. The organizers were quick to remind people to wash their own glasses/cups and return them to the people manning the stall. A few buckets of water and washing soap were available for the cleaning of the utensils. The idea struck a chord in the heart of many, with its environmental consciousness and feminist inclusivity. The dhaba had no owner, and the roster was prepared of the students to prepare a list of students who would volunteer each night. It became an utopic space—enthusing many people on campus to come out in the night especially to experience the activity around tea as a protest, of course, but also as a campus event and a performance of claiming space for and through the very act of sharing tea.

Once the dhaba got popular, the administration took note of the popularity and made the 'T'-point unavailable, first by putting huge posters covering the view to the space, and then actually making it difficult for the students to continue at that space. That only goes to show the strength of such 'guerrilla' activities, which often are ridiculed by the very people against whom they are organized. That the small, seemingly inconsequential, entity of a temporary tea-stall could be considered a significant threat to be stopped from functioning, is something that is strange in a space like a university campus known for its vibrantly diverse activities and performances. The student organizers, of course, made alternative arrangements. The shifting of space had a particularly performative quality that consisted of painted footsteps on the road, leading/indicating the changed location, whereby people followed the footsteps and indicators and arrived at the changed location. The dhaba thus became an ensemble activity, choreographed and dramatized, resisting the process of being taken for granted as any other daily activity of the other 'normal' food/tea joints. On social media it was spoken about often, beyond the student community, highlighting its functions as a meeting place for socializing and exchange of ideas and debate, a regenerative space to keep the campus vibrancy alive and also as a structure providing security and freedom of mobility for those (especially girl students) who feel uneasy walking down the deserted roads of the campus at night.

The decision to open the Guerrilla Dhaba also rested on another larger issue. One of the principal reasons that created a deep sense of anxiety in the female students' minds was also the fact that the GSCASH was replaced by the University administration without any discussion with the campus population. According to the coordinators of the Dhaba, the replacement of GSCASH with what students felt to be an inadequate and inappropriate Internal Complaint Committee (ICC) also led to many students feeling vulnerable, with means of redressal of harassment becoming vague and unclear. The students felt that stalking and other offences that threaten lives and freedom of female students would only be kept away with 30–40 students gathering around all areas generating public gatherings, including the tea stall. While it functioned, its precarity is what made its appeal greater to the students who found its presence comforting, even if just as a symbolic space they could identify as their own, within a hostile environment.

The Guerrilla Dhaba first became irregular and then was discontinued as the winter became severe in Delhi and many students went back to their homes during the winter vacation. The pressure of the semester work also made it difficult for the volunteers to sustain the effort. The Dhaba's birth has to be read as one of the efforts of resistance by the students to protest against the changing nature of the university space—from an internationally acknowledged institution of higher education and research into a policed and undemocratic space where the larger political plans of a conservative political dispensation are being implemented through various measures of control. One is pushed here to analyse the manner in which the Dhaba came into being but could not survive. I would like to look at the appearance and disappearance through the affirmation of the idea that protests using food or around food are almost always rooted in other important issues, such as politics of identity, religious choice/freedom, economic constraints, choices and freedoms that are accorded to individuals as well as communities. I would also like to see its appearance and constructive zeal as a feminist affirmation—as an inclusive and assertive initiative to empower all—and not only the women students—who felt uncertain by the suddenly changing campus-scape rather than what it was projected as, that is, an agenda to rescue women from men.

The Hunger Strike

Oliver Grojean (2013) writes:

> From a social movements' perspective, 'violence against oneself' can be defined as deliberate action that consists in damaging or even destroying one's own body to protest or support a cause … these actions, often understood as nonviolent (Gandhi), can actually be analysed within the frame of violent practices.

According to Grojean, hunger strike along with self-immolation and self-mutilation may be considered as violence against oneself and can be taken as part of an 'action repertoire'. To complicate the categorization of hunger strike as a political weapon, I would like to use the term 'self-weaponization' coined by Banu Bargu in her book *Starve and Immolate: The Politics of Human Weapons* Banu Bargu writes:

> By the weaponization of life, I refer to the tactic of resorting to corporeal and existential practices of struggle, based on the technique of self-destruction, in order to make a political statement or advance

political goals. I coin the term human weapons to designate the actors who forge their lives into weapons of political struggle by a resort to self-destructive techniques. (2014, 14)

Bargu (2014, 11) also talks about mass hunger strikes in Guantánamo in 2002 that were relatively short in duration and were generally organized in relays, whereby the possibilities of serious harm to participants could be reduced to the minimum. It also was to give a choice to the protesters to terminate or continue their participation as per their own decisions. They mention that it was up to the individuals to decide the duration of their participation that sometimes continued till they were force-fed by non-consensual and artificial feeding methods. This actually refers to two kinds of hunger strikes that have been witnessed in the university spaces in the last three years.

As a common form of resistance, hunger strikes have been the mode of student protests in Indian universities quite often, especially in the recent past, many student movements in the universities such as Hyderabad Central University (HCU), Film and Television Institute of India (FTII), Jawaharlal Nehru University (JNU), Jamia Milia Islamia University and many others.

Restricting my observations to JNU, I would like to put forth two categories of goals common to hunger strike plans witnessed recently. The first one is a death fast—planned to be carried on till either the demands are met by the administration, or to continue to fast until death. The second method is that of a time-bound fast or a relay, whereby student protesters are relieved by their replacements who carry on with the fast for the next slot of time.

On 27 April 2016, 20 students of JNU, including the important members of the then Students' Union sat on an indefinite hunger strike below the vice chancellor's office. The group included Kanhaiya Kumar, Umar Khalid, Anirban Bhattacharya—the three students who were arrested on 9 February the same year and jailed immediately after the doctored video on anti-national activities in JNU campus was broadcast by Zee Television network. The site for the hunger protest was one that has been historically used by students for hunger strikes and other forms of protests in JNU, which was until a few days back an open space below the main administrative building that houses the vice chancellor's office. It is also a space where former vice chancellors and administrative officers have many a times come down to meet protesting students, often on hunger strike, in the past. The students were protesting against the punitive actions of the High Level Enquiry Committee (HLEC) that struck down on a large number of students based on the allegations made by the media houses on the basis of the fake video. The space[1] was filled by the mattresses and utility items used by the hunger strikers, and the students on strike were passing their days and nights there with their laptops and phones. On one hand, they were finishing their academic work of writing assignments or reading, as well as lying down, as the mid-April heat started getting to them. The atmosphere alternated between hope and complete hopelessness, as the long tradition of hunger strikes by students in JNU, was encountering a new reception—of total silence and non-response from the administrators and the highest authorities of the university. The sombre mood of the days were replaced by a sense of rejuvenation in the evenings as there were a host of cultural functions such as protest songs, recitations, stand-up comedies, plays, film shows and political gatherings such as protest marches and slogans along with inspiring talks by scholars and the academics who openly extended their support to the hunger strikers.

The strike site was made into an arena that had large portraits of B. R. Ambedkar, Rohit Vemula and Bhagat Singh painted on the wall behind. It also became a hub for protests and its supporters to gather in.

The strike was called off on the 16th day after the High Court directed the Vice Chancellor of JNU on 13 May 2016, to hear and respond to the appeals made by the students. All punishments were stayed by the court until the appeals were heard. The High Court order also stated that in case the students' appeals were rejected the JNU administration could not implement the punishments before the students are given a period of two weeks to approach the Court once again.[3] The student community and the supporters celebrated the Court's stay order and the ending of the hunger strike with a ceremonial offering of fruit juice to the remaining strikers.

This hunger strike was considered a part-victory. It contributes an important element in this chapter as by revisiting the events during the hunger strike, there was a consistent possibility, a threat and a dread to all its participants and sympathizers—of it becoming a spectre of a struggle lost in public view and under full media glare.

The power of turning one's own body into a weapon means that one has to be ready to accept all losses that may occur as a result of such a decision. One wonders what the students would have been forced to do if the court order had not given them a reason to withdraw the hunger strike. Till the court decision came as a part-relief for the students, even if not a total victory, the vice chancellor had not met the students on hunger strike. He had not revoked any of the punitive measures imposed by the administration or by himself. He did not negotiate any discussion between the concerned communities. Before the strike ended, some of the students had to be given medical attention as their health condition deteriorated due to the lack of food. They had to break their death fast as a result.

Does one then take the power of the protest, mobilized by fasting and weaponizing of one's own body, and what it tries to achieve, as subordinated and subjugated to the power of the administration which holds the key to the possibility of the fulfilment of the demands of the protestors in this case? Is the choice of violence directed towards self, such as hunger strike, self-immolation, always more vulnerable than violence directed towards others, in the struggle to obtain visible ground in terms of power or control over making and changing of decisions of the authorities such as university administration?

Grojean argues that hunger strike and similar violent acts against oneself 'can support an individual cause with a collective purpose, a collective cause, and can even be collectively organized...'. According to him, it is the most resourceless actors who usually resort to violent acts against their own selves, using their own body—in the process, often deciding to go into a hunger fast to change the course of history (Grojean 2013).

Following Bargu's (2014, 16) argument, I would like to argue that hunger strike may be taken as a political intervention, in which the body is used as the tool for weaponization of life. The vulnerability and mortality of the body is the precise reason that its utilization makes the intervention significant and noticeable. The basic argument that comes through seems to be that the body is of no use if there is no reason for life to continue, hence prioritizing the politically meaningful life over mere biological continuation of bodily existence.

Body, Performance and Corporeality in Modes of Protest Using Consumption/Non-Consumption

The two spectra that remain common in my two examples in this chapter are the spectrum of embodied protest or resistance and the spectrum of control or power. In case of the Guerrilla Dhaba, there is a clear effort in the part of the students to establish a sense of control over night life within the JNU campus, and thereby actually resisting the administrative bid to be the supreme controlling agent. This resistance—by not physically offering resistance but activating resistive behaviour through a symbolic but apparently everyday 'normal' act of drinking tea, in an alternative tea shop—defied the temporal control on life in campus set and acted out by the administration. It generated a political message for the student community in general and the women students in particular that the campus is safe for one and all, as long as the students, regardless of their gender, consider it their responsibility, right, duty to make it a safe one. The hunger strike, on the other hand, foregrounds an assertion of rights to take one's own life, and through this political act, draws attention to the acuteness of the crises perpetrated by the JNU administration.

In both cases, the necessity to bring in a performative element to the event, as a strategy to 'stage' it as much for the benefit of the participants as for the larger student community, is understood clearly by the protesters.

Bargu argues:

Corporeality of these performances presents a paradoxical combination of instrumentality and the abolition of instrumentality. On the one hand, the body is an intermediary, a means of staging a protest that advances certain specific demands as the political ends of that protest. On the other hand, the body is not an empty, mediate vessel to achieve political ends precisely because its deployment only by way of its destruction defies the distinction between means and ends and obliterates instrumental rationality. (2014, 16)

Configuring the argument around corporeality for both the cases I would like to use Foucault's anti-essentialist understanding of the body and corporeality as developed through his concepts of 'biopower' and 'biopolitics' whereby his assertion about rights to foster the potential quality of life is read into these protests using consumption strategies. To quote Foucault in this regard one must then go back to his words:

The 'right' to life, to one's body, to health, to happiness, to the satisfaction of needs, and beyond all the oppressions or 'alienations,' the 'right' to rediscover what one is and all that one can be, this 'right'—which the classical juridical system was utterly incapable of comprehending—was the political response to all these new procedures of power which did not derive, either, from the traditional right of sovereignty. (1990, 145)

In his conceptualization of biopolitics, Foucault conceptualized mechanisms to develop a complex social theory to understand and analyse the processes and strategies utilized by the state or other regimes of power to control and channelize processes of socialization, subjectification through knowledge and discipline. In this chapter, I have argued that it becomes evident that both the manipulations of human life through such controlled structures and the resistance of the same fall under the biopolitical negotiations—deployed either to control or to resist. Both resistance and the controlling authorities strategize around life as a political object and the body as the corporeal tool to control.

To conclude it is important to state that in this chapter, it has been an effort to read the developments around assertion of biopower through certain performative acts of resistance. The assertion of power is located in the making and selling of tea in defiance of a campus rule and the refusal to consume food in protest of decisions considered unfair and draconian in JNU as performance and a public declaration of a struggle against hegemonic assertions of power. Moving beyond strategies of protest, the idea is also to create a sustainable discourse about life and the right to exert control over it as a public declaration of strength and conviction about the sense and space of the self and its existence within the collective.

Notes

1. The said site was an open space till then that has since been completely enclosed by the administration into an extension of the built area. It has been included within the concrete structure of the building and made into an extension of the office space, reducing the idea of accessibility and freedom both literally and conceptually.
2. After its first *avatar* closed down in the midst of severe winter in 2018, the Guerrilla Dhaba has become an excepted form of protest, and keep popping up in different locations intermittently since then.
3. In a related and preceding hearing, the Delhi High Court heard a petition filed by Umar Khalid and thereafter stayed the coercive enforcement of a fine of ₹20,000, which had the deadline of 12 May 2016 imposed on him after an enquiry by a high-level committee.

References

Bargu, Banu. 2014. *Starve and Immolate: The Politics of Human Weapons*. New York, NY: Columbia University Press.
Cooks, Leda. 2009. 'You are What You (Don't) Eat? Food, Identity, and Resistance'. *Text and Performance Quarterly* 29 (1): 94–110. doi:10.1080/10462930802514388.

Foucault, Michel. 1980. 'The Politics of Health in the Eighteenth Century'. In *Power/Knowledge: Selected Interviews and Other Writings, 1972–1977*, edited by Colin Gordon, 166–182. Brighton: Harvester Press.

Foucault, Michel. 1990. *The History of Sexuality: Volume I: An Introduction* (Trans. Robert Harley). New York, NY: Vintage Books.

———. 1997. 'The Birth of Biopolitics'. In *Ethics, Subjectivity, and Truth*, edited by P. Rabinow and J. D. Faubion, 73–79. New York, NY: New Press.

Grojean, Olivier. 2007. 'Violence against the Self: The Case of a Kurdish Non-Islamist Group'. In *The Enigma of Islamist Violence* (Trans. John Atherton, Ros Schwartz and William Snow), edited by Amélie Blom, Laetitia Bucaille and Luis Martinez, 105–120. New York, NY: Columbia University Press.

———. 2013. 'Violence against Oneself', in David A. Snow, Donatella della Porta, Bert Klandermans and Doug McAdam (eds), *The Wiley-Blackwell Encyclopedia of Social and Political Movements*. Blackwell Publishing Ltd.; https://doi.org/10.1002/9780470674871.wbespm217, accessed on 20 March 2018.

Haslanger, S. 2012. *Resisting Reality: Social Construction and Social Critique*. UK & USA: Oxford University Press.

Wordpress. n. d. *The Anthropology of Biopolitics*. Available at https://anthrobiopolitics.wordpress.com/2013/01/21/biopolitics-an-overview (accessed on 21 March 2018).

http://www.dnaindia.com/india/report-how-jnu-s-guerilla-dhaba-helped-students-recapture-the-night–2552096, accessed on 24 April 2018.

http://www.millenniumpost.in/delhi/guerila-dhaba-the-new-hotspot-for-dissent-and-discussion-in-jnu–266083, accessed on 24 April 2018.

http://www.thehindu.com/news/cities/Delhi/poets-musicians-keep-the-hunger-for-justice-alive-at-jnu/article8564087.ece, accessed on 2 May 2018.

10

Food Culture and Power Relations in Nepali Society

A Case from Chepang Community

Om Gurung and Uddhav Rai

Tell me what you eat, and I will tell you what you are.

—J. A. Brillat-Savarin, French lawyer and politician (1755–1826)

Introduction

Food is the most essential element to the survival of all beings. But the concept of food among human communities differs across the cultures and geographical regions. For some communities, food means anything that is edible, but for others, foods are those commodities/materials which consist of utmost social and cultural values. In some communities, foods are cherished, but in others the same foods are tabooed. Similarly, food preparation process and food preference also differ across communities and cultures. So, consumption of the same item is unique across people and places. Different people prepare different foods with the same material and ingredients with different presentations: shape, size, colour, taste, aroma and flavour. Some communities prefer to eat raw food, other eat cooked, roasted and steamed. Eating food is not only a matter of survival imperative, it is also a matter of social and spiritual pleasure. The Sherpa community of Nepal, for example, feel that eating food in general is one of the major pleasures of life, and eating good quality, tasty and aesthetically prepared food in particular is considered to be the epitome of enjoyment (Ortner 1978). So, food is a way of living and it has become an intrinsic part of culture. In this chapter, we will discuss the food culture in Nepali society with particular reference to the Chepang community, who consider food as a matter of survival and therefore it is precious, a luxury and blessing.

Asking about food consumption is an everyday phenomenon in Nepal. In certain communities, asking about eating is common. 'Did you eat rice?' 'Did you have snacks?' 'What curry did you have?' 'Did you drink tea?' are some of the regular questions people pose to break the silence or start a conversation. It becomes a courtesy address in most cases. Even if the person responds 'no', the enquirer does not expect a definite meaning on it. Food is treated just as a commodity which is needed for every day to every momentary life. But in some cases, such queries mean more than what it is. It has exploratory and interpretive meanings that situate the peoples' state of being. At first, such queries reflect that people care for others by enquiring about food or eating. If it is an eating time, they may offer and share food, and can chat more on other matters. Second, they want to understand their state of well-being by entering into a conversation on food. If the answer is 'no', queries follow: What happened? Are you not well? Is it not the time yet? When are you going to eat? Are not you eating today? If not, why? Questions go on and on, and the interpretive meanings of such queries also vary as of circumstances. Although the main discussion is about food matters, people indulge in talking and assessing their well-being through food talk. Who eats what variety of rice? Which taste is better than others? Who plants and eats which variety of rice? Who consumes what food with which curries? These are some of the queries which help to assess people's well-being. Sometimes, it reaches to very detailed questions such as how many times you eat meat in a week, what meat and so forth. Meat consumption ultimately becomes a symbol of their affluence.

Food has a ritual hierarchy and it is associated with social status and ethnic identity. In the Hindu society of Nepal, certain foods such as rice are considered to be pure and millet impure. Food also has both social and economic values. But all types of rice are not equally valued. Consuming *marsy* (local species of rice grown in a high-altitude land) and basmati rice are valued high and they reflect affluence in societies.

Although rice is considered a staple food of Nepali people, but among many communities rice is not a commodity; for them rice is life, it is culture and dignity (Perfecto et al. 2009). Similar patterns follow in eating meat. Traditional Hindu Brahmins eat goat meat, but they taboo buffalo, chicken, pork and beef. Meat also has social hierarchy and it is associated with the socio-economic status. Thus, goat meat-eaters are thought to be affluent than chicken, pork and buff eaters in Nepal. Above all, they assess the well-being of the households through food talk. They weigh *khandani* or *haisiyet* (social and economic power) of people and even rank and stratify them in hierarchies according to their food consumption patterns. This shows how food becomes a way of social assessment in the communities in Nepal. Therefore, apart from physical properties, the types and quality of food consumption becomes social determinants to weigh the socio-economic status in various communities in Nepal. McMichael (2009) finds similar cases of food consumption in South Korea, Mexico, China and India.

Food has a power of exchange and social relations. People bring food and drink souvenirs as an honour while asking for a favour, even while asking the hand of a girl for marriage. In case of marriage, after discussion of the purpose, if the house owner agrees to the deal, they happily open the food brought as souvenir and share with all present on the very occasion. People get happy and share good moments with drinking, singing and dancing. If the deal is not accepted, food is not opened or distributed but rather returned with regrets and excuses. Exchange of food strengthens social relations. Nepali people grow different food items in different ecological belts. They exchange their produce and share them. Food has a social stigma as well. For example, those who eat a lot of rice regularly are called *bhate* and those who eat gruel all the time are called *dhide*. In order to escape from such social stigma, people offer soft food of rice to their guests and they eat coarse and dry food of millet and buckwheat. It is a common saying in Nepalese hills that people give rice to pets while washing their hands after their meal just to show off that they have eaten rice even though they have eaten *dhindo* in the meal. Thus, rice is closely related to affluency in Nepalese society. Chepangs who feel affluent and cultured pretend to be rice eaters. Love for rice among Chepangs is simply based on its palatability, cleanliness and ease to cook. We hear and understand that many people in the West take rice as a poor people's diet. This concept may have developed simply because 'roughly 900 million of the world's poor defined as those with daily income below $1.25 in terms of purchasing power parity depend on rice producers or as consumers' (Pandey et al., 2010). This speculation may be true due to larger population dependency, but the larger chunk of poor people may not be eating rice; even if they are, they may have been eating poor quality rice which supplies low calories to the eaters.

With this brief conceptual background, let us examine the food culture of the Chepang community of Nepal.

Short Ethnography of the Chepangs

Chepangs are of Mogoloid stock (Bista 1967; Hodgson 1972), who speak Tibeto-Burman language. They are one the 59 ethnic groups officially identified and legally recognized as indigenous nationalities of Nepal. Based on human development indicators and topographical conditions, National Foundation for the Development of Indigenous Nationalities (NFDIN) has classified them as one of the 10 endangered indigenous communities of Nepal (2004). According to the National Census (2011), the total population of Chepang is 68,399. But Nepal Chepang Association (NCA), the national organization of Chepangs in Nepal, claims that their population is more than the number reported by the national census report 2001.

Chepangs are inhabitants of steep and sloppy marginalized rocky foothills of Central Nepal, and therefore they are called the people of stone (Rai, 1975). Their settlements are dispersed around the southern hills of Dhading, northern hills of Chitwan, north-western hills of Makwanpur and southern part of Gorkha districts in Nepal. Chepangs are native to these foothills and they are believed to be the first settlers of Mahabharat and Chure Hills.

Traditionally, Chepangs are semi-nomadic people and depended upon hunting wild animals and gathering wild roots and fruits for their survival. Although they claim themselves as *bhumiputras* (sons of the soil), legally, they do not hold much land in their names. They own very little marginal land which is not good for agricultural production. They practise slash and burn cultivation and produce limited amount of cereals, such as maize, millet, buckwheat, potato and little green vegetables just enough to feed their families for two to three months. So, they heavily depend upon hunting and gathering for their subsistence economy. They move up the hills for hunting and gathering and down the rivers to catch fishes. Hunting wild birds, gathering yams, tubers and catching fishes are their routine works. But in the name of *praja*[1] development, the government has forced them to live a sedentary life without ensuring alternative means of livelihoods. Thus, the government's policy of forced sedentarization has negative impacts on Chepangs' socio-economic life. Moreover, the rapid process of Hinduization, modernization, legalization, and politicization has pushed the Chepangs at the verge of extreme poverty and marginalization.

Chepangs are a socially excluded, culturally discriminated, politically dominated and economically exploited group. They are disadvantaged peoples and deprived of basic social facilities. The Nepal Multidimensional Social Exclusion Index (economic, social, cultural and political) prepared by Lynn Bennett and Dilip Parajuli and published by Himal Books in 2013 and The Nepal Multidimensional Social Inclusion Index (social, political, economic, cultural and gender discrimination) prepared by Arun Kumar Las Das et al. and published by the Central Department of Sociology/Anthropology of Tribhuvan University in 2014 ranked Chepangs as one of the four (Raji, Raute, Kusunda and Chepangs) highly excluded and thereby most deprived ethnic groups in Nepal. Although Nepal is proud to declare the drastic reduction of poverty rate from 32 in 2011 to 18 in 2018, the incidence of poverty is surprisingly high among the Chepangs (40 per cent).

Chepangs live in a state of chronic food deficiency and they suffer from food starvation every year for 3–9 months. More than 60 per cent of the families have food that does not last for more than six months. For the rest of the time, they eat wild food items, namely, fruits, yams, *sisnu (urtica dioca)*, tubers and the meat of wild animals and birds. The shortage of food appears primarily due to small size of landholding, traditional methods of slash-and-burn cultivation, low yield of marginal land and government's anti-people nationalization policy of forests, land, water and mineral resources. All these factors have made Chepangs as one of the poorest groups in Nepal (Riboli 2000).

Despite the economic hardship, culturally Chepangs are a happy people in Nepal. They have a high degree of cultural resilience to adapt difficult socio-economic environment. They are always happy whether or not they have food, shelter and clothes. Chepangs create pleasure and they never worry or never feel sad (Soveet 1992). They are simple, hardworking and care-free people, live in communal harmony and have a culture of sharing food and drink with others. Chepangs do not want to eat food received free from others without reciprocating. If they receive food from someone, they will reciprocate in giving them a gift either comprising food or any other item of equal value. The gift culture is strongly embedded into Chepang communities, even though they severely lack gift items.

Chepang Food Culture

Human food is a composition of cereals, vegetation, meat and dairy. Some people eat all of those, whereas others have no such choice. Food consumption is associated with culture and mostly chosen by the consumer. You can eat by cooking at home or go out to eat in restaurants. You can buy food from the takeout stores or order cooked food delivered at home. You can go for a pizzeria or a sushi restaurant, a burger house or a Chinese buffet. It is all the choices a consumer has. It is a situation, a choice and a culture that guides a consumer which food and where to eat.

Food is an everyday necessity but has interpretive meanings in societies. The values of food vary according to circumstances and associations. Hosting a banquet in honour of dignified personalities has different meanings than everyday eating in a house kitchen. Eating out in a date with a fiancée has different meaning than eating in a school hostel. Eating certain food in some occasions has different value than eating a regular food. Cooking and eating everyday meal in a house reflect a status different from scavenging food in a street rubbish bin. So the place from where you get food underscores your status and from which you interpret the being and purpose of the food in a society. So, it is rational to argue that feeding has symbolic and commoditized meanings in human actions. Symbolic meanings motivate to seek for additional meanings, while commoditized approach ends with everyday eating. Sherry Ortner (1978) considers that feeding has a cultural power in which the host has an immediate 'manipulative' or 'non-manipulative intent'. The host for some reasons has manipulative intents in the given examples mentioned above, whereas in the wedding and funeral parties, there are none.

Eating has a cultural and economic meaning to Chepangs. According to an old informant, who was born and grown up in a neighbouring Brahmin family of Chepangs and still lives in the same vicinity, Chepangs, whether they are food-sufficient or insufficient, cannot live without eating wild foods, namely, yams, bats, birds, vegetables and fruits. He did not elaborate why Chepangs are fond of wild items while he was not. But he was sure that Chepangs were fond of wild foods due to their cultural habits. They like wild foods because their liking is embedded in their culture. It is the way they were brought up by their parents together with hunting, gathering and feeding wild items from their childhood to adulthood. Of course, Chepang people prefer to eat foods cooked by their mothers. However, they cherish wild foods which they have been getting from hunting and gathering since the time of their ancestors. Thus, wild foods have become an integral part of their culture and identity. At present, the food-sufficient Chepangs' liking to wild foods reflects cultural reliance than economic need, whereas the poorest Chepangs' reliance on wild foods has become both cultural and economic dependence. This positions the former group into 'live to eat', that they intend to eat for pleasure and esteem, whereas the latter into 'eat to live' group compensating and meeting their daily necessities. Most of the Chepangs situate themselves in the latter group.

Per Lodwin (1998) has classified Newari food into three main categories: (a) *ja* or daily rice meals, (b) *baji* or midday snacks and (c) *bhoye* or feasts. Chepang meals can also be classified into the same categories—morning, day and evening meals. The intent of the categories in the Newars and Chepangs are the same. However, the ingredients are different. Chepangs cannot afford to have rice every day, which is mostly substituted either by other cereals or wild yams, as mentioned above. The same applies to snacks; Chepang snacks are mostly roasted corn, yam, or *jaand* (beer-like fermented slurry) only. About the feast, the culture and purposes are different as per ethnicity. Chepang big feasts are *Chhonam* and *Maghe Sakranti*, where they invite home their *chhori cheli* (daughters and sisters) and feast for some days. During their visit to maternal home, the chhori cheli bring food items; namely, meat, chicken and liquor as their gift. The maternal hone compensates their chhori cheli with similar types of gifts when they return to their home.

Chepangs normally eat their food with washed right hand. Unlike in Western culture, when people start eating meals, Chepangs normally do not speak. You can only hear some rattling utensils, chewing, swallowing and gulping of drinking water. Such etiquette was noted by Toffin (1975) among the Newars of Kathmandu valley, which Lowdin (1998) corroborate in his studies among the same ethnicity. Both Toffin and Lowdin observed that the etiquette of evening and morning meal taken together with the family members at home was silent, whereas midday meal in the field was conversational. It is observed that patterns of silence while eating exists in almost all communities in Nepal. This also follows hierarchy as the eldest eats first than others. Women, daughters-in-law and the cook, mostly a woman, eat at the end. However, among Chepangs the exception is that they all eat at the same time by dividing the food equally, as stated earlier. This manifests the sense of equality among family members which normally exists in an egalitarian society.

Alan Holmberg (1960) noted such eating culture in Siriono community in Bolivia in the 1960s, where eating took place without benefit of etiquette or ceremony. Food is bolted as rapidly as possible, and when a person is eating, he never looks up from his food until he has finished to avoid the stare of onlookers (Holmberg 1960). These eating habits could be interpreted in several ways. The first obvious reason is that people might be so hungry that they cannot or do not have time to think of anything other than eating hurriedly to satisfy their hunger. This also purposefully avoids potential lookers. Once they are full, they might think of other things such as taste, quality and servings. Second reason could be that people are eating in hierarchy (wherever applies). If the elder breaks the silence, others can respond, but elders think it is not appropriate to talk while eating, so silence continues. Another reason in some communities is that if people speak, they might spill over some food or liquid to others since they are sitting too close due to limited space while eating. The spills are normally taken as *jutho* (impure). If one spreads jutho to others, the food is polluted, and others do not eat it. The concept of jutho might have been imported from the Hindu concept of purity and pollution. The fourth reason could be that the food is served and eaten by the side of hearth which is quite dark, and people can hardly see another's face while they eat. So, face-to-face communication becomes ineffective while eating. Hence, it is not worthy to talk. Whatever the reasons are, this practice of silence while eating is observed in most of the communities, including Chepangs in Nepal.

Unlike Holmberg's (1960) observation among Siriono, Chepangs take food as essential necessity, but they are not aggressive to have it. They can wait with starvation for some time to get food in the lean seasons. Even the starving kids, as Rai observed during his fieldwork, were not in a hurry to grab food once the food was ready in the kitchen. They obeyed and waited their parents to serve them. Normally, they enjoyed if they had ample food in their home; if not they walked out and sought for other alternatives: foraging wild fruits, yams and berries in the forests. They were sad if they did not have food to cook for the day or night, but they kept it secret within the family as far as possible. They cheered up the food when they found it. In case there was no food item at home, they alternatively arranged borrowing from a neighbour or village head, went for wage labour, or hunt and gather wild food. They were not serious about food supply and savings. Neither did they care about nutrition requirements for children, pregnant women and elderly people. This could be due to low awareness.

Unlike other communities in rural Nepal, all Chepang family members eat together. Irrespective of age, all are served equal share of food before they start eating. The adults normally finish up the allocated food, whereas children store the leftovers or allocate it in a separate place before they start eating and eat the saved food later as *khaja* (snacks). Some are additionally served if the food is remaining in the pot. However, Chepangs serve foods first to the guests and elders on special ritual or festive occasions. During these occasions, the utmost priority is given to the guests. The guests and elders get the lion's share. The children come in the second priority followed by women who normally cook food and eat last. From gender perspective, it looks like a malpractice, as women are subordinate to men; but from Chepangs' perspective, it is customary for women to serve foods and drinks first to their guests and elders by women to serve themselves at last. This portrays one of the interesting facets of the Chepang cultural ideology that certain rituals, festivals and occasions call for special attention of food preparation and food serving by women.

Chepangs treat their guests usually as their relatives, and offer them good foods and drinks, no matter wherever and whenever they meet their relatives. For instance, if a guest reaches a Chepang house, the owner by all means tries to honour and satisfy the guest by serving the best food the household can offer. On many occasions, we were offered the esteemed food of the community—*bhaat* (cooked rice) with chicken curry, while they, including the children, ate dhindo with pickles. Even if we asked for the dhindo, they did not serve us because we were special guests. This practice symbolizes honour and respect in their culture, though this may vary in other cultures. One can also find Chepang hospitality to their guests even at small restaurants erected along the roads of Chepang settlements. Chepangs work hard and earn some money, but they spend their earnings treating guests without any hesitation. Uddhav Rai during his fieldwork in Bangti village of Chepang in 2009 found that one of his informants named Bir Bahahdur Chepang while treating his brother-in-law by serving chicken and beer at a restaurant spent half of the money which he had earned from sale of tomatoes at the local market. According to Rai (2012, 2014), Bir Bahadur was very happy to treat his brother-in-law out of his home. In such occasions, there are no 'manipulative purpose'. Chepangs' offer is guided by honouring and pleasing the guests with the notion that 'guests are gods'. But there might be manipulative purposes on other occasions. For example, in a Yangdzi transaction of Sherpas, an individual brings a token of gift of beer and/or food to another in a culturally formalized manner, and then asks the other for a favour—anything from lending a small sum of money to giving some sort of extended lessons, from promising to dance at one's wedding to dropping a legal suit, from selling something at a cheap rate to giving a daughter in marriage (Ortner 1978). Thus, Sherpas' food offering has a manipulative purpose; their offer has the intent of advance compensation to please the owner or master in the notion of fulfilling self-interests.

Chepang Food Concept

Food among Chepangs is always 'a commodity' which one needs to 'eat to live'. But sometimes it becomes pleasure and prosperity. During festivals, they spend their income from the sale of vegetables lavishly for food. They enjoy a lot with the foods they buy and eat like they are living to eat in this planet. They have a reason to do it. The reason of high expenditure on food is associated with their socio-economic status. However, their priority is the purchase of food. Within food choices, staple food receives the first priority, then the subsidiary items such as meat, vegetables, dairy products and drinks. As household income raises, so does access to food varieties, quality, and even quantity. The high-income groups eat lesser calorie fresh and more income elastic food. High-calorie food taken before becomes inferior food now. For example, in Nepal, poorer households mostly consume coarse grains like millet, buckwheat, barley, and corn. The middle-income group consume coarse to medium rice, while the richer households consume fine rice and other processed food products (Koirala 1997). But now the foods of millet, buckwheat and corn are considered to be organic and they become luxurious foods even for rich people for health reason. Many restaurants in Kathmandu, Pokhara and along the highway serve these foods at high price to their customers. Chepangs eat these organic foods at home, but they do not eat such foods in restaurants, if they have a chance to go to restaurants to eat. They think that eating such foods in restaurants is not only a waste of money, but also a degradation of their social status.

As said above, the simple meaning of food for Chepangs is a commodity or a *khana* in Nepali. But it is also an honour and respect to the guests. Food is protection, it is a growth and a development. Food is status, it is a well-being. Food is overall livelihood and life. Food is pleasure and prosperity. Food is respect and love. Food is a culture because this reflects manners. For Chepangs food is a basic need to be fulfilled, but at the same time, food is a gift of the god. Foods are the blessings of Mother Earth. Therefore, they perform *bhumipuja* (worship of mother earth). However, the ultimate morality of food is a reward of work. Therefore, Chepangs commonly say that the aim of work is to eat two meals a day: *kam garnuko udeshya akhir bihana beluki hat mukh jodnu nai ho* (the purpose of the work is to bring hands to mouth for two times a day). Thus, the output of a person's work is manifested in the consumption of food.

The meal of Chepangs normally consists of rice, mush or gruel with a local vegetable or meat curry, a pickle, if not green and red chilies, in the morning and evening, and at the most a bunch of snacks in the late afternoon. They cannot think of a few varieties of items from one material; for example, one can make only curry or fry from a pig or buff meat. Same is true with rice, as they either boil it or make a slurry of it. They have only understood about food sufficiency and insufficiency because that is the everyday, monthly and yearly phenomenon for them. About one-third of their food items still comes from wilderness. However, the quantity is significantly less than what it was 10 years ago. The understanding of *gauma anikal chha* (there is famine in the village) means food is severely scarce in the village. People have long experiences of food availability versus scarcity in the community. Chepangs often do not get enough to eat. Just filling the stomach is a major concern. They generally rely on cereal crops for five to six months, and for the rest of the months, they have to live on wild resources (Gurung 1989). These days they import rice from nearby market with the income from vegetable sale; however, *anikal* (famine) is the most used term to food insecurity. People have to remain half-filled or filled with *khole fando* (flour slurry) and *sisno* soup during famine season from March to May.

The meaning of food differs from people to people as per time and situation. If we ask a Chepang *'bhaat khanu bho'* (did you eat rice or whether you have food)? They normally understand that we ask them whether they have had rice. So, they might answer no. Because the literal meaning of bhaat is rice or the vice versa and Chepangs cannot afford to buy rice for daily meal even though rice is the most staple and widely eaten food in Nepal. So, rice becomes a synonym of food in common Nepali parlance, but for Chepangs rice becomes a symbol of affluence which they cannot afford, nor grow it by themselves. When we ask categorically about the items they eat from morning to evening, they realize all items are food. But if we ask them in bulk, they perceive it as rice but no other food. Even if they understand that they are being asked about what food they eat, they respond back to strangers meaning rice.

Food comes from various sources—self-growing, buying and borrowing. Until recent decades food of most of the Nepali people used to come from their farmlands grown by themselves. But now, food of most Nepali people come from markets. Until the recent past, Chepangs used to get their food primarily from hunting, gathering and fishing. But in present times, Chepangs cannot get food from those sources as a result of government's restriction to hunting, gathering and fishing. After the sedentarization process, they have started to cultivate land, but they produce food which is not enough to feed their families even for six months. So, they need to buy food from markets. At present, more than 80 per cent of the Chepangs (including children of school going age) are engaged as wage labourers at a meagre amount of daily wage and more than 60 per cent of the income is spent for purchasing food (Central Bureau of Statistics 2011). This obviously indicates the type of food the Chepangs eat. Thus, Chepangs' objective food situation can be well characterized by what the French lawyer and politician Brillat-Savarin (1826) wrote nearly two centuries ago, 'Tell me what you eat and I will tell you what you are' in his famous book *Physiology of Food*. By writing this, Brillat-Savarin has not only accepted food as a necessity, but also has explained that food symbolizes a category, status, group, level, class, culture, identity and well-being.

Chepang Food Regime[2]

The concept of 'food regime' is an analytical device of global food relations that emerged after II World War. It is the rule-governed structure of production and consumption of food on a world scale (Friedman 1993). The notion emerged in the 1950s, especially due to 'internal contradictions' in agricultural trade policies of the USA. The scale of food regime changes because of the political economy of states, which includes the policies, programmes and activities implemented by the state. Changes in certain policies may increase or decrease the food regime to a deeper extent. The notion of food regime emerged somewhat at the global level, especially in the USA and Europe. It is not about food per se but about relations within which food is produced, and through which capitalism is produced and reproduced (McMichael 2009). This is related to large-scale economies, particularly the booming US agriculture production and funding of the food aid provided to the war-torn European nations through Marshall Plan. The trend and analysis of food regime then was somewhat between the recipients and the donors. While analysing the procedures and substances, it is a whole matter of understanding the food system in a large or even a small scale. It is therefore worth to use the concept of food regime in a small community of Chepangs in Nepal. This deals with the food production and consumption systems among Chepangs in the Bangti cluster.

It is important to discuss whether Chepang food regime exists. Chepangs produce some of their food on their own, some they fulfil through scavenging, and recently they have been importing it from nearby market, though the food miles is not so long. Chepang food miles is rather short, mostly within walking distance from their homestead for their own production and for hunting-gathering. However, it is the rice, lentil and salt that come from outside the community, mostly from Tarai areas of Nepal. Their food regime, 50 years ago, was different from the regime now because their reliance on forest was much higher than now. However, there is a system of food-getting among Chepangs, which they have been following for quite long within some boundaries and practices. Even in the world food regime, not many food items cross national boundaries. While most food products are still consumed within a radius of 15 km from the place where those are produced—and only 15 per cent of food products across national boundaries. Local market places are now strongly subordinated to, and indirectly controlled through, the world market, and the food empires operating within it (Weis 2007). Chepang food regime is located within a distance of a day's walk.

Chepang foods are prepared from raw ingredients. They consume very few processed foods, though they have been eating a lot of instant noodles recently. The instant noodles are travelling steadily in the remote villages. This can be seen and realized by the wrappers thrown along the trails in the Chepang villages. While talking about instant noodles, people feel esteemed to eat those because they are easy to cook and tasty. More importantly, they are imported and attractive to offer to someone. Thus, consumption of instant noodles manifests the changing Chepang ways within their habitus. This not only portrays Chepang's passion for changing food habits but also presents their exposure to global food regime, ultimately changing their food culture.

As communicated by Hari Sharma (2011), Chepang's photos were displayed in the headquarters of Coca-Cola in Atlanta in 1996, which advertised the reach of their drink even to the remote caves of the Chepangs in Nepal. This not only signifies the reach of the product to remote areas but also furnishes the changes in Chepang's ways of living, eating and drinking. More importantly, this represents symbolic images of Chepangs globally, who despite their hardships can enjoy the products of the market wherever they are. Philip Deloira (2004) portrayed American Indians as central symbolic elements in American culture for a very long time. Native Americans and the Singer sewing machine picture puzzle carried powerful messages about the durability and reach of Singer (Deloria 2004). Thus, there is a big glamour of Chepangs as hunter-gatherers and staying in caves not only in Nepal but also in other parts of the world. Despite their dominant food system, there is a great deal of influence of globalization in the food habit of Chepangs. Eating instant noodles, drinking Coca-Cola and beer, smoking manufactured tobacco products are some of the visible instances of changing food habits among them. There are several influencing factors for it. Since Nepal has a shared border with both India and China, there is an influence on food habits from both sides—both rice and chapati (bread) are the major meals along with noodles as snacks (Bhattarai 2008). Apart from influence in the cereals, with the passion for change among people with aggressive marketing strategies, the overall changes in consumption are inevitable. Due to globalization and liberalization, the distance between markets and consumers in the world has become narrow, and food culture is becoming global. Consequently, Chepangs stand on the threshold of traditional and modern food regimes.

There are mainly three sources of food supply in Chepang villages—own production, scavenging and importing. In peasant communities producing own food is usual, importing also is usual, but scavenging makes Chepang food regime somewhat unique. The former two applies to Amartya Sen's (2000) capability entitlements, whereas the third one is somewhat associated with labour-based entitlement. The 'production entitlement' is mainly addressed but not to the extent to meet the requirements simply because the main cereals produced in Chepang villages (rice, maize, millet, wheat, sorghum and buckwheat) are not enough to meet the needs. The larger farmers produce rice and wheat, whereas the small farmers like Chepangs rely more on maize, sorghum and buckwheat produced in the marginal and slash-and-burn land. They also produce small amount of soyabean, horse gram, chickpeas and black gram. Broadleaf mustard, radish and pumpkin are some of the vegetables grown in the community.

The most hunted food items are non-toxic yams—bharlang and tyaguna. There are 13 types of yams foraged between January to July by Chepang people in the cluster. In addition, many wild vegetables—sisnu, cress, fern, asparagus, shoots—are collected from the forest. Recently, there are many vegetable items, namely, tomato, cabbage, cauliflower, bitter gourd, aubergine, pumpkin, cucumber produced in the community for sale. Those are partially consumed in the household, but mostly sold to the market. People purchase rice and other necessities with the income of their scale. It is hard to delineate the most important domain of the regime as they are not permanent but fluid due to their nature. However, it can be argued that all three food regimes are important for Chepang livelihood trajectory because practices of 'own production' and 'foraging' have been and are integral part of their culture, whereas 'food import' is one of the recent ways of food resilience.

People normally do not venture out to prepare and eat new food, rather they follow the tradition of predecessors. In the case of Chepangs, maybe due to the heavy influence of outsiders, things have been changing gradually. However, this trend was substantially explained by Holmberg (1960) in case of snake meat eating among Sirionos in Peru, where despite all efforts and demonstrations, the Siriono chief did not eat the snake meat. Secondly, food culture is a by-product of identity and ethnicity which guides to demarcate locality, space and food-making practices. Many food items are eaten only by Chepangs and not by others simply because they know how to eat and savour. Thirdly, Chepang ethnicity is not a process, it is a tag, name or brand of a certain group of people who are identified as Chepangs. They are a group of people who follow common patterns of livelihood and eat common food items than others. Most importantly, it is a community who define their identities and kinship related to their practices on food, clothes, shelter and well-being, ultimately making them one of the distinct communities in Nepal.

Food Culture and Power Relations among Chepangs

Food has a power of love, honour and respect. This sometimes establishes further networks among people. Hosting a banquet in a state visit of a country representative or organizing a dinner or tea party of influential and politically powerful people in Nepal are some of the functional examples of the food power at the macro level. Food is the primary exchange item that is given and received in the communities. There are reasons for keeping it and giving away, reasons for wanting it from others and not wanting to want it. The semantic ambiguity of food grows largely out of this social ambivalence (Ortner 1978). The system of give and take has been long embedded into the Nepali society, where the traditional service providers—particularly tailors, blacksmiths, cobblers, and singers—used to come to their patron's house and attend celebrations and festivals as a part of the *bista* system.[3] In this system, the patrons enjoy the feasts and the service renders also join as part of it. The clients show their loyalty and solidarity to the patrons with their presence and at the same time enjoy the festive meals especially made for such occasions. They also get additional food from their patron's house and take to home for family members. This relationship has socio-psychic reciprocity between the two parties. The patrons feel that they are respected and honoured, and they expect their fellow service providers' presence in such occasions to add on the affluence, whereas clients feel close to their patrons and show their loyalty. Such events bring them close and bind them together.

There are several connotations of food offering and eating according to its nature. If someone works in the field as a wage labourer, he or she gains some 'wage food', which is absolutely gained due to the service provided. Similarly, some workers work in a white-collar job, and the reward they get from the work could be called 'salary food'. If the food is collected from the forest, it is called 'wild food'. Due to the nature of processing, some foods are attractive, quick and tasty to eat for snacks and are called 'twinkie food'. Some high protein, not readily prepared food is called 'junk food'. In the bista system, food offering is closely associated with wage food. Furthermore, it is a reciprocity based on socio-psychological closeness between the patrons and clients in Nepali society.

Chepang food basically and mostly can be called as 'wage food', which has no hierarchy and just meets the essentialism. Though there used to be a patron–client relationship between Chepangs and the village head in the past, this is no more existent in most of the Chepang villages because the patrons, mostly Brahmins and Chhetris, have migrated out from the village. Food exchange between other groups—Gurungs, Tamangs, Magars and Newars—are reciprocated, though the so-called 'affluent' do not easily accept food from Chepangs. This is mainly determined by the status and the intent of the person the Chepangs interact with. If they are expecting a benefit from the food, they will enjoy the meal together with Chepangs; if not, they pretend to be full or not feeling well so they cannot eat right at the moment. However, it is reciprocal with the so-called lower castes called Dalits in every respect.

Food has a power of exchange in Chepang community. As Ortner (1978) underscored among Sherpa community, Chepangs bring food and drink souvenirs as an honour while asking for a favour, even while asking the hand of a girl for marriage. In case of marriage, after discussion of the purpose, if the house owner agrees to the deal, they happily open the food and share with all present on the very occasion. People get happy and share good moments with drinking, singing and dancing. If the deal is not accepted, the food is not opened or distributed but rather returned with regrets and excuses.

Another way of expression of power, love and respect is women bringing food items as *koseli* (gift) to maternal home in special celebrations such as Maghe Sakranti, Saune Sakranti, Chhonam, Dasain and Tihar and on occasions of invitation in marriage, birth and death ceremony in the household. Bringing and receiving koseli is voluntary, but it is a strongly embedded requirement when daughters and sisters visit their parental home. Some Chepang daughters and sisters do not visit their parental home for many years failing to arrange the deserved koseli but manifest reasons could be different than real. Many ideas and principles are to be noted in a system of this type. The most important of these social and emotional mechanisms is clearly the one which obliges us to make what Mauss (1967) calls a return gift for a gift received. If the daughters and sisters do not come to their maternal homes, the parents and brothers understand that there are some problems in their families, one of the causes of which could be inability to arrange gifts. Married daughters and sisters come to maternal home with seasonal foods and drinks carrying on head-load baskets. On all occasions, they are compensated with similar food items. The more koseli carried, the more is the affluence assumed. Bronislaw Malinowski (1984) observed such a situation among Trobriand Islanders where each year a man grows yams for his sister and his daughter if she is married. The husband does not provide yams to his wife. The more yams a woman receives, the more powerful and rich she is. The husband is expected to give his wife's father or wife's brother a gift in return of the yams they give to his wife (Malinowski 1984). In the same way, in a Chepang community, there is positive correlation with gift food items and affluence. If the sister or daughter has taken bigger *koseli*, she is thought to be well off and settled nicely, and vice versa.

Food has a power of politics as well. Nepali politicians use food to attract the vote of poor people. Food politics was evident during the time of World Banks' Food for Works Programme in the decades 70s and 80s. The shrewd Nepali politicians distributed wheat and corn to the workers and gave the impression that food was there because of their personal endeavour for their people. It is still in practice. The naïve and innocent people trust them and cast their votes during election.

Chepangs eat a large variety of foods which come from forests, farmlands, water and market. During his fieldwork for a PhD dissertation research in a Chepang village named Bangti-Cluster, Rai (2009) has collected 89 food items consumed by the Chepangs. However, the forest-based food items dominate their food variety (see Table 10.1).

Out of 89 items consumed by the Bangti households in a year, 24 items were wild, the highest number was for meat items, followed by vegetables. However, in terms of quantity, cereals such as rice, maize and buckwheat are the major contributors, followed by tubers and vegetables. Consumption of farm-produced vegetable items is greater than that of wild items. This signifies a recent increase in vegetable cultivation in the area. However, more wild meat products are consumed than locally available meat items. This indicates that a considerable number of hunting practices are still pursued among the village community.

TABLE 10.1 *Number of Food Items Consumed in the Bangti-Cluster*

Food Items	Number of Items	Items
Cereals (own and imported)	10	Rice, beaten rice, maize, wheat, millet, buckwheat, sorghum
Legumes (own and imported)	5	Pulse, lentil, grams, soyabean
Vegetables: domestic	13	Beans, cauliflower, cabbage, broadleaf mustard, leafy vegetables, fermented vegetables, mushroom, pumpkin, bitter gourd, cucumber, aubergine, capsicum, radish, colossi, bamboo shoot, gourd
Vegetables: wild	7	Nettle, water cress, tank (bauhinia), figure (fern), silicon, chichi do
Root crops: domestic	5	Potato, colossi, domestic yam, chayote, sweet potato
Root crops: wild	4	Wild yam, gather, *bhakur*
Meat products: own	7	Pork, mutton, buff, fish, chicken, duck, egg
Meat products: wild	8	Bird, bat, crab, *paha* (wild toad), wild boar, porcupine, deer, *bachhiun* (wild bees), *aringal* (hornet)
Fruits: own and domesticated	15	Banana, coconut, litchi, orange, pineapple, mango, grapes, plum, peach, papaya, apple, pear, guava, jackfruit, pomegranate
Fruits: wild	5	*Kafal, chiuri, amala, aiselu*
Milk products	5	Milk, yogurt, butter, kurauni (concentrated milk), slurry
Drinks	4	Tea, *jaand* (local beer), *raksi* (local spirit)
Total	**89**	

Source: Field Survey 2009.

Chepangs eat rice, meat and alcohol on festive occasions such as Dashain, Tihar, Maghe Sakranti and Saune Sakranti. On the other hand, they starve in the lean seasons with less quantity and quality. Milk products are also consumed in the cluster as per their availability. Drinking alcohol mainly *raksi* (local spirit) and *jaand* (slurry fermented beer) is most common. They do not have any time preferences for drinking.

They drink alcohol whenever they find it. They prepare drinks, mostly raksi, near forests and streams where water and firewood access are easier. They keep on preparing drinks from grains and tubers. Even children and women drink enough and get drunk. When they drink, all of them sing and dance pleasantly and enjoy much (Soveet 1992).

Rice is the highest consumed item per year in the Bangti cluster, as they are easily available in the market. The average per household consumption of rice was recorded to be 167 days. Although rice eaters are thought to be affluent in Nepali society, Chepangs believe that rice is not good for people who work physically very hard. Their experience is that rice tastes good, but it runs out quickly and leaves the person hungry while working in the field. So, they prefer to eat millet, maize, and wheat, but they cannot grow them more in their farmlands. They are also not available in the market in abundance. So, corn flour followed by millet, wheat, sorghum and buckwheat has been the other major food item.

Summary and Conclusion

Chepangs are one of the 59 indigenous communities of Nepal. They are simple and honest. They still live in an egalitarian and sovereign society in terms of their food getting and consumption patterns. Despite market penetration in the community, respect, love, honour and culture of food sharing persist among them. The food is commoditized and it has manipulative meaning among Chepangs because food manifests social status, respect and love. Irrespective of their well-being, all Chepangs savour wild food items, mostly in hard times of scarcity. Thus, it can be said that forest foods have remained and will remain an integral part of their lives.

Hunger is an everyday phenomenon among Chepangs, and anyone can assume that they should be angry, unhappy, and unpleasant. An example can be drawn from the Tharus of East Chitwan where people did not enjoy significant degree of satisfaction, happiness and sense of well-being due to shortage and quality of food and life (Pyakuryal 1983). On the contrary, Chepangs are always happy. Unlike Bob Marley's song 'A hungry mob is an angry mob', Chepangs are happy whether they get food to eat or not, whether they get quality food or not. They cheer their being there, even if they eat and live with slurry or vegetable soups, yam or berries. They are happy if they are fortunate to hunt any wild edible products, whether plants or animals, and celebrate it once they get to eat. The happiness among them is unparallel to the human society elsewhere, which attesting to Soveet (1992) anyone can openly see if they visit Chepang villages and meet Chepang community. An additional research on the sources of happiness among them seems worth for humanity in the future.

Chepangs are nature-loving people. They are quite adaptive to nature culturally, physically and economically. At present, Chepang livelihood has been greatly influenced by the penetration of capitalism which Marx calls metabolic rift (Marx cited in Foster 1999). The development of towns, the availability of imported rice and vegetables in the market and its penetration into even the remote and isolated villages of Chepangs have significantly disrupted the communal life of Chepangs. Due to these factors, Chepangs are now the poorest of the poor and from being a very cheerful people to much distressed and remorseful poor. A progressive Nepali song of 1980s nicely furnishes this irony of Chepangs:

> *Anikal lagyo bhanchhan, khoi kasalai lagyo?*
> *Jasle kheti gareko chha usailai lagyo.*
> (People say there is famine, but who is the victim?
> Those who cultivate are the ones).

This song rightly depicts the situation of the most of the Chepangs simply because they are the ones who till the land and do farming but are the victims of hunger. They do not have alternatives other than struggling with the nature for survival. Despite several institutional policy provisions, Chepang deprivation continues unabated.

Notes

1. Chepangs are also called *praja* (subjects). This ethno-name was given to Chepangs by the state.
2. Food regime is a global notion of food production, distribution and consumption mainly devised by the idea of capitalism which describes the relationships between capital, commodity chains, various forms of forced labour and the policies formed by the struggle between capitalistic and labour. Here, the food regime is interpreted as a social logic of food production, distribution and consumption within the contemporary state of economy.
3. Bista system is the traditional patron–client relationships between village heads and craftsmen. The patrons pay some amount of food grain to the craftsmen as annual wage, called *bali*. Apart from a bali, the client goes to the patron's house in festive occasions and celebrations to enjoy their company and partake in the events.

References

Bennett, Lynn, and Dilip Parajuli. 2013. *The Nepal Multidimensional Exclusion Index: Making Smaller Social Groups Visible and Providing a Baseline for Tracking Results on Social Inclusion*. Kathmandu: Himal Books.

Bhattarai, U. K. 2008. *Food Consumption Pattern, Quality and Safety*. Kathmandu: Department of Food Technology and Quality Control.

Bista, D. B. 1967. *People of Nepal*. Kathmandu: Department of Information.

Central Bureau of Statistics. 2011. *Nepal Living Standard Survey (NLSS) III*. Vol. 1 and Vol. 2. Kathmandu: Central Bureau of Statistics.

Deloria, P. 2004. *Indians in Unexpected Places*. Kansas: University Kansas Press.

FAO. 2006. *Statistical Year Book*. Rome: Food and Agriculture Organisation.

Food Security Monitoring Task Force. 2010. *The Food Security Atlas of Nepal*. Kathmandu: Food Security Monitoring Task Force.

Fortier, J. 2009. *Kings of Forest: Cultural Resilience of Himalayan Hunter-Gatherers*. Honolulu: University of Hawaii Press.

Foster, J. B. 1999. 'Marx's Theory of Metabolic Rift: Classical Foundations of Environmental Sociology'. *American Journal of Sociology* 105 (2): 366–405.

Friedmann, H. 1993. 'The Political Economy of Food: A Global Crisis'. *New Left Review* 197: 29–57.

Gurung, G. M. 1989. *The Chepangs: A Study in Continuity and Change*. Lalitpur: SB Shahi.

Hodgson, B. H. 1972. Republished. *Language, Literature and Religion of Nepal and Tibet*. Varanasi: Bharat-Bharati.

Holmberg, A. 1960. *The Nomads of the Long Bow: The Siriono of Eastern Bolivia*. Chicago, IL: University of Chicago Press.

Holmberg, D. 1989. *Order in Paradox*. Ithaca, NY: Cornell University Press.

Koirala, G. P.1997. *Food Security Challenges: Where Does Nepal Stand*. Kathmandu: Winrock International.

Las Das, Arun Kumar, Tika Ram Gautam, Chaitanya Subba, Yogendra Gurung, Kusum Shakya. 2014. *The Nepal Multidimensional Social Inclusion Index: Diversity and Agenda for Inclusive Development*. Kathmandu: Central Department of Sociology/Anthropology, Tribhuvan University.

Lowdin, P. 1998. *Food, Ritual and Society: A Study of Social Structure and Food Symbolism among the Newars*. Kathmandu: Mandala Book Point.

Malinowski, B. 1984. *Argonauts of Western Pacific*. Illinois: Waveland Press.

Mauss, M. 1967. *The Gift: Forms and Functions of Exchange in Archaic Societies*. Norton, MA: Norton Library.

McMichael, P. 2009. 'A Food Regime Analysis of the "World Food Crisis"'. *The Agriculture, Food, & Human Values Society (AFHVS)* 26 (4): 281–295.

National Foundation for the Development of Indigenous Nationalities (NFDIN). 2004. Classification of Scheduled Indigenous Peoples of Nepal. A Report Prepared by a Research Team led by Om Gurung, Lalitpur.

Nestle, M. 2007. *Food Politics*. Berkeley and Los Angeles: University of California Press.

Ortner, S. 1978. *Sherpas through Their Rituals*. Cambridge: Cambridge University Press.

Pandey, S., D. Byerlee, D. Dawe, A. Dobermann, S. R. Mohanty, and B. Hardy. 2010. *Rice in the Global Economy: Strategic Research and Policy Issues for Food Security*. Manila: International Rice Research Institute.

Perfecto, I., J. Vandermeer, and A. Wright. 2009. *Nature's Matrix: Linking Agriculture, Conservation and Food Sovereignty*. London: Earthscan.

Pyakuryal, K. 2012. 'Land and Agriculture in 2030: Low Performance amidst High Potentials'. In *Nepal 2030: A Vision for Peaceful and Prosperous Nation*, edited by S. Sharma, B. Upreti and K. Pyakuryal, 127–140. Kathmandu: NCCR North-South and Department of Development Studies, Kathmandu University.

Rai, N. K. 1975. *People of the Stones: Chepangs of Central Nepal*. Kathmandu Centre of Nepal and Asian Studies, Tribhuvan University.

Rai, U. P. 2012. 'Peoples and Policies: A Case of Food Insecurity among Chepangs of Nepal'. In *Readings in Anthropology and Sociology of Nepal*, 118–149. Kathmandu: SASON.

———. 2014. *Food Security and Exclusion among the Chepangs: A Case Study from Central Nepal*. An Unpublished PhD Dissertation Submitted to the Office of the Dean, Faculty of Humanities and Social Sciences Tribhuvan University for the Fulfilment of the Requirements of the Doctor of Philosophy in Anthropology.

Riboli, D. 2000. *Tansuriban: Shamanism in Chepang of Southern and Central Nepal*. Kathmandu: Mandala Book Points.

Sahlins, M. 2006. 'The Original Affluent Society'. In *The Politics of Egalitarianism*, edited by J. Solway, 79–98. New York, NY: Berghahn Books.

Sen, A. 2000. *Poverty and Famines, An Essay on Entitlement and Deprivation*. Delhi: Oxford University Press.

———. 2000. *Social Exclusion: Concept, Application and Scrutiny*. Manila: Asian Development Bank.

Soveet, P. 1992. *The Happiness in the Wilderness: The Chepangs: An Uncivilized Ethnic Group with Interesting Cultures*. Kathmandu: Bluerays Publications.

Toffin, G. 1975. *Nepal Past and Present*. New Delhi: Sterling Publishers.

Weis, Tony. 2007. *The Global Food Economy: The Battle for the Future of Farming*. New York, NY: Zed Books.

11

Sustenance in the Margin

Food Ethnography of Kolkata Brothels

Chhanda Mukhopadhyay

Introduction

Sex workers belong to a marginal section of almost all contemporary societies. Heterogeneous societies are often built on principles of inequality and distinction between core and margin. There can broadly be two types of marginalized groups in a society; those who have not been fully integrated or assimilated in 'core' society in spite of their own efforts or efforts by others, and those who have been pushed away or have been stopped from participating in the 'core' culture and its institutions (Roy 1992, 104). It has been argued that marginalization can be manifested in multiple forms, some of which cannot be readily comprehended by observers or even by concerned individuals. Marginalization may occur at different levels—formal or informal; may be located within time and place; and become part of the lived experience of the individual if internalized (Mowat 2015, 456). In India, there are Dalit groups and de-notified communities who experience marginality and are often associated with stigma, as part of their being. Sex workers belong to another type, each one of them gets marginalized and stigmatized only when she joins the occupation of sex work. This, however, is not true for the children of sex workers—their experiences of marginality are of the first kind, they start feeling it since their early childhood.

In case of female sex workers, marginalization is not restricted to social exclusion, the situation is further complicated by an overriding moral code dictated by certain patriarchal preferences. Though the usual relation between a sex worker and her client is consensual, the dominant view is to look at the woman as provocateur who pulls the man down from high seat of morality (Mukhopadhyay 2012, 199–209).

The process of marginalization creates a situation where the marginal ones not only differ from others socially, culturally or morally but remain politically weak too (Battaglia 1999, 119). In case of India, the political weakness is significant because sex work has not been legalized by the state, yet they are allowed to pursue their work. Such a self-contradictory standpoint on part of the authorities adds to the vulnerability of the marginal ones. At times they are denied the basic rights promised to citizens by the state. Under such circumstances, the condition of sex workers living in brothels is more vulnerable as their place of stay too is stigmatized. Brothel is a confined space where life of the residents is often controlled by police and local toughs. Many sex workers of Kolkata city live in brothels with their children, therefore marginality and stigma of the space where they grow up influence the children significantly.

Under normal circumstances, individuals facing difficulties in life seek help from their respective families, extended families and kin groups. Sex workers living in brothels often lack such support groups. Having normative conjugal life and carrying out household chores including preparation of food, rearing children are some activities where they differ a lot from rest of the society.

This chapter has discussed food and beverage-related practices in brothels of Kolkata; those practices are closely linked with lifeways of sex workers and their dependents. Under effect of such lifeways, many of them consume intoxicants frequently and at times habitually, which has also been discussed. The ethnographic account presented here is based on study of two red light areas—Sethbagan in northern part of the city and Munshigunj in the south. Resident sex workers at both locations are economically weak; they primarily cater to immigrant workers and less-affluent residents of the city. The 'high class' sex workers have been excluded from this discussion because they can afford to hire residential space better than brothels, therefore are not much affected by typical brothel environment.

Residents of the studied brothels primarily are female sex workers and their children; there are a few male sex workers at Sethbagan who do not differ from the rest in their food habit. Their ideas and practices about food differ from other sections of society for two reasons. Firstly, being located in a marginal and stigmatized part of the society their worldview is not supposed to be identical with those located inside or close to dominant sections of the society. Secondly, sex workers lack fixed work hours or definite time for domestic works and get limited support from others in their daily life. Children living in brothels do not get that kind of support from caregivers that are available to children living in normative families. This exercise has taken note of food-related ideas, thoughts and practices among the children as well.

This ethnographic study does not make any claim to be realist; it is not 'objective' as it does not claim to be free from all kinds of pre-disposition, political views and judgements. The very selection of the subject and locations of study were driven by certain judgements on the part of the author. The work rather leans towards critical ethnography (Creswell 2013, 93–94); although the study is not part of any activist agenda, the author wanted to describe the deplorable condition in which some marginalized and stigmatized persons of the society are living.

The world of brothels is not known to many, so the residents and their living condition have been described in the following paragraphs for better comprehension of context of the present study.

Residents of Kolkata Brothels

In the formative years of Kolkata, British administrators were very mindful of division of Indian population into religious and caste groups; they wanted the city to be segregated that way. Localities were created for artisanal groups like Kumhar (potter), Kansari (bell-metal worker), Shankhari (conch-shell worker), Moochi (hide worker), Jele (fisher), Dorji (tailor), Koloo (oil trader) and many others. They even differentiated the sex workers of the city on similar basis. There were Brahmin prostitutes who could be maintained by rich patrons, while prostitutes of non-Brahmin higher castes could receive a limited number of clients of their own or of superior castes. The third category of Hindu prostitutes resided in rented accommodation; they could be visited exclusively by Hindu clients from all castes. There were the dancing girls of both Hindu and Muslim origin who could be visited by customers of all castes and creed. In addition, there were public prostitutes of Muslim creed, low-caste Hindu prostitutes and Christian and European prostitutes.

According to an enumeration of 'registered prostitutes' in 1872, there were 6,871 of them, of whom Hindus were 5,804, Muslims 930 and the remaining were Irish, Polish, Russian, Hungarian, Italian, French and Spanish (Banerjee 1998, 72–103). The presence of non-European foreign nationals among the sex workers has also been reported elsewhere, there were some Japanese and Chinese sex workers in the city (Joardar 1985, 9) as well. It can be assumed that actual number of sex workers in the city was much larger than that for the registered ones.

The segregation of sex workers and their clients on the basis of religion and caste could not be found in the city during the present study. At both locations selected for study, sex workers were found to reside in rented accommodation. There were women from different castes and religious groups, and nobody bothered about ethnic identity of their clients.

Most of the sex workers of Kolkata brothels are females, only a handful of male sex workers were found. The female sex workers are referred to as *khanki* or *raandi*; their job is referred to as *khankir kaaj*. Male sex workers are known as *chhakka* or *mouga*. In recent years, a Bengali term *jauna-karmi* has come into vogue, which literally means sex worker and is considered to be more respectful towards the persons and their occupation.

Some sex workers of Kolkata city do not reside in red light districts; they stay with their respective families or as single persons and work at various locations like hotels and brothels. They are commonly known as 'flying'—many female sex workers and most of the male sex workers of Kolkata city belong to this type and have been excluded from the present discussion.

The sex workers residing in brothels are divided into several categories on the basis of what work they do and their relationship with other sex workers. Years back some retired sex workers used to provide furnished rooms, food, clothing and other necessities to younger practicing ones against share of their income. They usually were owners of the premise and were known as *bariwali* or *mashi*. In recent years, the arrangement has changed. Now *malkins*, *gharwalis* or *didis*, who are relatively senior sex workers themselves, hire rooms at a brothel and sub-let the same to girls working as *chhukri* or *adhiawali* under them.

A *chhukri* is a new entrant into the trade, she has probably been sold to the *malkin* by a trafficker. For the malkin, a chhukri is an investment, so all her earnings including the tips she receives are taken away. She is provided with essentials like food, clothing and some cosmetics till the malkin feels she has realized her investment with sufficient profit. The girl is kept under strict vigil to ensure she is not hiding any part of her income or is not trying to run away. To discipline the girls, a malkin would often resort to physical violence, sometimes she would be assisted by local goons.

Chhukri system is not much different from bonded labour, for long it has been opposed by sex workers and their organizations in Kolkata city. In recent years, the chhukri system could not be traced at both the studied locations, if there was any its existence was denied. Reportedly, the chhukri system exists in some brothels of the city. In view of strong opposition to the system, such girls are described as dependent sister, cousin or niece by the employer sex workers. In spite of some exceptions, a fresh entrant into the trade can start working with more personal and economic freedom these days.

An adhiawali is a contractual tenant working under the malkin. She is supposed to pay half or *adha* of her income to the malkin, who in turn provides the girl a room or portion of a room to stay and work. Food and other essentials are to be arranged by the tenant. Sometimes a room is divided into two parts with a curtain and given to two adhiawali girls. In some cases, owners of the house rent rooms out to adhiawalis directly and collect payment without any intermediary malkin in between.

An independent sex worker is known as 'brothel', she takes a room on rent from the landlord and keeps her entire earnings to herself. While moving from chhukrihood to independence through adhia arrangement, a sex worker grows old. Majority of the women belonging to this category were found to be above 40 years of age. By this time, usually a woman finds a partner and lives with her nuclear or extended family. A few of them were found to live in brothels with son, daughter-in-law and grandchildren.

Some of the senior sex workers become malkin or gharwali if they can save enough money to invest in hiring space. Whether they continue to be in active sex work or not, they remain part of the trade. Some of the senior women shift residence out of brothel but in the same locality. Some of them remain connected to the brothels indirectly. While a few run creches for children of sex-worker mothers, others cook food and deliver the same to clients in brothels. A few of them run shops in the red-light area, some shift away from the area altogether.

Babu is partner of a sex worker. Ground realities may not be as simple as the statement, such relationship can have many shades. A customer can have preference for a particular girl and can become her babu—he can visit her daily or once in a few days. A married babu may leave his family and shift to the brothel to stay with the girl. Some of the men allow the girl to entertain customers and earn her livelihood, some others provide total economic support and seek exclusive attention. Then there are babus who are economically dependent on the sex worker paramour and live a parasitic life; they eat, drink and gamble at the expense of the girls. Some sex workers, especially some Nepalese girls, were critical about such relationship. Those girls had plans about their retired life; they wanted to save some money, go back to the natal village, open a shop and build a house there. With a babu on toe such plans may go astray.

There was a time when a sex worker required protection from violence purported by pimps and local goons, it could be helpful for a girl to have one of them as her babu. That reason has become weak in recent years, but the lonely social existence of a sex worker often seeks emotional attachment with a person who would be different from the rest of the men she comes in contact with.

A *bherua* is also a male companion, but his status is below that of a babu, he is more like a domestic help and is dependent on the sex worker for his subsistence. Such a relationship is not much popular these days; there was only one bherua in two studied locations.

Children of sex workers can be divided into two categories—those who were born out of wedlock before the mother became sex worker and those who were born to a sex worker mother. Same mother can have children born before and after she became a sex worker. It is preferred to have children fathered by a husband or a babu than becoming pregnant by some customer with whom there is no emotional attachment. Customarily, the babu is known as father of all children of a sex worker. Some mothers send their children to boarding schools or to their natal families to keep the children away from brothel environment. Such arrangement involves expenditure that all mothers cannot afford.

Dalal or pimp is closely associated with the trade, but they serve the high-class sex workers who do not solicit their customers directly. Locations studied for this work are inhabited by relatively poor sex workers who go out to streets to negotiate with their customers themselves.

Residents of Kolkata brothels are frequently visited by customers and policemen, with whom the residents have love-and-hate relationship. Most of the customers at studied locations are factory workers, office goers, traders and shopkeepers. Some of them are from the same city, even from the same locality, while others are immigrants. A sex worker prefers repeatedly visiting customers as they treat her with kindness. There are violent customers too, who beat up the girls on flimsy grounds. Reportedly, some customers stole money or cell phone from sex workers.

Some policemen harass customers to extract money and scare them away. But the sex workers find the police indispensable when subjected to violence by musclemen, babus, customers or co-workers.

In the 1990s, sex workers of Kolkata city created several organizations working for their health, rights and respect. At the studied locations, an organization called Durbar Mahila Samanwaya Committee (DMSC) was active. Unlike earlier days, when sex workers or their clients are threatened or harassed by local toughs or by policemen, the women protest collectively. The peer persons among them spread awareness about health and socio-economic issues and command respect of entire localities. Those organizations have been instrumental in changing the mindset of sex workers. From consciousness of being part of a 'lumpen mass' they feel to be a 'working mass'.

Studied Locations

In the 19th century, there were fourteen red light districts in the city—three in the central part, which were Kerani Bagan, Bowbazar and Mechuabazar; seven in the north, namely, Rambagan, Jorasanko, Dharmahatta, Ahiritola, Chitpur, Sonagachi and Baghbazar; and four in the south, Kalighat, Bhowanipur, Kareya and Watgunge (Joardar 1985, 8–12). In recent years, some of those have closed down but the total number has increased for two reasons. Some of the older districts have sprawled into new locations while some suburban and contiguous rural areas have become part of the city along with their red-light districts.

Red light districts at both locations discussed in this work, Sethbagan in northern and Munshigunj in southern parts of the city, are more than a century old. Sethbagan Lane emerges from Rabindra Sarani, which was formerly known as Chitpur Road. This road predates the city and eventually became the earliest arterial road of Kolkata. The locality developed as one of the oldest parts of the city; it also was hub of different trading and cultural activities since long. There are two red-light districts located close to Kolkata Port, Munshigunj and Watgunj; those places owe their genesis to the port. Red-light districts close to the port were primarily dependent on patrons from among industrial workers and sailors from other states and other parts of the world.

At Sethbagan, there are several brothels on both sides of the narrow 100-yard long lane. Brothels are known as line-*bari* as sex work is also known as line. All houses in Sethbagan Lane are not brothels; there are 16 more-than-a-century-old houses that are functionally line-bari. There are two other types of houses; some are *grihasthi*, exclusively occupied by *grihastha* or householders, some are half-grihasthi where sex workers can reside as tenants but are not allowed to practise their trade. Almost all buildings in Sethbagan Lane are three- or four-storied brick houses; architectural style suggests people with moderate means constructed those houses. On an average, each room measures a 100 sq. ft, staircases are narrow and dark, courtyards small.

In 2011, there were about 190 sex workers at Sethbagan, excepting nine adhiawalis, all of them were independent. It suggests that women residing in Sethbagan brothels were staying there continuously for many years; initially they must have been working as chhukris and adhiawalis before getting promoted to independent status. It may also be noted that about two-third sex workers at that location had children. All of them were living in 16 buildings so there were less than 12 sex workers per building. Most of the sex workers at Sethbagan were Bengali speaking; they were from Murshidabad, Birbhum and Bardhaman districts of West Bengal.

At Sethbagan all sex workers had a room to herself. While some of them were single occupants of a room, there were others who were staying with their children, some with mother, dependent niece or grandchildren. Some had their resident babu staying in the same room. Each household, whatever be its size, had a single room to it. Each room served as bedroom, living room and kitchen. None of the rooms had any adjacent or exclusive toilet; the facilities were available on the ground floor and were shared by all residents of the building.

Some residents of these buildings were sex workers formerly; they were usually engaged in occupations related to major activities of those buildings. Some of them were bootleggers; others had one or two adhiawali or flying girls working under them.

There were a few grihasthi houses at Sethbagan Lane where some service holders, automobile mechanics, and car drivers were living singly or with their families. In addition, there were a few half-grihasthi houses.

Munshigunj Road is in southwest part of Kolkata. It is about 30 ft-wide with a row of single-storied buildings with terracotta-tiled roofs.

There are a few two-storied buildings too. This red-light district has Kolkata Port, several warehouses and small-scale industries in the vicinity. Earlier sailors from different parts of the world used to visit Munshigunj and neighbouring Watgunj brothels; in early 1930s there were between 20 and 40 Japanese sex workers, whose brothels were very nicely decorated with paper lanterns hanging on the veranda (Mukherjee and Chakraborty 1936). Cosmopolitan character of the brothels has been lost to a large extent; in recent years, sex workers in Munshigunj were from Indian states of West Bengal, Sikkim, Bihar, Chhattisgarh and Odisha, there were some women from Bangladesh and Nepal.

There were 15 line-baris at Munshigunj. While only three of those were two-storied brick and mortar structures, the rest were single-storied buildings with terracotta tile roof commonly found in Kolkata slums. From the standpoint of improved structure and design of the buildings, Sethbagan gives the impression of a middle-income-group locality, while Munshigunj could be considered a low-income-group neighbourhood. Between the two localities, Munshigunj shows a much higher density of residents in its brothels. Five of the line-baris with ninety rooms had a population of about two hundred resident sex workers. On an average there were more than two girls living in one room, sometimes the number was three. In the other 10 line-baris there were about 150 rooms; out of those 123 rooms were occupied by the 129 sex workers; rest of the rooms either had single occupants or family units.

Most of the rooms in Munshigunj brothels measured eight by eight feet; some rooms had just enough space for laying two narrow cots side by side. Some of the rooms had so little space that it was not possible to lay two cots parallel to each other, so the cots were laid perpendicularly by raising the height of one cot with bricks and allowing the other to come partly under it. Sometimes curtains were hung between the cots to allow resemblance of privacy to the sex-workers and their clients. In some of the rooms even that arrangement was not possible for lack of space; in such cases when a woman served her client, other women stayed out. Four out of every 10 sex workers in Munshigunj were adhiawali, for obvious reasons they could not afford to have single occupancy rooms. Sometimes even the malkin shared room with one or two adhiawali girls. In one case, a malkin, her babu and her child were sharing a room with one adhiawali and her child.

In Munshigunj also rooms were multi-functional, but there the space crunch was much more in comparison to Sethbagan as there were more occupants per room. With more than 320 sex workers residing in 15 houses, per house density in Munshigunj was above 21 while it was less than 12 in Sethbagan.

The houses at both Sethbagan and Munshigunj are pretty old, still owners of those houses rarely undertake any repair work on the pretext that the rent they receive is not enough for regular maintenance jobs. The occupants experience insufficient water supply and lack of toilet facilities. One line-bari at Munshigunj had a broken doorway and the landlord refused to repair it; this created a sense of insecurity among the resident sex workers of that building. Their apprehension came true when some local goons physically assaulted two girls one night entering the premise. Though the girls screamed loud, nobody came forward to resist the toughs. Next day, all sex workers of that building were seen to be very agitated over the incident and some of them were considering shifting to other houses.

Though there was a large market nearby at Khidirpur, the residents of that locality, including the sex workers, prefer to buy many commodities from hawkers visiting them throughout the day. Items like fish, vegetables, glass bangles, garments, make-up items, flower, utensils, sweetmeat, different types of cooked food are sold by the hawkers.

Eating Habits

Eating habit of sex workers residing in brothels is influenced by multiple factors. Their working hour is one important issue—duration of work time varies with age and position of a person in the system. A younger girl will possibly be in higher demand among clients, so she will be working for longer hours. A malkin would definitely want the chhukris and adhiawalis engaged by her to work more so that her earnings would increase proportionately. The chhukri or the adhia would hardly get any recess to eat her meals in time; cooking for herself would be more difficult. Relatively older women would supposedly be in less demand, so they would be spending less time with customers and more in supervising younger girls. So, the latter would have shorter working hour and more time to spend for cooking and feeding others.

Secondly, the living space allowed to an individual in a brothel is barely sufficient for entertaining customers and sleeping, accommodating a kitchen within that limited space is often a luxury. It has been mentioned earlier that sex workers convert a portion of their room or corridor leading to the room into impromptu kitchen. It would hardly be possible for each person to have her own kitchen even if she has time or will to cook her food.

The third factor is the lifestyle of sex workers. A large number of them, especially the younger ones, having no child are not bound by familial responsibilities. They have the liberty to decide what they will do with their free time, when there is any. Rarely an average sex worker would prefer to cook in her leisure hours; she would prefer to buy her food and spend the available time gossiping and watching movies. This sense of freedom among sex workers is significant; though they experience innumerable problems in their daily lives, they know the kind of freedom they enjoy is not available to most of the women burdened with household responsibilities. Mousumi of Munshigunj left brothel to live in some other locality with her partner. She was trying to mould herself into the role of a housewife in a grihasthi locality but then felt she was being dominated over by her partner. Mousumi went back to the brothel with the realization that as a housewife she was missing her personal freedom.

That the brothel dwellers and their visitors buy much of the food they eat has helped small-scale trade in food to crop up in the neighbourhood. Roadside food stalls that mostly sell fast food make good business round the day. Itinerant food vendors visit the area with rice, roti, vegetable and meat curry in metal pots. Those vendors seldom visit grihasthi parts of the city. Some former sex workers residing in brothels and half-grihasthi houses cook food commercially; few of those establishments sell alcoholic beverages too.

Journey of a girl from her family home to brothel is often prompted by the quest for two square meals a day. The girl herself may want to escape from poverty at home and earn a decent livelihood for herself. In her childhood, Mina Singh felt deprived as a girl child; she wanted to eat fish-head, but those were always served to her brothers and other male members in the family. She thought of a future when she would earn enough money to buy fish-head and other good food for herself.

Often a senior sex worker would visit her native village to recruit young girls from families with low income. She would impress the people with her big-city-woman appearance and her sweet talk promising better future for the girl(s). Manju was brought to Sethbagan by one of her senior colleagues when she was 14. For 15–20 days she was fed good food, new dresses were purchased for her. Once the undernourished look was gone, she was forced to do sex work. This was the story of almost all fresh entrants in the world of sex work.

A chhukri had to entertain customers with little respite. One woman, who was a chhukri a few years back, recounted that on some evenings two or three customers used to wait in queue when she was attending somebody. She could have her lunch at four o'clock in the afternoon and dinner at one o'clock in the morning. There are on and off seasons for sex workers. During Durga Puja, Kolkata's major festival of the year, the number of customers goes up. On the other hand, when migrant workers from rural areas go back home to attend agricultural operations like transplanting or harvesting or to attend festivities, it affects the number of customers. Muslim clients visit brothels less frequently during the month of Ramadan.

Sometimes working hours of the chhukris was prolonged further as they had to entertain babus of their respective malkins in addition to customers. Understandably, they had no time to cook for themselves, malkins or gharwalis cooked or purchased food for them. As a result, the chhukris had no scope to have food of their own choice, they had to eat whatever they were served. Moreover, as the malkins took away her entire earning, she had no money to purchase food of her liking.

Condition of adhiawalis is relatively better; though one has to hand over half of her income to the malkin every day, she has the freedom to cook or purchase food of her choice. Sometimes the adhias eat lunch or dinner cooked by malkins or gharwalis and pay for the same. Anita took lunch from her malkin against payment and purchased chapati and sabzi for dinner from food stalls.

Relation between a malkin and her adhia is not always determined by the contract between them, it often transcends that limit. Mita Singh, a malkin of Munshigunj, said one particular adhia girl did not always pay for her food. But the malkin did not stop serving her as she was mother of an infant and had to spend money to keep her child from morning to late night at a creche run by an ex-sex worker lady in a half-grihasthi house.

Some adhias prefer to cook their food; often two or three of them do it together. This kind of cooperative cooking is not just fun, it helps to reduce the workload on each participant. Munni was lucky, she used to bring her meals from her babu's house in the same locality. Radha was even luckier, her babu took care of lots of household chores and also cooked for two of them.

Malkins and independent sex workers behave more like householders, many of them have children, babu and sometimes a few adhiawali girls to be fed. They usually have a kitchen and are sometimes helped by girl children and girls working under her. Those kitchens, however, are generally used during day hours; during evening they seldom get time to sit down and cook a meal. For the above reasons, dinner is usually purchased. Food and drinks consumed while entertaining a customer is paid for by the customer. During this hour, local cooking and food delivery system becomes active; whether food or drinks, anything can be arranged within minutes. While asking a customer for tips, a sex worker would often say 'leave some extra bucks for a bottle of aerated water'.

Matter related to food takes a different shape when a sex worker becomes pregnant and subsequently gives birth to a child. Most of the sex workers are deprived of any help from their natal families, generally other sex workers and the malkin take care of her. Between the seventh and ninth month of pregnancy, a would-be-mother is treated with lunch by other ladies of the brothel; this custom of baby shower is called *saadh*. Sometimes the treat remains restricted to fried street food and sweets.

After birth of a child a mother abstains from doing household works and sex work; the period is 21 days for Hindu and 40 days for Muslim women. One sex worker of Sethbagan was married to the son of a former sex worker. The mother-in-law used to cook food for the girl for a few months after the child was born, but the mother had to pay for the service. In a few instances, the girls are assisted by their babus. Though co-workers extend some help, a mother takes care of her baby almost singly.

When a mother attends her customers, her co-workers and sometimes the malkin babysit for her. One adhia of Munshigunj, a mother of two children, was keeping her seven-month-old baby in a creche. She had to visit the creche intermittently to nurse the baby. At Sethbagan there was an evening creche run by a social welfare organization where babies up to one year of age could be kept from six to eleven in the evening against a payment. Similar facility was available in some other parts of the city too. At Munshigunj senior women used to keep children from early morning to eleven at night for payment. The mother may provide food for the baby; if it is arranged by the babysitter the mother has to pay for it separately. In reality, many sex worker mothers could not afford to put their babies under care of creche or of babysitters.

Once the children are beyond infancy, single mothers cannot look after the children all the while and the kids often feel free to do whatever they like. It is difficult for the mothers to serve them cooked food several times a day; from the age of three to four years they are given money to purchase their breakfast.

Children attending school often face other kinds of predicament. They realize the stigma attached to their mothers' occupation and of localities where they stay. They avoid mixing with schoolmates from other localities as that helps to hide their identity. When other children share lunch and prefer to eat together, children from red light areas do not do so as that can disturb the strategy of maintaining distance. Moreover, the other children often share homemade food among them while children of sex workers are given some money to buy their lunch. After the exhausting nights the mothers find it difficult to wake up early and cook food for the children.

Mothers try to keep their adolescent girl children out of way of the customers; in evening hours those girls huddle together in some room. Boys of same age, school-going or dropouts, usually spend evenings outside brothels. Mothers, however busy they may be, arrange to buy rice, chapati and sabzi for dinner of their children. When some customer buys costlier food like biriyani, a mother usually shares her portion with her children.

Children have a 'love and hate' relation with customers. Reportedly, a boy was fonder of a particular customer than the babu of his mother as the customer never forgot to bring him a pack of chocolate. All customers are not that generous, so some children learn ways to extract certain advantage from them. Reportedly a nine-or ten-year-old boy of Munshigunj blocked the path of a customer and said, 'Buy me a bottle of soda, then I would allow you to enter the house'. In another case, a boy in his early teens told a customer from the same neighbourhood, 'either you buy me some *nashta* (snacks) or else I'll tell your wife that you visit my mother'.

Intoxication as Way of Life

Drinking alcohol, smoking *ganja* (marijuana) and chewing tobacco is quite common among customers of sex workers. When in brothel, they ask sex workers to drink and smoke with them. Freshly recruited girls, who have been catapulted into a world almost unknown to them obey their patrons to keep them happy. Several sex workers have stated that their initial sense of being compelled to drink or smoke turned into a feel-good state of mind. Not only they started to enjoy being intoxicated, they considered it part of their liberty to decide what they would do with their lives. 'The girls drink whenever there are customers, for them it is the way of life', said one bariwali of Sethbagan.

The freedom sometimes enables the marginalized sex workers to challenge the idea of morality prevalent in society. Kalpana of Sethbagan had a babu, who told her he would be away for a few days. The babu of another sex worker used to flirt with Kalpana often. With her babu away Kalpana invited the other man to a night-long private booze party. Two of them drank a lot and made fun till Kalpana fell unconscious. Next morning, she discovered some of her money was missing and she raised alarm; she was suspecting another sex worker of the same brothel of stealing her money. That is how the entire locality came to know about the incident; Kalpana, however, had no remorse about it.

Papiya of Munshigunj was addicted to ganja. Once she had a drunk customer who assaulted her physically, the girl immediately moved out of the room. The customer was shouting that his money has been wasted; he also threatened to tell his acquaintances not to visit this brothel as the girls here are not well behaved. Other girls took notice and rebuked Papiya. One of those girls said, Papiya was standing outside the room nonchalant smoking ganja; she did not care about a customer or two as she was in high demand.

Such lifeway extracts its toll, some of the girls become addict and pay the price. One sex worker of Sethbagan became severely addicted to alcohol and her earnings dropped drastically. She was borrowing money from moneylenders at very high rate of interest. Other sex workers of the area were apprehensive; she would have no savings left for her future.

Though the girls are accustomed of entertaining customers who have consumed alcohol but try to avoid drunkards. Such persons, the sex workers said, often refuse to use condom. In such cases, the girls throw the person out after collecting some money from him to compensate the wasted time. Drunkards are liars too; they will pay a small amount as advance and at the end will claim to have paid the entire sum. A pregnant woman would try to avoid a drunkard as customer, he can be careless in bed and hurt her. All mothers having infant children cannot afford to keep them in creche; they prefer to keep the baby with the malkin or some other sex worker for the time she is busy with a customer. In case nobody around is available to babysit, the mother would keep the baby on the bed she is sharing with the customer. Such mothers too try to avoid drunkards as they might hurt the baby.

The sex workers prefer to have babu for multiple reasons. Girls estranged from natal space and family often feel an emotional void, there is nobody around who can be called her own. They seek some permanence of relationship in an environment where almost all relations are contractual and short term. Moreover, in a male-dominated situation, a girl would prefer to have a man who would stand by her in hours of need, support her in rearing the children. However, a babu can be a liability when he is addicted to alcohol or is a habitual gambler. Shandhya's babu was an alcohol addict, she got rid of him. Purnima of Rambagan, a locality adjacent to Sethbagan, threw her babu out after tolerating him for many years; he used to exhaust his own earning in buying drinks; for food the household was dependent solely on Purnima's income. Anjali, however, adjusted with her alcoholic babu, he was a qualified technician working on board a ship and earned handsomely.

Children of sex workers experience several oddities in life; they often learn about poverty, stigma and segregation at a very young age. While mothers try to keep the girl children away from the brothel once they reach adolescence, girls are often put into residential schools or shifted to hired rooms in grihasthi houses, boys tend to start earning early to gain economic independence. Though some of them continue to study till graduation, some learn one trade or another as apprentice and join the workforce when in their teens. A few boys showed signs of depression; they felt their life was worthless. Reportedly, those boys were found to be prone to substance abuse. A babu from Munshigunj said, boys pick up habits of drinking, chewing tobacco and gambling mostly from the customers.

Thoughts about Food

While listening to narratives of sex workers and their children, existence of several counter-thoughts could be felt. Experiencing marginalization, stigmatization, oppression, discrimination and separation from kin and other support groups at an early age can be quite difficult to assimilate. Many sex workers try to suppress thoughts about the gruelling present by thinking and speaking about pleasant memories, however few such remembrances might be. At times, those memories sound unreal, possibly those have been created to enhance feelings about the good times that never was. In some cases, the boundary between real and fiction is vague. Thoughts about unpleasant experiences have also been expressed in words. Food has often remained the central object in many such narratives; ideas about good life has been equated with good food, traumatic experiences with grimy food.

Shanti of Sethbagan told that her first husband used to beat her so much that she was compelled to leave home. That person came to where she stays now many a times and asked her to go back to him. She never patched up with him but used to visit his family. Shanti's mother-in-law and sisters-in-law treated her well; they always threw open the fridge, offered different kinds of food, and asked her to take rest in their living room. Wife of her present babu likes her too and invited her to their house frequently; her one-and-a-half-year-old son by the babu lives in that family.

Munni Begum of Munshigunj had her in-law's house in Jessore, Bangladesh. After a legal battle with that family she left that home, but they have kept her three-year-old son with them. Sometimes Munni visits their place. Though her ex-husband does not talk to her, he always brings chicken from the market for her. His present wife cooks the chicken for Munni.

An old lady, a bariwali of Sethbagan, said her late babu loved her very much. He purchased the house where the brothel is located and gifted it to her. Family members of that babu, especially his two sons, also loved her and used to visit her often. Her babu used to bring lots of delicacies for her from his natal place in Bardhaman. In course of the interview, the author asked the lady, 'As you have grown old now, why don't you go and stay with them?' Her response was, 'discarded plates cannot go to heaven'.

Several children living in brothels were asked separately, what their dreams were about the future. In majority of the cases their dreams revolved around their mothers. They wanted to provide her a good life somewhere away from brothels, and lots of good food will be part of that life. They were also asked, what they want to do if they are given lots of power for a few days. Manirul, a 17-year-old boy of Munshigunj said, 'if I'm made chief minister of this state, first I'll sack all corrupt policemen because they harass innocent boys, put them behind bars. I'll also eat good food to my satisfaction. And I'll create good playgrounds, so young boys can play.'

Thirteen-year-old Bappa of Sethbagan was a school dropout. After his baba's death, his baba or father was his mother's babu, Bappa had to leave the boarding school for want of money. The death left a deep scar on him; though his passion was photography, he became addicted to online gambling to earn quick money. Some day, he had meat for dinner, that night he dreamt of a butcher shop where a carcass was hanging. Then he realized, he himself was the meat.

Conclusion

Discussion in preceding paragraphs has shown that food practices of sex workers and their children living in brothels of the city of Kolkata are characterized by irregular eating habit as well as high dependence on purchased food, including street food. In addition, a large number of sex workers and some of their adolescent and young adult children are accustomed to regular smoking and drinking.

Such practices are closely related to certain anomalies in brothel environment, which include poverty and economic uncertainty, irregular and indefinite working hours, sense of social and physical insecurity, lack of emotional support from family or kin groups.

Sex workers, living at studied brothels, worked for relatively low payment, most of their customers were from low-income groups. Those customers always bargained hard and rarely paid tips. A sex worker beyond her prime had to wait for a customer for the entire day and sometimes for several days. Sex workers who maintained relation with natal families had to extend some financial support; those having children had more liabilities, they had to bear cost of accommodation, food and education of the children. Professional career of a sex-worker lasts for limited number of years; with so much economic burden, she tries to work for a few extra hours each day to earn little more. She may be required to work round the clock because customers may turn up any time. So, she cannot decide when she will cook or eat. Economic hardship compels them to limit their choice of food to the bare minimum. Once a woman is beyond her prime, she can have some time to cook food, sometimes commercially.

Unlike many other marginalized communities, sex workers do not feel they are simply socially excluded; quite a number of them, especially the elderly ones, felt to be morally degraded too. Many of them still refer to their occupation as khankir kaaj, a lowly job. Thoughts about self as 'wasted' or 'discarded' and debarred from having a 'good life' are allegorical statements that place one not just on the margin of society but somewhere outside its boundary. Even the children who do not belong to the occupational group themselves maintain noticeable social distance from other children who have both parents to take care of them. Following Mowat (2015, 456) it can be said that sex workers and their children have internalized marginalization, stigmatization and social exclusion to such an extent that those are part of their lived experience. For them life is a confined existence, it is difficult for them to come out of the seclusion keeping their identity intact.

Soon after joining the profession, sex workers of studied brothels experienced vulnerability in the hands of local toughs and policemen, loneliness in hours when they required emotional support, and realized that scope of improving their living condition and social position is almost impossible. Internalization of those experiences often compels them to look at certain common ideas and practices of society differently. It has been mentioned earlier in this chapter, the idea of 'freedom' among sex workers is not identical with that of the average women in a patriarchal society. The idea of having 'fun' too is different among them in comparison to women of similar economic standing but engaged in other jobs; few hours of good fun for sex workers may mean night-long booze party with friends of either sex.

For obvious reasons, sex workers' idea of 'freedom' and 'fun' is not socially approved under usual circumstances, they and their ideas are kept in the peripheral space allocated for lumpen elements. Still, very little is done to instil 'good' values in them because the society is incapable of rewarding them even if they behave 'well'. Passivity of society is rooted in the fact that it cannot deny irreversibility of their marginal or even excluded position. Under such circumstances they are not expected to live orderly life which is appreciated at the centre, even in matters of food and intoxicants.

Organizations like 'Durbar Mahila Samanwaya Committee' have tried to create a closer-to-centre space for sex workers; these days when sex workers or their clients are threatened or harassed by local toughs or policemen, the women protest collectively. Peer persons among them work to spread awareness about health and socio-economic issues in neighbourhood and command respect of the entire locality. Such efforts, however, could not pull all sex workers out of marginality; effects of marginalization on their lifeways are still strong.

References

Banerjee, Sumanta. 1998. *Under the Raj: Prostitution in Colonial Bengal*. New York, NY: Monthly Review Press.

Battaglia, D. 1999 'Towards an Ethics of the Open Subject: Writing Culture in Good Conscience'. In *Anthropological Theory Today*, edited by Henrietta L. Moore. Cambridge: Polity Press.

Creswell, John W. 2013. *Qualitative Inquiry and Research Design: Choosing among Five Approaches*. Lincoln, NE: University of Nebraska–Lincoln and SAGE Publications.

Joardar, Biswanath. 1985. *Prostitution in Nineteenth and Early Twentieth Century Calcutta*. New Delhi: Inter India Publication.

Mukherjee, S. K., and J. N. Chakraborty. 1934. *Prostitution in India*. Calcutta: Das Gupta & Co.

Mukhopadhyay, C. 2012. 'Children of Sex-workers of Kolkata City: A Study on a Marginalized Group'. *Journal of the Indian Anthropological Society* 47 (2): 199–209.

Mowat, Joan G. 2015. 'Towards a New Conceptualisation of Marginalisation'. *European Educational Research Journal* 14 (5): 454–476.

Roy, S. 1992. 'Applicability of the Concept of Marginality in a Mono-caste Slum in Calcutta'. *Journal of the Indian Anthropological Society* 27 (2).

12

Hearth to Heaven
Ritualization of Food

Shibani Roy

The Indian subcontinent is the salad bowl of diversified communities, traditions and religions; this diversity has generated a large cultural wealth. Over the years, this wealth has been polished by daily use, best reflected in its art of culinary refinement which can be tasted and experienced from the mud plastered rural kitchens to the *rasoi*, *chowka* and *bawarchikhana* of urban centres. The highly ritualized and sanctified Indian kitchen produces delicacies that have gained popularity the world over.

The geographical diversity and six diverse seasons accompanied with distinct agricultural and horticultural produces have accentuated the diversity. Despite variation in culture and language among them, the people share the basic condiments for cooking that have fascinated the world for centuries.

In this treatise, case studies have been presented from the heartland of India—the Indo-Gangetic plain. The narration is from a person who was born in the age of radio sets, bicycles and *chulha* (hearth), and has witnessed the arrival of gas oven, refrigerator and microwave oven. The depiction of ritual, sanctity, paraphernalia and nuances associated with food and its transformation has remained the focus of this chapter. The case studies have been presented in a narrative form first to present the general rule or custom. The structural aspects have been derived from it as inductive reasoning. The complex events or series of events give rise to a social situation, which show that different conflictive perspectives interplay and are enjoined in the same social system. Moreover, the qualitative comparative analysis leading to situational analysis has brought forth the social changes within the system. This has exhibited morphology of a social structure, often held together by conflicting ideologies. It has also examined social relations between individuals and the logistic staff drawn from specific occupational groups for maintaining the hearth and running the kitchen on daily basis and their gradual disappearance. The following case studies present a collection of human experiences that lead to human responses and ultimately give expression to cultural mores and manners.

Case Study: Narrative 1

Locale

As a child in a middle-class household of *Purani* (Old) Delhi, my world during the preschool days was centred on the small *angan* in front of the kitchen and a long stretch of balcony overlooking Dr Ansari Road. The rows of shops lining the street varied from barber, *pansari* (grocer), *mithaiwala* (sweetmeat seller), *bangali mithaiwala* (dealing with sweet specifically from Bengal region), *koeleywala* (coal vendor), *doodhwala* (milkman), doctor's clinic, chemist, stationary shop, paanwala, press-wala, all in a row. The road was a world by itself made livelier by the presence of a municipality tap connection, the urban water hole for the pulsating populace, especially for those who lacked water connection in their residence. In this category were the shop owners who converted back portions of the shop into living room-cum-kitchenette while sleeping on the footpath at night. Further, my balcony faced a wide expanse of a tree-lined lawn; this was my exclusive forest area. Winter nights were thrilling with cries of *papadwala* (man selling salted wafers made out of gram/rice/arrowroot), *gajjakwala* (man selling candy bar made of sesame/jaggery/sugar) and *moongphaliwala* (man selling pea nuts). The mornings were unique blend for the Purani Dilliwalas. The four o'clock *azaan* from Jumma Masjid and *mangal arati* at the temples were distinctly heard and reverberating in the sky, along with the flapping of wings of hundreds of pigeons flying through the morning sky. This was followed by the swish of the safaiwala sweeping the road. The mashakwala was soon to follow filling the mashak with municipality water and sprinkling the tarmac roads to settle the dust.

Family Orientation/History

Inside the house the small angan was a virtual stage for me where I could sing, dance and draw on the blank wall. The lone spectator was ma in the kitchen, sitting and cooking on the portable chulha. She was the perfect picture of happiness, fair complexion, ruddy cheeks flushed by the heat of the chulha. The red vermillion mark on her forehead used to be the only adornment besides the shiny nose pin. She was popular for her cooking in the neighbourhood. She used to sing while cooking; her voice was sonorous and rich; she could render the difficult notes very smoothly. The two songs which I still remember *'amibonophul go chhondeychhondey…'* and *'megher porey megh jomechhey…'*, the second one a Rabindra sangeet. During the morning cooking, I had to sit in front of the kitchen with a slate and chalk. Ma would write a Bengali alphabet and I had to trace on the alphabet with the chalk. She was my first teacher who introduced me to Bengali language.

Ancestors of this family migrated from Bengal during the 18th century; they hailed from the village Moyurpukur (Noorpur) of the then 24 Parganas District. Ancestry of this family has been mentioned by Das (1925) in the Aligarh chapter of his book '. The family belongs to Mukhopadhyaya clan of Srirampur and this has been authenticated by the family's matriarch Sanyasini Sarojbashini Roy (Mukhopadhyaya), popularly referred to as 'Pagol Ma', in her book. The title Roy was adopted from the *khetab* (title of honour) bestowed upon the family by Mughal emperor.

Bengali Diaspora in Delhi and NCR

It appears that the first influx of Bengali Hindu settlers came to Delhi between late 18th and early 19th centuries. An essential requirement for those settlers was that of a Kali Bari for the worship of the mother goddess. The first one was established in 1826, but the temple was destroyed during the 1857 revolt. The idol was later salvaged and a temple was built in Roshanpura. The space within the temple could not accommodate a large number of devotees, so land was bought, and a temple was built at Tis Hazari in 1917, which still exists. There are more than 25 Kali Baris and few Durga Baris in Delhi. Moreover, many other temples have been built in different parts of New Delhi and NCR by Bengalis. The first private Durga Puja in Delhi was celebrated in 1842 by one Majumdar of Rajshahi, while the first *baroyari* (community-based) Puja is that of Kashmere Gate, started in 1910 and still celebrated with fervour and tradition. The Kali Bari in Mandir Marg temple was built in 1930 (Roy, Siddarth 2011, Smith, R.V. 2018).

A sizeable population of Bengalis settled in Delhi when Calcutta and Delhi were first connected by train in 1864; thereafter, with the shifting of capital to New Delhi in 1911, the shifting of government employees ensued. The next big wave of migration was in 1947 and then in 1971. Initially, employees from central government departments were settled in Timarpur; later in 1924, another government housing came up near Gole Market. Shops came up in Gole Market to cater to Bengali taste and needs. Chittaranjan Park today is home for many Bengalis. It was established as EPDP Colony (East Pakistan Displaced Persons Colony) and has shops catering to all the needs of Bengalis from fish to books and saris.

Bengalis spread over Jaipur, Ajmer, Alwar, Delhi, Lucknow, Kanpur, Allahabad, Moghulsarai to Patna were referred to as *probashi bangali*, who have moved away from Bengal and settled in other parts of the country. After Kali Bari, the other essential requirement was of schools where Bengali as a subject would be taught; now there are several such schools. Once learning of language and script was confirmed, parents were assured of retaining their identity amidst the vibrant multilingual populace. The languages prevalent in Delhi were Hindi, Urdu, Punjabi and Haryanvi.

The Neighbourhood Rasoi, Chowka and Bawarchikhana

I have been one of those fortunate women who had been taught to cook by my mother—Ma, mother and Amma, my mother-in-law. Ma hailed from Allahabad and Amma from Lucknow; both were excellent cooks. Being born and brought up in the walled city of Delhi I had free access in the rasoi, chowka, chulha, bawarchikhana of the neighbouring families. My childhood memories have vivid image of the great patriarch of Bhatnagars, my Bauji, cooking mutton in the angan during weekends. The aroma emanating from his concoction used to be the topic of discussion among the ladies of the neighbourhood. When in mood, Bauji would allow me to partake evening meals from his table, and they tasted like something I had never eaten before. Cooking by the male members was never a surprise for us. Bauji's wife Maaji would not allow non-vegetarian dishes inside her chowka, since all the ladies of the house were vegetarian. Whenever Maaji would sit on her chowki to make *take paise* (a curry of gram flour dough shaped like coins), we would extend our hands for a piece of the crisply item. A huge wooden casket in the corner of Maaji's bedroom was like a pandora's box for me. It was referred to as the *baksa*. It was opened twice daily, during morning breakfast and evening tea. When opened, it was a sight to behold and the aroma to be sucked deep in the lungs. The box was partitioned, and it used to be full of homemade snacks ranging from *namak pare*, *shakkar pare, sawal, gujhiya, namkeen sev, meethay sev, pappad, mathree, besan kay laddoo, atey-ki-pinni*, etc. This was a joint family of three married sons, parents and their children (Roy, Shibani 2007).

Prior to Diwali celebrations, the ladies of the household would get busy with flour, gram flour, semolina, dry fruit, sugar and various kinds of condiments. The snacks were made under the strict guidance of Maaji and carefully stored in the wooden box; those lasted beyond the festival of Holi during the month of March. I have never seen it empty since, it was opened in front of us to dole out some delectable while we played in their house. Maaji's pappad was the hit item among the neighbourhood women, they also joined in this melee to learn pappad making. On the day of Diwali, after the propitiation of Goddess of wealth, Lakshmi, platter full of eatables was exchanged between the households. The main item on this was parched rice along with *batasha* (sugar candy), which was offered to the Goddess along with all the home-made snacks. With time, this tradition has totally eroded and has been replaced by boxes of sweets purchased from the market. With increase of health awareness, people developed aversion towards sweets with high sugar content. Sweets were replaced by dry fruits and other utility items as gifts.

Mitra mashima, a Bengali lady, had a separate stove for cooking fish. On the other side were the Garg's and Biji's chulha and her *karhi* was the most popular item; she would always send a bowl of it to Ma. Maa tried to cook the karhi herself and it was Biji who not only tutored her but introduced her to *kasoori methi*, the wonder herb, which can make mutton or potato attain an absolutely an ethereal taste. Beyond Biji's house was the serene and sombre flat of Miss Mukherjee, a grand personality with a loving Christian soul. She was the school principal of one of the prestigious girl's school of the walled city which paved the way for giving basic training to the girls. She hailed from Calcutta and her steaming and baking procedures are still followed by many of us. Though her students were awestruck by her gravity, I was her darling. She used to entice me with a variety of chocolates and cookies in lieu of getting admitted in her school (referred to as Kali Phatak, due to its huge black gates). I used to devour all the sweets and replied that I would attend the school which had buses without the nose (engines of which were fitted next to the driver's seat and not in front of the bus). I still follow her method of making the pudding.

Across the road was Nikko Apa's sprawling Pili Kothi and her bawarchikhana was no less than a wonderland for us youngsters. The *niyamat khana* of Nikko Apa and Ma's meat safe were yesteryears' ventilated cupboards in which leftovers and freshly cooked food were stored.

Refrigerators have taken over those net closets. Niyamat khana is a term prevalent in Lucknow and Delhi among the Muslim households. The word niyamat in Urdu means all the material goods bestowed by God. Its origin can be traced back to the 15th-century treatise of Mughal recipes titled *Niyamatnama*. This was composed by a Malwa king and dedicated to a Mughal king. It is also a precursor of evolution of food preparation to suit the taste buds. Today, the niyamat khana, a net closet is omnipresent in the trousseau of a Muslim bride in North India. However, the affluent families have replaced the niyamat khana with a refrigerator. Ma's meat safe served the same purpose, but its name was highly anglicized. This might have been borrowed from the colonial rulers, to keep the mutton safe from cats.

In Lucknow, Amma till recently used to have a maid whose work was only with *silbatta* (grindstone). Prior to cooking she would come and grind all the masalas beginning with haldi and ending with garam masala as per Amma's instruction. Freshly grind garam masala is the essential part of cooking and it does make a sea of difference. In these different kitchens with their varied heritages, I learnt the difference between *chhowka, baghar, tarka, dum* and *phoran*. Mind it, all are different unique methods of seasoning and capable of giving different taste and flavour.

These grand ladies Ma, Amma, Maaji, Mashima, Biji, Mrs Mukherjee with their experience and expertise had opened a vast arena of knowledge regarding food and its preparation. For them cooking was a pleasurable job and they used to put their heart and soul into it. They cooked with care, love and compassion and that was their trade secret. They did not have exotic herbs, sauce and ingredients in their kitchen, nor any of the modern gadgets to curtail on time and labour. Yet, even the roti from their kitchen had the special taste and flavour; or am I being partial to them?

The Hallowed Precincts: Rannaghar

Unoon and Types of Fuel

Looking back in those childhood days, I distinctly remember that Ma entered the hallowed precincts of the kitchen after her morning rituals and bath. Lighting the portable *angithi*/chulha (referred to as *unoon* in Bengali) itself was a piece of art. The chulha was designed with a 10–15 litre iron bucket with horizontal iron bars set in the middle. Making two chambers in it, in the lower portion a small window was cut out. Inside of the chulha was plastered with hard clay which was neatly painted with wet mud after a day's use. It was sacrilegious to light a used chulha.

It had to be cleaned of all the ashes and a fresh coat of wet mud had to be painted on it. The paraphernalia for the chulha were dried cow dung cakes or kanda, charcoal, soft coal/pathar ka koela, kerosene or newspaper optional. The cow dung cakes or kanda were to be broken into pieces and neatly arranged on the upper part of the chulha. Few drops of kerosene were dribbled on it and it was lighted. As soon as the cakes became red charcoal was arranged on it. The topping was always of soft coal. The smoke from the chulha used to be plentiful, slowly traversing upwards and disappearing in the blue sky. When the smoke subsided, the chulha used to be carried in the kitchen and the day started with boiling of milk in a huge iron wok, that is, *kadhai*. After completion of cooking the first morsels of each food item were offered to the Agnidevta by symbolically dropping them in the chulha. The chulha entailed the purchase and storage of charcoal, coal and the cow dung cake. The Koeleywala was a dark version of the hunchback of Notre Dame. He was always covered with coal dust from head to toe; he had a limp and was always bent over with the load of coal. The outstanding part of his personality was a pair of red eyes and a set of white teeth. The Kandewali came from the village near the city wall dressed in ghaghra choli and an array of silver jewellery adorned from head to toe. Her shrivelled old face with a hooked nose was clearly outstanding but the antiquity and the design of her ornaments fascinated me immensely.

Janta kerosene stove came much later and became popular in all Delhi households, since it could be lighted in a jiffy, limited emission of smoke and single fuel usage. However, the smell of kerosene was undeniably a deterrent. Further, the management of the stove required repeated changing of the wicks and durability of the tin stove was very questionable. Since heat and moisture used to erode the tin, a leaking stove had to be thrown away. Despite all its negative points the kerosene wick stove was a boon for the housewives during late night or early morning cooking in winter and rainy season. During the 1950s, liquid petroleum gas was introduced in Delhi, in our neighbourhood we were the first to subscribe for it. Since Ma was used to cooking while sitting, she opted for a single burner stove which was placed on the floor of the kitchen. The white stove became the prime exhibit in the kitchen; battalion of *mausiji, taiji, mashima* and *chachiji* were ever eager to view its performance and analyse the ills of cooking on the gas stove; especially, the making of roti was the centre of the controversy. They believed, baking roti directly on gas flame had several ill effects on health. The alternative arrived at was to bake it entirely on the tawa or pan. The onset of gas era meant ouster of coal and cow dung cakes. Kerosene was the exception since a spare stove was always kept ready for emergency and economizing on the fuel.

Purity and Pollution

The two most contentious aspects of our household towards which I was vehemently critical were ritual purity/pollution centred around the kitchen and toilet. After entering the toilet for defecation, one was required to take a bath, wash the attire which one is wearing and then enter the household premises. During inclement weather, we were spared the bath and a change of clothing was enough. However, exceptions to this military diktat were the men of the house adorning the sacred thread. They could move about have a cup of tea, shave, read the newspaper and then bathe. My repeated remonstrations against this gender bias did not bear any fruit except a loud response from Ma saying that they are wearing the sacred thread. In retaliation I used to run up to Ma after my exit from the toilet and dance around her, threatening to touch her which would entail her unfit to pray and cook in the kitchen. For my revengeful antics mother would say, 'No, don't'. Though the toilet was situated in one corner of the angan, yet it was considered to be the most polluted area of the household. For convenience, the bathroom had an extra pair of dress hung for visiting the toilet during odd hours. In many households, the women would drape two towels one around the waist and the other on the torso to enter the toilet. All concepts of purdah, ghunghat, *lajja* were kept at bay on this issue, it used to be quite a free show for occupants of the family who used to ignore such exceptional diversions. However, having witnessed such semi nudity at an impressionistic young age, while visiting family and friends, I had vociferously raised the issue at home. In my lifetime I have experienced the concept of pollution surrounding defecation with such severity that I still have the feeling of guilt after my exit from the washroom. Egress from the washroom entailed a bath and change of attire.

The daily visit of Thappo to wash and clean the toilet and carry away the household garbage was one of the regular features in our house. Thappo was a hazel-eyed dark beauty with half a dozen children. The most outstanding aspect of her countenance which attracted me as a child was the set of silver buttons adorning her kalidar kurta. The dupatta used to be folded on her chest and all the eatables and leftovers collected from the households were kept there. Since her hands were soiled she would extend her dupatta and we would drop the food items in her makeshift bag. Refrigerators being a rarity most of the households had something or the other to contribute to the food kitty of Thappo.

I have never seen my family members cleaning the toilet. Another astonishing and annoying feature was that of urinating in the bathroom and not in the toilet, since defecation was considered polluting and not the urination. The sacred haven in the house was the kitchen. As a child and adolescent, I could never grasp the protocol of working in the kitchen. The most sanctified area was *bhanraar* or *bhandar* (storage space) where all the spices and condiments, oil, flour, rice, cereals and jars of pickle were kept. This area at times housed the pooja closet of the family—the most sanitized zone.

The first clear distinction between food items were *amish* and *niramish*. Under amish came food items like fish, mutton, eggs, onion and garlic. Chicken and chicken eggs were never cooked in the kitchen. However, duck meat and eggs were allowed. On repeated enquiry as to the reason for this dichotomy my query was brushed aside as chicken being a foreign entry in our food item. By foreign entry it was implied imported by British colonials, thus a *mlechha* food item hence to be barred from the kitchen. On enquiry, it was found that besides onion, garlic, chicken, chicken eggs, pork, beef, even tomatoes and masoor dal were prohibited in some of the households. A lot has been written on Indian and specifically Hindu food habits and I do not intend to go into its polemics. Yet, within my lifetime I have seen and experienced the strict taboo associated with these food items. In most of the urban households, beef and pork were unheard of items. For cooking other non-vegetarian items, separate utensils and stove were allotted. The actual cooking was done outside the kitchen in a corner of the angan or secluded spot of the verandah.

The other concept is that of *entto*, in English it would mean which has been touched by the mouth while eating. Thereby, the right hand with which one eats is entto while eating. The serving bowls with food items kept on the dining table are not to be touched by the right hand. As per Bengali etiquette even a glass of water served to the person has to be lifted by the right hand. I abhorred this, since the tumbler would be smeared by the food item I was eating as we eat with fingers. Whenever I used my left hand for lifting the tumbler, I was reprimanded for making both my hands entto. In temples and during Puja partaking of *charnamrit* (holy water) rendered the right hand entto and it must be immediately washed with water. Certain food items were also classified under entto category. Cooked rice was entto and the other food items like vegetable and cereals, sweet dishes, chutney and pickles were always kept away from it. In case any of the items accidently touched the *bhaat* container, mother would yell by saying keep it aside it has become *bhaater entto* (bhat is cooked rice). Similarly, roti also falls in the category of cooked rice/bhaat. In some families, even *chirey*/flattened rice is kept outside the pantry since it is first boiled and then flattened to flakes. The plate of food from which one eats is also considered entto—*pater entto* (pater or platter). Due to all the above restrictions, food is doled out by the matriarch who eats after everyone has finished eating. These restrictive rules extend to the preparation of *bhog prasad* (food offerings to the deities) as well.

Another significant aspect of our religious observances is abstaining from eating bhaat/roti on specified days; to mention a few— Ramnavami, Janam Asthami, Shiva Ratri, Purnima (full moon), Ekadashi (eleventh day of lunar cycle) and Shashti (sixth day of the lunar month). During these days, after fasting for the entire day, *pukka khana* is taken which includes *luchi/puri* (deep fried flour bread). Thus, the dichotomy of pukka and *kachha khana* (rice and chapatti versus luchi) is common among various linguistic groups in the northern belt.

In our kitchen, all the vegetarian items were cooked first and kept aside, while non-vegetarian dishes were cooked at the end. After this the stove or unoon was kept out for fresh coating of mud paste to revive its ritual sanctity. The ritual sanctity was essential since prior to serving the food to the family members Ma used to offer it to Agnidevta in the chulha.

The *rannaghar* being a highly sanctified domain, it had set rules regarding bhadar/bhandar where pickles and wheat grain and pulses were stored. The ritual purity and pollution concept of kachha and pukka khana was very rigid and confusing for me then. Now after years of travel around India and world over and in trying to understand each culture, I realize there is this ritualistic mode and overtures surrounding the kitchen. Sweeping the kitchen floor with bucketful of water twice a day, bathing and entering without shoes, and lastly, offering the cooked food to the God in the hearth, before serving. Why? That is because till we breathe our last it is the food which sustains us and being human beings bestowed with the best of the faculties in the animal kingdom, we have refined the art of food intake as per our need, taste and requirement. The variety of cuisine developed so far has been achieved due to the discovery of fire; venerated as Agni Dev.

The Household Menu

The menu of our house was a blend of West Bengal and Uttar Pradesh food items. Morning breakfast was a glass of buffalo milk and desi ghee (clarified butter) parantha with egg. To this dry fruit was added, especially during the time of examination. During summer, Ma would soak the almonds and make almond *sharbat* (almond milk) by rubbing each almond on a rough stone (Chondonpidi – mainly used to make sandalwood paste for puja) painstakingly. During summer *lassi* (yoghurt sharbat) was made to keep us cool. The Delhi winters were severe and to keep cold and cough at bay father would bring goat trotters. Soup was made from the trotters after hours of boiling. Lunch used to be tuar/ arhar dal, rice and crisply fried potato chips, along with some seasonal vegetables. Salad of raw onions with vinegar or lemon juice was always served. On festive occasions luchi and pulao were added.

We did not have knives for cutting vegetables but three set of *bontees* (indigenous cutter/scraper held by foot-stand that was used either by squatting or sitting cross-legged)—one for vegetables, one for non-vegetarian items like fish and a third for cutting fruits during puja. Ma was an expert in using these and her potato chips could be used conveniently in the botany lab for section cutting. The variation in pulses was minimal. Only alternative was masoor, chana dal and urad. *Moong dal lauki (gourd) ki khichri* was served with when we were sick. The glass of milk was turned into freshly made *chhana* (cottage cheese) by squeezing lemon over it. This curdled milk was supposed to be easily digestible. Further, the domestic help would be requested to bring fresh small fish from Jamuna River. Small fish was considered light on a weak stomach. Evening tea was a royal affair, Ma was excellent in churning out snacks in a jiffy; they ranged from *nimkee/namak parey, goja/shakkar-parey (jibheygoja, elojhelo), chhanar jilipi, sandesh, bhapa sandesh, pithay,* cutlet, fruit salad, *payesh, mithey chawal, halwa* and pudding. Though as children we were never served tea, yet teatime used to be the prime time as far as food was concerned.

Dinner was always chapattis and mutton curry. The variation in the dish was brought about by cooking mutton and *keema* (minced meat) with either potato, shalgam, tinda, peas or any seasonal vegetable. When in special mood father would bring specially dressed mutton called *pasinda*, which was marinated and fried. Fish was not a staple for us, since; father was not an alert and smart buyer. He never learnt to select the fresh fish and was handed over a stale item, Ma would complain and argue to no avail. Hence, our fish eating depended totally on the visit of Kallu, the fish monger. Unlike his name, he was not dark but very fair with kohl-lined bright eyes and a black mark on his forehead. A sign signifying praying five times a day. Maa would select the fish and get it dressed as per her requirement. The standard Bengali items cooked in our house were *aloo bhate* (mashed potato), *shorshey batamachh* (only rohu and katla), *kosha mangsho, chorchori* and *doi mach.* *Shukto, ghanto* were never hot favourites with children, so rarely cooked. Ilish was not purchased since the smell was not conducive to our taste. Rice was eaten only on weekends, since chapati was preferred by all.

Another significant feature of our home was the partisan attitude of mother towards her sons. The son and male members always got the larger portion of mutton, fish and sweet dish. Though the girls were not deprived of these items, yet, the portion served to them was always less than that of the male members of the house. I had vehemently opposed this practice and demanded an equal portion for myself. My militant behaviour was tolerated with laughter, light banter and as a sign of intense sibling jealousy. This feature of unequal distribution of food extended to her own platter, she would dole out everything if need be, keeping nothing for herself. However, one aspect of food intake which intrigued me was mothers feeding their children till the age of seven/eight years. Irrespective of the gender, the children were fed all the major meals by the mother. It used to be time consuming since intake of each morsel required lot of cajoling, cuddling, singing, storytelling and play acting as well. There are several two to four-liner *chhora*/folk verses which have been often recited by generations Bengali mothers, while feeding the child.

Aye ray aye meni
Khokar dudhey chini
Dudh khabena raag korechhe
Khokon jadumoni

(Come pussy come on
There is sugar in the milk
My boy is annoyed
And refused to drink the milk)

To sum up the seventh-generation Bengali family under study residing in North India had largely adopted to local food items. The standard Bengali menu referred to as '*teto, tok. jhal, mishti*' beginning with bitter veggies followed by *jhal* (hot and spicy) and culminating with sweet and sour chutney had been abandoned at the altar of time, place and people. However, sweat dish preparations were continued with all earnesty by Ma and we never had to pine for chhanar jilipi or sandesh.

Gondush and Panchgrasmantra: Partaking of Food After Ritual Offering to Gods

The male members of our household after receiving the platter of food used to first offer food and water to the panchdevta and then start partaking of the food. I give an abridged version of the same. They first use to do the *achman* by uttering the mantra *Om asmakamnityamshvetat*. Achman was a process by which the things and surroundings were purified. After this they would keep the hand on the food and utter the following mantra:

Brahmarpanang brahmhavirbrahmaganau brahmanahutam
Brahmau ten gantavyam brahmakarma samadhina
Om annang brahm raso Vishnu bhokta devjanardanah

Few morsels of the food items were picked up and placed at five places in a geometric pattern on the floor besides the platter. Water was poured in the palm of the right hand and the following mantra was uttered thereby offering the food to the five deities.

Om nagaynamah
Om kurmaynamah
Om krikaraynamah
Om devdattaynamah
Om dhananjayaynamah

On each utterance a drop of water was poured on each morsel arranged on the floor. Half of the leftover water was poured in the mouth by uttering the following mantra: *Om amritopasturanmasisvaha.* Few drops of the water left in the palm were sprinkled on the floor. After this offering the actual eating began.

The daily offering of food to the god prior to each meal by the twice born entailed that the food be cooked by maintaining ritual purity of the kitchen. This ritual was strictly followed by male members of the household. However, our male siblings discontinued this ritual due to various factors, such as not being initiated (*upanayan*/sacred thread ceremony) during their pre-teen and teenage. For the sake of bringing about brevity in life cycle rituals, upanayan was performed during marriage. This led to non-compliance of various practices associated with Brahminic tradition, for example, adorning of the sacred thread, maintaining a tuft of hair on the occiput and offering of food to the gods prior to each meal. Boys, when initiated at a tender age, abide by the diktats of the pundit. Elder and younger siblings who were initiated during their youth, conveniently bypassed those customs attributing it to their urban living and fast pace of life.

Lunar Phases and Restriction on Food Items

Another important aspect which influenced our kitchen was various food restrictions depending upon the month and the lunar position.

Lunar Position	Food Restriction
Pratipad (new moon is the 12 angular degree after syzygy)	Kumra/pumpkin
Dvitiya (moon is the 24 angular degrees after syzygy)	Brihati (*solanum indicum*)
Tritiya	Potol/pointed gourd
Chaturthi	Radish
Panchami	Bel/wood apple
Shashti	Lemon
Saptami	Taal
Ashtami	Coconut
Nabami	Gourd
Dasami	Kalmisaag
Ekadashi	Sheem/beans
Dvadashi	Puinsaag/Malabar spinach
Trayodashi	Brinjal
Chaturdashi	Mash kalai/white pulse/black gram lentil

During Amavasya, Purnima and Sundays non-vegetarian food like fish and mutton were forbidden. During the month of Magh (mid-January–mid-February), radish and berry were forbidden. During Bhadra (mid-August–mid-September), gourd and elephant yam were not allowed. All these restrictions were there but not followed verbatim. As per the shastra, besides fish and mutton, the main non-vegetarian food items, masoor dal/red lentil, black gram lentil, onion, garlic, beetle leaf, red leafy vegetable, a variety of lemon and any roasted vegetable are also considered non-vegetarian.

Life Cycle Ceremony and Food

I would like to mention two items which I have continually encountered in our religious performances conducted at home—*panchgabhyya* and *panchamrit*.

Panchgabhyya is a mixture containing *gomoy* (cow dung), *gomutra* (cow urine), *gabyaghrita* (clarified butter made from cow's milk), gabyododhi (yoghurt made from cow's milk), *gabyodugdh* (cow's milk) and *kushodok* (water soaked in *kush* grass (*Desmostachyabipinnata*). This is made when *sthal shuddhi* (purification of a place) or *deh shuddhi* (purification of the body) is required.

Panchamrit is a mixture containing *dugdh* (milk), *dadhi* (yoghurt), *ghrita* (clarified butter), *madhu* (honey) and *sharkara* (sugar). Idols of deities are bathed in it and it is used as *charanamrita* by the devotees who drink it after completion of the worship. Each item is identified with a human emotion. Milk signifies *moha*/desire since the cow gives milk only after its calf is held in front of it. Honey signifies greed of the honeybee while collecting the honey. Yoghurt symbolizes anger, while clarified butter signifies pride and sugar glory. Thus, by drinking it the devotee tries to free himself from the materialistic worldly responses. Besides, this mixture is highly nutritive and has a regenerative effect on the body. After fasting panchamrit tastes like heavenly elixir.

On the birth of a child honey is rubbed on the tongue of the newborn. During the *annaprasan* (solid/cereal food) ceremony of the child, *payesh* (rice cooked in milk and sugar) is fed to the child. During the sacred thread ceremony, the boy is fed chirey (rice flake), curd, and sweet prior to sunrise. The same applies to both bride and groom on the day of their marriage referred to as *dadhimangal. Shraddha* ceremony is performed by the children of the deceased. In this ritual, *pind daan* is performed. Pind are round balls made from boiled rice and black sesame, which are offered to the deceased and his ancestors. On the death of a family member, the entire household is considered polluted, the hearth is not lighted and nothing is cooked. The entire house must be swept clean with water and any cooked food item in the kitchen is thrown away, along with the bedding of the deceased. After cremation, when friends and relatives return from cremation ground, they have to walk over a lighted lamp, chew a neem leaf and have a piece of sweet. It is worth mentioning here that the sweet has to be made from milk and is mostly a *burfi* (solidified condensed milk and sugar). Sweets made of wheat, rice and other cereals are not allowed. The family members can take milk, fruit and sweet on the day of the death. For the next 10 days, the family members of the deceased eat *hobishanno* cooked once a day. It is one pot cooking, cooked by a family member and include boiled rice, matar dal (split pea lentil), unripe banana and eaten with clarified butter made from cow's milk and *soindhablavan* (rock salt). For dinner, milk, sugar, sweets and fruit are taken. Some of the families allow moong dal (green gram), job's tear, sesame, leafy vegetables like *bettor shaak* (amaranthus) and various kinds of edible roots. On the 13th day of death, *niombhango* (literally meaning breach of the observance) is performed, when all close relatives are invited to a feast of vegetarian and non-vegetarian food items.

One does get nostalgic while thinking of childhood. However, growing up and entering the world beyond Dr Ansari Road was also exciting.

As a teen I used to enjoy spending a day at my friends where we could enter the kitchen and make merry while cooking without any supervision and restrictions. As a working woman on waking I dash to my kitchen to make breakfast, pack lunch for office goers and children. Everyone in my house has access to the kitchen—children for making their favourite noodles, husband for his coffee. Ritual purity has been replaced by maintenance of personal hygiene: ample use of hand wash. Moreover, the modern kitchens are standing kitchens and there is no facility to sit and cook on a *piddhi* (low stool used for squatting). In the gas burner, there is no scope for offering the food to Agni Dev, the burners would get clogged. Within the limited space of a six-seater dining table it is difficult to attempt panchgras. Instead, a recent phenomenon has been witnessed in the city of Delhi which is called *gaugras*. A person from the *gaushala* (cowshed) makes a round of each locality collecting chapati, vegetable and fruit peelings (minus onion and garlic). Most of the households contribute, since feeding a cow is considered a sacred duty. Writing about the changing norms I am reminded of a touching instance which had become a memorable landmark in our household. During that period, we were posted at Shillong and my daughter was attending the Loreto Convent School. Dinner used to be the only meal when the family assembled. One evening after being served, my five-year-old said, 'Let me say the prayer before we eat:

> *Our father in heaven hallowed be your name; Your kingdom come, your will be done, on earth as it is in heaven; Give us this day our daily bread.'*

The prayer was said with such earnestness that we were all touched and then onwards, my mother made her say the prayers before every meal. Mother had also attended a convent school as a child and despite her Brahminic leanings, prayer to the almighty in any language or form was pious to her. She hailed from Allahabad, a product of *ganga jamni* culture.

As regards current eating norms, my family eats together, there is no supervision on distribution of food. The children are no more 'force fed' by the grannies; they have total disregard for such feeding habits. The child's individual likes and dislikes are given more weightage. The family deities are closeted in a room or niche. Till date it remains sanctified, retaining its ritual sanctity. My kitchen doles out salad, mixed sautéed veggies on daily basis. Food is now associated with maintenance of health: one eats to live and does not live to eat. The breakfast *parantha* has been replaced by porridge; lunches are either packed *roti sabzi* or frugal *dal, roti sabzi*. Dinner times are family time when all are present, hence slightly elaborate. Weekends are the days of indulgence when lunch is served with rice and fish. My family loves

Ilish and relishes it. On special occasions biryani is made and I am an excellent biryani maker. However, when it comes to cooking during fasting or making prasad, all the ritual sanctity of the kitchen is maintained as taught by Ma. Thus, to wrap up the experience of a lifetime with respect to cooking, cuisine and partaking of food, it can be said that elaborate ritualization has been practiced by cultures to emphasize its importance for existence.

Case Study: Narrative 2

Though the girls of Pilli Kothi were not allowed to visit the mutton shop, yet during childhood I had held on to Bua's dupatta while she was on her morning errands. Being the omnipotent housekeeper, nanny, cook, storyteller and 'lady in waiting' of our household, she was an indispensable figure in our domesticity. The members of our household and our home were her entire world. She had accompanied Amma to the household of Nawab Ali Mian along with the trousseau. Bano bi had been like a shadow of the *dulhan* (bride) initially, but with time and her managerial expertise Bano bi had become the handmaiden of Amma huzur, my grandmother. Later, she was the designated Bua or nanny for the children born to the dulhan she had accompanied. Abbu was the exception; he would address her as Bano begum when in good mood.

On her way to the market she would stop at Hafizji's shop ordering for one *pao kaleji* (250 g liver) exclusively for Nawab sahib's *nashta* (breakfast), half a *ser keema* (about 1 kg minced meat) mixed well with ginger and fresh coriander leaves for making *kofta* (meat balls) for Amma *huzur* whose teeth seem to have worn away due to constant chewing of paan. After placing the order for two ser mutton, half for *korma* (curry) and half for biryani for the day's requirement she would begin her chat with Hafizji. He was a tall, very fair, blue-eyed man with a goatee. Dressed in Aligarhi *pyjama* (trouser) under a long shirt and topped with a starched *dupalli topi* with the finest of the *chikan* work done on it, he had a black mark on his fair forehead which added to his grandeur. Bua would often teased him saying he has not got it by rubbing his forehead on the *jaanamaz*, that is, prayer carpet, but his wife has put the kohl mark to protect him from the evil eye of the shoppers. Hafizji had a gentle soothing voice to go with his personality. He mostly nodded and smiled while handling the cash and listening to Bua's constant chatter. I would tug at her dupatta at which undeterred she would pick me up and perch me on her waist.

Next halt of Bua was at the *halwai* (sweetmeat seller) for purchasing dahi or yogurt for the *raita*. Dildarhalwai was the heftiest man I had encountered. The huge milk-filled kadhai that he constantly stirred seemed to be his regular work and milk his diet. As a child I used to imagine Dildarhalwai drinking milk from the huge kadhai with his handlebar moustache dripping with milk. His topless body with the immense fair belly hanging over his pyjama made him look like the jinn of Aladdin's lamp. The days she had to purchase vegetables, Noora, Abbu's *chhilumburdar* (tender of tobacco pipe) would accompany her with a huge basket on his head. She would never enter the *mandi* (market) premises due to the crowd, instead patronized the makeshift hawkers. She had the prowess to haggle over the smallest item reducing the price by 50 per cent, arguing and gesticulating with her henna tipped fingers in the background of colourful glass bangles. The hawkers would always succumb to her persuasive techniques. Though at home we were not vegetable lovers, yet, potato, onion, ginger, garlic, green chilli, coriander leaves and tomatoes always remained omnipresent. Depending upon the time of the year leafy vegetables like *methi, bathua,* soya, *palak* (spinach) were favourites, since those blended tastefully with either potato or mutton. Besides, cauliflower, *arbi* (taro), *gajar* (carrot) *tinda* (apple gourd), *shalgam* (turnip), *chukandar* (beet root), green peas were the other vegetables which Bua purchased for making *tehri*, that is, vegetable biryani or *salan* (mutton curry). Salan was a common factor in both the meals; it had multiple vegetables cooked with mutton. However, the children used to prefer the korma and kebab. During childhood, helpings of vegetables always appeared like bitter pill. Poultry, chicken were the other items popular in our *dastarkhan* (dining table). Poultry was never purchased from the market. Instead, we had our own poultry farm at the rear end of the house in a corner and Gabru oversaw it. In one of the listless hot summer afternoons I had stepped out and wondered near the pen. Gabru was getting a chicken out of the pen for *halal*. With the utterance of the Kalma and the movement of the knife on the slender neck, somehow the chicken managed to slip out of Gabru's strong grip, splitting blood on the dry earth. Gabru was as quick as lightening, he caught up with it, dressing it with all the vengeance for trying to save his neck. I was awestruck and frightened. I had never seen Gabru at his work earlier. That was the day I refused to have chicken; I was eight then. It took me seven long years to get over this incidence. Our locality was devoid of a beef shop. I do not remember to have seen or eaten *barre ka kabab* or *salan* on our dastarkhan. Abbu, who had been educated in London for his degree in law, used to say that in India cattle were not reared for the table, instead the draught animals which were too old to work were sold to the butchers. During Haseen Bhai's *dawatwalima* (marriage feast) the slaughterhouses in and around Delhi were shut down protesting against certain legal measures. Mutton and poultry were not available in Delhi. The only solution to the problem was getting selected cattle slaughtered stealthily. Amma huzur was furious at the suggestion saying Ali Mian's *aukat* (status) has not reduced to such a level that beef has to be served in his grandson's dawatwalima. Abbu had to send the old station wagon with Peer Mohammad, the driver and the head bawarchi to Ghaziabad to bring chicken and mutton. However, in that dawat, mutton seekh kebab and chicken biryani excelled the rest of the preparations. The *misrain* (Hindu lady chef) and *maharaj* (Hindu cook) who had come to prepare the vegetarian dishes had a hard time. The vegetarian section was for our old family friends from Bazaar Sita Ram and Daryaganj, who were mostly Jains or Khatri business families. Since, the *dahi bara* (cereal ball dipped in yoghurt) was relished by all, maharaj ran short of it. However, Bhaijan's friends who were a mixed group made a beeline for the biryani. This dawat was talked over for months in the neighbourhood. The ghazal recital by Nazo Jan continued till the dawn. I was too young to appreciate and had fallen asleep.

The coming of fufeejan to Delhi for her delivery used to be eventful, exciting and dramatic—she was much pampered with special food; instances of false alarms prior to the delivery; then rushing to Machhliwala Hospital (Saint Stephens Hospital); and finally anxiety of the elders culminating with fufee's return home with her bundle of joy. Amma huzur never allowed feeding bottles and powder milk in the house. She insisted, mothers should breastfeed their children and took special care for the diet of nursing mothers. Suthora and panjiri were prepared with *desi ghee* (clarified butter) and *mewa* (dry fruit). Sunthora is a sweet dish popular in north India. It is made in the house for the lactating mothers to gain back strength and for easy lactation. Its main ingredients are wheat flour or *suji* (semolina), dried ginger, coriander seeds, *kamarkass* (*Palash gond*/Salvia plebeian raisin), *lajwanti* (Mimosa pudica), *jaiphal* (nutmeg), *javetri* (Myristicafragrans), *saunth satva* (dried ginger), *bura* (sugar), *magaz* (seeds of pumpkin and musk melon), *makhana* (puffed lotus seeds), *safed mirchi* (white pepper), *khuskhus* (poppy seeds), *ajwain* (bishops weed), *methi dana* (fenugreek), *satawari* (Asparagus racemosus) and *gond* (Tragacanth Gum). The dry fruits include coconut, almond, cashew, *chironjee* (Buchananialanzan), *kishmish* (raisins), *akhrot* (walnut), *chwara* (dried dates) and *pista* (pistachio). All these were available with the local *attar, pansari* and *kirana* who dealt in grocery. For the other members of the household almonds, black pepper, poppy seeds, raisins were soaked in water overnight. These were grinded to a paste in the morning, fried with desi ghee and poured on a warm glass of milk. During our student days, Amma huzur would personally supervise drinking of *nishashta* by school-going children.

During childhood school and studies were important. Nursery classes were a rarity, but preschool grooming was rigorous. Learning the first holy sentence: '*Bismillah Ir Rahman Ur Rahim*' with the fanfare of bismillah ceremony at the age of four years four months and four days was a great event. The feature of this ceremony, which was dear to me as a child, was the new dress—replica of an adult woman's attire, which included a *garara* (flared pyjama), kurta and dupatta. Putting the dupatta on head I had not realized this piece of cloth ensnares a woman's entire being. From that day onwards I could confront Maulvi Sahib only if I was attired in long pyjama and dupatta. Bua had taught me how to encircle my face and crown with the dupatta so that it does not open while I am reading the Quran. My school uniform was sky-blue tunic and white blouse of Presentation Convent situated at the heart of old city was surrounded by high and thick walls. All the girls of our family had been inducted here. Amma huzur herself had been a product of Loreto Convent, Lucknow. I presume convents manned by British and European nuns were considered the safest haven for girls from elite Muslim families. Formal education was given top priority; both Fufi Amma and Lado Fufi graduated from Indrapastha College. Till recently, their lecturers residing in the columned house of Faiz Bazaar, very graciously received the *sewain* (sweetmeat) during Mithi Id and *hissa* of *qurbani* (sacrificial mutton) during Bakr Id. The Bose family had come to Delhi as civil contractors. However, none of the children took up contractor's work. They were teaching in the premium schools and colleges of Delhi. Bua mentioned that they used to tip her handsomely on receiving the Id delicacies. Nothing less than five to ten rupees was kept on the tray and returned to the servant who had brought it. The other recipients of the Id delicacies were from Bazaar Sita Ram. These were sent especially for the women members, who could not always make it to our place on the day of Id. Nevertheless, their men folk never missed a single Id. Till Abbu was alive, besides the relatives and our own community members of the neighbourhood, receiving and serving these non-Muslim friends almost had a ritualistic fervour. Since some of them were non-vegetarian, Ammi herself supervised serving them.

The grandest part of Id celebrations was Amma huzur seated on the *takht* (divan) under the *anjeer* (fig tree) with her *khandani paandan* (container for betel nuts and leaves) having four wheels and two velvet purses. One was filled with coins and the other with currency notes. Abbu's classmates would come and wish her Id Mubarak. She would reply to them with her charm adding the entire blessing due from a matriarch. Then they would extend their palm to her for the Eidi. The prosperous business tycoons on receiving a silver coin or currency note would say, '*Amma huzur apkii di maibarkathaiise main sandook main rakhunga*' (the cash received from her would be his talisman which he would keep in his cash box for growth and prosperity). They worship money as Goddess of Wealth. Amma huzur would retort not to forget to have kulfi from the idi. Since, during childhood they used to spend it on iced candy.

The yearly events of Mithi Id and Bakra Id in the household were prime. The delicacies prepared for the occasion were first offered to Allah by an elderly family member after a bath and adorning clean clothes. The *takht* for namaz was cleaned, a clean sheet was spread on it and all food items prepared for eating were arranged at a corner facing west. On the other end of the takht a person stood and read out the *fateha* (first verse of Quran) aloud; it is the *nazrana* (gift) for the almighty prior to the feast. *Nazar* is practiced on happy occasions like birth of a child, getting a job and on Yaumay viladat, that is, birthdays of all Imams. On the demise of a family member, fateha is read out on the 3rd, 13th, 40th days and on yearly basis on the food items. A part of the food items is distributed among the fakirs. Many families perform fateha on weekly basis, that is, on every *jummey raat* (Thursday) for the deceased person and a portion of the food (hadia/gift) is given to fakirs. Shab-e-barat is observed on the night between 14th and 15th days of Shavan, the 8th month of Islamic calendar. It is a night of forgiveness and a day of atonement. It is the night when God forgives the sinners. Sweet dish *halwa* (semolina cooked with sugar and dry fruits) along with *puree* (deep fried flour bread) are offered to the dead. There is no gender bias regarding nazar and fateha, any ritually clean man or woman can perform it.

However, it is important to note that ritual offering of the daily food in the Muslim households is a practise followed without fail. To accommodate all the members of the family during the daily meals, the dining table was often abandoned and the dastarkhan was spread out on the takht. All the food items were

'*Bismillah fee awalihiwaakhiri*' (In the name of Allah in the beginning and the end). After finishing the meals, the following is uttered thanking the God:

'*al humdul illah lazi itmana wa sadkana wa jallana mina muslimeen*' (All praise and gratitude are due to Allah who has fed us and given us drink and who has made us Muslims).

This was engrained in us and even while on duty having a working lunch, I would recite it and then start eating.

I suddenly wake up from my reverie. I had to slow down my car and change the gear from third to first. The Ring Road has ended. I turn to left, I have to park the vehicle near Agra hotel since the parking spots on Faiz Bazaar were full by now. I am returning to Pili Kothi for the installation of a pump set. Granddaughter of Nawab Ali Mian is now the proud owner of a chain of beauty parlours in Delhi. 'Nazneen Beauty Parlour gives personalized service to its clients' is the main slogan on huge billboards. Nobody remains in the haveli now except for the family of Noora, who is now an octogenarian. Despite all the traumatic upheavals we could never part with the haveli, since, each tree, each brick and the nook and corners had a story to tell. For family events and get-togethers, we still use the haveli and once again the silent haveli comes to life with the laughter and scream of our children, clatter of utensils from the kitchen. The aroma of kewra sprinkled on the *zarda*/ mitha *pulao* with the women members reclining on the takht once used by Amma huzur, known to a select few as Shafiunnissa Begum, whose demurring smile was only for Nawab Sahab to behold and none other. I, Nazneen Ali, her granddaughter, had inherited her regal carriage and aquiline features. I cater to hundreds of Delhiites who aspire to look beautiful. Till date, at night Bua comes trudging in my room with a bowl of milk and cotton wool. That is the secret of my complexion. Bua, an octogenarian now, still remembers the last item before retiring to bed. She is the retainer of bygone days and time. Bua's reminiscence of *'haveli mein to...'* is still heard with rapt attention by me and my children. I never allowed Bua to retire in the village house, when one by one we had to leave the haveli due to our respective economic pursuits, I brought her to my flat with due deference towards her love and dedication for dulhan's children. The spacious flats of New Delhi were more economical than maintaining the haveli. And Bua! Well! She is a part of my growing up and who does not like to be pampered occasionally.

Nazar and niaz are considered un-Islamic by some schools of Islamic jurisprudence like Shafi, Hanafi. However, Shiasm and Sufism propagate such practices. Reciting dua before and after the meal is common among all Islamic sects.

An Introspection

Food: The Prime Mover

The narration of two case studies from two different linguistic and religious groups within the same geographic area amply reflects upon the commonalities, synchronization and discord in the sphere of food. In the first case food items are categorized as per their quality and availability. Further, an iron curtain is drawn between niramish (vegetarian) and (amish) non-vegetarian food. This was essential since a large section of the community abstained from non-vegetarian dishes depending on their religious orientation, marital status, rites de passage and rites of intensification. In the second case, there were no hardcore boundaries between categories. Despite this vast difference, there was a common ground where both met. It has been mentioned in the first case, mutton shops were all located on Faiz Bazaar Road and Muslimqasai were owners of those shops. Their clientele included non-Muslims too; according to the elders of the house those people knew how to dress the meat. *Jhatka* shops were not found around this place till my teens. The difference between halal and jhatka was basically method of slaughtering the animal. Halal in Islam meant permissible and involves slitting animals' throat without stunning it. A cut is made in the jugular vein, carotid artery and windpipe. During this operation Quranic verse is read. In Hindi, jhatka means swift; in this method an animal's head is severed in one single stroke. It is generally associated with animal slaughter in Sikh tradition; Guru Govind Singh prescribed killing an animal quickly without causing prolonged suffering. In Hindu tradition, *bali* or animal sacrifice is a relatively recent practice, as it finds no mention in Rig Veda where some hymns have indicated slaughter of animals for food and sacrifice. It is mostly practised in Shakti cult, while Puranas and the Gita forbid animal sacrifice.

Milk: Animal Product?

First case study mentions milk and milk products as the most sanctified food for gods, hermits and humans. In our worship, we still use unboiled milk as offering to the deity. My greatest trepidation is considering milk as a vegetarian food as it is an animal product found among mammals to nourish the newborns. The flow of milk from the udder or mammary glands is a purely psychosomatic process. The mother, on seeing and feeling the child suckle, develops compassion and milk oozes out. On milking the bovine and consuming the milk, we deprive the newborn from its mother's milk. Moreover, we fool the bovine by tying the calf in front of her and releasing it only after the udder has been emptied. In case the calf dies, its skin is stuffed and the same is hung in front of her. Thus, the deprivation and deceit induced by the dairymen makes milk an unfair animal product. Categorizing milk as a vegetarian product is an erroneous concept prevalent in the food culture of our society and religion. Raising the status of cow to dizzying height of mother and making Yam to ride a buffalo and Shiv to ride on an ox in no way reduces the wrong of partaking this animal product.

The Vedic hermits were basically cattle breeders, and their wealth was measured by the number of cattle owned. Thus, the economic valuation of cattle, which was assessed by its milk and milk products, along with the cattle dung used as fuel and fertilizer and the skin used for various purposes raised the status of cattle to the hallowed and sanctified heights. During the Puranic period, the earth goddess Prithvi on being chased by the first sovereign Prithu takes the form of a cow. She is milked by Prithu to generate crops and end famine. Further, Krishna worshippers are devoted to cows since Krishna was a cowherd. Goddess Kamdhenu, the miraculous 'cow of plenty', the 'mother of cows' in certain versions of the Hindu mythology, is believed to represent the generic sacred cow, regarded as the source of all prosperity. In the 19th century, a form of Kamdhenu was depicted in poster-art that shows all major gods and goddesses in it. Presently, statues of Kamdhenu abound the market and almost all temples and religious organizations use this as a piggy bank to collect money for the maintenance of gaushala.

As per a 2014 survey,[1] India produced 140 metric tonne milk per year. This is 50 per cent more than United States of America. On an average a bovine gives 10 litre of milk daily. As per tradition, three-fourth of the milk is taken away by the milkman and quarter of it is left in the udder for the calf. The cowherds also profess that milking the cow greatly relieves her from the distress of heavy udder. However, this is true only when milking is manual. In mechanized dairy farms, the bovines undergo a lot of pain. This includes repeated artificial insemination manually done by the dairymen. This amounts to recurring rape of the bovine. Daily dose of oxytocin injections to produce more milk is another evil. This injection induces uterine contraction and is very painful. The calf is not allowed to suckle, and the bovine and calf are left bellowing for hours. Moreover, the oxytocin laced milk leads to premature puberty among girl child and gynaecomastia (enlarged breasts) among the boys. Further, it must be noted that only 25 per cent of the bovines are productive and the rest 75 per cent are non-productive. These non-productive bovines make the beef and buff industry flourish in the country. The ethical vegetarian thereby supports the beef industry without realizing it. The male calves are left unattended while the female calf has the same fate as its mother. The 'green dot' that signifies food obtained is cruelty-free, as stamped on the milk packets needs to be authenticated and then used.

On reviewing animal milk consumption by the humans, we find that starting with cow, buffalo, yak, camel, horse, goat, sheep, llama, donkey are popular among different communities. However, dietary pattern of most communities of Cis Himalayan region shows that milk as a staple food is alien to them. The dairy products like cheese, butter and ghee, despite being animal products, are consumed as vegetarian diet from time immemorial and offered to god during rituals. The vegans are now opting for soya milk, almond milk to replace the animal product.

Jeeva: Seed of Life

Another astounding factor is the perception of life form. The experiments done as a child in the botany laboratory with cereals left a deep mark in the young mind. Later, while sprouting the cereals in the kitchen and serving them for breakfast, I had the same feeling of beholding life form in the bowl. The sprouted seeds would cling on the wet cloth wrapping and one needs to spoon them out. When transferred in the bowl one can see the distinct movement of the seeds, as if each seed is trying to anchor on to something. Thus, the varieties of seeds and fruits we consume have the potential to rejuvenate and grow into a plant. So how is it different from an egg? The latter is imbued with a life force like the life force of germinating seeds. This life force is referred to as *jeeva* in Sanskrit literature. The word itself originates from the Sanskrit *jivás*, with the root *jīv*, meaning 'to breathe'. Hence, the sprouting seeds and an egg are manifestations of jeeva/*prana*.

Here it is worth mentioning that for plucking leaves of *tulsi* (basil) and *bilva* (wood apple/Aegle marmelos), specified shloka are recited recognizing and accepting the plants as life form with prana.

The presence of life force, energy, prana, its constant regeneration, cyclical birth and death are the underlying philosophy of not only Hinduism but also of indigenous belief patterns often described as animism (from Latin anima, 'breath, spirit, life'). Animism is the religious belief that objects, places and creatures all possess a distinct spiritual essence. Potentially, animism perceives all things—animals, plants, rocks, rivers, weather systems, human handiwork and perhaps even words as animated and alive. Tylor (1871) has explained animism in detail. Most of the world religions are animistic in nature in simple or in complex form. In Christianity it is the spirit (the holy spirit is a member of the Trinity, the triune God, manifested as father, son, and holy spirit, each person being God). Among the followers of Islam, it is the *ruh* (man's immortal essential self). In Hinduism, it is the atman (it is the concept of essence) which exists in all matters congregating into *Param Atman* (the supreme self). The concepts of *maya* (illusion), *karma* (action), *dharma* (divine and worldly duties that are followed to maintain harmony between man and nature). Through the cycle of birth, rebirth and moksha, the chain of events carries the atman from one life to the next till moksha is achieved and the atman submerges with the Param Atman. The above concepts are not as simplistic as they appear, rather their interpretation and analyses differ from one philosophical school to the other. Taking into consideration the above factors, the compartmentalization of amish and niramish becomes superfluous in the sphere of food and intense ritualization of certain food items.

In my career as an anthropologist, I have not come across any vegetarian tribal community. Eating some plants and killing certain animals might be a taboo for some due to their affiliation to a certain clan, lineage, or family. Those living forms are thought to be guardian spirits and symbols representing the people. This phenomenon is associated with animism and found worldwide in several cultures. Such practices are not only sustainable, it helps in protecting those plants and animals from extinction. The dichotomy of herbivorous and carnivorous animals are evident in the animal kingdom, while human and some primates are omnivorous and are located on top of the food chain. While some animals are herbivore and some carnivore, humans and some other primates are omnivore and located on top of the food web. Thus, survival of the omnivorous human species depended on the sustenance of the ecosystem. The philosophy of animism was a way to create a bond with nature; it was a bond based on deference, its bounty and utility, and lastly, fear of the unknown. Nature's fury was irrevocable; hence, natural resources were used with caution, prudence and complex ritualistic overtures. Varied festivals and rituals observed during hunting, fishing, sowing, harvesting and building structures were such few instances. Even while partaking of food, God has been thanked in different languages by man around the world.

Assay

The concepts and practices of purity and pollution within the kitchen and outside appear to be interrelated. The cooking stove, the kitchen, pantry, and entry of the matriarch in the kitchen centred on religiosity of the family where the first morsel of food goes to Agni Devta. Food served is first offered as panchgras to the five deities. Rice is an ingredient that remains a constant from birth to death—payesh to pindi. Though milk and milk products are basically animal products, those are placed at the top in food hierarchy and are offered to God. Despite the entto concept, honey collected by bees is considered ritually pure, though it is an animal product. Various food restrictions on the death of a family member and lunar cycle require further research and verification by nutritionists and horticulturists. I can add that habishanno is a sign of mourning, while periodic avoidance of certain vegetables could certainly save it from overuse and total extinction. I do not want to substantiate any of the practices by *scientific reasoning*, since a ritual based on belief pattern is arrived at after a lot of contemplation, thought and introspection by learned and knowledgeable persons. While the gradual erosion of the traditional rituals within a lifetime and over the centuries implies the changing social environs along with change in lifestyle of the individual which restrains and restricts him from carrying out the traditional mode of living.

On the contrary, in the second case study we find, with the change in language and religion, there is a lot of dilution in terms of ritual sanctity, gender bias and sanctified precincts of kitchen. Yet, dishes for nazar and niaz are cooked with special care and devotion and during fateha ritual sanctity is maintained. Can it be attributed to chronological age of the two religions? However, the food emanating from the hearth of each home not only sustains the family members in this world, it also helps the living to keep hold of the departed members. Thus, foodstuff is the link from this world to the next and is assumed to be reaching God through daily propitiation.

Note

1. https://www.news18.com/economic-survey-2015-16-ind (accessed on 1 April 2020).

References

Das, Shri Gyanendra Mohan. 1925. *Bonger Bahire Bangali*. Kolkata: Anath Nath Mukhopadhyaya.

Roy, Shibani. 2007. *Indo Pak Cuisine—Food Anthropology*. New Delhi: Star Publications.

Roy, (Mukhopadhyaya) Sanyasini Sarojbashini. 1935. *Lojja Pabey Tumi* (Brahmadarshan). Delhi: IMH Press.

Roy, Sidhartha. 2011. 'From Bengal, but Staunchly Delhiites'. *Hindustan Times*, 1 September.

Smith, R. V. 2018. 'Bengali: The Diaspora in North India', *The Statesman*, 26 July.

Tylor, E. B. 1871. *Primitive Culture*. Vol. 2. London: John Murray.

13

Materiality of Boro Food Culture
Social and Cultural Meanings

Dharitri Narzary

Hokhangafa, Khobaifa!
These two words are cultural expressions related to food and lifestyle of Boro people. Hokhangafa is an act of fishing in shallow water using a bamboo-made *jekhai* (fish-catching tool) and *khobaifa* (a basket full [of fish]). There are plenty of such expressions that the Boro people use in their everyday life, including folk songs around activities related to food, that inform us about their culture and worldview!

Seeing culture as the interface between tradition and innovation (Montanari 2004), this chapter provides an insider's perspective and looks at food culture of the Boro people as the marker of social category, ascribed identity and cultural tradition.

Introduction

Living away from my native place since before adulthood could not erase the memory of the taste of traditional Boro food that I relished during my childhood. This intimacy with food, I realized, cannot happen with 'other' food and is strongly embedded in my cultural being. The phrase, 'we are what we eat' holds true for me, though as an expression different people may interpret it differently. While a scholar may interpret such an expression as a way of understanding how a particular society is organized socially and culturally, a layman will see it in literal sense (Kohn 2013, 50). Acknowledging food as part of cultural history or cultural studies is still very new. While many writers have produced some very interesting work on food per se, studies around the historical and social relevance of food carrying nuanced meanings remain much to be desired. This is particularly true when we look at the literature produced over the decades on the importance of food in communities who struggle to negotiate for social and cultural space owing to their food choices and lifestyle. Such negotiations are subtle in some cases but are increasingly becoming more assertive in the times we are living in, forcing us to pay attention to the larger issues emerging out of contested identity politics.

It cannot be denied that the regional and peripheral cultures received little attention and appreciation in modern period due to the dominance of metropolitan cultures that spread along with the pace of development, and in the process, the regional or peripheral began to be seen as 'exotic'. This exoticization is not limited to people as cultural group and has extended to everyday lifestyles, which include food and food habit. Food habit is very community specific and with it are the associated material aspects that play an important role in shaping the socio-cultural position and identity of a group. As Ronald Berthes rightly says, food is 'a system of communication, a body of images, a protocol of usages, situations, and behaviour' (Berthes 2008). However, it is surprising how we limit ourselves to knowing about the food that we eat per se and pay little attention to the associated meanings and materiality of food culture in the larger social context. To illustrate, food offered during religious and social rituals require use of special and different kinds of material objects identified with rituals specific to a community. Depending on the nature of food, they are adapted to utensils and other associated paraphernalia. Here the food items dictate the usage of the objects; in the same way, certain material objects teach us a particular kind of social behaviour leading to symbolic value creation. It is also interesting to see how traditional food habit is undergoing change due to influence coming from other cultures, locally and externally, as a result of migration, globalization and popular media. Food is thus one way of understanding the cultural trajectory and social positioning of a community in given social and historical contexts.

Food itself is one component of tangible culture and is reflective of the environmental surrounding from where it is sourced. While it has spatial relevance, it is also intrinsic to the production of an intangible cultural wealth and knowledge system unique to the community. Food is not only for survival but has significance associated with the spiritual world of the community and is related to their world view. In contemporary times, therefore, any discussion on food habit is seen as representative of cultural sensitivity or lack of it. Discussion on food can happen at multiple levels but the important factor is to see the greater link it provides to understand the hierarchy that we so often talk about in academics. Mostly studied by sociologists and anthropologists, the topic of food has remained in the periphery of mainstream studies for a long time. This attitude towards the subject changed with an increase in the interest for a multidisciplinary approach to understand the changing global phenomenon. Particularly, post globalization changes in people's lifestyle posed challenges to scholars and researchers to adopt new methods to study the way fast changing global communities are communicating in a transformed world. In this changed world commodities, ideas and people moved faster than one could imagine earlier. Interestingly, with this change one gets to notice in food culture across societies the entry of the 'exotic' in the popular culture. This corresponds to the human psychology of self-upgradation in a constant effort to stay ahead in a distinctive way. This is also seen in the way traditional food items are being reinvented and presented today by groups in a conscious effort to mark and assert their cultural identity. For instance, there was a time when Naga food was completely unknown outside the state of Nagaland but today it is one of the most popular 'exotic' dishes in some of the metropolitan cities of India.

Boro Material Culture of Food

Before going into discussing the material culture of food among the Boro (anglicized as Bodo), it is imperative to understand the geo-cultural conditioning in which the Boro people live. Historically, the Boro people, spread across different parts of the north-east of India but presently concentrated in the state of Assam, belong to the ruling clan of the great Kachari tribe. The community is the largest plains' tribe of Assam in terms of population. Having lived amidst nature and natural surroundings, their lifestyle is connected with the flora and fauna of the land they inhabit. The main occupation and livelihood being agriculture, they have been dependent on nature for self-sustenance and preservation, developing a symbiotic relation with it. They originally formed clan-based societies living in units of villages identified and named after natural characteristics of the surrounding landscape, or particular incidents that happened in the past history of the place. The

Boro village names such as Belguri, Narabari, Mwiderkhoro (also known as Hatimatha), Amguri, Samoguri, Lokhra, Sijoubari, Samthaibari and so on evoke affinity with nature. In earlier times, one could visualize the natural surroundings of a village by its name, though spatially there is a rapid transformation as urbanization has spread like in any other place of today. Despite such rapid transformational processes, the Boro community, particularly in Assam, has managed to keep its cultural identity alive by reinventing their traditional practices in the face of pervasive commercialization post globalization.

In discussing the Boro material culture of food, this chapter will also highlight the manifold socio-political dimensions that operate to create the marginalized in the cultural context. The hypothesis here is that such marginalization based on discriminatory evaluation of cultural practices provides the foundation for reinventing traditions. The Boro food culture is a case in example that will allow one to understand this process. Having grown up witnessing the everyday social interactions between the Boro and the non-tribal, it becomes easier to articulate the social discrimination that emanated due to food habit. On the contrary, experiencing the method of food production in a Boro familial space helps one to resonate with the sentiment associated with food by the community as well as to understand the way Boro society is structured. The traditional Boro society is egalitarian in essence with no social hierarchy and this fact can be understood simply by looking inside the kitchen of a Boro family. For example, before adopting modern time dining tables practically everyone in the family, including the servants, used to eat together sitting around the open area within the kitchen on the floor-mat-like wooden stool called *khamplai* (pira in Assamese). Sharing food is the biggest example of social commitment and trust between the master and subordinates. However, from such traditional practices and sitting arrangements for meal, what comes across is the very patriarchal character of the society as all male members are first served by the female members who often eat after feeding the children, men and older members. Women of the house including the maids sit together in the second round for meals in the same fashion. Such practices though are no longer seen in urban homes, this tradition is continued in the villages with some modifications. The changing material life of the urban Boro has affected the social values too, particularly giving birth to class consciousness which maybe also understood in the context of the urban and rural divide in contemporary time.

For a long time, the Boro people faced social and cultural discrimination on the basis of their food habit, which is interestingly closely connected with their everyday lifestyle. One of the reasons for such discrimination had been the Hindu notion of purity that consider certain food items as pollutant and inappropriate for human consumption. In traditional Boro society, pig rearing has been one of the most important economic activities precisely because of its market value as a favoured food. *Oma bedor* (pork) or Gahori in Assamese was considered a taboo by Hindu caste society till a very recent time. Therefore, activities like pig and silkworm rearing along with various traditional methods of food production was seen as uncivilized practices.[1] Silkworm larvae is a rich source of nutrients and a Boro delicacy, and rearing of it served both economic and cultural purposes.[2] Prior to the strong influence coming from various Hindu sects, perhaps vegetarianism was unknown to the Boro people. The external influence brought in by Gurudev Kalicharan Brahma in early 20th century by introducing Brahma Dharma has great socio-political significance and the time coincided with the historical movements Assam witnessed as a response to the anti-colonial movement across India. Gurudev Kalicharan was born in 1860 and in early 20th century, he was deeply influenced by the teachings of Swami Shivanand Paramhans of Calcutta where he had an opportunity to meet the later. A large number of Boro people by this time had already converted to neo-Vaishnavism who came to be known as *sarania* (to take *sharan* or shelter). This period also saw the rise of few individuals who managed to get higher education and become aware of their socio-political standing in the larger Assamese society. It is perhaps through these individuals that Boro society was exposed to the prejudicial view that the non-tribal Assamese and Bengali society held towards the Boro people.[3] Many educated Boros tried to assimilate into the larger Assamese society in order to avoid the social and cultural discrimination by consciously giving up Boro cultural traits and lifeways, eventually following the path of the saranias. This included changing food habits, giving up speaking in Boro language, wearing the Boro traditional attire (mostly by women) and traditional practices among other things. This had alarmed Gurudev Kalicharan who feared extinction of Boro identity as a distinct cultural people. Inspired by the teachings of Swami, he began to preach Brahma Dharma among the Boro people living in the villages and committed to devote his life for the upliftment of his people. He served as a social reformer taking a leadership role to guide the Boro society against social and cultural discrimination (Basumatary 2017). As a reformer he advocated education for all children and doing away with traditional practices which brought ill reputation to the community, mainly brewing/drinking alcohol and pig rearing. Adopting Brahma Dharma though did not necessarily mean giving up Boro identity, this brought the Boro closer to the Hindu tradition of the non-tribal Assamese society, which played a very crucial role in shaping the religious identity of the Boro people. Today, the non-convert Boro people consider themselves to be the followers of Hindu religion, especially the ones who perform *jagya* and are followers of Brahma Dharma, but this is a topic far more complicated than understood and require deeper engagement with *Bathou*, the traditional belief system of the Boro people, which is understood by its practitioners as the core of their cultural existence. But despite the concept of vegetarianism entering the Boro kitchen, the association of it with the notion of purity is limited to those who have consciously assimilated to the larger society. For the majority of the Boro population, the idea of vegetarianism is more to do with restraining oneself for religious, spiritual and medical reasons by opting to eat vegetarian food only on certain days of the week.

Materiality of Boro food is not limited to ingredients and raw materials used in cooking which lend a distinct taste, colour and texture to the food. It also incorporates materials obtained through processes like fermentation, smoking, drying and roasting to arrive at the desired taste and for preservation of food. In addition, tangible aspects include material objects like utensils, storage containers, baskets, pounder, and other wooden and bamboo items that are related to and used in food production. Such objects have in due course of time become representative of the Boro people as a cultural group and can be called community 'artefacts'. Though some of these objects bear similarities to the ones used by other indigenous communities, what makes them distinctively Boro is the way they are used. The important aspect is not about what Boro food is but what makes a food Boro as said by the well-known cultural historian of Philippines, Doreen Fernandez, in describing Filipino food culture. Whether cultural imperatives shape material life or material surroundings contribute to cultural development is subject to scrutinizing as well as interpreting the multidimensional aspects of a cultural community. The material objects have a purpose which is not limited to the end use of it but extends to producing a whole range of experiences associated with the use of it in a given time and space. These experiences are not purely individual and private but linked to one's sense of belonging to a shared culture so important for articulating identity.

Material Objects and Food

In Boro food culture, certain material objects are necessities and have become integral to the community identity. Most notably, the use of bamboo in everyday life around food is often overlooked as insignificant. Here, bamboo may simply be seen as a medium of creating something unique to the culture in discussion, but their irreplaceability is what makes the difference. The opening line of this paper, 'Hokhangafa, Khobaifa', is an example of cultural nuances associated with the food habit of the Boro people. These two words do not mention about fish but clearly are an expression of fishing activity. For performing this act most important objects that become tools are the jekhai and khobai, both made from bamboo and are representative of Boro culture. These are no extra-ordinary objects and are used by many communities in Assam for fishing mainly by women. But it is only among the Boro that a specific term and expression, *na gurnai*, is used to refer to fishing by women using these two objects, which makes it distinctly Boro culturally. Here, the term na gurnai can be seen as a cultural appropriation of the fishing activity. There are folk songs around this particular activity using jekhai and khobai, which become the symbolic representation of community identity. Though there are other bamboo-made objects for the purpose of fishing, jekhai and khobai occupy special place in the cultural imagination of the people, and na gurnai, the act of fishing, is romanticized as an idyllic lifeway of Boro women in the midst of lush green open nature wearing *dokhna*, the colourful traditional attire of Boro women (see Figures 13.1 and 13.2).

FIGURE 13.1 *Jekhai*

FIGURE 13.2 *Khobai*

Boro food culture cannot be imagined without some material objects, which are used for preparing, cooking, storing and for preserving food, and these items have been locally made using bamboo or wood. *Sandanga* is a common object made from bamboo and used for drying as well as smoking fish and pork. It is also often used for washing green leafy vegetables as it allows water to drain quickly through the sparsely woven bamboo knits. Sandanga can be found in all Boro households. Another object that is no longer in much use but has been very much a part of each and every household kitchenware is the humble *khadou*, a flat and plain bamboo stick used for steering boiling rice. *Khadou thunai* (khadou push) is a famous proverb among the Boros used to express the less time consumed while returning home after a wholesome meal at a relative's place living far away. Though khadou is a slowly disappearing object from the Boro kitchen, especially in urban homes where pressure cooker is an absolute essential, the proverb continues to remind the relevance of it in a cultural context as there is a tradition of occasionally visiting close and distant relatives living in different villages for which there is a term, *Alasi janai*. It is believed that the Assamese word, *Alohi khowa*, is derived literally from this Boro expression to describe 'going to eat lunch/dinner as a guest'. Khadou thunai is the term used to express the return from Alasi janai for which there is no equivalent term or expression in any other language perhaps.

The tradition of *bathwn* (kind of chutney) continues in every household because of the convenience provided by *thousi* (khundani/pounder) in preparing it. Thousi is not just an object for making bathwn but has reminiscence of an ideal and organized village life. The iron thousi creates a pounding sound like *think-tho tho,* which is audible in the quieter evening time to the neighbours and announces the preparation of dinner early in the evening, like a cue indicating the time, as dinner by sunset was the norm in earlier times when Boro people mostly lived in villages. Bathwn may be made of practically anything edible pound together with green chilli, salt, ginger and garlic. Traditionally, it was to be served with hot sticky rice before men left to the fields for the day's work. Though there is a change in people's lifestyle, no kitchen is complete without thousi despite the presence of modern amenities (see Figure 13.3). But unlike the thousi, *uwal-gaihen* for pounding paddy grain into rice is disappearing though rice is the

FIGURE 13.3   *Thousi for Pounding*

FIGURE 13.4   *Uwal-gaihen Seen on the Platform of a Traditional Granary, Made from Clay and Used for Storing Paddy*

Note: Uwal is the base, and gaihen is the pounder.

staple food of the community (see Figure 13.4). Every time I come across this pair of names, I am reminded of a famous folk song that the younger generation probably will not know any longer as the tradition of pounding rice using uwal-gaihen has become a rarity:

Dumbru kaosa ni uwaljwng
Sal sirini gaihenjwng
Bihari sanwijwng dum dum
Daam daam swolaibai
Honwi Alongmwnha...

In the song, the sound of paddy grain pounding by Along's two wives on uwal made from *dumbru* log and gaihen obtained from *sal* branch allows one to get a glimpse of traditional Boro society and family. The importance of uwal-gaihen in a typical Boro family is communicated through this song while also informing about the practice of polygamy as an accepted social norm. Though uwal-gaihen is not generally linked with the food tradition of the Boro, it is simply not possible to imagine the role it plays in the preparation of some food items apart from pounding to de-husk paddy grain. Ondla, a distinct Boro curry, made from rice flour or *sobai* (black lentil, which is first roasted and then pounded before cooking into a curry), or the making of rice cakes like *pitha* and *sithau* during harvest festival cannot be imagined without the use of uwal-gaihen. Along with uwal-gaihen comes the *songrai-sandri*, also called *dala* in Assamese language (songrai helps to air-clean grain from husks, dusts or tiny pebbles) and *saloni* (for sandri is a circular-shaped strainer made from bamboo) to complete the act of pounding. The acts associated with these objects too have unique terms of expression, *jaonai* and *salinai*, respectively. But these are multipurpose objects and used in the kitchen for washing vegetables and drying fish; likewise the *kherkha* is a deep strainer like circular utensil made of aluminium or bell metal (Kax in Assamese), which is used for washing and rinsing rice.

The most favoured cultural beverage among the Boro is a rice brew called *jou*. Jou is an integral part of Boro identity, but the Hindu society in Assam saw this cultural tradition of brewing and drinking as unproductive, as a sign of backwardness. It is used not merely for recreation purpose but has a spiritual significance and considered essential for religious and social rituals. Brewing is one aspect of Boro culture that requires expertise. Traditionally, an earthen pot called *thinkli* or aluminium pot called *dw* (dekchi) have been used for brewing, and a bamboo strainer called *jantha* and bamboo spoon called *laothai*[4] are used for scooping rice beer out of the pot. Laothai is also made of dry bottle gourd in some places. These objects are used primarily when making jou, the wet rice beer, popularly also called as *gishi* and *bidwi*, sweeter than the *jou gwran*, which is stronger and contains pure alcohol. The sticky rice of white and red varieties are the most favoured ingredients for making jou especially during festival times like Bwisagu (Boro new year in Baisakh). The rice is first cooked and this particular rice for brewing is called *jumai* (see Figure 13.5). The cooled down jumai is then mixed with the fermenting ingredient called *emao*, which is a concoction of several edible leaves and herbs prepared into a cake using rice dough (see Figure 13.6). Emao is the main ingredient that gives the alcoholic character to jumai. The emao-mixed jumai is kept to ferment for two to three days, which is called *jou dabka* (see Figures 13.7 and 13.8). Traditionally, jou is served from dabka thinkli (pitcher) during all social gatherings, including wedding, by one elderly person from the village who seem to guard the dabka, rarely leaving it alone.

When we talk of material objects in food culture, generally we focus more on pots, pans, spoons, bowls and so on. Among the Boro people, the use of earthen pots has been limited to pitchers and rarely have they been used for cooking purposes. Most commonly found in the Boro kitchens have been utensils made either of aluminium, iron or bell metal.

FIGURE 13.5 *Jumai (Broken Rice Cooked for Fermentation) Taken Out Using Khadou and Spread on Songrai for Cooling*

FIGURE 13.6 *Emao (the Fermenting Cake) Being Crushed Using Khadou*

FIGURE 13.7 *Emao-mixed Jumai Which Will Become* Dabka, *Stuffed into an Earthen Pitcher and Will Be Sealed for Fermentation for 2–3 Days At Least*

Thwrsi gubei (bell metal plates), *lotha gubei* (bell metal drinking vassel), *khurwi* gubei (bell metal bowls), khwrsli (serving spoon) and *gamla* (big bowl) are the basic kitchen items traditionally used along with *sarai* (iron wok, kadai) (Figure 13.11) and aluminium *dw* (pot/big saucepan) including *garha*, also called *dwihu* (ghara, pitcher) for storing water (see Figures 13.12 and 13.13). Though bell metal objects are used in some households, largely they are being replaced in contemporary times by steel because of the cost factor and easy maintenance required. Bell metal utensils have been the most favoured gifts during special occasions especially for wedding and the first meal ceremony called *wngkham dwounai* (annaprasan) for a child. Whether this tradition pre-existed the first rice eating ritual practiced by larger society in Assam is difficult to tell. It is believed that eating food from bell metal utensil, made from an alloy mix of copper and bronze, keeps a person healthy (see Figure 13.9). One of the most common utensils found in every household is the bell metal *bata*, a

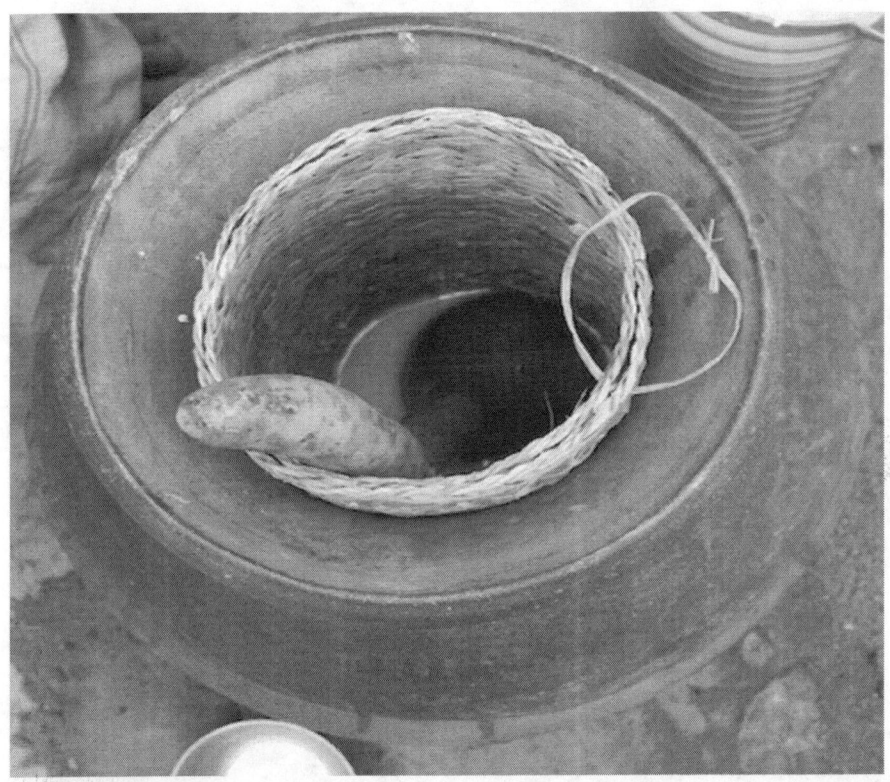

FIGURE 13.8 *Fermented Dabka Ready for Extracting Jou Using Jantha (Bamboo Strainer) and Laothai (Dry Bottle Guord/ Wooden Spoon)*

FIGURE 13.9 *Bell Metal Glasses and Bowls*

FIGURE 13.10 *Bata with a Serving Spoon*

FIGURE 13.11 *Sarai, Iron Wok, Found in Every Boro Kitchen*

serving plate with a stand (Figure 13.10). This is used by the Boro people to serve *goy-pathwi* (betel nut with paan and lime) to all visiting guests as a welcome gesture irrespective of the mealtime. Bata is also used for serving dry food items and accompaniments on special occasions, especially by other communities in Assam. The use of metal objects reflected social status in Boro society. These utensils carried rich economic value as family assets and at times were used even for mortgaging.

FIGURE 13.12 *Bell Metal Garha (Pitcher)*

FIGURE 13.13 *Aluminium Garha*

FIGURE 13.14 *This Is a Pair of Hatha, with Bent Handle for Female and the Straight Handle for Male*

One unique pair of objects slowly disappearing is the *hatha*, wooden saucepans made of gambhari log (Figure 13.14). The gambhari tree has a spiritual and social significance in Boro worldview since it meta-phorically represents of wisdom that comes with age and experience. Hathas are specially made for solemnizing marriage in traditional Boro style, which is called *hathasuni*. The traditional Boro marriage custom underwent a change due to the influence of Brahma dharma under Gurudev Kalicharan Brahma in the early 20th century. As opposed to the present time ritual of performing *ahuti* or jagya during marriage ceremony according to the Vedic tradition, in hathasuni marriage, there is no jagya but offerings made to the indigenous and formless almighty, *bathou bwrai*, who dwell in the bathou alter present in most households. It is understood that before the conversion to other religions, all Boro households maintained and worshipped the bathou altar, around which all important social and religious rituals were performed. In hathasuni marriage ritual, a pair of male and female fowls is sacrificed in front of the bathou altar by the *oja* (shaman or priest) and the same fowls are cooked using only a pinch of salt to signify purity and simplicity in harmony with nature. It is from these hathas that the sacrificed fowls meat is offered to the bathou bwrai along with jou and from the same hathas the guests are served. There is an effort nowadays to revive this tradition of marriage, which is much simpler and economical. This, of course, has its own complications located in the larger socio-political framework in present Boro society.

Raw Materials for Boro Cuisine

What makes a food distinctively Boro is completely dependent on the ingredients and raw materials used in addition to the method of cooking. As mentioned earlier, vegetarianism among the Boros is a recent concept that spread as a result of influence coming from external factors, primarily associated with religion conversion. Though majority of the Boro people practice and follow bathou worship, the traditional belief system involving animal sacrifices as well as performance of jagya (ahuti, offerings made to fire) in accordance with Bhrahma Dharma practices are also prevalent. Further, there have been converts to Christianity and many have become followers of Sai Baba, Joyguru (followers of Anukul), Krishnaguru, Vaishnavism, including smaller sub-sects of indigenous faith. The conversion to more established religious sects may be seen among the upwardly mobile Boro middle class trying to dissociate themselves from the more primitive-style bathou worship in an effort to assimilate with the larger Assamese society. With the conversion, some of them consciously turned to complete or partial vegetarianism. Generally, it is difficult for Boro people to imagine food without fish or meat and dairy products were never a part of Boro food until the concept of vegetarianism entered. Even though many kept cattle it was for agricultural purpose of ploughing, manure and selling the milk in the market. Rarely did any household engage in making milk products like curd, ghee (clarified butter) or paneer (cottage cheese) consumed primarily in other parts of the country. One reason why the Boro people consider themselves to be closer or even followers of Hindu religion is because beef eating is tabooed among the Boro though buffalo meat is very much a part of traditional Boro food. There is no other explanation to abstaining from beef eating by the community. But being primarily non-vegetarian does not mean that people ate meat or fish every day. The vegetarian food items had never been seen as 'vegetarian' food per se, rather it meant non-availability, lack of resource or inability to procure non-vegetarian food. Under such circumstances people simply relied on their backyard to collect varieties of green herbs and edible plants for the day's meals.

Raw materials in Boro food are primarily of two types—seasonal and all time—of which seasonal type dominates in terms of popularity. While most winter vegetables, called *Mesengni Mwigong*, are grown in the backyard, spring and summer ones come from backyard garden as well as the mountains and forests. Boro people love leafy green vegetables and the most popular leafy vegetables are *lai, lafa, mwitha, deosrem, pathw* and *besor bilai* to name a few, which are grown domestically. The wild favourites during spring are *sibru* (kind of asparagus but with tiny thorns) found in plains and foothills, *olodor* (a variety of yam plant) stem generally found in tropical hills during spring, *kheradapini* which is a dark green leafy grass type shrub found around marshy paddy fields and *ajnai bibar*, the light mauve-coloured flower of a plant called ajnai that grows in marshy plains available all through the summer. These vegetables and edible plants are generally prepared either with meat or fish, pork being the all-time favourite combination. One ingredient, which is obtained from *pathw* (jute leaves) through drying process is *narzi*, which is rich as a medicinal nutrient. Narzi is an all-time favourite, especially among the adults because it is bitter in taste but goes extremely well with pork. It is recommended for diabetics and believed to be full of nutrients, also working as a great medicine for deworming. The jute leaves are collected after the felling of trees and dried for days till they become so crispy that when crushed one gets a pale green powder like *kasuri methi*, but when cooked, the colour turns darker. As a preserved food item, it can be eaten any time of the year and there are different methods of preparing narzi.

An interesting part of Boro culture related to seasonal food is called *gwkha-gwkhwi janai*, literally meaning eating bitter-sour food. It is a tradition to mark the year end before welcoming the vernacular new year, Baisakh, by performing certain rituals that involve gathering of edible plants of 13 kinds including the sour and bitter ones from the neighbouring forests and mountains (see Figure 13.15). This activity, which generally is observed on 14 April every year, is very community oriented as members of one or two villages collectively venture out to gather the plants and leaves to perform the ritual of gwkha-gwkhwi janai just before celebrating the spring festival, Bwisagu (Bihu in Assamese). The most well-known and must-have ones are *kheradafini, sibru, lafasaikho, onthai bajab, mwisungkha*, to name a few. My own knowledge about many edible plants found in the forests and mountains come from such expeditions that I had accompanied during childhood times. It is the most ideal way of passing community knowledge to the younger generation. Unfortunately, with urbanizaton and changing lifestyle, this practice is gradually declining. Also, because of the pervasive commercialization most of these food items are sold in the markets. Interestingly, it is mostly the womenfolk who collect such food items from foothills and neighbouring forests to sell in the local markets where they fetch good price. This aspect of Boro society is thought provoking as a reflective of social dynamics where women play a crucial role in sustaining family economy as well as the cultural tradition. Majority of women engaged in such commercial activity

FIGURE 13.15 *Gwkha–Ghwkhwi Janai Tradition: Thirteen Perennial Vegetables Chosen on the Day before Bwisagu (First Day of Baisakh)*

do not have the required education to be absorbed in formal work sector and therefore, supplement family earning through use of their knowledge about food resources alongside other traditional skills.

While discussing sources of food other kinds of green vegetables found in backyard gardens must also be highlighted, including weeds like edible plants, which grow in abundance and do not require seasonal planting. Most Boro houses typically have open yards around their houses where even without much effort several kinds of edible plants grow, which are very local to the environment; one of the reasons perhaps, why Assamese people in general do not like to work very hard is because nature has been very kind to them, supplying all necessities of life in plenty. The term *mwidru-mwila* is used to refer to a mixture of varieties of edible plants collected from the surroundings but it also carries certain social meanings. Though Boro people are fond of mwidru-mwila in general, sociologically it can be linked to the economic condition of a family as it carries a subtle meaning of lacking in resources where mwidru-mwila connotes the last option when it comes to food choice based on availability of resources and has a tendency to influence the social image of the family as unproductive. Traditionally, Boro people did not consume several of the lentils generally used by non-tribal people in everyday meal. For example, *dal* or *dali* as it is called in Assam was considered a luxury item by many in the villages as certain types of cereals did not grow or were not cultivated in Assam and were brought from other parts of the country. Dal was considered expensive and, in their place, local types, mainly kesari dal and sobai (black lentil) became predominant, but not for daily meal.

The two most popular grain-based curries are sobai and *ondla* using home-made alkaline called *kharwi* (khar) for taste and colour. Both the items are generally cooked with fish and meat. While sobai is more like dal, ondla is made of rice flour and is a very typical Boro curry, traditionally favoured in large families due to its volume. Ondla is also prepared with certain kinds of herbs and flowers, most common being papaya flower. Generally slight bitter tasting edible flowers are used as combination with ondla and sometimes a handful of *nathur* (fresh or dry shrimp) is thrown in. Among the most favoured combinations are *meowai* (fresh bamboo-shoot), *oma gwran* (smoked pork), *dao* (chicken) and *shamo* (shallow water shelled muscles). Traditionally, it is prepared during all community occasions including marriage feasts and *wnkham gwrlwi janai* (first harvest feast or natun/nou bhat khowa). Wnkham gwrlwi janai is an important annual occasion among the Boros where the entire village folks are invited for the feast to celebrate the good harvest and is like thanksgiving to the community in appreciation of their support to the family in times of need. My memory of it is that of all the children of the village sitting in one row on the floor and eating from banana leaves amidst much merry making while elders enjoying the rice brew. Interestingly, the cooking expertise of a Boro girl is judged from her ability to prepare a smooth curry of ondla.

Food Preservation

Food preservation among the Boro is more for the taste than for the purpose of preservation per se. Fresh food is generally preferred but there are few items, which are processed for acquiring the desired taste and can be preserved for long as well. The materials and ingredients used for processing food items are easily available and the methods simple. The most common being dry fish, fermented fish, smoked pork and dry leaves which are also considered delicacies and consumed occasionally. Varieties of fish sourced from the neighbouring water bodies are dried for domestic consumption as well as for commercial sale in the local market primarily by women. *Na gwran* (dry fish) is an important ingredient of Boro cuisine as it gives a distinct flavour to the curry when used with particular type of vegetables. For example, *mwitha* (Meshta or Gongura), which is a sour leafy seasonal vegetable grown during the summer, tastes different when prepared with dry fish and is a typical Boro food. *Napham* (similar to Hidol) is fermented fish and can be preserved for long time. The saying is that only a real Boro can eat napham without difficulty because of the very strong smell. Napham is made of small fish generally that are dried then pound together in uwal-gaihen with yam stems. The mixture is then stuffed into a bamboo tube, the mouth sealed tightly using banana leaf and clay to make it air proof and kept to ferment. Use of bamboo tube is slowly disappearing as glass and plastic bottles have become available for preserving napham in airtight condition (Figure 13.16).

The idea of smoking and drying of meat is not always for preservation purpose but for acquiring the taste so popular in Bodo cuisine. Oma gwran (smoked/dry pork) is the all-time favourite meat of the Boro people (Figure 13.17). The best smoked pork comes from local home-reared pigs. Smoked pork is generally not sold in the market and processed at home just one or two days before use. Buffalo meat is dried and smoked for preservation in villages but it is rarely visible in urban areas.

Traditionally, beef eating among the Boro people is not heard of. Historically, whether it has any link to the practice of Hinduism is difficult to say though in present time there

FIGURE 13.16 *Napham in Bottle*

Source: The author.

FIGURE 13.17 *Pork Smoked on Bamboo Sandanga in the Sun for Duel Effect for Drying the Meat Using Fire and Sun*

is clear indication of not consuming beef due to religious reason. But buffalo sacrifice has been common among the followers of traditional belief system, bathou (see Figure 13.18). However, with the conversion to Christianity, it is assumed that beef is part of the festivities among Boro Christians.

Epilogue

Food is the most intimate aspect of a culture and associated with it are the many-layered human relationships with living and non-living things in the environment. Food is representative of a collective sentiment and individuals become agents for carrying forward the tradition. What is visible in the material culture of Boro food in present time is the consistency in the use of raw materials and ingredients but gradual disappearance of a whole range of objects and items associated with food culture due to external influences, especially in private kitchens. It is interestingly in the more community-oriented public spaces that the traditional artefacts linked with Boro food culture continue to get prominence and this may be linked with the existing socio-political dynamic in the state of Assam. This may also be read as a response to

| FIGURE 13.18 | Dry Buffalo Skin Preserved (It Is Generally Minced and Cooked with Black Lentil Sobai) |

Source: The author.

the conversion and assimilation question faced by the community. Contestation over certain cultural heritage is inadvertently leading to groups getting conscious and aware of the need to preserve and promote tangible and intangible aspects of their culture, wherein material objects become symbols. Festivals are organized to reinvent traditions with an objective to make statements and to reclaim the 'legitimate' place in larger society. The recent development is the efforts being made by various sections of the larger Assamese society, particularly the Assamese speaking, to appropriate certain cultural traditions of the Boro and other tribal communities in order to legitimize their indigeneity. As a result, eating pork is no longer seen as impure or a taboo. Claims and counter claims to indigenous food culture have seen mushrooming of eating joints and restaurants named as *Tribal kitchen* and *Boro kitchen*, inadvertently helping the food culture of the Boro people to get recognition. However, such efforts may bring in the crucial question of what is claimed as patent as well as seen in the case of other aspects of indigenous traditions and knowledge.

Notes

1. This is connected with the desire to bring about a change in the status quo by few educated Boro individuals, particularly Guruduv Kalicharan Brahma who was the founder and preacher of Brahma Dharma among the Boro in early 20th century. To be accepted by the larger society he initiated early social reform activities including change in lifestyle by giving up pig rearing and brewing.
2. Endi (silkworm) rearing traditionally was practised in every household for procuring the endi silk for which Boro women have been well recognized and weaving has been one of the most visible cultural acts among Boro women.
3. The coming of Bengali clerical staff and officials to work for the colonial administration transformed the social and cultural landscape of Assam. This introduced the tribal population of Assam to the nuances of cultural discrimination.
4. Laothai is also used as a nickname by some people in villages, though it has no link with a person being a drunkard.

References

Basumatary, Kumud Ranjan. 2017. 'Gurudev Kalicharan Brahma: The Emergence of Bodo Ethnic Consciousness in the Early 20th Century'. *International Journal of Social Sciences and Humanities* 4 (2, March–April): 21–32.

Berthes, Roland. 2008. 'Toward a Psychology of Food and Contemporary Consumption'. In *Food and Culture*, edited by Carole Counihan and Penny Van Esterik. New York, NY: Routledge.

Kohn, Tamara. 2013. 'Stuffed Turkey and Pumpkin Pie: In, Through and Out of American Contexts'. *Cultural Studies Review* 19 (1, March).

Montanari, Massimo . 2004. *Food Is Culture*. Columbia University Press.

14

Food, Tradition and Politics among the Santals

Kanchan Mukhopadhyay

Introduction

> Immediately after our forefathers established this village there was a
> severe famine in the area. It was 1280 as per the Bengali calendar (cor-
> responding to 1786–1787 AD). The famine was caused by less rainfall
> and lasted for several years. There was no crop in the fields, even grass
> did not grow. Many residents of our village died; livestock perished.
> The survivors could not dispose of the dead, they were too weak from
> starvation. Another reason was the belief of those people that who will
> dispose of the dead would also die. Corpses decomposed in open, stink
> of starvation and death hung in the air for a long time. (Upendranath
> Saren, resident of Saraspur village, told the author in 1995.)

When Santal residents of Saraspur village were asked about history
of their village, they recollected memories of a series of famines the
community had experienced. Tales about how the people survived
through periods of acute scarcity of food and had to depend on wild
resources for survival are part of their collective memory.

When a group of people remember their past largely in terms
of availability or scarcity of food and where that food was sourced
from, food becomes an important component of their 'tradition' and

'identity'. Association between food and intra-as well as inter-community relationship is often reflected in local and regional political nexus—food practices are used as symbols and used to compete for power.

Food-culture of the Santals remained closely linked with their physical environment as well as the social-cultural milieu. While asserting their identity in a pluri-cultural situation where they mostly remained dominated by others, socially and economically, people often picked up cultural markers that conformed to dominant socio-cultural ethos. Sometimes they picked up such markers that highlighted their distinctiveness from others, especially the dominant ones, and in this way they articulated their disagreement with the hegemony to which they were subjected. A noteworthy part of both kinds of exercise had been the selective presentation of their food practices to others. In order to conform to the foodways of the dominant sections of the local society, they even abstained from what their community had been eating for long. To challenge the hegemony on the other hands, the Santals decided to eat such food that are tabooed for the dominant communities.

A 'tradition' may encompass multiple ideas that can be opposed to each other. It becomes further complicated when those ideas are politicized to derive economic and other advantages in a pluri-cultural situation. This chapter has examined how food and beverage traditions have been used by the Santals to advance their social and political rank. The history of politicization of cultural practices by the Santals is a little less than a century old. Though the events discussed here started in the 1930s, the ripples reached the studied location of the south-western part of Bankura District in West Bengal, India, much later. Study of that location offered a chance to examine the relation between politicization of traditional lifeways and the role of an emerging group of neo-elites among Santals inhabiting this rural area. Further, the ways by which politicization process has influenced common people's views about traditions, especially those related to their collective identity, has also been explored.

Politicizing Tradition

A number of factors influence food practices of a group of people. Availability is a significant factor, but people do not eat everything available to them. Unless they face severe scarcity of food, distinction is made between what is suitable for eating and what is not. Deciding appropriateness of food can be a multifactorial and elaborate process. When resources are abundant and the people have freedom to decide, their choice of food would often be influenced by certain 'traditional ways'.

Tradition has been described as 'the passing on of customs and beliefs from generation to generation' and as 'long-established custom or belief passed in this way' (Soanes, Spooner, and Hawker 2001). In the above description, temporal dimension of tradition and processes of its transmission have been emphasized. Hobsbawm and Ranger (1983) have shown many cultural practices recognized as tradition are not as old as they were thought to be, those have been invented or constructed rather recently with some implicit purpose. Such a view challenged non-critical imagination of antiquity in many traditions. Pelikan, on the other hand, was opposed to pulling down 'traditions' indiscriminately because humanities, especially anthropology, have shown how tradition plays both positive and negative roles in making people what they are (Pelikan 1984). Whether old or of recent origin, a tradition cannot simply be described as a bundle of beliefs and practices experienced at a given point of time. It can also be assumed that when a tradition is constructed, the vehicles of its transmission are also designed.

Sources of new ideas that have been accepted and internalized by a society can be exogenous (Hobsbawm and Ranger 1983). Whatever be the source, in a plural situation a tradition can have far-reaching consequences; it can create a new identity or conversely can help people to get assimilated into a pre-existing identity. Consequently, it can redefine and restructure relations, especially power relation between different sections of society. The abstract ideas and imaginations contained in a tradition cannot be effectively communicated unless those are translated into symbols representing the thoughts. Symbols encompass 'public, communicable meanings which are derived from a society's culture and tradition and are shaped by the degree of unity and differentiation present in the society' (Rothman 1981, 286).

While discussing the significance of symbolism in everyday politics, Edelman emphasized on how and why the 'elites' and the 'mass public' perceive symbols differently. For the 'mass public',

> politics is a spectacle in which they ritualistically seek symbolic reassurance that they live in a meaningful world. But for the 'elites' ... politics is merely an instrument for manipulating the objective world to win certain tangible benefits—money and power .... The utilitarian politics of the few is a rational calculation of material interests. The mythical politics of the many is an irrational evocation of abstract ideas. (Edelman [1964] 1985)

It can therefore be argued, if a society is divided into unequal sections on the basis of social status, wealth, knowledge or skill, there would be multiple and dissimilar views about its tradition, symbolic representation and political manipulation.

Perceptions of commoners and of the elites about the significance of tradition in public life can sometimes be opposed to each other yet linked through overriding structural arrangements. Similarly, traditions and symbols used by nations and at a much smaller scale by village communities may look different though those would possibly follow the same organizational principles.

Tradition and Food

Food-centric cultural practices occupy significant place in political discourses on India and rest of South Asia. Food, especially those which are perceived as traditional, not only are closely related to identity of many communities, but are considered to represent ideas and emotions of the people and eventually gain political significance.

Politicization of food practices in South Asia has a long history—many political battles have been fought over beef, pork and other kinds of meat; many violent clashes have taken place between communities over appropriateness of food. A sarcastic narrative on post-independence India describes a violent clash between people from one part of an imaginary province and those from another part. Ethnic identity was the rallying point in their fight for larger share of political power. A family fleeing from an alien part of the province hiding their identity were intercepted and lynched because a jar of pickle gave away their identity (Rao 1987).

At the micro-level too, domination of one section of local society over another is often manifested through food practices. The way the dominated ones accept their subservient position or sometimes resist the hegemony contributes significantly towards understanding local social dynamics. Srinivas noted that sharing drinking cups at a toddy shop in Rampura village indicated social ranking in the late 1940s. In spite of their claim for higher social status, the community of smith had to drink from cups that were earmarked for the 'Harijan, Swineherd, and Muslim' because the smiths are a left-hand caste (Srinivas 1976, 172).[1]

Even in areas where Santals have a large population, socially and politically powerful non-Santals have often tried to influence Santal lifeways. In the face of hegemony of those of the 'others', Santals could be seen to conserve and at times restore their exclusive identity and reinstate social cohesion that was perceived to be impeded.

When those 'others' were establishing domination over the Santals and the community was either adjusting to or resisting the domination, the role of certain cultural practices including those related to food remained crucial. It may be noted that food was neither exclusive nor the principal issue while adjusting to or in resisting hegemony, it always was part of a larger assemblage. The following discussion on the use of traditional cultural practices by the Santals to achieve political ends has treated food accordingly.

Conversing with Self

Santal lore narrates mass migration of the community at different points of time. A people that was largely dependent on hunting, food gathering and shifting cultivation in the past rarely stayed at one place for long. Whenever they felt a settlement had too large a population to sustain, some of them used to move out and settle at a new location. They also used to leave a place whenever subjected to the whims of non-Santal elites, especially when the rule of community endogamy was threatened (Mallik 1993, 26). Though the Santals took up intensive plough cultivation rather late, they learnt the skills thoroughly and rapidly. After the enactment of the Permanent Settlement in late 18th century, zamindars often engaged Santal peasants to reclaim and cultivate forestland. As soon as such land became productive, zamindars used to impose tax on Santal tillers. The idea of paying tax and the crooked ways of tax collection often compelled the Santals to leave the land they had reclaimed.

The Santals divide their non-Santal neighbours into two groups; some are 'friendly' while others are 'hostile' (Gautam 1977, 37; Sachchidananda 2001, 162–175). Artisan groups like *tantubay* (weaver), *karmakar* (blacksmith) and *kumbhakar* (potter), cultivators and wage-workers like bagdi and bauri are included in the friendly category. The Santals often participate in festivals of their friendly neighbours and maintain economic relation with some of them. The higher-caste Hindus, who often were zamindars and mahajans and still own large tracts of superior quality agricultural land, are detested for their exploitative and coercive treatment of the Santals. The latter group of people are referred to as *diku* [2]; they used to treat the Santals as well as Bagdi, Bauri and several other groups of people of the area as *chhoto jat* or lowly folks. Exploitative treatment meted out by zamindars and moneylender mahajans compelled the Santals to stand up in rebellion several times in the 19th century, those rebellious activities always targeted the diku and the state, as the latter was the protector of the dikus.

The *hul* or rebellion of 1855–1856 AD surpassed all previous ones in scale and intensity when the Santals took up arms against zamindars, moneylenders and armed forces protecting the zamindars and money-lenders. Local police forces failed to stop the rebels and the British army was called to fight the scantily armed people. Atrocities committed by the colonial armed forces made some British army officers feel ashamed (Abdullah 1964). Many friendly peasant and artisan communities joined hands with Santal rebels.

Though the Santals are an oppressed people who repeatedly tried to protect their material and ideological possessions with whatever military force they could muster, they never compromised with their tradition of music and dance. Santals have a rich heritage of folklore describing both joyous and gloomy times of the past. The people spend long hours singing, dancing, playing instruments and narrating lore. *Raska* is the Santali word for pleasure, it is an essential part of life for them.

Simultaneous presence of their rebellious and pleasure-loving nature may appear contradictory, but those have been found to be intensely interconnected. Culshaw (1949, 39) noted that raska helps the Santals to escape from difficulties and sorrows by providing some comfort. Orans (1965) showed how element of pleasure helps to promote Santal social cohesion. While discussing the personality structure of the Santals, Mahapatra (1986, 35) identified 'pleasure-principle' as a driving force in Santal life. He argued, on some occasions pleasure can be equated with happiness and at other times with the absence of pain.

When they offered armed resistance to the oppressors, they did so to shield them from disintegrating forces. When they gathered in village square to sing and dance after a day's work, they asserted the integration that they had. In either case, the people did not attempt to convey their ideas of social solidarity or of any political aspiration to others.

Communicating with Others

Adivasi or indigenous communities of Chhotanagpur region, including the Santals, initiated a movement for political autonomy in the 1930s. Principal demand of the movement was creation of a new state called Jharkhand in a region where Adivasi groups were present in large numbers. They adopted a 'political rank path' for the purpose; it was designed to communicate their desire to others. On one hand, they had to build solidarity among different Adivasi communities, on the other the non-Adivasis had to be told about their political aspirations. During this period a movement for resurgence of indigenous socio-cultural elements was initiated; the movement challenged and eventually reversed the earlier trend of cultural transformation largely based on acculturation and assimilation (Orans 1965, 93).

Different Adivasi groups of the region could aspire for greater partici-pation in the then prevalent political structure for multiple reasons. By the 1930s, certain reforms in the system of governance in the country revealed what advantages a people can extract if they judiciously use their numerical strength. Moreover, by this time, a group of neo-elites emerged in those Adivasi groups who were educated in western systems and were politically articulate.

Elites have been defined as persons who influence the course of poli-tics with the help of their strategic position and resources controlled by them, while neo-elites are those who transcend the national level of politics to act globally (Pakulski 2012, 10, 17). While using those terms in the Santal context, the concepts need to be scaled down sub-stantially. In a conventional sense, Santal elites in a village society are members of the village council, who neither had much authoritarian power nor plenty of resources at their disposal. A village council is headed by *majhi hadam*; he is also the successor of the principal founder of the village. His deputy is known as the *paranik*. *Naeke* is the spiritual head of the village, he acts as the village priest. His deputy is known as the *kudam naeke*. *Jog-majhi* is the moral guardian of young boys; *godet* is the messenger. In addition, in some of the Santal villages there is a seventh position called *bhaddo*, designated for one senior male person of a wealthy Santal family. Possibly the position was created to have representation of the nouveau riche in the village council.

The Santal system of social control beyond the village level existed in the person of *parganait*, one who is knowledgeable in customary law and looks after affairs of several villages. The supreme council of the community is called *Lo Bir*; all councils beyond the village level have ceased to exist. Disputes concerning multiple villages are mitigated by the assembly of several majhi hadams. Traditional system of social con-trol is not effective when persons of other communities are involved.

Santal neo-elites were not entirely concerned with nuances of tradi-tional social control, they were trying to popularize the 'political rank path' to consolidate their own people and to articulate their political aspirations to a larger world. Position and status of the neo-elites were achieved on the basis of certain universal attributes like formal education and scholarship. This possibly was the first time that some Santals were articulating their views and aspirations in non-military language to other Adivasi and non-Adivasi communities.

The transition from hul in 19th century to Jharkhand movement in 20th century showed several phases of oscillation. When people realized that military options were closed to them, some of them opted for a ritual rank path. Through a popular movement known as Kharwar or Kherwar, they adopted several religious symbols from the Hindus in their effort to improve their rank. Kharwar is believed to be the ancient name of the Santals and is often connected with a period of political autonomy. The movement was launched in 1871 by Bhagirathi Majhi or Babaji; he claimed that economic and social impoverishment of the people was a divine punishment for the sins they have committed. By adopting monotheism and cleanliness, the independent status of Santals can be restored. There was a political dimension of the movement too. Babaji instructed the Santals to stop paying tax on the land they cultivated. Subsequently, the movement got engrossed in religiosity and adopted more Hindu elements in its body before splitting into three sects—Sapai or Safa, Samra and Babajiu (Das and Mitra 2013, 140).

While hul has been identified as contra-acculturative because it took the Santals away from Hindu influence, the Kharwar movement was targeted to cause more acculturation. However, the emulative character of the Kharwar movement could not qualitatively change the attitude of the Santals towards dikus, the latter were still loathed for 'their attitude of superiority and exploitation' (Panchbhai 1983, 31–33).

Till the 1960s and sometimes even later, a large number of Santals took part in Hindu festivals; they could be seen to dance and be possessed by Hindu deities. However, there was never any mass conversion to Hinduism (Orans 1965, 88–89). The Jharkhand movement altered the process of acculturation by opposing the process with ideas and activities. However, during that movement, it was the most acculturated members of the community who opposed acculturation vehemently while the least acculturated people in most remote villages offered very little resistance to the ongoing process of acculturation (Orans 1965, 97).

Neo-elites in the community tried to identify an alternate set of ideas which would help them to move away effectively from Hindu influences. Orans observed a conscious effort to create a 'great' tradition which was preceded by 'rank concession syndrome' or acceptance of social inferiority by the subservient community. He also talked of 'power incorporative borrowing', the belief that the more powerful society possess traits that instil special efficacy, hence it is worth emulating them. The dominant section of the society, the powerful dikus, brought 'external pressure' on the Adivasi groups so that they fall in line. Possibly, the oldest and most continuous of such pressures on the Santals had been governmental interference with their custom of cow sacrifice and beef eating (Orans 1965, 97).

While community endogamy and raska helped maintaining intra-community solidarity among Santals, common cultural practices of different Mundari tribes were highlighted to create an inter-community solidarity. Those practices included sacrifice of the cow, consumption of beef, speaking their own languages and worshipping their specific deities. A Santal political leader asked his community to stick to their own religion and worship deities at the sacred grove. In other words, they were asked not to convert into any other religion. The community should also continue to consume *handia* or rice beer and beef. Once these practices are stopped, the Santal identity will be gone, said the leader (Orans 1965, 205).

To prevent the community from conforming with views and practices of the dominant, leaders of the resurgence movement picked up such identity markers that would accentuate distinctiveness of the Santals in contrast to the dikus. Added to that was their emphasis on the use of Santal language at all levels of formal education and use of a script called Ol Chiki; the script was invented in the early 1940s by Santal scholar Raghunath Murmu. Till that time, Santali was written in Roman or Devnagri in Bihar and Bengali in Bengal. Soon the new script became the symbol of distinction for Santal elites. Initially, interest about the script remained largely confined to Santal neo-elites, the issue gained popularity and political significance in later years. In 2011, Government of West Bengal declared that Santali language would be recognized as a medium of instruction at school level and books would be printed in Ol Chiki. Several years later, some Santal organizations complained that the state government has failed to fulfil its promises and asked members of the community to agitate against the government. It was noticed that the rural Santal masses participated in the programme in large numbers (*Anandabazar Patrika*, 23 September 2018).

The issue of religion was operational at a different level altogether. While Charulal Mukherjea highlighted trends of assimilation of Hindu traits in Santal religious tradition, Dutta-Majumder noted resilience of the Santals and their efforts towards formation of exclusive identity (Dutta Majumdar 1956, 62, 114, 127; Mukherjea 1962, 379–381). Kochar emphasized a high degree of self-awareness among the Santals; he observed, when some Santals adopt a different religion, they lose societal status and cause displeasure among others. Both Hinduized and Christianized Santals are considered socially inferior and are rebuked openly (Kochar 1970, 32).

Saraspur: A Village

This author has studied the village located in south-western part of Bankura District of the state of West Bengal in India in several phases since 1995. The area where Saraspur is located was described as 'liable to famine' in early 20th century. There the people were largely dependent on cultivation of different varieties of paddy, many of those require large amounts of water. However, no facility of artificial irrigation was available to them excepting a few *baandh* or check-dams to hold monsoon water (O'Malley 1908, 106). Geographical conditions like undulating terrain and porous soil were found to be responsible for little moisture content in earth and for frequent crop failure in the area (Banerjee 1968, 265). This part of Bankura District experienced repeated famine situation and worst sufferers were the landless Bauri labourers, the poor Santals and Samantas (O'Malley 1908, 107).

Those days the Santals used to cultivate quick-growing varieties of paddy that could grow without much moisture. They also cultivated *musna* (linseed), *eeri* or *shyama* grass, *gundlu*, *janra* (Indian corn), *bajra* (pearl millet), *jaanhe* (kodo millet), *kode* (finger millet or *ragi*), legumes like *ghangra* (cowpea), *birhi* (black gram), *malhan* (flat bean), *rahir* (red gram) and *harech* (horse gram).

In the given situation, they did not depend on any single crop but cultivated several varieties and types. The diversity allowed higher cumulative yield and better opportunity to cope with the failure of one or two crops in a given year. Even then they had to consume the produced food with care as those were almost always insufficient for their requirement. They rarely ate grains directly during periods of acute scarcity—cloth-sachet of cereals were dipped in boiling water and the broth was consumed; the sachet was kept aside for future use. Livestock could rarely be killed for meat.

The Santals made extensive use of numerous non-cultivated items of food since long. Fruits, tubers, roots and leaves of different wild plants as well as *genri-gugli* (snail, periwinkle) and *chhatu* (mushroom) were collected. They fished and hunted varieties of birds and animals. All those gathered and hunted items are integral part of the Santal culinary tradition.

Since early 19th century several bandhs were erected in the area to catch runoff precipitation; such arrangement helped to irrigate a small part of agricultural land under their possession. With that limited rise in the yield of paddy, sometime in mid-19th century rice became the staple for Santals of this area. Other than those sporadic check-dams determined by geo-morphological conditions, no large-scale irrigation work was undertaken before the 1970s.

The suffering of the Santals from scarcity of food compounded further due to sharp inequality in the local social order; they have long been treated as chhoto jat or lowly people. Though the Santals are not placed in the Hindu caste hierarchy, they are nevertheless treated at par with the lowly placed caste groups by their high-caste Hindu neighbours. This is reflected in the general pattern of acceptance and non-acceptance of food and other spheres of social interaction where such notions of hierarchy are reflected.

In matters of food, the Santals were treated as untouchable by dikus; eating with the Santals was out of question; a diku would not even buy food from a shop run by Santals. People of Saraspur narrated experiences of a Santal youth who established a shop at Khatra market. Nobody told him he cannot sell cooked food; he was evicted from the place by some diku persons on the pretext that he was encroaching government land. There were dozens of other shops standing on government land and nobody ever tried to evict them.

The Santals showed some dilemma in this matter. Unlike the Bagdi, Bauri and other caste groups who were accorded low rank, the Santals did not always agree to accept inferior status. They expressed their disagreement by refusing to accept cooked food from non-Santals. The idea of rejection of food was not of recent origin, it was reported in the 19th century (Dalton 1872). At the same time, many of them conformed to diku practices by not sharing food with them.[3]

Maintaining social distance by avoiding food sharing was not restricted to their transaction with dikus alone; at a Santal marriage in Saraspur in the 1990s, the hosts handed over raw food items to their mahato guests from the same village, the guests cooked the food for themselves.

A gender difference also could be noticed; while Santal men sometimes broke the rule and dined with others or ate cooked food at the employers' place when working as wage workers, generally the women abstained from eating such food.

It may also be noted that the above scheme of social hierarchy is almost concomitant with relative economic position of the social groups involved.

More about the Village

The economic situation discussed above changed in several villages located in the area, including Saraspur, when irrigation facilities were created by Kangsabati River Project in the early 1970s. With the availability of water round the year, the drought-prone area changed to a large extent. Higher soil moisture made cultivation of certain high-yielding crop seeds possible, which were hitherto unknown to the people. To grow such crops, new varieties of fertilizers and insecticides were introduced by government agencies. The people were exposed to elaborate technological know-how required for new methods of agriculture. Large tracts of mono-crop land became multi-crop, some cultivators could produce surplus food grain and vegetables for selling those in the market. The nearby township of Khatra metamorphosed into a bulk-market for agricultural produces. The town witnessed phenomenal growth in construction activities; new roads were laid; masonry houses constructed. Many stone quarries and rock crushing units were established. Those dependent on wage work could get jobs closer to home round the year; their seasonal migration to irrigated regions in the east in search of jobs decreased to a large extent.

To understand the influence of transformed agricultural practices on the residents of Saraspur, a rough sketch of the demographic and economic profile of the villagers has been presented in the following paragraphs.

Santals were more than half of the Saraspur population; there were several mahatos and a few Tantubay, Pramanik, and Bhumij households. Not many households of the village were exclusively dependent on agriculture for their livelihood; the size of agricultural land held by a household delimited or even determined their choice of occupation. Among the Santals, there were a couple of landless households while little less than half of them had less than 5 bigha[4] of cultivable land, one quarter households had more than five but less than ten bigha of land, one-tenth households had more than 10 but less than 20 bigha of land.

Irrigation, new varieties of seeds, fertilizers, and pesticides were not of much use for several Santal households; small landholding and expensive agricultural inputs made agriculture a not-so-viable option for them. Under the circumstances they were earning part of their livelihood from wage work. Irrigation of land resulted in marginal increase in yield of crops but better opportunity for wage work in and close to the village for such households. Those small producers did not grow crops commercially, but they had to sell out portions of the produce to earn cash. Wage work remained another major source of cash income. Cash was required to pay the grocer, buy clothing, and to purchase agricultural inputs like seeds and fertilizers.

An essential difference between the Santals and the Mahatos could be noticed. While the Santals were largely dependent on wage work for additional income over agriculture, Mahatos generally opted for trading activities for the same purpose. Aversion of the Santals towards trading activities was admitted by them; they found dealing with the 'cunning' diku traders a difficult task while working as a wage worker for an employer was easier.

Some Santal women of the village used to run small-scale trade in food crop; they were known as *bhachati*. The women collected paddy a household wanted to sell, parboiled and husked the same to sell it in form of *muri* or *chirey* at the local weekly markets. Though agriculture did not become predominantly a commercial activity in Saraspur post irrigation, the overall quantity of marketable food crop increased. The women bhachatis, with basket on head, were replaced by bicycle riding men with sacks of paddy or rice tied to their bikes. The job of husking paddy became mechanical; small power-driven husking machines replaced the wooden husking levers. The women, who once were self-appointed traders, were now engaged by the new breed of male bhachatis in the drudgery of soaking and parboiling paddy. The husked rice was not taken to weekly markets anymore; those were sold to bulk dealers at Khatra.

Social and economic stratification among the Santals have undergone certain changes in recent times. There was no social stratification in the community in the true sense, though some degree of gender inequality was present. Previously rights of inheritance and succession were denied to women, in recent times, their inheritance rights have been acknowledged to a large extent. In comparison, economic inequality was found to be sharper and more complex.

Earlier the Santals used to divide their own people into two divisions on the basis of accumulated wealth, *kishar* or wealthy and *rangech* or poor. Santals of Saraspur claimed that these days they have a third group, positioned between kishar and rangech and described as *madhyabitti*.

They admitted that there was no term in Santali for the middle-income group; hence, they use a term that possibly has been derived from the Bengali word *madhyabitta* or middle class. It is difficult to equate the middle-income Santal villagers with Bengali middle-class economically, socially or culturally. This categorization created by the villagers is indicative of their relative affluence among them of late. When asked to distribute the Santal households in those three categories—they identified one out of every ten households as kishar, about a quarter as rangech and the rest two-thirds as middle-income group. It may be noted that landholding was not the sole criterion considered for placing a household in a particular category, one of the two landless Santal households was placed in middle-income group because they had several wage-earning members (Mukhopadhyay 2013, 204).

Emergence of the middle-income group suggests that quite a few Santal villagers could become relatively affluent even when they had little land to cultivate, insufficient capital to invest in cultivation and were largely dependent on wage work. Not just higher yield from land, even availability of wage work closer to home allowed the people to spend more time in village. Those transitions helped the emergence of a group of neo-elites in the village, who have been discussed later in this chapter.

Food, Pleasure and Ideology

Recent transitions mentioned above were preceded by a series of trans-formations in the past when interplay of food, tradition and politics was evident. Santals were attracted towards and repelled from the religious beliefs and practices of their Hindu caste neighbours to varied degrees at different points of time. The acculturative Kharwar move-ment gained popularity immediately after the failed rebellion in 1855 and boosted further owing to the prolonged hardship caused by the dikus (Dutta Majumdar 1956, 114; Orans 1965, 205; Panchbhai 1983, 31–33). The process of repulsion and resistance can also be connected with certain material conditions that apparently took place in times of political stability and absence of extreme food scarcity.

In south-western Bankura, the Santals had Hindu caste groups as their neighbours since long and their religious beliefs had been sub-jected to Hindu influence. Kharwar movement was so influenced by Hindu religious ideas that Santal followers renamed their supreme god Thakur or Chando as Rama Chando. Shridharma, another religious movement, became popular in Bankura district and found a large follow-ing among Santal, Kora, Kharia, Lohar, Maghaiya Dom and Bauri. This puritan movement borrowed ideas from Gaudiya Vaishnava Bhakti cult, followers were asked to abstain from liquor, beef and pork (Banerjee 1968, 163). The period of popularity of Shridharma roughly corresponds with a time when the Santals and their non-diku neighbours were experiencing prolonged scarcity of food and occasional famines.

The trend started many years back. During a severe famine in 1874, the founder of the Kharwar movement told the Santals to purify themselves, as only then would god rescue them from distress. One way of doing so was not allowing the rice distributed by the government as famine relief to get contaminated by fowls and pigs (Das and Mitra 2013, 140). In this case, one category of food has been perceived as 'purer' than another category of food, which is the 'contaminator'.

Construction of several check-dams in the 19th century though increased crop production marginally, but failed to end food scarcity entirely; puritan movements under Hindu influence were going strong during that period. Several Santal houses of Saraspur built in those days had *tulsi mancha*—fixed holder of tulsi (basil) plant in their courtyard. Some brick-built houses had the Vaishnava chant 'Hare Rama Hare Krishna' engraved on plaster in Bengali script.

During the period of relative affluence in the 1990s, many tulsi manchas in Saraspur were lying empty, others had some flowering plants like marigold and portulaca planted. The engraved Vaishnava chants were often damaged and covered with moss. Though Santals, subscribing to the Kharwar movement and later to Shridharma in 19th and early 20th centuries, developed strong faith in Hindu deities, their devotion towards Hindu gods weakened. They were still attending Hindu fairs and festivals in large number, but such participation was more a source of raska than act of faith.

Christianity also had conspicuous influence on the worldview of Santals of this area. The programme for distancing Santals from Hindu beliefs and practices was initiated in the 1930s by a few Santal persons who were not Christians but attended schools run by Christian missionaries. Those persons and their associates went around the countryside and urged Santal villagers to strengthen traditional village councils and reduce the number of broken marriages. People were asked to abstain from drinking alcohol except on rituals and festivals. They were also asked to prohibit women from dancing at Hindu festivals. Such persuasions received partial attention, people continued to take part in Hindu festivities and drink alcohol as those were part of raska. For the same reason, puritanism preached by Christian missionaries was not well accepted by the Santals (Culshaw 1949, 167–168).

Changing Food Practices

One Santal political leader equated their indigenous religious practices, drinking rice beer and eating beef with the core of Santal identity (Orans 1965, 106). Different accounts have highlighted the significance of drinking handia or rice beer in Santal life. In Mayurbhanj District of Odisha, rice beer is considered to be the most important cultural trait and self-image of Santals (Mahapatra 1986, 40). The same phenomenon was observed at Kuapara village of Birbhum District, West Bengal, where it was served at rituals, social gatherings, festivals, informal visits, ceremonies and meetings, offered to the bongas or gods, and was paid to the village council as fine (Kochar 1970, 35–36). Villagers of Saraspur remembered that some influential diku persons used to visit them to taste good liquor. However, the guests were not supposed to accept cooked food from the Santals.

Santal neo-elites, faced a certain dilemma in identifying rice beer as an identity marker. In Odisha, it was noticed that excessive drinking ruined many Santal families (Mahapatra 1986, 40). In Bihar, reportedly, half of the annual consumption of rice by the Santals went into preparation of rice beer and addiction was rampant (Thakur 1989, 89). Raghunath Murmu, who provided the Santals with one of their major identity markers by inventing the Ol script, was considered a spiritual leader for the people. He had to tell the community to restrict drinking of handia to rituals and occasions only (Mahapatra 1986, 40).

In Santal households of Saraspur home-brewed beverages were prepared and consumed during rituals and festivities. Friendly non-Santals were also invited during Sohrae or other major festivals; drinking of handia was an integral part of the celebration. There were a few addicts among the Santals but that was not discussed in public, though it was not denied as well. In the assembly of men, the habitual drinkers were not deprived of a seat, but sometimes others made fun of them. This way of expressing social disapproval was used with some prudence; persons of same age or older to the person are supposed to cut jokes, the younger ones are expected to keep silent.

Though preparation and consumption of rice beer was never stopped among Santals of this area, under the impact of several reformist movements, consumption of beef was not common among them. Most senior persons of Saraspur said they have never eaten beef, nor have they seen their elders to do so. While most of the villagers refrained from eating beef, some of them used to consume carrion. In those days, when a bovine animal died, some Santal men carried the carcass to a desolate place away from the village. *Moochi* or hide-workers were informed, they de-skinned the carcass and took the hide away. The Santal men divided the meat among them, no extra share was given to the owner of the animal. At another village of the area, the rule was different. Villagers de-skinned the carcass themselves; the owner of the animal was given the skin and one-third of the meat. At both villages, the assembled men used to cook and eat the meat in the open, they could enter home next day after taking the purifying bath.

The situation has changed in the studied area since the late 1980s. In recent times, beef was being cooked in kitchen at some Santal house-holds. They argued, when beef is an edible item why should they treat it as unclean? Roughly one-third villagers of Saraspur were found to eat beef at home in 2010. Around that time Santals and reportedly some 'low-caste' Hindus used to buy beef at weekly markets. Till that time, Santals preferred to avoid buying beef butchered by Muslims, they slaughtered the animals themselves. For the purpose, they hit the animal on head with a blunt end of an axe; this method is called *kutaam*.

The situation has changed further, in 2019 beef entered more Santal kitchens and many Santals do not hesitate to buy beef from Muslim shops. Itinerant Muslim vendors can be seen to hawk beef in some Santal villages.

It may be noted that the situation found in West Bengal may not hold true in other states of the country. Even in the neighbouring state of Jharkhand where the indigenous socio-cultural movement took its shape, situations were observed to be quite different in recent times.[5]

Practices of food avoidance among Santals of West Bengal have also become weak. While all high-caste dikus do not accept food from Santals, Bauris and Bagdis, some high-caste and many middle-caste Hindu individuals have started to do so. On part of the Santals, the total refusal of cooked food from others is a matter of past; even Santal ladies were found to attend non-Santal marriages and eat food there.

Traditionalizing Politics

Some residents of Saraspur were critical about members of the Santal village council for different reasons, one strong argument against certain members was their lack of leadership quality. The village structure of Santal council was incomplete; there was no separate naeke, the majhi hadam was functioning as priest and had no paranik to assist him. The naeke of a village is supposed to be appointed through divine intervention and not by humans; in this village the convention was violated, and the position was succeeded in male line. It appeared that the villagers were not taking the council seriously and occasionally they defied instructions of the majhi hadam.

The traditional elites did little to increase their political influence beyond the village; they usually acted as the bridge between villagers and local leaders of national and regional political parties. Acquaintance with political leaders, especially those belonging to parties in power, can earn some admiration among co-villagers. It was noted that almost all traditional elites of Saraspur were aligned with 'mainstream' parties when some political groups were focused primarily on Adivasi issues.

The neo-elites could appropriate the role of opinion makers in the village by virtue of their relative economic solvency, education, salaried job and ability to articulate. They picked up identity markers once popularized by leaders of the 'native socio-cultural resurgence movement' in forms of language/script, religion and food/beverage. The pre-independence resurgence movement was partly re-enacted in the village in post-irrigation days, owing to the creation of limited economic prosperity.

Residents of Saraspur took interest in learning the Ol script for the first time in the 1990s when one person hailing from a kishar family and holding white-collar government job took initiative. A year-long course in Ol literacy was organized with the help of an organization called Adivasi Socio-Educational Cultural Association (ASECA).[6] At that time, Ol literacy was of little use to general villagers, the situation changed in later years when Santali language and Ol script were recognized by state and union governments. People realized that Ol literacy can help the Santal youth to pursue higher education and create employment opportunities. The movement for the recognition of language and script was not an abstract identity issue anymore, there were a series of popular agitations led primarily by Bharat Jakat Majhi Pargana Mahal, a political platform for the Santals.[7]

Hindu fairs and festivities continued to be part of raska for Santals, only a few of them adopted Hindu religious ways with devotion. Santal village council members could not convince their co-villagers to stay away from Hindu festivals. On the other hand, observance of village-level traditional Santal religious rites was discontinued in Saraspur for a while because some villagers were not happy with the performance of the majhi hadam, the traditional village chief. Such factionalism helped the neo-elites to make their position stronger.

Culshaw noted in the 1930s that very few Santal village chiefs knew the Santal story of genesis which they were supposed to learn and recite. The myth was disappearing and losing its significance, he observed (Culshaw 1949, 64). As part of the socio-cultural resurgence movement, a group of culture specialists called *gurus* emerged in the 1970s and 1980s. They were masters in Santal mythology who could recite the *binti* or narratives and explain the same. Those gurus were encouraged by the neo-elites; in fact, the gurus and naekes were included among the neo-elites.[8]

Shridharma and other reformist movements could not stop the Santals from consuming alcoholic beverages though slaughtering cow and eating beef was a different proposition. While many diku men expressed their taste for beverage brewed by Santals, they interfered with Santal practice of eating beef (Orans 1965, 97). Barring occasional eating of carrion, the Santals did not eat meat of slaughtered cow till the late 1980s. When efforts were made to popularize beef as a traditional food in the course of the Jharkhand movement, Santals of south-west Bankura did not respond positively. They probably were not aware of the resurgence movement at that time – food scarcity was continuing and Vaishnava influence on the people was strong.[9]

Conclusion

The preceding discussion shows that Santal residents of Saraspur village perceive traditionality of their food in multiple ways. Narratives about prolonged scarcity of food and repeated famine, which are part of their collective memory, have been transmitted across generations but remained primarily confined within the community. During socio-cultural resurgence movement initiated in the 1930s, traditionality in certain items of food was highlighted. In this case, the idea of traditionality was supposed to be shared both within and beyond community boundary.

In the first instance, construction and transmission of ideas of traditionality was largely spontaneous; almost nobody, including the village-level traditional elites, was much bothered about how the narratives would be remembered and transmitted. The process was not so impulsive for the group of nascent and politically articulate neo-elites; they picked up such socio-cultural elements that could further their political programme. Method of transmission ceased to be exclusively oral, a section of the neo-elites scripted the discourses and it began with Raghunath Murmu establishing the first Santali printing press in

Jamshedpur. In 1952, he published a Santali language magazine and in 1964 established ASECA to popularize the language and script. Through non-oral transmission of discourses, the neo-elites could reach out to newer audience; it helped to change their relationship with members of the community.

It is evident that the resurgence movement did not happen everywhere simultaneously. In south-west Bankura, where the studied village is located, as well as in the entire south-western part of West Bengal, it started roughly in and after the 1970s. This development can be equated with end of acute food scarcity and beginning of relative economic ease for cultivators with small landholding and wage workers. Such a situation helped the emergence of neo-elites in the area.

Revitalization of ASECA amply illustrates the developments during that period. The West Bengal chapter of the organization was revived post 1970, working towards popularizing Santali language and Ol script not only in the state, but at the national level too. Other organizations like Bharat Jakat Majhi Madoya, later renamed as Bharat Jakat Majhi Pargana Mahal, and Bharat Jakat Majhi Dhram Baisi were established during that period.

In the revitalized resurgence movement of south-west Bankura, very few words were spoken publicly by the neo-elites regarding food practices. It has been noticed that beef consumption among rural Santals has gone up in the last few decades, but that has happened without much ado. When Santals started accepting food from others ignoring their earlier practice of not doing so, neo-elites often remained silent. A probable reason of the silence was that the neo-elites wanted to get certain other communities, the Dalits and minorities, as their political allies. They did not want to send a wrong signal by encouraging members of their own community to treat all others as untouchable in matters of food.

That the same political phenomenon may be interpreted and manipulated by elites and masses quite differently (Edelman [1964] 1984) was evident among Santals of Saraspur and adjacent areas. The process of 'native socio-cultural resurgence' shows that the cultural markers used to assert 'Santalness' were initially picked up or constructed by the neo-elites; commoners did not always identify their own interests with those markers immediately.

Neo-elites, who had no locus-standi in traditional Santal society, were using 'traditional' symbols like language, religion and food to build community solidarity in non-traditional forms. Such a situation illustrates the presence of stratification within the community, and it also shows that internal divisions are glossed over when people rally behind 'traditional' cultural markers, especially when those are identified with their mundane interests.

Notes

1. I visited the village in 2015 and saw several villagers were drinking tea at a shop. On enquiry it was revealed that there were persons with different religious and caste background among them. The shopkeeper, however, was serving all of them tea in similar cups, thanks to the introduction of disposable plastic containers.
2. In recent times, the term diku is not always used to identify the 'undesirable' and 'exploitative' non-Santal persons; any non-Santal stranger can be described as diku. In such instances, however, diku is used as a term of reference and not as a term of address.
3. In my early days of fieldwork in Saraspur I tried hard not to behave as a typical diku who often looks down upon the Santals as inferiors. On their part, the villagers never treated me as a marketplace diku out to make fun of the 'lack of intelligence' and 'simplicity' of Santals. In spite of all my efforts not to appear a diku, I was never offered cooked food at any Santal household in that village. Whenever I asked them for food, which I shamelessly did when I worked for longer hours and felt hungry, they served me good quality chire and *gur* (molasses). Chire is an uncooked item that can be taken as substitute of cooked rice. Only once I was given some cooked food to eat, it was boiled egg.
4. One bigha is equal to 1.66 decimal or 67.43 m².
5. State government of Jharkhand banned cow slaughter in 2005 though several communities in the state, including the Santal, used to eat beef for long. The enactment was followed by several instances of aggressive cow-vigilantism and lynching of suspected beef traders in that state. A Santal theatre activist was arrested in May 2019 for a Facebook post defending right of his community to eat beef. Immediately after, several tribal communities stood in support of the activist and demanded their rights to be restored.
6. Pandit Raghunath Murmu established ASECA in 1964 to demand government recognition for Santali language and Ol script. The organization became almost non-functional within a few years, but it was revived later as a platform for a movement on inclusion of Santali in the official schedule of Indian languages and recognition of Ol as script of that language.
7. Bharat Jakat Majhi Madoya was established in 1970s as an apex organization of Santals across state boundaries. It had certain political agenda and often dealt with Adivasi issues that have political consequences. The organization was renamed later as Bharat Jakat Majhi Pargana Mahal that actively organized agitation over language and script issues between 2016 and 2018.

8. An organization called Bharat Jakat Majhi Dhram Baisi was established in 2000; it remained engaged in resurgence of certain cultural items, especially indigenous religion of the Santals. They ask people to follow that religion and train gurus and naekes in rendering spiritual and priestly services.
9. In 1995–1996, very few Santal villagers of Saraspur were even aware about hul, the Santal rebellion of 1855–56. When I came to know this, on one of my trips to the village I took with me a couple of books on the history of hul for the villagers.

References

Banerjee, Amiya Kumar, ed. 1968. *Gazetteer of India, West Bengal, Bankura*. Calcutta: State Editor, West Bengal District Gazetteers.
Culshaw, W. J. 1949. *Tribal Heritage: A Study of the Santals*, 39. London: Lutterwoth Press.
Das, N. K., and S. Mitra. 2013. 'Tribal Religion, Sectarian Movement and Religious Syncretism in Santal Society'. In *Syncretism in India: Multidisciplinary Approach*, edited by A. V. Arakeri, Kakali Chakrabarty, and Bibhu K. Mohanty, 112–175. Vol. 1. Kolkata: Anthropological Survey of India.
Dutta Majumder, N. 1956. *The Santal: A Study in Culture Change*. Calcutta: Manager of Publications, Government of India.
Edelman, Murray. (1964) 1985. *The Symbolic Uses of Politics*. Urbana: University of Illinois Press.
Gautam, M. K. 1977. *In Search of an Identity: A Case Study of the Santal of Northern India*, 37. The Hague: Leiden.
Hobsbawm, Eric, and Terence Ranger, eds. 1983. *The Invention of Tradition*. Cambridge: Cambridge University Press.
Jha, D. N. 2002. *The Myth of the Holy Cow*. London: Verso.
Kochar, Vijay. 1970. *Social Organisation among the Santal*. Calcutta: Editions India.
Mahapatra, S. 1986. *Modernization and Ritual: Identity and Change in Santal Society*, 35. Calcutta: Oxford University Press.
Mallik, S. K. 1993. *Transformation of Santal Society: Prelude to Jharkhand*. Calcutta: Minerva Associates (Publications).
Mukherjea, Charulal. 1962. *The Santals*. 2nd ed. Calcutta: A Mukherjee & Company Private Limited.
Mukhopadhyay, K. 2013. 'Culture-Contact and Emerging Middle Class among the Santals'. In *Exclusion, Discrimination and Stratification: Tribes in Contemporary India*, edited by N. K. Das, 198–207. Jaipur: Anthropological Survey of India and Rawat Publications.
O'Malley, L. S. S. 1908. *Bengal District Gazetteers: Bankura*. Calcutta: State Editor, West Bengal District Gazetteers, Education Department, Government of West Bengal.

Orans, Martin. 1965. *The Santal: A Tribe in Search of a Great Tradition*. Detroit, MI: Wayne State University Press.

Pakulski, Jan. 2012. 'Introduction: John Higley's Work on Elite Foundations of Social Theory and Politics'. *Historical Social Research*, 37 (1): 9–20.

Panchbhai, S. C. 1983. 'The Jharkhand Movement among the Santals'. In *Tribal Movement in India*, edited by K. S. Singh, 31–33. Vol. 2. New Delhi: Manohar Publications.

Pelikan, Jeroslav. 1984. *The Vindication of Tradition*. New Haven, CT: Yale University.

Rao, Ranga. 1987. *Fowl-Filcher*. New Delhi: Penguin Books.

Rasul, Md. Abdullah. 1964. *Saotal Bidroher Amar Kahini*. Calcutta: National Book Agency.

Rothman, R. 1981. 'Political Symbolism'. In *The Handbook of Political Behaviour*, edited by Long S. L., 285–340. Boston, MA: Springer.

Sachchidananda. 2001. 'Change and Continuity in Santal Worldview'. In *Santhal Worldview*, edited by Nita Mathur, 162–175. New Delhi: Indira Gandhi National Centre for the Arts.

Soanes, Catherine, Alan Spooner, and Sara Hawker. 2001. *Compact Oxford Dictionary, Thesaurus, and Wordpower Guide*. New York, NY: Oxford University Press.

Srinivas, M. N. 1976. *The Remembered Village*. Delhi: Oxford University Press.

Thakur, R. N. 1989. *Social Matrix of a Tribal Village*. New Delhi: Archives Books.

15

Food Tradition of Chandal Community

Saradindu Biswas

Mere rice, whole or broken or pest infested, just any rice. Mutton-fish, milk-ghee, oil-salt, these were not asked by the dying. They had to be given just some rice, without worrying over substantial food. Trees have leaves, forests have taro. They wouldn't have died. One doesn't die if he chews on some rice grain, without boiling. You might not agree, but Baboo, it's true that they don't. They might get weak, but the throbbing of heart would still survive. (Bandyopadhyay [1947] 1998, 104)

Food is the driving force of life. Quest of food results in the evolution of life. Food scarcity, for natural or manmade reasons, creates an enormous stress on life. A widespread scarcity of food may result in famine. Lakhs of people and cattle may die in the consequent epidemic. How survival of human life is totally dependent on food is evident from Manik Bandyopadhyay's short story '*Chhiniye Khaini Keno*' (Why Didn't They Snatch and Eat?) on the Bengal Famine of the 1940s. We also get to know from the story that if food is a natural resource available to all, then life can sustain through critical period; but if 'food' becomes a commodity in the market, then its availability is restricted to the affluent class only, it is hoarded in the storehouses of the rich creating artificial food shortage.

Energy is the source of life, and animals acquire energy from food. Hence, pursuit for food, selection of appropriate food and food consumption are woven intricately with the struggle for survival. As a result of lack of rainfall and consequent droughts, there was a dearth of food production in Bengal during the 1950s. To compensate for the deficit in rice produced in Bengal, Rangoon rice was imported from Burma, present Myanmar. In 1942, Japan occupied Burma and threw away the British and Chinese. As a result, import of Rangoon rice stopped. The British hoarded huge amount of foodstuff for their army fighting the war, and the food scarcity took the shape of an endemic.

A series of Churchill's decisions between 1940 and 1944 directly and inevitably led to the deaths of some three million Indians. The streets of eastern Indian cities were lined with corpses, yet instead of sending emergency food shipments Churchill used the wheat and ships at his disposal to build stockpiles for feeding post-war Britain and Europe. (Mukherjee 2010, 498)

In her book, Mukherjee mentions what Churchill said about Indians. 'I hate Indians. They are a beastly people with a beastly religion. The famine was their own fault for breeding like rabbits'. It was considered more important to store food for the warring soldiers in Asia than saving the lives of Indians.

On the contrary, the Indian wholesalers started hoarding food crops for long in their warehouses. As a result of this man-made crisis, the undivided Bengal suffered a famine, which gradually started spreading.

The survival struggle started off with reduction of food intake and then families started selling jewellery, ornaments, and other smaller items before selling or mortgaging their immovable properties. Matters worsened that witnessed disintegration and abandonment of families, prostitution, sexual exploitation and child selling. Many children became homeless and orphans. Small children were seen begging. Mass displacement led to decline of sanitary conditions and hygiene standards while disposal of corpses in rivers and water supplies contaminated drinking water giving rise to diseases. Dead bodies were also left to rot and putrefy in open spaces which attracted vultures and jackal. (Mukherjee 2010)

Natural disaster, in most cases, causes greater damage to the economically impoverished. From the 'Famine Enquiry Commission Report' published by the Government of India in 1945, we come to know that right from May 1943 there was a dearth of food procurement in six districts of Bengal. These districts were Rangpur, Mymensingh, Bakharganj, Chittagong, Noakhali and Tipra (present Tripura). Because of cutting down of boat services, the famine started spreading across the districts along the course of the Ganges. The islands of Sundarbans suffered the greatest blow in the famine. By October 1943, the famine took a mammoth dimension, killing lakhs of rural poor.

Contemporary mortality statistics were to some degree under-recorded, particularly for the rural areas where methods were rudimentary even in normal times. Thus, many of those who died or migrated were unreported. It appears that from May to October 1943, starvation was the principal cause of excess mortality, filling the emergency hospitals in Calcutta and accounting for the majority of deaths in some districts. 'Deaths by starvation had peaked by November 1943; by December, disease had become the most common cause of death' (India Famine Enquiry Commission 1945, 203–207).

The report published by the Famine Enquiry Commission declaring that 1.5 million people died in the famine of the 1950s was later discarded by researchers. In 1943, the Bengal Public Health Department published a report putting the death toll to 1,873,749. Around this time the Department of Anthropology of Calcutta University, under the leadership of Professor K. P. Chattopadhyay, published a field survey report stating that the death toll was 2.7 million. This report has been considered most acceptable. Chattopadhyay's study was based on surveys of sample groups in the worst-affected areas, where mortality rate was 10 per cent. It was assumed that two-thirds of the population of Bengal was affected by the famine (c.f. Sen 1981).

In later years too, researchers considered this report to be most valid. Economist Amartya Sen (2000, 197) put the death toll to somewhere between three to four million. He mentioned several surveys in his work—according to the Famine Enquiry Commission the total mortality was 1.5 million, K. P. Chattopadhyay calculated it to be 2.7 million, Pakistan Census assumed it to be 2.62 million for Eastern Bengal, for combined Bengal it was 3.05 million.

The districts where the famine became endemic were thickly occupied by Chandals, Poundra, Rajvanshi, Malo, Koibartya, Muslims and other poverty-stricken communities. Although the Chandals were found in almost all districts of Bengal, they were most concentrated in Bakhargunj, Jessore, Khulna, Faridpur, Gopalgunge, Noakhali, Barisal, Dhaka, Mymensingh, Chittagong and Sylhet. In the Ganga-Padma, Brahmaputra, Meghna, Madhumati-washed plains, Chandals were the largest community in undivided Bengal (see Table 15.1).

District	Population
TABLE 15.1 — District-wise Chandal Population as per the 1872 Census Data	

TABLE 15.1 *District-wise Chandal Population as per the 1872 Census Data*

District	Population
Mymensingh	123,252
Bagura	7,647
Pabna	50,126
Jessore (including Khulna)	271,325
Faridpur	156,223
Sylhet	122,457
Dhaka	191,162
Tipra (Tripura)	81,155
Noakhali	12,947
Barisal	326,775

Source: Census of India (1872, Bengal, Vol. V (Part 1) Caste Tables, Calcutta).

The Chandals of Dhaka were known as Bhaowal. They were followers of Buddhism and were famous since the Pal Dynasty. The Chandal population of 797,422 was larger than the other three influential castes, namely, Koibartya, Brahmin and Kayastha, which had a combined population of 706,487 in 1901 in Dhaka division. In the census report of that year Commissioner Edward Albert Gait mentioned that the Namasudra (Chandal) aggregate was about 1,861,000 and the Pods (Poundra) nearly half a million, but a large number have been converted to Mohammedanism and call themselves Sheikh. There were ten and a half million Mohammedans in Dhaka and Chittagong Divisions at that time and a great majority of them were descendants of converts from the ranks of those two castes (Census of India, 1901, Vol. 1-A, Part II, Calcutta).

It is evident that in earlier days, this community was autonomous like a tribe or a nation. In the Indian Census report, C. J. O'Donnell, Herbert Hope Risley, Edward Albert Gait and other commissioners had described the Chandals as a tribe, and their internal social structure similar to the 'Alpine' tribes. They were expert in agriculture, fishing, navigation, internal and external trade. Since the Sen Dynasty, they became victim of social ostracization. Trapped in Ballal Sen's castist social order, they lost their social esteem and turned into marginalized destitutes. The Zamindari system of Bengal turned them into landless citizens and menial labour became their only means of livelihood. The production system and food chain to which they belonged was effectively destroyed.

In the 1911 Census, attempt was made to bring many social groups of Bengal under the aegis of Hinduism. The severally divided Chandals joined the rat race which was framed in the name of social progress. Many accepted the four-caste varna system prescribed by Manu and resigned to being clubbed with the Sudra. The Chandals became untouchables, the castes belonging to the top three varnas treated them with so much hate that the Chandals considered this identity as a foul abuse. Counter efforts also were made; 40 famous Brahmins of Bengal declared that the caste Namasudra was Brahmin by origin and had descended from the great Brahmin sage Kashyapa and they were not Chandal (Biswas 2004, 48).

In April and August 1901, the Chandal leaders made two appeals to the government to recognize them as Namasudra. In 1911 census report, the Chandals acquired the new identity of Namasudra as a caste group under the Hindu system. The famine of the 1940s again devastated the Chandal community of economically poor rural Bengal.

When the production system and food chain is destroyed, there is an adverse effect on biodiversity, labour and production organizations suffer a setback. Long-term depression makes human population economically and then physically weak. Natural hazard and artificial food crisis deprive the poor further. Churchill's food regulation, inhuman hoarding of food by the wholesalers within the country and their non-cooperation turned Bengal into a graveyard, the result of which made people suffer for long. The strike was on humanity—whether Chandal or non-Chandal is inconsequential. This weakened the ethics of humanity, the economy and the nation as a whole.

Chandal Nostalgia

The ancient Chandals would often say that at some point of time in the past, they had 'cowshed full of cows, pond full of fish, and field full of grains'. There was milk aplenty. In harvesting seasons, the crops were abundant. The *bratacharis* spread the word of the country's bounty to all houses through the Hulai songs, welcoming the Bastuthakur, the God of Domesticity. The merchants of Bengal would travel on their seven-tiered dinghies to traverse the seven seas to reach the enchanted lands of spices. The boatmen would sing Bhatiali. The newlyweds would weave sweet unfulfilled delicate dreams, on their embroidered kanthas. As the dusk turned into night, the grandmothers would spin the fairy tales of Madhumala, Kanchanmala and Sankhamala in their melodious voices.

Many of these memory-laden stories of the proud Chandal ancients are found in the accounts of the Chinese explorer Hiuen Tsang. He travelled through four *janapadas* in the East. Those were Pundrabardhan, Samatat, Tamralipta and Karna Subarna. He mentions that all these janapadas were led by prosperous communities. The people of Tamralipta and Karna Subarna were very rich. As the land was fertile, there were abundant crops, flora and fauna. The ports near the sea were very active. Hiuen Tsang mentions both inland and sea trade.

Rice was the staple food of most of the ethnic groups of India, including Kol and Chandal. Hiuen Tsang mentioned several varieties of rice cultivation in the eastern janapadas.

We get evidence of rice cultivation in a stone edict between third and second century BC, from near the ancient civilization around Karotoya riverbed. It is a royal directive ... the *Mahamatra* of Pundangal (Pundranagar) has been asked to follow the directive mentioned in the edict. (Ray 1996, 138)

Ray mentions that palaeographer Debdutta Bhandarkar considers this edict to be an inscription of a Mauryan emperor. It calls the *bhikshus* to contribute rice and money (*gandak mudra*) to the common people to tide over disaster and calamity. Once the people become food-secure, they would return the crop and money to the treasury.

The history of Bengal is mostly the history of Chandal, Kol, Dom, Pulinda and Shabar. Historians and ethnographers believe that the process of growing and processing wild rice varieties as local crop fit for consumption as staple food was a contribution of the Australoid communities like Kol, Chandal and others. In pre-partition Bengal, the famous rice-growing regions were Barisal, Jessore, Khulna and Bardhhaman. Barisal was famous for its tasty and aromatic varieties.

In the eastern janapadas, there is mention of an ancient boat named Balam which were involved in inland and sea trade. These boats traded aromatic rice from one port to the other. This scented rice variety, traded on Balam boat, was later renamed as Balam rice. (Biswas 1998, 168)

Upendranath Biswas (2005, 102) has quoted the list prepared by W. W. Hunter of the varieties of rice after traversing many districts like Jessore, Khulna, Faridpur, Barisal, Mymensingh, and Rajsahi. In Jessore alone, he had mentioned of 62 varieties of rice, which are: 1. Nepa, 2. Lakkhada, 3. Maita Chaul, 4. Kala Amon, 5. Bharuajata, 6. Gandha

Kasturi, 7. Pritthviraj, 8. Koch kolom, 9. Kuhulakh, 10. Bhojankarpur, 11. Gila mait, 12. Chhatrabhog, 13. Niyarphal, 14. Dulia, 15. Byarleja, 16. Lakkhikajal, 17. Phoolamon, 18. Kola, 19. Dudh kalam, 20. Diga, 21. Malbhog, 22. Surjamoni, 23. Jabra, 24. Bharuanega, 25. Haldibati, 26. Netpashra, 27. Durgabhog, 28. Chhirti, 29. Kartik shol, 30. Alambhog, 31. Balam, 32. Ajan, 33. Dayargur, 34. Gobindobhog, 35. Munar, 36. Panti, 37. Dantakali, 38. Pakkhiraj, 39. Khunematar, 40. Bharuakunri, 41. Haludkhar, 42. Kumar Goir, 43. Char, 44. Badsha Bhog, 45. Chingradhusi, 46. Jamai Puli, 47. Jhingashail, 48. Mantra, 49. Kalamkati, 50. Bikamla, 51. Nalita, 52. Sitahar, 53. Begaphool, 54. Muktahar, 55. Kandidhala, 56. Guyachhari, 57. Rajmorol, 58. Mahishkandi, 59. Dalkachu, 60. Porongi, 61. Gajibhog and 62. Shibjita.

The list of rice varieties prepared by Hunter is quite long, it comprises a variety from Faridpur and Barisal, which floats above 15–20 ft deep water. There were long and medium length creeper varieties. Among these, the Faridpur-Barisal floating creeper varieties had surprisingly strong survival character. Preparation for rice plantation would begin by mid-*Poush* (December–January). By *Kartik* (October–November) and *Aghrayan* (November–December) months, when the *amon* rice was harvested, the villages started celebrating *Nabanna*, the harvest festival. Land tilling started right from the month of Poush.

Use of Plough in Agriculture

A plough is made of four pieces of wood. The ancient farming communities had chosen the wood of acacia through trial and error. Even in present times, acacia wood is used to make bullock and horse drawn carts. The first of the four wooden pieces, which are joined to form the plough, is called *gada*. The spear-like sharp portion digs into the soil and makes it loose. When iron was invented, a sharp iron *phal* (plough share) was attached to this. The second part of the plough is *nijam*. The edge of this portion is strongly driven into the gada. The upper portion of nijam is L-shaped; it is called *guti*. The guti is pressed downwards while ploughing. The third portion is *ish*. This is a longish piece of wood which goes angularly into a hole at the junction of gada and nijam. The other end of the wood, which is long smooth and grooved in the front is attached to the *jongal*. A spool of rope in the middle of attaches the *angot* and the. Two strong young bullocks are tied to the *sonal* on two sides of the with *jot*. The left bullock is called *dere* and the right bullock is called *bere*. The dere waits (*dnarano* in Bengali) for the bere to take its turn when the plough takes a right turn. As the stronger bullock on the right takes a longer turn for the other bullock to join in the same line, it is called bere. The ploughman or the *halua* drives the bullocks with a bamboo stick or *haluanari* yelling '*dnay dnay dnay*' (right right right), '*bnay bnay bnay*' (left left left), '*hurrrr hnat hnatghorghorghor*' (turn turn turn), '*dnara dnara dnara*' (wait wait wait). At times, the musical halua enchants Barasia or the song of twelve months:

> *Winter passed and spring has come*
> *Phagun is here*
> *Yet he did not arrive*
> *The desolate lover's grief*
> *Sears through the twelve months*
> (popular Barasia song, Faridpur, Bangladesh)

The seedbed is prepared in low-elevation swamps. The young seedlings are known as *pato* in Chandali language. These patos are transplanted to grow the amon rice. Seeds of amon and *aush* rice varieties are scattered on dry land. Then a ladder or *chongo* attached to bullocks is run over them to cover the seeds with soil. This rice grows from moisture of the soil. By the end of *Jaistha* (May–June) and at the beginning of monsoon, the aush rice is harvested. The amon rice remains in the field with their trimmed stems. As the water collects in the field, these spread across the field.

By *Ashad–Shravan* (June–August), there is heavy rainfall and the paddy is submerged in water. The houses look like islands in the sea of water. If there is a strong wind, the water lashes against the houses in waves. The boats are the only means of conveyance. To tide over such deluge, each family has their own small and large boats. When the paddy is totally submerged, the worried farmer takes his boat to the field. Once the rain subsides, the same paddy raises its head again in sunlight. Pushing behind his unwarranted worries, the farmer is hopeful again. The green rice crop thrives with the rains in Ashad–Shravan.

Long creeper rice varieties of Faridpur: (a) Bagha, (b) Lepa, (c) Mahishkandi, (d) Baliyabet, (e) Lakkhideegha, (f) Dudhkalam, (g) Lakkhikajal, (h) Malaj, (i) Ranginalaaj, (j) Jhul, (k) Dulai, (l) Bagrail, (m) Dalkochu, (n) Gilamaita, (o) Garruya, (p) Bhojankarpur, (q) Boyra, (r) Kalahar, (s) Gandha Kasturi, (t) Pittiraj, (u) Maitchal, (v) Kachkalom and (w) Borodeegha.

Long creeper rice varieties of Barisal: (a) Pakkhiraj, (b) Kalamanik, (c) Lakkhibilas, (d) Rayeda, (e) Botar, (f) Kachkalom, (g) Lepa, (h) Khoimugri, (i) Nethapasha, (j) Bhojankarpur, (k) Jalkochu, (l) Chinaisa, (m) Boyrakola (n) Kalmona, (o) Kloura, (p) Betak, (q) Nepurkani, (r) Basmati, (s) Noloj, (t) Shatabhag, (u) Chhatrabhog, (v) Matchaul, (w) Kumragori, (x) Dudhkalm and (y) Ghritshail.

Staple Food of Chandal Community: Rice

It goes without saying that where so many varieties of rice are grown, the staple food is rice. The practice of having rice in several ways like boiled and fermented, eating broken rice and rice with bran is common among the Chandals. However, separating the husk from the paddy, and converting the grain to edible rice is a long process. Boiling the paddy and drying it appropriately, then converting it into rice by de-husking on a *dhenki* or wooden husking lever is part of the traditional skill of the Chandals. Dhenki was used in all households at one point of time and de-husking was a daily activity. Primarily, the maidens and the married women of the household engaged in this for a considerable time of the day. Earlier, there was no other way to de-husk other than using dhenki. A 4–5-ft-long piece of acacia wood was used to make a dhenki. In eminent and sophisticated families, the dhenki was made from the wood of *sundari* tree. Some even made it out of tamarind wood.

Dhenki Jantra

Dhenki is a popular machine to separate rice from the paddy. A round smooth piece of wood is attached to the headpiece of the dhenki. This wood is called *monai*. An iron-hold called *gula* is attached at the head of monai. Another round piece of wood is fitted in diagonally through the middle of the dhenki, this is called *sonai*. The sonai is attached on both sides to two grooved pieces of wood, called *katla*, which are tightly driven into the ground. The other end of the dhenki is made flat and smooth, where women press with their foot to de-husk paddy or make flat rice or grind rice for *pithey-puli* (sweetmeat). Below the flat portion, there is a pit dug in the ground. This pit is called *goda*. When the flat end of the dhenki is pressed with foot, it goes inside the goda and the head of the dhenki hauls up with the monai and thrashes the paddy kept in the *notey*. At the head end of the dhenki, the notey is dug inside the ground. The notey is made durable with rice husk and *chara* from earthen pots. The paddy is filled in the notey and de-husked by *paar* or paddling on the other side. At the tail end of the *dhenki*, two women stand on the *pothey* and rhythmically paddle the dhenki. In front of the pothey, a bamboo is placed crosswise above the head. When the women paddle, they balance their body weight against this structure called *bhara*. An experienced person turns over the paddy inside the notey. Once the rice is separated from the husk, the women raise the dhenki by balancing on the *bhara*. The husk and the rice are taken out from the notey and replaced with new grains. The husk is separated from the rice by winnowing with a bamboo *kulo* (winnowing fan). This process is called *kara.* Thus, the rice is separated from the husk through progressive win-nowing called *ekkara, dukara* and *tin kara* to get the white polished rice.

The song that women sing while they paddle the dhenki is called *'dhan bhanar geet'.* The lyrics are humorous, and the humour takes off the drudgery. The women of Faridpur would often sing, as they paddle:

I pound rice, as I paddle my dhenki
I dance and I waddle, along with my dhenki.
The monai says, I'm most vital
How would you de-husk if I wasn't there at all?

Thus, all parts of the dhenki are separately described to establish their significance in the de-husking process.

In the process of de-husking, some grains of rice get broken. The broken pieces are called *khud* and the powdered portion is referred to as *kuro.* When the rice is winnowed, the khud are separated. The rice made from the khud is called khudbhaat. Among the Chandals, it is customary to have khudbhaat with several boiled vegetables. Khud is soaked and mixed with kuro to be served as feed and fodder for the duck, hen, pig and cow.

Panta bhaat or fermented rice is a favourite food of the Chandals. Usually, it is eaten as breakfast. Rice cooked the previous day is soaked in appropriate amount of water and taken as panta bhaat the next day. The lightly sour panta bhaat is usually taken with salt and chillies. During the farming season, the farmers go to the field with their plough and other implements. As the day progresses, the women carry a pot of fer-mented rice on their head and a pot of drinking water on their waist to feed the men. Farmers claim, fermented rice keeps their body cool and they feel less tired. In recent times, fried vegetables and several types of *bharta* (mashed vegetables) are also taken with panta.

Vegetable Garden Palan

It is commonly said that pulses–rice–vegetable curry is the primary food of the Chandals. Vegetable gardening or palan farming is integral to every rural Chandal family. The women of the family oversee the garden. They collect various seeds and tubers to stock up their garden.

The leafy vegetables that are grown in palan are (a) radish, (b) spinach, (c) Indian spinach, (d) amaranthus, (e) *dnata* (stalk of plants), (f) bottle gourd, (g) pumpkin, (h) *bele* (white goosefoot), (i) *titey shaak* (bitter leafy vegetables) and (j) *pat shaak/noltey* (jute leaves).

The primary vegetables grown are (a) lady finger, (b) aubergine, (c) tomato, (d) bitter gourd, (e) turnip, (f) cabbage, (g) cauliflower, (h) giant taro, (i) elephant foot yam, (j) chilli, (k) snake gourd (snake gourd is usually put up on scaffold or *jangla*), (l) ridge gourd, (m) *turturi* (a dwarf variety of ridge gourd that grows in bunches) and (n) wild potato.

Floating Garden *Gatua*

Gatua or floating garden is a unique creation of the Chandal society. It is an organic repository made of clay and *nara* (stump of paddy) and a unique example of organic farming. Usually after harvesting paddy in the month of Aghrayan (November–December), the stump of paddy, which remains in the ground is called *nara*. There is almost knee-high water in the rice field around this time. Farmers make long hooked bamboo poles called *dalchhara* to collect these stumps from water. Those stumps get decomposed on the rice field. Once the water dries up, the stumps are stacked in piles. Over each pile, some soil is scattered. The 5–6 ft-high and 25–30 ft-long mound of stumps is called *gatua*. In the month of Ashad, when the rainwater rises, the gatua starts to float. Seeds are sown in the gatua according to the requirements in the family. In Dhaka, Faridpur, Jessore, Khulna, Barisal and other districts, the Chandals collect vegetables from gatua for about five months. The vegetables collected from these gatua are lady finger, aubergine, bitter

gourd, ridged gourd, Indian spinach, black arum, buffalo spinach, water spinach, etc. Before the water entirely dries up, these floating gardens are taken to palan or the main garden. When the palan farming begins, the gatua is razed to the palan soil. In this way, the palan soil is made more fertile and helps in the healthy growth of vegetables. Sometimes, the Chandal women remind the men that 'a piece of land is income in hand'. This is probably to emphasize the importance of home-grown food more than the profit at business.

Pulses, Mustard and Seed Crops

Moong, matar and *khesari* are especially popular among the Chandals. After the harvesting of *amon* rice in Aghrayan, matar and khesari are scattered in the rice field. The matar and khesari plants seek support from the stumps of the paddy and grow. Mustard seed is scattered in other fields. This natural cultivation gets very good yields of pulses and mustard. Moong dal is cultivated in elevated land. Moong dal and mustard is harvested around the end of the month of Poush (December–January). To meet the demands of oil, sesame and linseed are grown. Around the month of Ashad, sesame is harvested and stored to be used as oil during the monsoon months.

Milk, Curd, *Ghol*, Ghee and Butter

That this agro-based community have a close relation to cow farming is evident from their folk festivals and rituals. The cow and the calf get as much importance as any other member of the family. In the farming season, first ploughing is done by the cultivators without using any draught animals. This is done so that the cows of the household do not feel that they are being 'used'. The cattle are named like any humans in a Chandal family. The common names are Kali, Dhawli, Chitakpali, Mangali, etc. The bullocks are named Kartik, Ganesh, Lalu, Dholu, etc. Apart from a sturdy pair of bullocks, there are mostly cows in the cowshed. Hence, there is no dearth of milk and milk products like curd, butter, ghee and *ghol* (buttermilk). No Chandal sells milk to the market. The excess milk is distributed among neighbours and the rest is left for the calf.

It is not customary to rear goats or lamb among the Chandals. However, pig breeding has started. Pig is not kept in the cowshed; they have separate pigsty. Usually they feed on panta, *khud* (broken rice), roots and tubers. Chandals are very fond of pork.

Fishing by Chandals

The fish from the rivers, canals, water basins of the sea lying Gangetic Bengal is a huge food reserve for the Chandals. From the early hunting age, Chandals have managed to include fish as their primary food. They have developed several methods to catch fish since then.

> It is not surprising that in the waterfed Bengal with Pacific and ancient Australian influence on its civilization, where rivers and canals are aplenty, fish would be considered as a primary diet. If we look into the food habits of inhabitants of China, Japan, Burma, Southeast Asian countries and archipelagos in the Pacific Ocean, it is evident to which culture and civilization does Bengal (*Bangladesh*) belong. Rice and fish are primary food everywhere. (Ray 1996, 445)

The vast knowledge of fish hunting among the Chandals is fascinating. They studied the directions and depth of the water bodies and devised ways and means of catching any fish. They invented several instruments to catch small-, medium- and large-sized fish. This included harpoon-like contraptions to throw and impale the fish from a distance. The well-known among these are *era*, *jhupi*, *koch* and *juti*. This kind of weapons is used mostly for catching shol, shal, boaal and chital.

The bamboo-made contraptions, which are commonly used, are *ghuni*, *duari*, *aatol*, *dhorka*, *hocha and pawloi*. These apart, there were several forms of *barshi* or fishing hooks, *chhip* or fishing rods and *dang*. For a large catch, several kinds of nets like *kheola*, *gherjal*, *bhyasal*, *bhuri* and *sangley* are used. *Bhurijal* was used to catch big size *rui* (Rohu), *katla* (South Asian Carp), *mrigel* (white carp), *kalbaus* and *boaal*.

'The large fan-like net (*bhurijal*), framed on a triangular bamboo frame, is tied to the side of the boat,' writes Manik Bandyopadhyay.

> The bamboo at the far end of the net is parallel to the side of the boat. Two long bamboo poles from its two ends meets at the side of the boat and intersects each other as they enter the boat. These are the two handles of the net. The net can be propelled by using these handles. Two bamboos operate the big open mouth of the net which is dipped in 12–14-cubit deep water. When the fish enters the net, there is an indication on the rope held by the fishermen, and it is by manipulating the rope that the mouth of the net is closed underwater. (Bandyopadhyay [1948] 1998, 13)

The most important fishing net of Bengal, however, is *sangley*. This is the only net used to catch hilsa. Sangley is a bigger fishing net than bhurijal.

The hilsa season starts in mid-monsoon. The fishermen spend night and day fishing on Padma. Their livelihood is based on selling this fish. Fish selling, however, is strictly prohibited for Chandals; they catch fish only for food. If there is excess, they share with neighbours, and there is no wastage. They consider the hilsa season as the season of hunting celebration. This is an ancient tradition. If they are unable to catch hilsa, they do not buy it from the fishermen at a cheaper rate. This primitive hunting instinct lasted for a long time. Although the young Chandals went to the Padma to catch hilsa, the ancients preferred the fish from Madhumati. The hilsa from Madhumati is considered most delicious.

The Extravagant Food Assortment of Chandals

Barishal has balam rice
Khulna has cow ghee
What else do Chandal's need?

—a conventional rhyme, Faridpur, Bangladesh

Typically, in the 'big farmer' family, there is abundant fish, meat, pulses, fried vegetables, chutney and milk products with aromatic rice. The first course starts with mashed vegetables with ghee. This is followed by *chacchori, ghyant* (both are different types of mixed vegetable preparation), potato and pointed gourd fry cooked in ghee. Guests are served the big fish-head of katla in a big bowl, and several fish and meat items, typical of Chandal food platter, displayed around the bell metal plate in one, two, three stacks. The grandeur of this food scenario is enhanced by the delicate waving of the palm-leaf fan by the women of the household. A great spread of food and the care bestowed by the hostess makes the Chandal food tradition glorious.

This apart, the Chandal women prefer to cook several recipes with different types of fish. Fish curry is cooked with vegetables. *Machher jhal* (fish with mustard), *machher paturi* (fish and spices wrapped in banana and other leaves), *machh sidhho* (boiled fish), *machh bhapa* (baked fish) are some preparations of fish. Mouth-watering dishes are prepared with ground mustard and boaal (a variety of catfish), chital (knife fish) and bata fish. It is customary to have piping hot rice with the fried fat of ilish (hilsa). Bata cooked with the small variety aubergine called *salua begun* is also delicious. The fish-head is cooked as *murighanta*. Moong beans cooked with the fish-head of katla is considered a delicacy. The last course is a preparation of a sour condiment of fruits/vegetables with spices, sugar on a sour base, usually called *ambol* or chutney. This would indicate that the food course is at its end.

Salua Aubergine

This extravagant food course also adds yoghurt, chhana (Indian cottage cheese), and other sweet milk products like *sandesh, kheer* and *payesh* (rice porridge). Fruits like banana, mango, ripe jackfruit, and melons are served. Mango and milk concoction were favourite in Chandal households. Food connoisseurs prefer a concoction of milk, *aamsatto* (dried mango strips), banana and cottage cheese.

Food during Festivities

Sankranti, Sakrat, Poush Parbon

The new year begins at the end of Poush and beginning of Magh. The golden rice grains fill the granary. The cow and the bullocks get some rest. There is a celebratory mood in all village households. The mud walls are decorated with *alpana*. Several varieties of rice are spread out in the courtyard in the bright sunlight of winter. The Chandal women toss and turn the grains with their *alta* or red dye decorated feet. The experienced ones press some grains with their feet to remove the husk and taste whether the grain is ready for *pithey-puli* (sweetmeats), *payes* (rice porridge), puffed rice, popped rice or parched rice. Puffed rice from *urki* variety and popped rice from *binni* variety are famed for their superior quality. There are traditional poems and songs defining which strain of rice is famous for which by-product. One such poem says:

> *Grace my house, my friend*
> *Will give you a pira to sit upon*
> *Will serve you flattened rice*
> *Made from shalidhan*
> *Will serve you sweetened parched rice from urkidhan*
> *And parched rice from binnidhan*
> *And ripe sabri banana,*
> *And yoghurt wrapped in gamchha.*
> (*pira*, a raised platform made of wood; *dhan*, rice grain; *gamchha*, thin cotton towel)

As night descends, one can hear the sound of frying puffed rice. In Chandal dialect, puffed rice is better known as *hurum*. This can be attributed to the 'hurum' sound that emanates from stirring the hot rice grain thrown into a hot sand-filled earthen pot, after the rice grains are fried in an open earthen vessel. Thereafter, the sand-mixed puffed rice is transferred into a perforated earthen vessel called *jhanjhor* which is placed above another earthen vessel called *chhabna*. A bamboo made *naruni* or stirrer is used to stir the puffed rice and sand anticlockwise so that the sand empties out into the chhabna through the perforations, and the puffed rice remains in the jhanjhor. Such an advanced procedure to fry puffed rice is rarely seen elsewhere.

As Poush Sankranti (last day of Poush) approaches, the women get busier. *Ala chal*, rice that is not parboiled, is turned into rice powder on dhenki. Jaggery is mixed with puffed and parched rice and fried rice grain to make *moa* and *murki* separately. Coconut and sesame mounds called *naru* are made.

Huloi, Uloi or Huloi Songs

Dusk sets in, night falls. Night of cicadas and fireflies. The women are busy in the kitchen processing and preparing food. And all of a sudden, the community youth break the silence as they arrive with the victory message of uloi or huloi songs.

> *Bless us the god of domesticity*
> *Fill your store with the harvest*
> *From this room to the other*

As they arrive, the mistress of the house comes out to the courtyard with a lamp. The other women join her. The children who have not gone to bed yet also join in the audience. Huloi is a *bratachari* (a spiritual and social movement) group. The group sings of man's struggle and victory against the adversities of nature, and his aspiration to create a prosperous society. They take this message from village to village, house to house. Every member of the huloi group has a bamboo pole about a man's height. They wear a turban made from *gamchha*. They sway their bodies, move their left and right feet, and dance to the rhythmic beats of the bamboo poles struck on ground along with the huloi song. The lyrics tell about the recent developments of the country. They also narrate stories from history.

Huloi or uloi is derived from the Santhali word *hul* or Mundari *ul*. Both words are from Austroasiatic source. The original meaning is war or struggle. It is rare to find such a popular expression devoted to the victory of Man over Nature and the celebration of prosperity. The war fought by Sidhu Kanhu (known as hul) and by Birsa Munda (known as *Ulugulan*) marks the unique history of struggle of the tribes of India against the dikus (outsiders, here the British). In some places, this song is known as *halui* or songs of the *halua*. Those who till the land with the *hal* (plough) are called halua. The band is created with youth who are experienced in farming and cultivation.

At the end of the performance, the group asks for *madhukari* or *mangaon* (begging for small amount of food). The mistress of the house gives rice, pulses, vegetables, etc., on their extended *dhama* (flat cane baskets). The huloi continues till before the Poush Parbon. On the first day of Magh, an elaborate hodgepodge is cooked with the cereals and vegetables acquired from madhukari. All young and old males in the village have hodgepodge on banana leaves together. Women get it delivered at home.

Just before Poush Parbon or the Poush festivity, every corner of the entire house is swept clean of all remains from processing rice grains. Every member of the family gets new winter garments, colourful drapes. The old get monkey caps.

On the first day of Magh, the cowshed is cleaned and plastered with cow dung. The hoofs and horns of the cattle are polished with oil. Designs are drawn on their bodies with rice powder dabbed in water. *Sindoor* or vermillion is applied on their heads. Chandals do not have pithey-puli on the first day of Poush Parbon. Only the cows of the house are entitled to sweetmeat on that day. They consider the cow as their means to prosperity.

From the second day of Magh, there is a surfeit of pithey-puli in every household. The Chandal women spend nights preparing several types of pithey. The ones in which the rice batter is pressed in earthen moulds are called saanch pithey. When this saanch pithey is dipped in condensed milk mixed with palm jaggery, it is called *bhijano pithey*. In many houses, the bhijano pithey is made from aromatic rice dust. *Chandosa* and *bora* are oil-fried pithey. *Patisapta* is made by spreading a thin layer of rice batter in an iron pan and wrapping it around a filling of coconut. Steamed pithey includes *pooli* and *choosi pitha*. *Chhawrar jau*, *payesh* and *kheer* are also prepared.

The women of the house get set from the breaking of dawn. Even before the children wake up, they sprinkle cow dung water and plaster with cow dung to create a pious environment. The whiffs of pithey-puli fill the air. The guests sit on wooden plank and are served on bell metal platter. Endless items! Boundless joy! The food fiesta continues from one village to the next, from one house to the next. The gastronomical carnival continues for four to five days. It is not merely limited to pithey-puli. Rice, pulses, fries, mixed vegetables, fish and meat are added to the fare.

The Sankranti of the Chandals and the Sakrat of the Santhals have many similarities. These two ethnic communities have the same calendar and calculations of days, months and years. In both communities, the children have their bath immediately after sunrise. A fire is lit near the pond or at the corner of the courtyard. To drive away all germs and diseases, people bask around the fire, which is termed *agoon pohano*. The Santhals believe that if one basks before the fire lit in the *kumbaghor* (a thatched room next to the pond), no evil can touch him throughout the year.

Go Phaguna and Bhagwati Puja

Go Phaguna is a festival in the month of Phalgun (February–March), and Bhagwati Puja is held on the first of Baisakh (April). The cattle are primarily responsible for the creation, production and prosperity of Chandal society. The cow is Bhagwati, and so the milch cow is worshipped by putting vermillion on its forehead. The cows are worshipped by the woman inside the cowshed. Parched rice with yoghurt, flat rice, banana and palm jaggery are mixed together as prasad (devotional offering). Payesh and kheer are prepared. The puja is held in every cowshed of the village. Once the prasad is distributed in one cowshed, the women move to the next and start the puja with ululation. The teenagers crowd around to get the prasad.

Arong: A Folk Festival of Autumn

The most popular folk festival of the seafaring Bengal is Arong. It is the biggest get-together of relatives and an occasion to establish new friendships. It is also the largest carnival of Bengal. The autumn is also a significant time. The natural calamities waive off during this time. The paddy defies the rising water to raise their head high. The home is stacked with aush rice. The rice fields, with digha and amon, fill the farmers with pride. There is less work, a lot of leisure. The much-desired daughter comes home to her parents. The parents are thrilled by the visits of the son-in-law, daughter, grandsons and granddaughters. There is a five-day celebration with food and frolic.

Arong mela is on *Dashami* (10th day of the festivity). The preparatory mood is since morning. After lunch, everyone gets set to go to the fair. At the edge of the river, the family boat is ready to take off. At the other end is a *Bachari*; it is a fast-moving *dinga* (dinghy). Once the *madhukars* (merchant vessels) of Bengal were guarded by seven such war dinghies; the fleet was called *Saptadinga Madhukar*.

Once the boat is ready, members sit according to age group on the plank. The women of the household come with a winnowing fan decorated with ritualistic items like mustard oil, vermillion, unhusked rice grain and trefoil grass to worship the boat. After the ritual, the Chandal women push the boat lightly with their feet to set it free. They call out 'be victorious'!!

All go to the Arong mela, except the elderly. The river is traversed with fluttering sails of boats. Boats of several shapes and size bring together a variety of food and an array of attractive materials to be sold at the Arong mela. Boats like *korfai, sampan, pansi* and *balam* are some examples of the ancient marine-centric culture of Bengal.

Usually the Arong mela arranges for the provisions of agro-based working class. The participation of women, along with men, is equally striking. On the return journey, several sweets like sandesh, rasogolla, pantua, chomchom, danadar, jilipi and gawja are bought, also bundles of sugar cane.

Before the dusk sets in, the boats are on their return. The elderly women await the arrival with unhusked rice grain and trefoil grasses on winnowing fan or bell metal plate. As the party returns, the women welcome them in ritualistic style and feed them several types of sweets and mounds of sweetened coconut or *naru*. Everyone visits every house in the neighbourhood, exchange greetings and engage in a brotherly embrace, putting aside all differences, if any. By the end of the 15th century, the immersion of Durga idol was clubbed with Arong mela, and as a result, Durga Puja gained more prominence than the ancient ritual. Gradually, the memory of Arong has been wiped away from the folk rituals of Bengal.

Gasi

> Cook in the month of Ashwin, and eat in the month of Kartik
> Desires of the lady are fulfilled
>
> —a traditional Gasi poem

It can be easily assumed from the poem that Gasi is a food festival. The specialty of the festival is that the food is cooked on the last night of Ashwin (mid-September–mid-October) and consumed on the morning of the first of Kartik (mid-October–mid-November). The food includes panta bhaat, *korkora bhaat,* and a preparation of water spinach. Several leafy vegetables like *beleshaak* (white goosefoot), *laushaak* (bottle gourd leaves), *kumroshaak* (pumpkin leaves), *dnata shaak, knata-notey shaak* are fried separately. Fried *punti machh, pona machh* or hilsa adds to the platter. Potato, pumpkin, sweet potato, and Indian spinach are made into a mishmash. No curry or soup or stew is cooked during Gasi.

Apart from rice, the women prepare a variety of pithey. Palm pithey wrapped in banana leaves is popular during Gasi. The fried pithey prepared are *talbora* (palm dumplings), *kalabora* (banana dumplings) and *chandosa. Sannch pithey* and *puli* are popular steamed pithey. Patisapta is primarily among fried pithey. Soaked pithey in gur (jaggery) or milk is also common, and so is payesh. The most popular food of this festival is the seed of palm fruit.

There is a relation between the Gasi Parab festival of the Chandals and the Kak Brata. The mistress of the house gets up before dawn, arranges portions of food prepared for Gasi Parab on a banana leaf and takes it to the bank of the ponds or to the tomb of the ancestors and offers it to a raven. She calls it out by addressing as 'Baba Kalachan'. Once the raven comes, she offers *pronam* from a distance and returns home. Chandals believe that the ravens or *kalachan* are social messengers who indicate good and evil times. We come to know from Chandal folklore that these birds would indicate direction, sitting on the masts of the madhukars or merchant ships. They indicated the forthcoming dangers or informed about new countries.

In a similar manner, all the food made for Gasi is arranged on a banana leaf and spread in the courtyard. Turmeric and neem leaves are ground and put in a big bowl. Green tamarind is roasted and put on the leaf with some mustard oil. *Kajal* or lamp black is made by burning an oil lamp at the edge of a banana leaf.

The participation of the young and the old is also significant in the Gasi Parab. The small children wake up very early on the festival day. They loiter around in nooks and corners, and strike the fences with a stick and recite:

Run along, you mice and mites
Have Mona's mother's rice in bits and bites

Or

O credulous mosquito
Knot in your ear, you tie
All mosquitoes fly away
To Panchi's mother nearby

After their bravadoes over mosquitoes, flies, mice and mites, the kids gather in the courtyard. They rub the turmeric and neem paste on their entire body. After about five minutes, they go to the nearby pond, river or some waterbody to bathe properly. Even the grownups do the same. Thereafter, they gather around the banana leaf in the courtyard in their wet bodies. They rub the tamarind and mustard oil under their heel. They put kajal in their eyes. The Chandal community believes, *Gasir snan*—the ritual bath—prevents *gasua* or impurities and infections.

The food course begins with having the palm seed first. This is followed by pithey-puli, payesh and panta bhaat with ghanto and fish fry.

Chandal Drinks

Palm syrup, date syrup, green coconut water and coconut water are popular drinks of the Chandals since early times. Treating the hosts to a sherbet made from palm candy or sugar candy with *gandhoraj lebu* or *kagji lebu* (two varieties of lime) is an age-old tradition prevalent even now.

Ghol

Among the drinks made of milk, ghol or buttermilk is most popular. Unpasteurized milk is poured and kept in an earthen vessel for a few days. This turns into curd. The curd is poured in an earthen vessel called *kadia* and mixed with small amount of water. The mixture is then churned with a bamboo-made *sodoi* or *ghol dnati* to bring out butter. The watery liquid left after lifting the butter is called ghol. It is a very satiating drink in the summer. Chandals believe that ghol keeps the body cool and compensates for water loss from body. The traditional doctors or *kobiraj* advise ghol for diabetic patients.

Doli

Doli is a delicious drink of the Chandals. This has similarity with the handia of the Santals. During the spring, as the sun mounts early and days become very hot, the farmers return home by the afternoon with bullocks. As they rest on the raised platform adjacent to the courtyard, after washing their hands and feet, this drink is served. If they feel drowsy after the drink, they take a short nap in the same place.

Doli is prepared in an earthen vessel. The preparation process is long and complicated. Good variety of rice is required to prepare this drink. Ususally, the rice variety used to prepare pithey and puli is used for preparing doli. The rice grain is soaked and then dried out in the sun by the women. The grain is pounded in dhenki to get rice. The husk, germinated paddy and broken bits of rice are separately soaked in water. The rice is soaked for a long period and made into powder by pounding on dhenki. As much rice powder is obtained from germinated paddy, the same quantity of powder is made from non-germinated rice, which is converted into duthi. Little by little warm water is poured over the rice powder and the mixture is stirred till the powder coagulates. This coagulated rice powder is steamed to form duthi.

The soaked husk, broken bits and germinated part are strained through a clean piece of cloth, and the liquid extract is poured in a medium-sized earthen vessel. Sugar drop candy is mixed with the liquid as sweetener. Then equal quantity of powder from germinated rice and duthi are mixed thoroughly with the liquid using a wooden ladle. After mixing, the mouth of the vessel is carefully covered and placed under the cot or under some raised platform inside the house. The processes are undertaken by Chandal women in all its austerity, wearing clean clothes. Although some women might extend help till the grinding of the rice to prepare rice powder, mixing of duthi and rice powder in the liquid extract and placing them under the raised platform is done by a single woman. After exactly 24 hours, she removes the cover from the mouth of the vessel after taking a bath, dressing in clean clothes and offering namaskar to the vessel. The young farmers, usually the brothers-in-law, gather around when they hear about doli. They sit on the raised platform adjacent to the courtyard. Doli is served in stone bowls. They wrap the bowls in their hands as they taste the doli.

Doli

Doli from Kauraada

There is another method of preparing doli. It is made from the tuber of *kauraada* or *kurada* plants collected from the forest by the women. This plant looks like a big turmeric plant. The tuber is washed clean and grated on an iron mesh. Then the ground tuber is put inside a piece of clean cloth and pressed hard to extract the juice. The juice is further sweetened with sugar drop candy. After putting it out in the sun for a few days, this tuber extract is used as a drink. Chandals consider this to be an energiser.

Crisis Food of the Chandals

Lives of the Chandals have been affected by various forms of socio-economic exploitation, natural disasters, battles and wars, eviction and displacement time and again. Several incidents of clash of interest of the independence loving Chandals with aliens and locally dominant groups have resulted in many crisis situations in the past. They had to seek new ways of living through acute unfavourable conditions. Thus, foraging and production of food among the Chandals is a long and complicated story. And their treasury of food for critical times is equally long and varied.

This list includes broken rice, flat rice, grass seeds, edible roots and tubers, pink water lily, mussle and cockles and *chiney*. Chiney is a variety of millet or grass seeds believed to have originated in China. In difficult times, this cheap substitute for rice is bought to meet the food requirement of the family. Many grow chiney in a small piece of land during Boro cultivation. There are popular rhymes among Chandals:

Dhin Dhina Dhin Dhina
The goat devoured china
Weaver bird has eaten the paddy
The country is flooded

Broken rice and rice with bran is on the top of the crisis-food list. The rice bran is cooked like pulses and is called *phyantelani*. It is served with *noltey pata* or *gutipater pata* (jute leaves), which is dried in the sun and lightly fried.

When there is a dearth of vegetables and greens, phyantelani is the only option. When the crisis becomes acute, stalks of water lily foraged from nearby water bodies are boiled and served with little rice. When the petals of the water lily wilt and drop, the disc of the flower forms *dhyap*. Seeds from the dhyap are cooked and served with boiled lady finger during extreme times. *Jau* is prepared by adding foraged vegetables to rice bran.

In such crisis, if mother's milk is not available, infants are fed on rice broth for survival. The broth is diluted to make *nothani*. That mix is put in the mouth of the infant with a *jhinuk*, a traditional infant feeding device. Custard apple, Indian mulberry, date, guava, *khoi* (fruit of gum arabic tree), black plum are fruits foraged from the forest. There is an increase in hunting of animals and birds during food crisis. Cranes are hunted with *fnad* or traps, doves are caught, *kora* is hunted from the paddy field. These hunted animals and birds, bird eggs and eggs of turtles provide food during unfavourable times.

That the absence of any form of rice, be it boiled, fermented, broken, or dehydrated cold rice carries a sad message, is evident from Buddhist *Dohakosh*.

> *My home is at stake*
> *There are no neighbours around*
> *As there is no rice in the pot, I'm starving regularly*
> *My family has become fragile*
> *The milk from the cow is returning to the udder*

Stigmatizing the People and Their Food

To reduce a community to nothing, it is not necessary to crush it by force; it can be done by denying food. Thus, it is possible to subjugate people in interest of state, religion and society by citing restrictive laws on behalf of the ruling class. The state can turn into an exploitative machine by condemning voices of resistance as seditious. Strict regulations begets instability, insecurity and fear of life, which compels many to submission. Many abide by the state policies and stay content by accepting the allocations. In India, the indigenous communities like Kol, Chandal, Naga and Rakshashas had been subjected to several such restrictions and regulations since the beginning of alien invasions.

There are several examples of such restrictions imposed on the free-spirited Chandals. Because Kol, Chandal, Naga and Rakshashas stood to oppose the Brahmanical hegemony, the dominant ideologies treated those communities in harshest terms. On several occasions, the Chandals had been severely victimized by the Brahmanical norms and laws. The chauvinistic mindset of Brahmanical ideologies was set to destroy the Indian civilization by destroying its history.

The Nagas, Chandals and Rakhshashas had been instrumental in defending the indigenous cultures of the land. Hence, primary objective of the Brahmanical narratives was to weave a mesh of religious regulations to make the Chandals weak and insignificant. In Sanskrit literature there are several evidences of food control over the Chandals. According to the Puranas, certain advices were given by Manu, son of Brahma, to save the animal world, crops, medicinal herbs and Vedas which are considered to be the repository of Aryan knowledge, during the time of deluge. The tenth chapter of Manusmriti mentions emergence of a hybrid race; it mentions the Chandals as the children born out of a union of Shudra man and Brahmin woman. Manu has excluded the Chandals from the four-caste system by condemning them to infinite hatred. Their daily life has been subjected to several restrictions. They have been dragged to the bottom-most step of the social ladder on the pretext of consuming inedible food. Food prepared or even touched by them has been considered impure.

> But the dwellings of Kandalas and Svapakas (those who eat dog meat) shall be outside the village, they must be made Apapatras, and their wealth (shall be) dogs and donkeys....

> Their dress (shall be) the garments of the dead, (they shall eat) their food from broken dishes, black iron (shall be) their ornaments, and they must always wander from place to place....

> A man who fulfils a religious duty, shall not seek intercourse with them; their transactions (shall be) among themselves, and their marriages with their equals....

> Their food shall be given to them by others (than an Aryan giver) in a broken dish; at night they shall not walk about in villages and in towns. (Sharma 2003, 51–54)

The Chandals are aware, how their food habits have been narrated in Balkanda of the story of Ramayana. It says, Raja Trishanku from the Ikshaku family expressed his desire to go to heaven in his mortal form. He told this to his Guru Vasistha, who considered this impossible and rebuffed Trishanku. Then Raja Trishanku went to the descendants of Vasistha and told them his wish. The angered descendants cursed Trishanku and said, 'You will become a Chandal'. Next morning Trishanku found his body turned blue, his hair short and he found himself dressed in blue. His body was covered with garlands and ashes from pyres and he was wearing iron ornaments. Trishanku then went to Viswamitra and narrated his saga. This angered Viswamitra and he cursed the descendants of Vasistha saying, for the forthcoming seven hundred years, they will be known as Mushtik or Chandals and will have to eat corpses. They will feed on dogs, and they will dwell in all lokas (worlds) as distorted forms among several adversities.

The worst suggestion regarding Chandal food consumption is stated in the Markandeya Purana. This is related to the story of Raja Harishchandra, who enraged Viswamitra and was compelled to sell off his wife and child. Thereafter he sold himself to Yama, the God of Death, disguised as a Chandal. He lived in the cremation ground, his regal ornaments were substituted with iron shackles, royal robe was replaced by the clothes worn by the deceased, his royal sceptre was replaced by a pole to manage the pyres and had food cooked on a pyre. Even his wife and son were separated from him. Instead of staying in a palace, he was made to roam around as a vagabond. He became untouchable. Looking at him was considered unholy. His touch could spoil everything. When Chandal Harishchandra was reborn as a dog, his food was excreta and vomit.

Concluding Remarks

The Chandal community though fell prey to acute social inequalities and some of them tried to raise their social and ritual status within the fold of the same Brahmanical system that was oppressing them, all of them did not surrender to subjugation for long. By reclaiming low-lying land in certain parts of eastern parts of Bengal for cultivation they could become relatively affluent in matters of food. Religious protest movement against Brahmanical supremacy in all aspects of life provided them with a platform to stand together against the hegemony of a few. When adult franchise opened the doorway to exercise voting right, they made use of their numerical strength to become a political power not only in pre-partition Bengal, but in national politics of India too (see Bandyopadhyay 1997).

Later, partition of the country, displacement of majority of the Chandals from their homeland in Eastern Bengal and dispersal of the dislocated population thinly over large parts of India jeopardized the social status and political might they once built. Still, the community has shown a great deal of resilience in face of all oddities, but that is a different story altogether.

References

Bandyopadhyay, Manik. (1947) 1998. *'Chiniye Khayni Keno'*, *Rachana Samagro*. Sixth Part. Kolkata: Paschimbanga Bangla Akademi.
———. (1948) 1998. *'Padma Nadir Majhi'*, *Rachana Samagro*. Second Part. Kolkata: Paschimbanga Bangla Akademi.

Bandyopadhyay, Sekhar. 1997. *Caste, Protest and Identity in Colonial India: The Namasudras of Bengal*. Surrey: Curzon Press.

Biswas, Saradindu. 1998. *'Sonar Dnar Pabaner Boitha'*, Ganashakti Sharad Sankhya. Kolkata: Ganashakti Printers Pvt. Ltd.

Biswas, Swapan. 2004. *Hari-Guruchand: Banglar Chandal o Bharatbarsher Bahujan Utthan*, 48. Kolkata: Orion Books.

Biswas, Upendranath. 2005. *Banga Mulnibasi Ekti Janagosthi*. Kolkata: Banga Pathak Publication.

Hunter, W. W. 1875. *A Statistical Account of Bengal, Statistics of Cultivation*, 242. Vol. 2.

India Famine Enquiry Commission. 1945. *Final Report*, 203–207. Madras: Govt. Press.

Mukherjee, Madhusree. 2010. *Churchill's Secret War: The British Empire and the Ravaging of India during World War II*. New York, NY: Basic Books.

Ray, Niharranjan. 1996. *Bangalir Itihaas, Adi Parba*, 138. Kolkata: Dey's Publishing.

Sen, Amartya. 1981. *Poverty and Famine, An Essay on Entitlement and Deprivation, Famine Mortality*. Oxford: Clarendon Press.

Sharma, R. N. 2003. *Manusmriti*. Delhi: Chaukhamba Sanskrit Pratisthan.

16

Place, Space, Identity and Transforming Cuisine among the Karen of the Andamans

Shiba Desor, Manish Chandi and Saw John Aung Thong*

Much has been written about food and its connections with various aspects of life and society. Food studies have been an important sub-field in anthropology and have helped in the advancement of anthropological theory and research by illuminating broad societal processes

* The authors acknowledge the support of Dakshin Foundation and Andaman and Nicobar Environment Team (ANET) in facilitating this research. They would like to thank Dr Meera Oommen for her comments on the draft. They are grateful to all the Karen of Middle Andaman who shared their stories, and especially to Saw Paung, Saw Zakious, Naw Roseline and Naw Namu for helping understand their local realities. They appreciate the invaluable role played by the data collection team (Saw Issac, Naw Cecilia and Naw Stella) for carrying out the socio-economic survey. Manish Chandi would also like to particularly acknowledge the encouragement, participation of his late colleagues Harry Andrews, Saw Shwether, Ravi Sankaran and the collective interest spurred on among them at ANET over several years in understanding the community from various perspectives.

(Mintz and Bois 2002). Looking closely at any food habit can reveal its linkages to not just economy and politics, but also psychosociology, history and culture, thus transforming the notion of food from a mere collection of consumable products to a system of communicating ethnic identity, social, economic and gustative preferences and also its connection with the past (Barthes 1961 [2013]). Lévi-Strauss (1966) considers cooking as a language through which society translates its structure or reveals its paradoxes. Douglas (1975) takes this further to show how the sequence in which meals are ordered and created, through the day, week, season or year, symbolizes particular social orders and boundaries. But beyond the cultural and symbolic attributes of food, there is also the political economy (Goody 1982) and the constantly changing societal aspirations and direct appeals (Mintz 1979) that influence food habits over time.

This multi-faceted nature of food cannot be discussed without understanding its connection to place. Place, through many varying definitions in academic literature, comes out as a multi-layered dimension, 'that often underlines the historical, cultural and social features' (AOF 2005). A nuanced understanding of place is particularly relevant to consider when talking about ethnic cuisine or a 'local' food culture. While calls for re-localization of food systems are becoming stronger by the day, issues of place (Feagan 2007) and knowledge (Fonte 2008) become important to handle. There is a danger of viewing 'ethnic' or 'local' as fixed and bounded but these are, in fact, in a constant state of flux. What is considered as appropriate eating may also be influenced by the behaviour of other people towards that food (Higgs and Thomas 2016).

The food culture of a community is thus an ever-evolving outcome of meaning-making based on place, memory and space. This chapter attempts to explore how the bio-geographical and the socio-political dimensions of place influence the present food culture of the Karen population that migrated from erstwhile Burma (now Myanmar) to the Andaman Islands in the Bay of Bengal nearly a century ago. The methodologies we employed include participant observation over several visits and lengthy periods of stay with the community, maintaining field notes, conducting interviews and analysing the socio-economic data collected through a household survey.[1]

The Karen Community of the Andaman Islands

The Andaman and Nicobar Islands in the Bay of Bengal are composed of 572 big and small islands lying at nearly 1,200 km from major ports of mainland India. In contrast, at its closest point, North Andaman is about 200 km from Myanmar, and southern Nicobar is about 150 km from Indonesia. While popular representations of this archipelago often focus on its connection to the pre-independence Indian freedom struggle or its portrayal as the home of 'savage' indigenous islanders, only a small number of recent publications (Anderson et al. 2016; Heidemann et al. 2016; Zehmisch 2017) have highlighted the commonly neglected historical processes of migration, settlement and place-making that had taken place. This chapter is an attempt to focus on one such settler community, the Karen.

The Karens are a distinct ethnic community brought to the Andaman Islands from erstwhile Burma in 1925 by the British during the colonization of the island archipelago. They came from different parts, chiefly Mawlamyine, Hinthada and Pathein and from different endogamous subgroups. In Myanmar, they are chiefly divided into three divisions—Sgaw, Bwe and Pwo (Marshall 1922). In Andamans, the Sgaw was the dominant sub-group and the population eventually formed a single endogamous community (Roy 1995), with the present population identifying itself as Sgaw (Maiti 2004). The settlement arose out of communication between the chief commissioner of Andamans Lt. Col. M. L. Ferrar and his cousin, the head of the American Baptist mission in Burma, Rev. Marshall (Roy 1995). The former communicated to Rev. Marshall about requiring a self-contained group of people to settle in the islands as labourers and cultivators. Following this, an advertisement was posted in the Burmese newspaper seeking 'poor landless Christian Karen' for settlement (Maiti 2012, 139). The first batch of 12–13 families arrived in 1925 under the leadership of Thra Sam Ba and Reverend Lyugi, followed by another batch in 1926.

This community chose to be surrounded by forests and were shown an area in the interiors of the Middle Andaman island being exploited for forestry by the then Andaman Forest Department. The area had rolling lands along the course of a freshwater stream and mixed forests. This site was chosen by their leaders and the village was called 'Webi' or 'hidden settlement'. The settlement has since grown to a population of about 3,000 individuals.[2] At present, the Karens are concentrated in eight villages (seven in Mayabunder Tehsil and one in Diglipur Tehsil) in Middle and North Andaman and are a minority among the settler population of the islands. Other dominant settler communities include former refugees from Bangladesh and various ethnic groups from mainland India in varying demographic proportions.

A Broad-spectrum Food Economy

Food often becomes a means of identifying and delineating a community. The boundaries of such cultural identities associated with food are not fixed, and instead evolve with time. In the eyes of the other settler communities of the Andamans, the Karen identity is closely associated with food items such as *ngapi* (fermented paste of dried shrimp or fish), *mohinga* (rice noodles with fish soup and tender banana pith), steamed or fried items made of glutinous rice and certain types of meat. The Karens of the Andamans themselves present these as their traditional food items during public events. However, these food items, exotic as they may seem in India, are generic dishes with variation found throughout Burma and North Eastern India too, and not exclusively associated with the Karen tribe in that place. It is also important to note that the Karen within Burma use other food items as distinct markers of their identity. *Me-to-pi*, prepared by pounding glutinous rice with sesame, is one such food item which is considered as a traditional Karen dish in Burma. In contrast, among the Karen of the Andamans, hardly anyone has eaten or prepared that dish in the past few decades and only a few people remember tasting it in their childhood. This indicates how what is considered as a 'Karen meal' in Andamans keeps evolving.

In recent times, a typical meal of the Karen of the Andamans, comprises rice with soup, ngapi, *taado* (raw, boiled or steamed vegetables) and an optional serving of fish or meat. They have a broad-spectrum food economy dependent on multiple sources such as forests, fields and oceans, each of which is described in some detail in this section. This aligns with the proposal that dietary diversity provides a higher probability of nutrient adequacy and energy intake (Ruel et al. 2013). Such diversification also provides a safety net for food security, particularly during periods of disconnectedness, food scarcity and famine as was seen in the intensified dependence on uncultivated foods during the Japanese occupation and food shortage period of the 1940s in the islands.

Forest Dependence

Many among the Karen are expert hunters, skills learnt from their forbears who sourced much of their nutrition from wildlife such as barking deer, spotted deer, wild pig, monitor lizard, civet, shellfish and frogs. Pork is a favourite among the Karens and wild pigs were hunted freely and relished during the earlier times before hunting was banned.

Apart from the commonly roasted pork, strips of pork are also dried and eaten as a frittered snack. Animal fat, especially pork fat, was also commonly used for frying and cooking before the advent of market oils. This was particularly so during the war years of the 1940s, when pig fat completely replaced cooking oil which was unavailable from the single store in Mayabunder.

Beyond hunting in forests, our surveys show that Karens depend on more than 58 types of wild plants for food and medicine which are con-sumed raw, boiled or in fermented form. Fermentation may be done by storing them in the water used for washing rice (as in the case of *chucha tha* or Oroxylum Indicum) and *gadde* doh (soap nut leaves). Boiled or roasted *geekadu* (cane shoots) are a particular favourite, supplementing a meal of rice, or cooked with meat to make a meaty broth called *tapopa*. In some cases, where cane shoots may be scarce, tender shoots of a mangrove palm, *Phoenix paludosa* (locally known as *bothalu*) are used as a substitute. A number of other plant species are also used as medicines for assisting digestion. For instance, tender leaves of *tenithi* (Pongamia pinnata) is used for deworming and tender leaves of *Kathephola* (Cassia alat) are used to cleanse the body of accumulated toxins.

Fishing

While common targets of subsistence fishing across communities of the Andaman Islands include shellfish, reef fish, holdfasts, eels, and many other marine organisms, the Karens specialize in what was once a subsistence fishery but given the growing tastes and demand have become a commercial activity. Tiny shrimps like krill are found in habitats abutting mudflats, mangrove creeks and shallows. The shrimps are collected, slightly fermented and salted to make ngapi. At least four varieties of krill/shrimp (among the Karens, these shrimp varie-ties are known as *tado gaw, tado wa, tado woh naw soo* and *tengo*) are identified by size, colour and flavour. Traditionally, ngapi was a staple of virtually every meal, but, at present, given the exogenous demand beyond the Karen villages, possible overharvests and land-upliftment post-tsunami of 2004, the krill/shrimp used to make the paste are not as easily available.

Ta-da-uh is a bay in the northern part of North Andaman island, where most Karen people travel and camp for ngapi harvests. Most of the ngapi harvesting is done between November and December. The initial steps of drying for ngapi-making are often carried out during the fishing trip itself.[3] Traditionally, ngapi is consumed directly with rice, either steamed with spicy chillies or with a dash of lemon juice or tempered with oil and spices. A similar fermentation process is also used for making fish ngapi or *nya-ou-ti*.

Apart from various forms of ngapi (*ngapi lemma, ngapi doun, nya-ou-cho, bal-chaun* etc.), fish is eaten as smoked, boiled, raw (tempered with lime) and lately, also as fried fish. Fish is also preserved for later by sun-drying the catch. Fishing is an important part of Karen lives and livelihoods and even an ordinary meal is made palatable to any Karen with some form of fish, fresh or pickled, used as an accompaniment to plain rice. From the household survey it was found that 77 per cent of Karen households in the Andamans engage in fishing activities primarily for subsistence. Prawns, crabs and fish are currently considered as common subsistence foods while decades earlier, larger fish, sharks, turtles and dugong formed the chunk of marine life consumed by Karens for nourishment. Different fishing techniques used by them include hook and line, skin-diving for shells and lobsters, spear fishing, plough-net for shrimp, cast-net and crabbing rods. Traditional woven baskets and traps made of bamboo are also used for fishing. Of late, some members of the community have also been engaging in gill netting or troll line fishing. Large nets are generally not used, although a few people have adopted the use of large gill nets recently from Telegu fishermen who traditionally use them.

The Karens of the Andamans introduced the concept of planked dugout canoes (locally referred to as *dungi*) to traverse mangrove and coastal regions of the archipelago, and eventually motorized these vessels (Chandi 2001). The dungi (called *khlee* in Karen) has become the mainstay of fishing, cargo operations and local intra-island passenger movement in the Andaman Islands. Fishing voyages on a dungi can last from a few days to a few months. Longer voyages usually take place from January to February, with a crew of between four to six persons onboard. On occasions, two or more boats accompany each other and sail for extended periods through the fair season fishing and sending fish to known trading hubs. While commercial fishing for export markets is rife across communities and the Andaman Islands, subsistence fishing and diversity of catch is a major contribution to nutrition and gastronomy of the Karens.

Agriculture

Often being known as simple rice cultivators and foragers by the outside world, the complexity in the repertoire of Karen kitchens and cuisine is only experienced through flavours of herbs, spices and condiments collected, cultivated and used in food. The Karens in the Andamans cultivate 14 varieties of rice, 31 types of trees, 42 kitchen vegetables and herbs and 14 medicinal plants. These figures indicate that unlike common perception, the Karens are not only paddy cultivators, but also avid gardeners dependent on kitchen gardens and orchards for many supplementary, medicinal and flavouring additions to their cuisine. Often the agricultural lands are fallow, only being used for the single crop of rice cultivated during the south west monsoon. Kitchen gardens are tended throughout the year.

Agricultural practices have undergone change with time. Previously, ploughing was undertaken using bulls. Now many families lease a tractor to till their lands. Rice-processing is now mechanized while hand-pounding and foot-pounding techniques as well as hand-grinding stones are now hardly used. When the Karen migrated to the islands from Burma they brought their own seeds of traditional rice varieties, a number of which continue to be grown currently and thus conserved at various homesteads at the hands of these farmers. Each variety has its own set of characteristics and is grown for different purposes. Many report a loss in the 'purity' of the varieties. 'The taste of rice has changed with time because people don't do seed selection carefully while sowing. Earlier, people used to do it patiently, separating grain by grain', remarks 75-year-old Naw Thusay. The most common traditional variety that continues to be grown by most Karen farmers is *Chowchiminai*. The word in Karen means 'it can grow without manure' (Ahmed et al. 2014, 98). It is locally known among other communities as *Khushbuya* because of its fragrance. Perhaps the reason for its continued prevalence is that it grows easily, gives good yield and does not require too much of special attention. A formal process of conserving such cultivars was initiated by Saw Saytha of the Karen Welfare Association by connecting with the Government Agricultural department. As part of this initiative, five varieties were registered in July 2017 and conserved in a seed bank.

Rice cultivation practices have also been affected by the availability of rice through the Public Distribution System (PDS). Over 90 per cent of the families have a ration card. As a result many families, even the ones that grow paddy, are dependent on '*card ka chaawal*' (literally translated as 'card's rice'). This could be because the present level of paddy cultivation is not enough to meet the required household level demands or perhaps it is a chicken-egg situation with cultivation reducing because of availability of PDS rice. A Karen woman, who was interviewed, spoke about how her children now prefer PDS rice to the local varieties. They are now more accustomed to the taste of PDS rice, whereas she herself still prefers flavours of the older varieties.

Glutinous rice varieties grown by them are known as *pe-ee* in Karen and as *Burma chawal* among other local communities. These are used for breakfast and powdered to make snacks such as *mosijo* (fried rings), *moloyebau* (boiled rice balls soaked in sugar water), *mophaito* (steamed rice flour packets stuffed with grated coconut and sugar or jaggery) and *molonji* (fried balls stuffed with grated coconut). The other rice varieties are used for cooking *mei* (simple rice), or occasionally, *ounthamei* (coconut rice) or *meichow* (fried rice). Rice is used for making *mohinga* (noodles), *molosaun* (a coconut milk drink with pieces of boiled, soft-pounded rice), *silemeki* (a sweet dish made from rice powder, turmeric, sugar) and *muchede* (made from rice powder and slaked lime). Rice cooked in bamboo is called *meiseepaw*; it is a method in use harking back from their former foraging and nomadic life when fresh bamboo found in forests was used for multiple uses including as a vessel to cook food and hold water too.

Apart from rice, the Karens plant 87 types of trees, herbs and vegetables. These are used for flavouring, medicines and find use as *taado*. Taado is a side-dish of raw, boiled or fermented plant parts, common in a traditional Karen meal. These may also be pickled or marinated in different ways such as using rice water (as in case of banana and radish), boiled saltwater (as in case of mango and dried lemon) and lime water (for unripe bamboo shoots). In earlier times, some of these foods were also used as common snacks, such as sun-dried unripe banana, fried lumps of jackfruit fibres mixed with rice powder, fried pig skin/fat and roasted tamarind seeds.

Livestock Keeping

A key resource in the past for the cultivation of rice was draught animals such as cattle and buffalo. Currently, they are not as common as they once were, given prospects of mechanized agriculture and a slow but definite increase in dependence on markets and the PDS. Livestock are an important source of protein and are assets that Karen families maintain in homesteads. This is especially relevant since hunting wildlife is banned, and wild pork and venison are scarce. As per the ANET/Dakshin Foundation survey, chickens and ducks are the most commonly kept livestock (kept by 80.5 per cent of respondents), followed by goats and pigs (55 per cent) and bovines (25.84 Per cent). Meat is an important component of Karen diet, and various meats (harvested wild and from domestic animals) are stored either smoked or sun dried, while livestock are used for especially important events and celebrations.

Geographical Influences on Food

Place, in terms of physical and ecological factors such as weather, climate, soil and the landscape, plays an important role in shaping a food system. The Karens came from the coastal areas of Mawlamyine, Hinthada and Pathein in Burma. Upon migration to the Andamans, there would have been a change in the food system in accordance with availability of food resources. At the time of their settlement in the islands, there were no markets to speak of, and apart from the initial assistance given by the then British Administration to aid their settlement, they were expected to eke out their own sustenance. The community began to farm paddy on their allotted lands and foraged for edible food including flora, fauna and fish from their surrounding environments to sustain their families. A section of the settler population was employed in contract labour for felling timber (Roy 1995). Very soon, community members established friendly relations with the few remaining indigenous forest dwelling islanders in those regions, collectively called the Great Andamanese.[4] By associating with them, the Karen community both learnt of their immediate geography and built their own knowledge of the island and various livelihood resources including plants and animals.

Given similarities in the flora of the Andamans and Burma, the Karen found edible forest products and also cultivated paddy varieties that were brought by them during their migration from Burma. Interviews with elders reveal their pleasant surprise at the profound abundance of boar, and their initial reluctance to incorporate the meat of spotted deer (a species introduced in the islands from mainland India) in their diet, with beliefs about it leading to disease and bad health. This belief was shed over time, and soon Karen began to enjoy venison. Forest wildlife such as pigs, deer and monitor lizard were used for protein while fish, shrimp and shellfish were harvested from forest streams, mangrove creeks, seashores and coastal waters. The geographical features of the islands would have also opened some opportunities while restricting others. Some maritime adaptations, like the crafting of the dungi also took place upon settling in the Andamans. At present, the dungi plays an important role in their fishing activities. The transition from shifting cultivation in Myanmar to settled cultivation in the islands, and from predominantly freshwater fishing to a mixture of freshwater and marine fishing would have also brought interesting changes in diet and attitudes, but there is at present insufficient data to understand the details and implications of these transitions.

This connection of food habits with place implies that changes in the physical condition of the place, for example through environmental degradation or climate change, would directly affect the cuisine. Correspondingly, people have reported a reduced availability of forest foods such as wild pig in areas where they were previously found in abundance. They connect this reduction to population pressure, over-extraction and over hunting. They have also reported a marked reduction in ngapi stocks which they associate with the land upliftment since the Tsunami of 2004.

With respect to agriculture, many people report a reduction in productivity because of loss of soil fertility. During an interview with us, Saw Polomein, who is 78 years old, recalls:

> Citrus fruits like oranges, and lemons were abundant. In the last ten years or so, their availability has dwindled, being destroyed by pests quickly. Earlier we didn't have things like chips and biscuits. We would eat fruits and relish those. Now this land has been used for too many generations, it has grown old.

This rationale of believing that land is growing old is a way of understanding ecology by shifting cultivators who feel that a piece of land cannot keep providing good yield under conditions of continued cultivation for too long. This is why traditional shifting cultivation practices used to follow long fallow cycles before returning to the same piece of land for cultivation. A socio-economic study conducted in North Andaman in 1999 also indicated a substantial decline in rice productivity in 40 years from 5.24 tonne/hectare to 1.57 tonne/hectare (cited in Ali 2000). The physical condition of the place, therefore, cannot be separated from the activities undertaken on it. This implies that the food culture of a group is influenced by not just the place, but by the 'space' of what is allowed and encouraged in that place.

Spaces for Continuity and Ruptures

> Saw Ather: People are more, and fish is less. And now we don't go too far. Earlier, we used to go to far off places in halis[5] dungi for fishing and hunting. Everything was free. Hunting. Farming. Fishing. Now my fishing license is cancelled since I am past 60 years of age. There will be no fun in going for fishing now-like thieves, with the threat of being caught hanging over.

> Naw Amelie: Restrictions were less. There was abundance of oil and meat of wild pig and turtle. Nobody to catch you—you could go

anywhere, clear any land. Now land is not available. Even if available we are not allowed.

Food systems are connected not just with the place, but also with the arrangement and accessibility of the place according to socio-cultural and political factors, something that we can loosely denote as 'space'. Space can be considered as a function of mobility and accessibility, thus being affected by what is promoted and what is restricted. For instance, along with reduced availability in recent years, the decline in the use of wild species such as wild pig, deer, civets, etc., is clearly linked to imposed laws that the Karens have to follow. Whether they agree with it or not, they have come under the ambit of the larger, restrictive conservation policies brought in from the mainland and imposed by the Forest Department. This lack of choice in the matter affects several food-related practices including fishing, ngapi-making, and foraging for forest foods. The two quotes given above reflect the nostalgia among Karen settlers in the Island about the relative freedom of movement and of use of forest resources in the first few decades after settlement. Voyaging across islands, beaches, mangroves and mudflats is a way of ensuring continuity of the nomadic and itinerant lifestyles of the past. Being static and rooted to one place gets boring, while travelling and foraging for articles of consumption, domestic use and to sell for income is adventurous and exciting, something that even young boys who accompany their elders for weeks like to endure. Restrictions and criminalization of many forest activities have increased with time, leading to an insecure access to the forests where they once wandered freely. Getting the necessary paperwork done is a daunting task to work through red-tape and harassment that many prefer to avoid. Because of the precarious and insecure nature of forest-based livelihoods, many prefer alternatives that take them away from their customary ways of life.

Such policies which try to exclude the forest dweller from their home environment or impose a range of restrictions affecting how they would have otherwise interacted with their forests have attracted some qualitative critiques especially in the context of the social injustice involved (e.g., Bijoy 2007; Johari 2007; Lasgorceix and Kothari 2009; Sarin 2005; Taghioff and Menon 2010). In 2006, the central government passed a legislation known as The Scheduled Tribes and Other Traditional Forest Dwellers (Recognition of Forest Rights) Act, which recognizes rights of forest dwellers and has the theoretical potential of enabling democratic governance in the forest (Pathak Broome et al. 2014). However, the Act is ambiguous in its implications for a community like the Karen who are not considered as traditional forest dwellers in the Andamans. The A&N Administration maintains that the Act is not applicable to the islands since the interests of the tribals (limiting the interpretation to the indigenous populations present in the islands) have already been protected by the A&N Islands Protection of Aboriginal Tribes (Regulation), 1956.[6]

Such legal interpretations overlook the history of settlement programs in the Andamans. Zehmisch (2012, 6) points out that 'subalternity appears both as a precondition for the transportation of populations as well as their continuous domination in the island colony'. He defines subalternity as 'a relationship of subordination as well as physical and epistemic violence, experienced by marginal groups in the modern state' (ibid.). Populations that were considered as hard working, sturdy and docile, or 'problem populations' were selected for settlement in the islands. Policy-making for the islands, in the colonial period through commodification and post Independence through development policies, has failed to give due consideration to inherent linkages between people and environment (Krishnakumar 2009). The programme of improvement through settlement, labour supply and moralizing taken on by the Chief Commissioner Ferrar, was continued by the Indian state, while merging it with the idea of nationalization (Mazumdar 2015). These larger processes can have had a great impact on food cultures worldwide. For instance, a more 'civilized' diet was imposed by Spaniards on Native Americans as an evangelizing exercise through a forced change in their foods and cookware (Vernot 2018). In Japan, the practice of having elaborately crafted lunch box (*obento*) can be viewed as a gendered state apparatus where subtle pressures work on mother and child to make them behave according to a certain set of expectations (Allison 1991).

'Space' is thus connected to not just physical arrangement and accessibility, but also dominant notions of what is considered as appropriate and how the subaltern reacts and responds to these. So, the state schemes that promote mechanization in fishing and agriculture, hybrid paddy varieties, free rice from ration shops or a 100-day employment in construction activities, all have an influence on the space allowed for a food system to continue and evolve. At an even more subtle level, ideas of cultural taste reinforce social and class divisions (Bourdieu 1979/2013), implying that this space is influenced by notions of purity and inferiority. Consequently, settler tribal communities like the Karen and the Ranchi[7] have always held an ambiguous state of identity. Pushed by notions of development and fitting in, the Karen of the Andamans have preserved certain aspects of their cultural identity while selectively discarding or transforming others (Mittal 2015).

Confronted with the notional dichotomy between the savaged and the civilized, there is a shedding or hiding of 'tribal' attributes that may be considered as socially inappropriate. For example, there is often a sense of reluctance and self-consciousness among the Karen about eating ngapi in its classic runny form (which has a characteristic smell) in front of people belonging to other communities. During weddings and birthday parties organized by the Karens within a heterogeneous village, the celebratory meals have shifted to mainstream fare such as chicken biriyani and paneer. This is in stark contrast to the customary rice meal served with ngapi, boiled vegetables, soup and pork. The Karens are also reluctant to pack some of their most distinctive or strong-smelling meat or fish preparations in school lunch boxes for their children because of a similar feeling of social awkwardness.[8] At the same time, they wholeheartedly enjoy consuming these articles in presence of their own kin.

Interviews with several Karen individuals have revealed a feeling among some of them that their community is 'backward'.[9] Some have even connected it to their folklore. One of the Karen origin stories talks about how the mythical boar-hunter Htaw Mein Pah who was blessed with eternal youth wanted to go ahead searching for more land for settling his ever-increasing family. His brother Sa Khai Khlo was left behind because he had put *khlo* (shellfish) in a pot to boil and kept waiting for the shells to soften (something that would never happen). The Karens consider themselves to be the children of Sa Khai Khlo and connect this story to their present status in development. 'He keeps waiting for shellfish to boil while others go ahead. This is Karen. While others get developed, Karen doesn't understand how to do such things,' narrates Naw Namu.

In this context, it is important to consider subordination meted out to people through the lens of what Pierre Bourdieu terms as 'misrecognition'; 'the symbolic violence of the most powerful groups that allows the naturalization of domination, thus creating passivity and conformity to a given social order' (Navarro 2006). This operates so subtly that individuals may not be aware of their own subordination.

Implications of spaces on food occurs not only at the landscape level (movement in the forests, seas and on land) but also at a more localized level, for instance, in the layout of the homestead space, and the clustering arrangement of the houses. As the size of the landholdings decreases, and as more and more houses get constructed in a line by the side of a road, some customary food processes, like spaces for pounding ngapi, or keeping livestock, become more inconvenient. Slowly, they go out of practice. The architecture of the Karen house has also changed from being a homemade predominantly from wood, bamboo and umbrella palm to a cement-dwelling with a tin roof. This change is because of restricted access and low availability of natural materials on the one hand, and easy availability of materials from markets (promoted also by government schemes) on the other. In traditional Karen architecture, the lower floor of houses was used for granaries and livestock, and the upper floor was the section to live, which had a kitchen with a wood stove. In modern dwellings, there is no space for grain or livestock, and the wood stove has also lost its place within the house, being replaced by a modern kitchen. Dominant and mainstream ideas of aesthetics, propriety and modernity can affect such important choices of house planning and layout, thereby affecting continuity and change in food traditions.

In a study of the Karen settlers in Australia, Bird (2013, 12) talks about settlement as 'a more tacit, intersubjective and ongoing process of belonging, longing and shifting loyalties, and finding meaningful ways to negotiate these alongside shifting identities and cultural frameworks'. She stresses that these aspects are as important as the material and practical aspects in terms of their implications for a person feeling settled. While ideas of social appropriateness may push a community towards a desire for assimilation, ethnic assertion sometimes becomes a political and strategic need. Ethnicity is understood as an acknowledgment of difference and a visibility of contrast (Mintz and Bois 2002). While on one hand, there is an attempt to blend in, on the other, there is a need to stand out. The articulation of Andamans as a culturally hybrid society, often called 'Mini-India' can be viewed as a strategic action for being heard (Zehmisch 2012). But at the same time, the provision of 'positive discrimination' since 2005 through reservation as Other Backward Class has led to a simultaneous assertion by various settler communities of a separate bounded identity (ibid.). Interest in cultural revival among the Karen may also be politically motivated, to get recognition as a Scheduled Tribe (Maiti 2012).

The process of change in the cuisine of the Karen of the Andamans is 'more syncretic than substitution' (Mittal 2015, 15). Despite the changes in food systems that have been brought about because of restrictions and dominant ideologies, many distinct elements of the Karen cuisine continue to exist and thrive. Although there is now a high dependence on the market among the Karens for packaged food like chips, biscuits and candy, they still depend on internal and local networks of purchase and exchange for commodities like fish and vegetables. Their rationale is that they want to avoid fish and vegetable which use chemical fertilizers and preservatives. The more laborious food items of Karen cuisine that are slowly going out of consumption are being revived through their preparation in local community markets and fund-raisers organized occasionally by different local self-help groups, cooperatives and the Karen churches. The most recent such initiative to revive Karen cuisine is a Karen Food Restaurant that has been initiated by the Andaman Karen Crafts Cooperative Society with support from the Andaman Nicobar Environment Team (ANET) and Dakshin Foundation. Through this restaurant, rice-based snacks such as mophaito, molonji and molosaun are regularly made available, thereby markedly increasing the consumption of these items by both the Karen community and other communities. The highly labour-intensive rice noodles called mohinga are also served on a weekly basis. Attempting to ensure demand and income through consistent sales, the restauranteurs have extended the food menu to include a number of mainstream fast-food items and *thali*-type meals as well. There is thus a blending of the old and the new within the Karen cuisine of the Andamans.

Concluding Remarks

Food sharing has significance and value in maintaining community membership, harmony and reciprocity in social relations (Quandt et al. 2001). The Karen cuisine, like that of many other agricultural communities, is an integration of choice, practice and need, and is continuously evolving with time. Rice being the staple, cultivation of rice in erstwhile Burma by many including the Karens was practised as a form of shifting agriculture adapting to the needs and terrain. By shifting from place to place within and around forests, their knowledge of edible wild foods from these forests supplemented the food that were cultivated and provided protein and other nutrients to the community. Such practices are prevalent even today in the way in which the diversity of food sourced and consumed by the Karens takes place. Foraging, fishing, domestication, cultivation and earning income to purchase food are the range of livelihood activities among this small ethnic community. While such a range is common among many other settled communities in the Andaman Islands, some food-gathering skills, knowledge and the ability to use a wide repertoire of locally found foods are unique to the Karens. Apart from a multitude of cultivated plants (including leaves and fruits of various trees) used in their diet, a wide range of wild plant foods are sourced from the vicinity of habitations. Consumption of cultivated vegetables and meat of domesticated animals are recent practices, and form just a part of their diet.

For a community with a history of foraging, migration, relative isolation, adaptation and assimilation, the availability and access to resources and cultural infusions have played an important role in shaping their present diets in the Andamans. Restricting access to the forest and its varied resources, regulating hunting and fishing activities, as also promoting other vocations by governmental and non-governmental agencies are common to all settled communities on the islands including the Karen. Such overarching control as an administrative requirement of the Andaman and Nicobar Administration influences the economic activity of the islanders. As a community which was formerly largely self-reliant for not just what is eaten at home, but what is accessed for economy, infrastructure, leisure, etc., such influence has transformed cultural notions and dimensions of well-being among the Karens of the Andamans. As mentioned earlier, part of Karen identity (as with any ethnic group and identity) is associated with continuity of traditional practices associated with life skills, food preferences, health and leisure. Cultural assimilation through inter-cultural marriage, mainstream employment and education and also migration beyond their natal villages has changed food preferences among many younger members of the Karen community in the islands. Modernity and mainstream ideas of propriety have infused perceptions of difference leading to changes in perceiving cultural identity, including embarrassment about openly eating certain foods which are considered as 'primitive', or 'unclean' by other ethnic groups in the Islands, even while the older generation affirms these to be healthy and nutritious. At the same time, there are emerging processes countering this homogenization by reaffirming pride in the traditional Karen cuisine and making it available to other communities.

It is clear from this study that the relationship of Karen with their food has evolved in the Andaman Islands with time, as a function of place and space, and still holds an important role in the cultural identity of the community. While markets and lifestyle changes have had an impact on what is cooked, notions of propriety and legality have also influenced the diet, especially what is eaten openly.[10]

Notes

1. The household survey was conducted by ANET/Dakshin Foundation between December 2017 and March 2018. The data was collected by Saw Isaac, Naw Cecilia and Naw Stella.
2. As communicated by Saw Saytha, Secretary of Karen Welfare Association which conducted a census in 2017

3. These involve cleaning the shrimp of other waste, sun-drying, pounding, drying again for two to three days and then pounding again with some salt to form a lump. At this stage, some people mix this lump with *ganji-rice* (watery rice gruel) in a proportion of 4:1, but this is generally done for self-consumption, not for distributing or selling to others. Otherwise, this lump is then dried again and stored in a special clay pot called *trey*.
4. It will be important to note here that apart from the Great Andamanese, the Karen also had a few encounters with the Jarawa, but these were ridden with conflict and violence.
5. Refers to rowboat.
6. As regularly accounted in the Ministry of Tribal Affairs' reports on Status of implementation of Forest Rights Act.
7. A term used to denote the aboriginal populations brought in the 1920s from the Chota Nagpur region of Central India.
8. A similar state of mind is depicted by Zai Whitaker in a children's story 'Kali and the Ratsnake', where a boy belonging to the Irula tribe packs his favourite snack of fried termites to school but sits away from other children fearing that they will make fun of him.
9. This feeling or opinion cannot be generalized as pervading to the entire community as there will be differing perspectives among them.

References

Ahmed, Z., R. Gautam, P. K. Singh, A. Singh, N. Bainsla, and S. Dam Roy. 2014. 'Special Features and Characterization of Rice Land Races of Karen Community in Andaman and Nicobar Islands, India'. *Journal of the Indian Society of Coastal Agricultural Research* 32 (2): 97–100.

Ali, R. 2000. 'A Socio-economic Study of the Villages Bordering Saddle Peak National Park, North Andaman'. ANET Technical Report (p. 20), Andaman and Nicobar Environmental Team, Port Blair.

Anderson, C., M. Mazumdar, and V. Pandya, eds. 2016. *New Histories of the Andaman Islands: Landscape, Place and Identity in the Bay of Bengal, 1790–2012*, 342. Cambridge: Cambridge University Press.

AOF. 2005. 'Local food'. *Anthropology of Food* 4.

Barthes, R. 1961/2013. 'Toward a Psychosociology of Contemporary Food Consumption'. In *Food and Culture: A Reader*, edited by C. Counihan and P. V. Esterik, 36–43. Translated by Richard Nice, 3rd ed., 1997/2013. New York, NY: Routledge.

Bijoy, C. 2007, July. 'Adivasis of India: A History of Discrimination, Conflict and Resistance'. In *This Is Our Homeland: A Collection of Essays on the Betrayal of Adivasi Rights in India*. Bangalore: EQUATIONS.

Bird, J. N. 2013. 'Talking with Lips: Settlement, Transnationalism and Identity of Karen People from Burma living in Brisbane, Australia'. Unpublished doctoral dissertation. Brisbane: Queensland University of Technology.

Bourdieu, P. 1979/2013. 'Distinction: A Social Critique of the Judgement of Taste'. In *Food and Culture: a Reader*, edited by Carole Counihan and Penny Van Esterik, 36–43. Translated by Richard Nice, 3rd ed., 1997/2013. New York, NY: Routledge.

Chandi, M. 2001, July. 'The Dugout Karen Dinghy "Khlee" of the Andaman Islands'. WWF Report.

Douglas, M. 1975. 'Deciphering a Meal'. In *Myth, Symbol, and Culture*, edited by Clifford Geertz. New York, NY: W. W. Norton.

Feagan, R. 2007. 'The Place of Food: Mapping out the "Local" in Local Food Systems', *Progress in Human Geography* 31 (1).

Fonte, M. 2008, July. 'Knowledge, Food and Place. A Way of Producing, a Way of Knowing'. *Sociologia Ruralis* 48 (3): 200–222.

Goody, J. 1982. *Cooking, Cuisine, and Class: A Study in Comparative Sociology*. New York, NY: Cambridge University Press.

Heidemann, F., and P. Zehmisch, eds. 2016. *Manifestations of History: Time, Space, and Community in the Andaman Islands*. New Delhi: Primus Books.

Higgs, S., and J. Thomas. 2016. 'Social Influences on Eating'. *Current Opinion in Behavioral Sciences* 9: 1–6. https://doi.org/10.1016/j.cobeha.2015.10.005.

Johari, R. 2007. 'Of Paper Tigers and Invisible People: The Cultural Politics of Nature in Sariska Tiger Reserve, Rajasthan, India'. In *Making Conservation Work*, edited by G. Shahabuddin and M. Rangarajan. New Delhi: Permanent Black.

Krishnakumar, M. V. 2009. 'Development or Despoilation?—The Andaman Islands under Colonial and Postcolonial Regimes'. *Shima: The International Journal of Research into Island Cultures* 3 (2): 104–117.

Lasgorceix, A., and A. Kothari. 2009. Displacement and Relocation of Protected Areas: A Synthesis and Analysis of Case Studies. *Economic & Political Weekly* 44: 37–47.

Lévi-Strauss, Claude. (1966, Autumn). 'The Culinary Triangle'. Translated by Peter Brooks. *The Partisan Review* 33: 586–596.

Maiti, S. 2004. 'The Karen—A lesser Known Community of the Andaman Islands (India)'. Paper presented at the Islands of the World VIII International Conference, Kimmen (Quemoy), Taiwan, November 1–7.

———. 2012. 'The Price of Progress: "Dying Arts" among the Karen of the Andaman Islands, India'. In *Moving Subjects, Moving Objects: Transnationalism, Cultural Production and Emotions*, edited by M. Svašek. Oxford: Berghahn Books.

Marshall, H. I. 1922, April 29. 'The Karen People of Burma: a Study in Anthropology and Ethnology'. *The Ohio State University Bulletin* 26.

Mazumdar, M. 2015. 'Improving Visions, Troubled Landscapes: The Legacies of Colonial Ferrargunj'. In *New Histories of the Andaman Islands: Landscape, Place and Identity in the Bay of Bengal, 1790–2012*, edited by C. Anderson, M. Mazumdar, and V. Pandya, 29–61. Cambridge: Cambridge University Press.

Mintz, S. W. 1979. 'Time, Sugar and Sweetness'. *Marxist Perspectives* 2 (4): 56–73.

Mintz, S. W., and C. M. Du Bois. 2002. 'The Anthropology of Food and Eating'. *Annual Review of Anthropology* 31: 99–119.

Mittal, T. 2015. 'The Karen of Andaman Islands: Labour Migration, Indian Citizenship and Development of a Unique Cultural Identity'. Anthropology Senior Theses. Paper 174.

Navarro, Z. 2006. 'In search of a Cultural Interpretation of Power: The Contribution of Pierre Bourdieu', *IDS Bulletin* 37: 11–22.

Pathak, Broome N., S. Desor, A. Kothari, and A. Bose. 2014. 'Changing Paradigms in Wildlife Conservation in India'. In *Democratising Forest Governance in India*, edited by S. Lele and A. Menon. New Delhi: Oxford University Press.

Quandt, S. A., T. A. Arcury, R. A. Bell, J. McDonald, and M. Z. Vitolins. 2001. 'The Social and Nutritional Meaning of Food Sharing among Older Rural Adults'. *Journal of Aging Studies* 15: 145e62.

Roy, S. B. 1995. *Bio-Social Change among the Karen of Andaman Island (Tribal Studies of India Series)*. New Delhi: Inter-India Publications.

Ruel, M. T., J. Harris, and K. Cunningham. 2013. 'Diet Quality in Developing Countries'. In *Diet Quality: An Evidence-based Approach*, edited by V. R. Preedy, L-A. Hunter, and V. Patel. New York, NY: Springer.

Sarin, M. 2005. 'Laws, Lore and Logjams: Critical Issues in Indian Forest Conservation'. *Gatekeeper Series* 116.

Taghioff, D., and A. Menon. 2010, July 10. 'Can a Tiger Change his Stripes?' *Economic & Political Weekly* 45 (28): 69–76.

Vernot, D. 2018. 'Changes in the Social and Food Practices of Indigenous People in the New Kingdom of Granada (Colombia): Through Artifacts'. *Journal of Ethnic Foods* 5: 177–183.

Zehmisch, P. 2012. 'A Xerox of India: Policies and Politics of Migration in the Andaman Islands'. Working Paper, Social and Cultural Anthropology 2, Munich.

———. 2017. *Mini-India: The Politics of Migration and Subalternity in the Andaman Islands*, 343. New Delhi: Oxford University Press.

17

Small Community and Large Industries

Food and Other Resources of Dandami Maria of Bastar

Amitabha Sarkar

Small-scale communities living in different eco-settings often depend on natural resources that are available in local eco-systems for their sustenance. Those resources are often utilized by them with the help of their age-old knowledge and techniques. Ways of using natural resources through application of technological knowledge help to create distinctive lifestyle of a community and are cherished by their specific ecological niche (Hardesty 1977, 289).

Undivided Bastar District that constitutes a large part of present-day Indian state of Chhattisgarh houses a rich cultural mosaic; presence of different ethnic groups, many of whom are small-scale communities and designated as 'Scheduled Tribe' contribute their respective cultural attributes to create the tapestry. Bastar is the homeland of Abujh Maria, also known as Hill Maria, who have been identified by the Indian government as 'Particularly Vulnerable Tribal Group'. Each of the communities of Muria, Dandami Maria, Dhurwa, Dorla, Halba and Bhatra occupies specific territory, has developed immense knowledge and emotional relationship with that space and possesses skill of eking out resources required for their survival from that given terrain. Relation between the people and their physical environment is not static; it undoubtedly is subjected to change—but rapid change caused by 'development programmes' like dam building, mining activities or other forms of industrialization in the space occupied by them has almost always caused immense distress among the communities. This chapter has discussed in some detail the relationship of the Dandami Maria of Bastar, who are also known as Bison-Horn Maria, with their environment. They traditionally were dependent on the local ecosystem for collection and production of both edible and non-edible items and made it part of their lifeways through beliefs and cultural practices. Probable consequences of industrialization in the region have also been discussed to understand how the food-procuring activities like gathering and hunting, and food production activities like horticulture and agriculture are impacted by unequal competition for same or kindred resources. Firstly, it has described how they exploit natural resources available to them for sustenance and how that relation tunes their socio-cultural life. Secondly, it has tried to assess how shrinkage of natural resources that were available to them traditionally, especially the food that they depended upon, can affect their lifeways and severely damage and even destroy food security.

Bastar experienced huge change in its ecological setting for the first time in post-independence years when large stretches of forest were cleared to make room for industry and mining. This resulted in eviction of tribal and other marginalized communities, for whom forest had been the habitat and resource base for centuries. People of Bastar lacked technical education and skill that the large-scale industries were looking for in employees; though several of them were employed in those industries, almost all of them were unskilled menial workers. They gradually became aware of the ruthless exploitation they have been subjected to and the ever-increasing alienation from resources they have been thrown into by the capital-intensive system. The ruling political parties devised a series of social and economic measures to placate the aggrieved feeling that ran high among the affected people. As most of those programmes were woefully inadequate to address their basic needs, failure was inevitable. As such, the growing resentment did not subside as expected; on the contrary, it rapidly escalated to a violent revolt (Sarkar et al. 2014).

It is true that capitalism 'freed the subaltern classes from the yoke of feudalism and its standard bearers, the bourgeoisie even promised a society based on rational principles with equal opportunity for everyone.

It is also true that under capitalism, with a centralized authority to maintain law and order, the forging of cultural unity and the emergence of the idea of nation, the modern state evolved. Nevertheless, the exploitation of the subaltern by the rich did not stop. On the contrary, it became more relentless under the guise of democracy. The capitalist class was especially keen on amassing colossal capital and reaping huge profit by siphoning off the surplus value created by wage labour into its own coffer. In the process, it alienated the labour force, which had no control either over the means of production or over the production process, from the economic, political and social mainstream. That is why Marx remarked, 'Capitalism, which had emerged as a liberating force, grew into a new system of exploitation' (Sarkar et al. 2014).

In India different tribal communities live in different eco-setting and for sustenance, they utilize the immediate natural resources with their traditional knowledge and techniques. Since physical environment is the key factor for using such resources, it is obvious that their social environment also flourished under such environment. The ecological setting reflected the technology, world view and the belief system of the communities. Their economic pursuits are usually linked with ecology, environment and technology that allow them to adjust themselves in different interactional situations. These interactional activities have crystallized to some extent in the form of cultural traits. As these communities have differential cultural setting, their response to the immediate ecosystem might be different. The present chapter highlights interaction of the Dandami Maria community with their natural environment for their survival and its impact on their social environment.

For collection of empirical data three villages were selected from Bastar District (see Figures 17.1 and 17.2):

1. *Koduli:* Here the people practise *penda* or slash and burn cultivation. It is in villages located in dense forest area where penda or shifting cultivation is practised along with plough cultivation. The village is situated in the forest area of Orcha Block of Bastar District. Here the Dandami Maria are immigrants settled in Abujh Maria tribal enclave.
2. *Burumpal:* The Dandami Maria practise wet cultivation in the plains. In this village they practise plough cultivation and are more exposed to the outside world. This village is under Tokapal Block of Bastar District. Due to protest by the villagers a steel plant could not be established here.
3. *Padapur:* This village is in National Mineral Development Corporation Limited (NMDC) mining area. Here plough cultivation is practised. It is under Dantewada Block of undivided Bastar District.

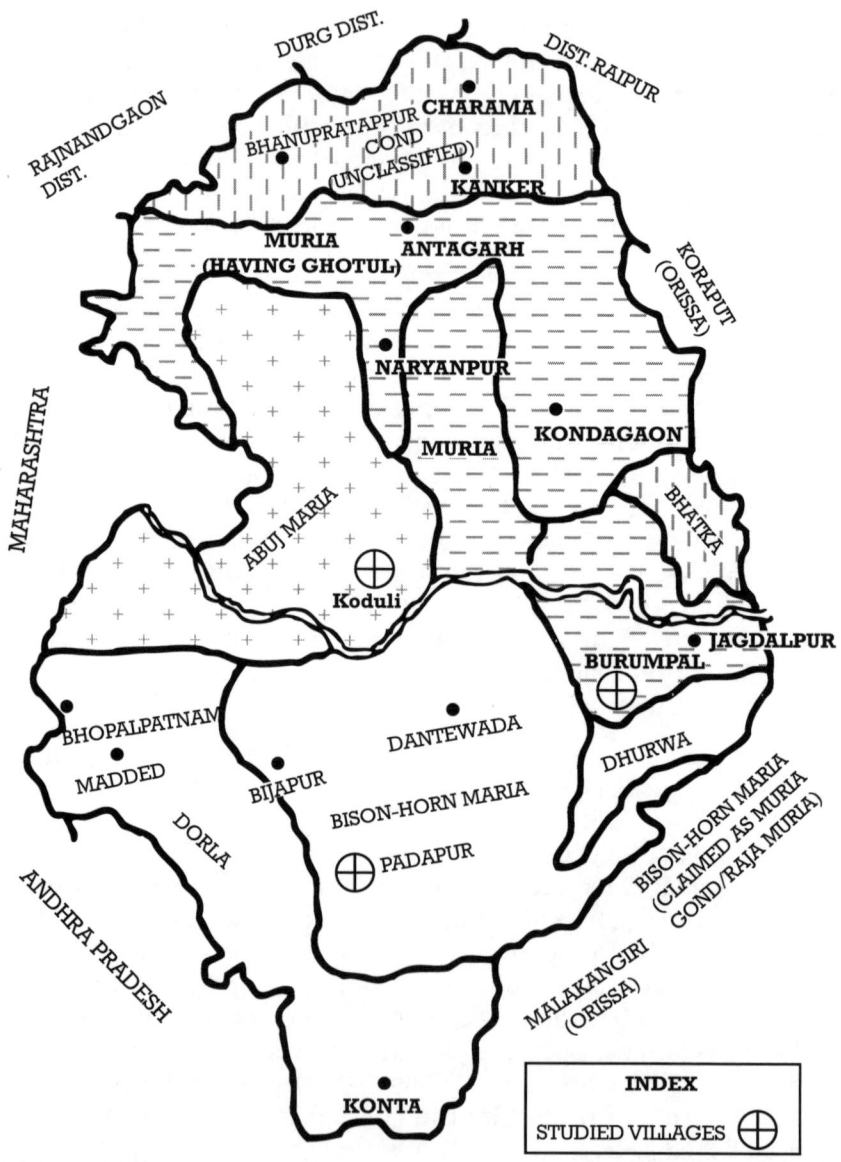

SKETCHMAP OF DISTRICT BASTAR (UNDIVIDED)

CONCENTRATION OF TRIBAL POCKETS AND STUDIED VILLAGES

FIGURE 17.1 *Sketch Map of District Bastar (Undivided)*

Source: Meteorological Office, Jagdalpur, Bastar, Madhya Pradesh.

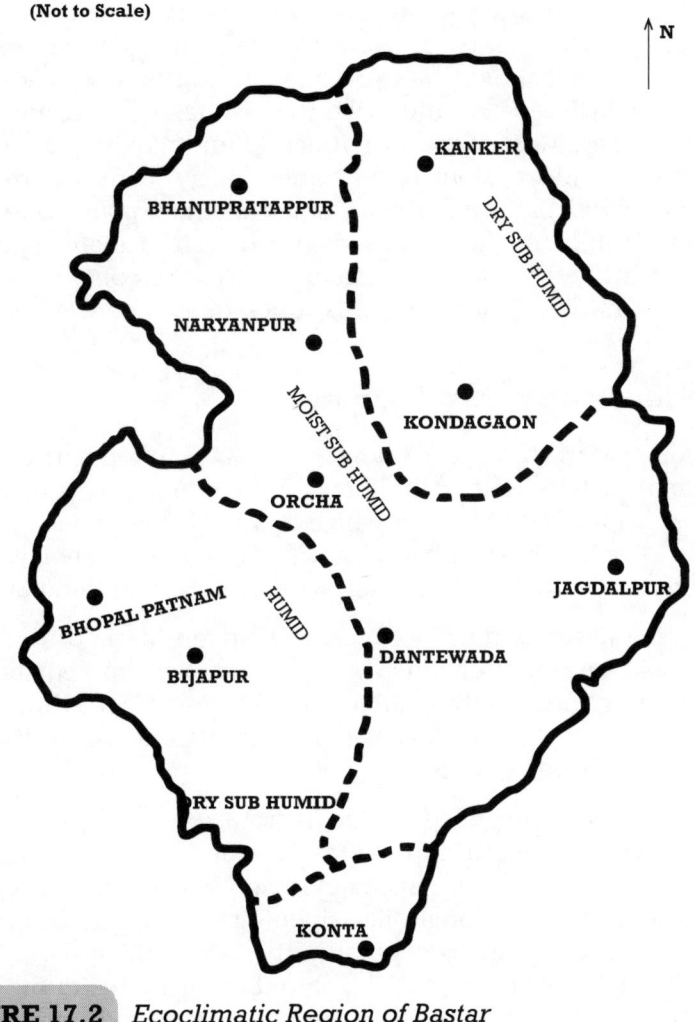

(Not to Scale)

↑ N

KANKER

BHANUPRATAPPUR

DRY SUB HUMID

NARYANPUR

MOIST SUB HUMID

KONDAGAON

ORCHA

JAGDALPUR

BHOPAL PATNAM

HUMID

BIJAPUR

DANTEWADA

DRY SUB HUMID

KONTA

| **FIGURE 17.2** | *Ecoclimatic Region of Bastar* |

Source: Meteorological Office, Jagdalpur, Bastar, Madhya Pradesh.

Ecoclimate

The ecoclimate of the district is estimated based on monthly rainfall and mean monthly temperature. Bastar District is divided into three ecoclimatic zones:

1. *Humid*: The Southern plateau—West of Bailadilla and Tikanpalli Hills, mostly constituted of Bijapur Teshil. Usur Hills lie south-west of this zone.

2. *Moist sub-humid*: Abujhmar Hills, north-western parts of Kotri-Mahanadi plains, eastern parts of southern plateau covering Dantewadi plains, right up to Sukma and southern parts of north-eastern plateau covering Indrawati plains of Jagdalpur region consti-tute this zone. Most of the area under Bhanupratappur, Naryanpur, Dantewada and Jagdalpur Teshil comes under it (Crookshank 1963).
3. *Dry sub-humid*: Eastern parts of Kotri–Mahanadi plain constituting Kankar Teshil, northern parts of north-eastern plateau covering Kondagaon Teshil and a very small region South of Golapalli Hills situated in Konta Teshil form this zone.

Dependence on Forest Resources

The Dandami Maria have been traditionally living in forest areas and are dependent on forests for their livelihood. Ecological setting of their abode makes a deep impact on their life, which gets adequately reflected in their economy as well as in their belief system. All the raw materials for hut construction are collected from the forest, especially in Koduli village.

Having a forest-based economy, the Dandami Maria of Koduli sat-isfy most of their requirements by exploiting their immediate niche. The forests not only supply a patch of land to construct a hut, but also provide them with wooden log, bamboo and thatching grass like *sadka* and *chand* or *ind kata* grasses.

They also collect various food items from forest, this is the major economic activity of the Dandami Maria, especially for women of the community, who often are assisted by their children. In the season of *mahua* flower (Madhuca longifolia), ripening of tamarind (Tamarindus indica), collection of kosa (cocoon of Antheraea moth) and *tendu* leaves (Diospyros melanoxylon), they devote much of their time to collect those items. Due to close association with forest environment, they possess intimate knowledge about edible roots, tubers, herbs, leaves, fruits, mushroom, wild animals and medicinal plants. Some of the food materials they collect are so bitter or sour that those are not suitable for human consumption in the state those are collected. The people process those items by washing for long in running water or by boil-ing and then washing repeatedly till those are rendered edible. Each morning the women move into the forest with a *tokna* (bamboo basket) and a *pushal* or *korki* (digging stick). Their competence in collection activities is recognized by all members of the community. They can assess presence of edible roots and tubers by observing the surface of earth and surrounding vegetation. They do not uproot the entire plant while collecting a tuber or a root but leave enough for rejuvenation. Collection usually starts in early morning and continues till mid-day. Throughout the year they collect various edible and non-edible forest products depending on seasonal variation in availability, a list of which is provided below in Table 17.1. They recognize three seasons, which are *garmi* (summer), *barish* (monsoon) and *jara* or *sardi* (winter). Blooming mahua flower indicates beginning of garmi; when sal seed

TABLE 17.1 *Seasonal Collection of Minor Forest Produces*

Season	Edible Items	Non-edible Items
Garmi (summer) (February–May)	*Mati* or tubers Kodo, kaska, gone, kotosh, kai, kaiman, keku, lekh, rasa, nangal, tule, gunga, rash, nager	Seed Sal
	Saag or leafy vegetables Velvetun, kodeli	Twig Sal, harra, neem, amba (mango)
	Phool or flower Velvetun, tund, mahua (eiru)	Leaves Siyari or elephant creeper, tendu, tummer, chhind, sabai, epur (for making brooms, collected by Dandami Maria of Abuj Marh region), bamboo,
	Phal or fruit Kohka/velva, amba (mango), char, phanos (jackfruit), ind, turguna, tendu, imli, harra, baira, tummer	
	Bija or seed Tora, sal, ghogha, gorga and chhind (palm)	Insect Kosa (silk cocoon)
Barish (Monsoon) (June–September)	*Mati* or tubers Kash, pad, kaiman, tule, kotosh, bada (a kind of tuber grown under sal trees).	Bamboo, fuel wood.
	Saag or leafy vegetables Kahak, mugur, erbor, koliari Basta (tender bamboo shoot) and various kinds of mushroom.	
Sardi (Winter) (October–January)	*Mati* or tubers Pidu, pad, gali	Sal leaves for *doni* (bowl) preparation, *sabai* grass and bamboo for basketry.
	Phal or fruit Harra or karka, bayra or jahka	
	Tree sap Sulphi and chhind	

Source: Author's fieldwork data.

falls and mango becomes ripe, it is about time for barish; when *kosra* and paddy is ready for harvest and when *chhind* (palm) juice becomes sweeter and tastier—it is the time for sardi.

Forest plays a significant role in deciding their substantial possession not only on the basis of material needs, but on spiritual requirements too. Materials required for construction of a house are usually procured from local forest. Since they consider *saja* or *aden* (Terminalia tomentosa) tree as sacred, they prefer to use some saja twig in house construction.

Household goods of daily use and various weapons and implements are mostly made of wood, bamboo, grass and leaves procured from forest. Handle of an axe, *mushal* or wooden husker, *gudari* or hoe is made of wood, hunting implements like bow and arrow are made of bamboo splits. Their cot is made of *bija* or *dhaman* wood, while netting is done with *siyari* creeper. Bamboo is used to prepare tokna or baskets of various shapes and sizes for carrying or keeping cereals other items (Sarkar 2004). Raincoats and hats are prepared with various leaves. Their personal tobacco pouch or *gota* is made of *timas* wood and lime container or *chuna goruli* is made of bamboo. They also make various types of musical drums with dried trunk of sago palm tree; for tonal variation they cover one side of the instrument with cow hide and the other side with hide of goat or deer. The Dandami Maria keep peacock and fowl feather in each house, it is believed that those items possess some magical power and can drive malevolent spirits out.

Near-absolute dependency of the community on forest resources has been daunted, while iron and other metal imported from distant places were part of their material culture since long, in recent times plastic objects are making inroad. Wood and bamboo containers for tobacco and lime are being replaced by plastic containers in villages close to mining sites.

Hunting used to be another major means of forest-based sustenance for the Dandami Maria; this activity is prerogative of the men. They possess vast knowledge about the forest terrain and about various animals. Nowadays due to non-availability of hunts, it is not considered an economic pursuit. Hunting is collectively done on certain occasions and festivals as a sports activity. But Dandami Maria men always carry bow and arrow, whenever they go to forest. If by chance they can hunt birds or larger games like wild boar, it offers them an occasion for a grand feast. Summer is the best time for hunting.

Trapping is another important activity for the community. They catch field rats with traps and use kosra grains as bait. It is a delicacy for them. Hare is trapped in night, but the trapper identifies the holes during day hours, lays trap and urinates there—the smell attracts the animal and pulls it to the trap. Birds are caught by using a gum that they make with extracts of locally available plants.

Relation between the Dandami Maria and their physical environment is not necessarily that of food consumer and food provider; they have several totemic clan groups and each group refrain from harming or killing their totem animal or totem plant. Thus, the relation transcends mere need-based transactions; elements present in the environment become part of their meta-physical existence.

Forest Resources in Treating Ailments

Apart from extracting food and material required for other necessities, the Dandami Maria make extensive use of forest resources to treat different ailments. Table 17.2 presents a small part of the huge repertoire of knowledge that the Dandami Maria use for the purpose (for a detailed discussion see Sarkar and Choudhury 2013). The traditional medicine man in Dandami Maria community is known as *gaita* or *wadde*; this is a hereditary post.

TABLE 17.2 *Use of Indigenous Knowledge for Treating Ailments*

S. No.	Herbs, Plants, Seeds Used	Ailment
1.	*Sarpagandha* (Rauvolfia serpentina)	Roots of the plant is used for high blood pressure, hysteria, snake bite and mental derangement
2.	*Charota* seeds	Oil is used for skin disease
3.	*Kali musli* (Curculiza orchiocdes)	Tuber is used for health rejuvenation
4.	*Sadabahar* (Vincarosea, Family-Apocynaccae)	Flower is used for diabetes
5.	*Sarpunka* (Indigofera angulosa)	Roots, fruits, seeds and flower are used for stomach pain, piles, deworming
6.	*Banjira* (Carum nigrum)	Seeds are used for rheumatic pain
7.	*Jamun* seed (Syzygium cumini)	Crushed seeds used for diabetes
8.	*Harra* fruit (Terminalia chebula)	
9.	*Behra* fruit (Terminalia bellirica)	Help digestion and clear stomach
10.	*Aonla* fruit (Emblica officinalis)	

(Table 17.2 Continued)

(Table 17.2 Continued)

S. No.	Herbs, Plants, Seeds Used	Ailment
11.	*Kala haldi* (Curcuma caesia)	Paste is used for treating leprosy
12.	*Chiraita* (Swertia chirata)	Used as blood-purifier, anti-diabetic and anti-malarial medicine
13.	*Shivalingi* seeds	Treats barrenness
14.	*Arjun* bark (T. arjuna)	It is soaked in water and water is taken for heart problem
15.	*Kakai* bark	Health rejuvenator for postpartum women
16.	*Jangli Kela* (Musa sepintum)	Seed used in smallpox
17.	*Jangli Payar* (Urginea indica)	Tuber used for diarrhoea and epilepsy
18.	*Bhui aonla* (Phyllanthis nurarii)	Whole plant extract is used for jaundice and anaemia
19.	*Hadjod* (Vitis quadrangularis)	Tip of leaf is used to treat bone fracture, rheumatism, acidity and worm
20.	*Kala dhatoora*	For asthma leaves are smoked
21.	*Tad/Sulphi*	Used for toothache
22.	*Bajradanti* root	Used for dental diseases and stomachache
23.	*Nirmali* grass (Strychnos potatorum)	Plant is used as water purifier
24.	*Velva* seed (Semicarpus anacardium)	Oil extracted from burnt seed is used to treat headache
25.	*Kusum* seed and bark (Schleichera trijuga)	Extracted oil is used for skin disease, rheumatic pain, and itches
26.	*Babachi* (Psoratea corylifolia)	Seeds used for leukoderma, leprosy, fistula, diarrhoea and promoting urination
27.	*Amaltas* (Cassia fistula)	Fruit and flower used for fever, piles, gastric and constipation
28.	*Dhaura* (Anogeissus latifolia)	Entire plant used as astringent, antidote for snake and scorpion bite
29.	*Kurchi* (Horlarrhena antidysentrica)	Bark and seeds are used in amoebic dysentery
30.	*Erand* seeds (Castor) (Ricinus communis)	Extracted oil used for snake bite and pulp used as purgative

Source: Author's fieldwork data.

The medicinal system that includes diagnosis and treatment has developed among the Dandami Maria over generations through prolonged association with their local ecosystem and is yet to be documented fully.

Custodians of Nature

As the Dandami Maria are dependent on forest and other natural resources for their physical and spiritual well-being, they try to protect their physical environment through certain traditional conservation ethics.

A major component of such ethical practices is preservation of sacred grove. Paranjpye (1989) described sacred groves as 'patch of forest ... which is undisturbed by the local inhabitants'. Buchmen (1992) noted sacred groves to contain 'a large number of species and is considered to be a true ecological jewel'. Gadgil and Vartak (1976) have thanked such traditional practices for their contribution towards preservation of biodiversity and have noted that such practices operate in various tribal pockets of India.

Among the Dandami Maria sacred groves or *tallin* are patches of forest usually left undisturbed by the local inhabitants. They can collect foliage and dry twigs from the sacred space but cannot cut any tree standing there. A grove is dedicated to their mother goddess *Deogudi*, who is supposed to protect and preside over the grove. Intruders who violate customary law related to sacred groves are punished by the village panchayat. Usually each village has a grove that is situated at the village periphery. Most of the community worship, annual worship, *pen* (clan deity) ritual and all celestial rituals are performed at the tallin.

Apart from rules related to sacred groves, there are prohibitions about cutting trees or burning certain trees at their penda field. They are also tabooed to eat certain fruits, flowers, leafy vegetables like amba, mahua, *koliyari bhaji* prior to the performance of specific rituals. Such seasonal abstention is related to overeating some items or protecting those plants when required for their conservation. Some trees such as *saja, jagdumar, dhura* (Anogeissus latifolia) and *bargat* (baniyan) are considered sacred. *Aden* or *saja* tree (Terminalia tomentosa) and its leaves are very important in Dandami Maria culture. When a *siraha* or priest is possessed by some deity, he keeps saja leaves in his hand; during the trance, the deity communicates with the priest through the medium of saja leaves. The Dandami Maria usually keep a dry twig or log of saja at the house in order to protect themselves from evil eye or malevolent spirits.

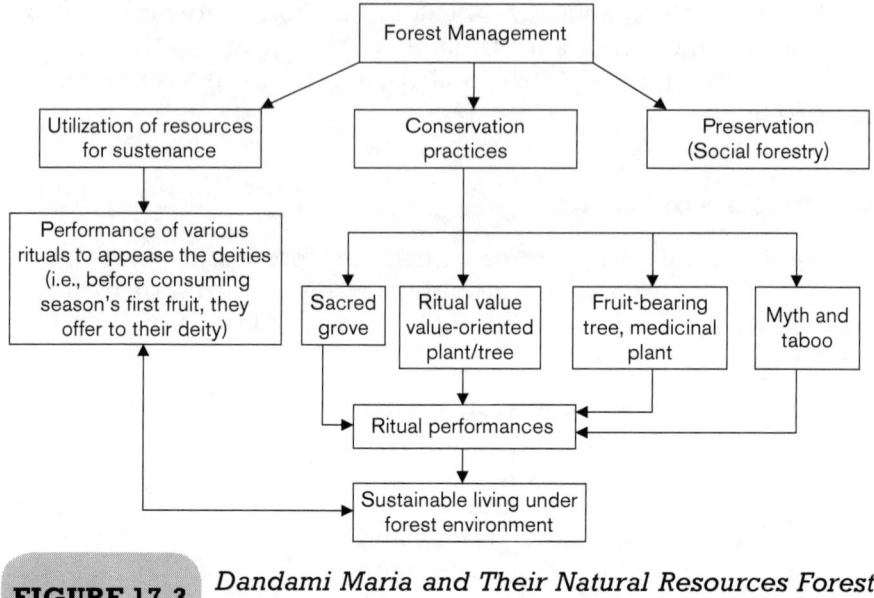

FIGURE 17.3 *Dandami Maria and Their Natural Resources Forest Management*

Source: Author's fieldwork data.

They also conserve some trees which have economic value like mango, tamarind, *aonla*, *bayra*, harra, mahua, char and sulphi. Possession of those trees signifies economic and social status in the village. Aden and dhaura are important because silk moths lay eggs on those trees, *kosa* or silk cocoon is a saleable item.

In the plains and in areas where mining activities are common, some trees have been planted as part of social forestry programme. There chiefly eucalyptus, arjun, sal and cashew trees have been planted with the idea that those plants can be sold when matured. Such relationship with plants does not go with traditional Dandami Maria ethics about their local ecosystem.

Figure 17.3 shows the apparent relationship between the Dandami Maria and the local ecosystem, which is their habitat. It also places exogenous programmes like social forestry in the scheme of traditional resource management of the community.

Cultivation of Land

At the outset, the typology of cultivable land needs to be described. Selection of crops to be cultivated is largely based on the type of land

TABLE 17.3	Nature of Crop and Land Type as per Retention of Water Capacity
Land Type	**Chief Cereals/Crop Produced**
1. *Maran/Marhan*	Kosra, oil seeds like tilli, korch; paddy, arba, kulthi, urad, chikma
2. *Bari*	Jendra, rahar, tomato, kulthi, chikma, sarsoo, tilli, gourd, pumpkin, barbati (yard long bean), jata (flat bean)
3. *Bera*	Paddy, wheat

Source: Author's fieldwork data.

(see Table 17.3). High land on the hills is known as *pahar* or *metajamin*; when such cultivable land is situated on a tabletop hill, it is called *maran* or *marhan*. Usually in the *marh* or hilly area they practise two types of cultivation—*erka* and *dippa* or *dahi*. The other variety of land on hill slope is penda, in comparison to higher land, hill slopes are much larger in terms of area. Third form of land is *chatan* or rocky surface, it is generally used as grazing field for their livestock. The fourth type of land is *bera*, which is comparatively flat and low and is suitable for paddy cultivation. Soil in this type of land is sticky and has the capacity for retaining water. They also prepare contour bunding between plots of land for water storage. Bera land is again divided into two categories according to its production capacity. The high land bera is known as *vedang*, where quick growing coarse variety paddy is cultivated. Low-lying *bera* land is known as *munda*, where finer quality paddy is produced; such land is tilled with plough. A munda land is usually situated close to *nallah* or rivulet, where plenty of water is available.

The other type of land is homestead land or *bari*; again, this type is classified into two according to its position. It has been observed in the studied villages that their huts are situated in such a manner that each one has some attached cultivable land. In this type, low lying land is known as *velum*, where crops like *jondra*, (maize), *madia* (millet), *setka* (a kind of paddy), *bhaji* (leafy vegetables) and sometimes *sarsoo* (mustard) are produced. Bari land is very fertile because the excrement of the livestock acts as fertilizer. Bari land located higher is relatively dry, it is known as *marhan*. On such lands they cultivate a kind of paddy known as *atwanji*, which requires less water, but the yield is rather high. The seeds are sown sometimes in April and mature before Dussehra. Apart from atwanji paddy, they also cultivate kosra of various types. In fact, this is also a table land situated above the level of velum homestead land.

Types of Cultivation

Penda

The Dandami Maria of the marh region practise penda or shifting cultivation. This mode of cultivation exists in various parts of the world with certain differences due to variation in the local ecosystem. Usually the most senior member of the family decides which part of the forest is to be sown in a particular year by examining the growth of vegetation. Penda involves several stages of operation. The first stage is selection of the site and this is usually done a year in advance. The patch of land is selected based on whether the vegetation is sufficiently dense or not.

Between February and March, the selected site is cleared by felling trees and shrubs and the wooden logs are left to dry. Before felling of trees and shrubs for penda land, they perform a ritual to appease the deity of tallin, the sacred grove. The dry woods and foliage are to be set on fire, but according to Dandami Maria tradition one is not allowed to light fire in the forest prior to the performance of Holi on new moon of the month *Phagur* or Phagun. Probable reason behind the restriction is that around that time they complete harvesting of *os kosra;* with the crop lying in the forest land, the lighting of fire in the vicinity may destroy the crop. The Dandami Maria of Koduli village, who migrated into this area, follow the norms of the original settlers of the land, the Abujh Maria, regarding selection of penda plots.

After successive cultivation for at least four years, the penda cultivators shift to another plot. Adjacent penda plots are demarcated by raising row of shrubs or planting sesame or with the help of some tree trunks. They receive three yields of kosra from a penda plot. During the month of *Mur* (April–May) after one or two showers they broadcast kosra seeds. This is known as *chhota kohla/kosra* or *ghatka*. They remain busy with their bera land for paddy cultivation during *Na* (May–June) and *Hai* (June–July). Harvesting of kosra is completed within *Eranj* (August–September), when they also harvest paddy grown on hilly plots along with kosra. There are various types of small kosra like *ghatka, chikma, kodon,* and *mandia*.

The other type of kosra, known as big kosra, is sown in *Hai* (June–July), and consists of varieties like *kutki* and *kang*, which are harvested during the month of *Pandi* (November–December). On the same plots they cultivate various pulses like *arhar, urad* and *jata* (*Dolichos lablab*).

During Eranj they sow os kosra in penda plots of *chhota kosra*. Along with this, they cultivate kulthi, and mung pulses, which are harvested during Pusi (December–January).

Erka Cultivation

In this type of cultivation some trees are fallen in the forest, then those are carried to a flat table land and spread out for drying. There the dried trees are burnt, usually before shower. The ashes are mixed with soil as fertilizer. Then seeds are broadcast. Erka cultivation is usually done in flat *marhan* land where they produce rice.

Dippa or Dahi Cultivation

This type of cultivation is similar to erka. It is also done on flat land, a dippa plot is cultivated for two years at a stretch. In the first year, they cut smaller trees, shrub, undergrowth of a plot and cultivate the land. In the second year, they cut big trees and those are burnt. It is believed, during the first year, fertility of the hitherto fallow land is high; therefore, they clear only small trees on the plot and burn the same. Next year, after harvesting of crops grown, fertility of the land is reduced. That is why, they cut big trees and the ashes act as a fertilizer for the plot.

Plough Cultivation

Plough cultivation is primarily done for paddy on bera land, which is usually reserved for paddy cultivation. In the month of May–June, they prepare the land by tiling the soil. After the first shower in the month of June they again till the soil and then sowing operation starts. The Dandami Maria have proved them to be good cultivators; they are well aware about technologies of plough cultivation.

The Dandami Maria of Burumpal village who are skilled in this type of cultivation also raise rabi or winter crop. As soon as they harvest jondra, they plough the soil again for rabi crops, which are primarily oil seeds like sarson and tilli, since in this area there is irrigation facility. On the marhan land, they cultivate *arhar (perhmi), urad*, chikma, kosra, kulthi and tilli etc.; in bari land they cultivate kulthi, jondra, sarson and tilli. While in bera land they chiefly practise paddy cultivation; the low-lying bera land located close to perennial water sources are used to produce rabi paddy and wheat.

In Burumpal there are seven hamlets attached to undulated cultivable land. Therefore, contour bounding between plots is prevalent for retaining water. Similar land is present in Padapur village (Figure 17.4).

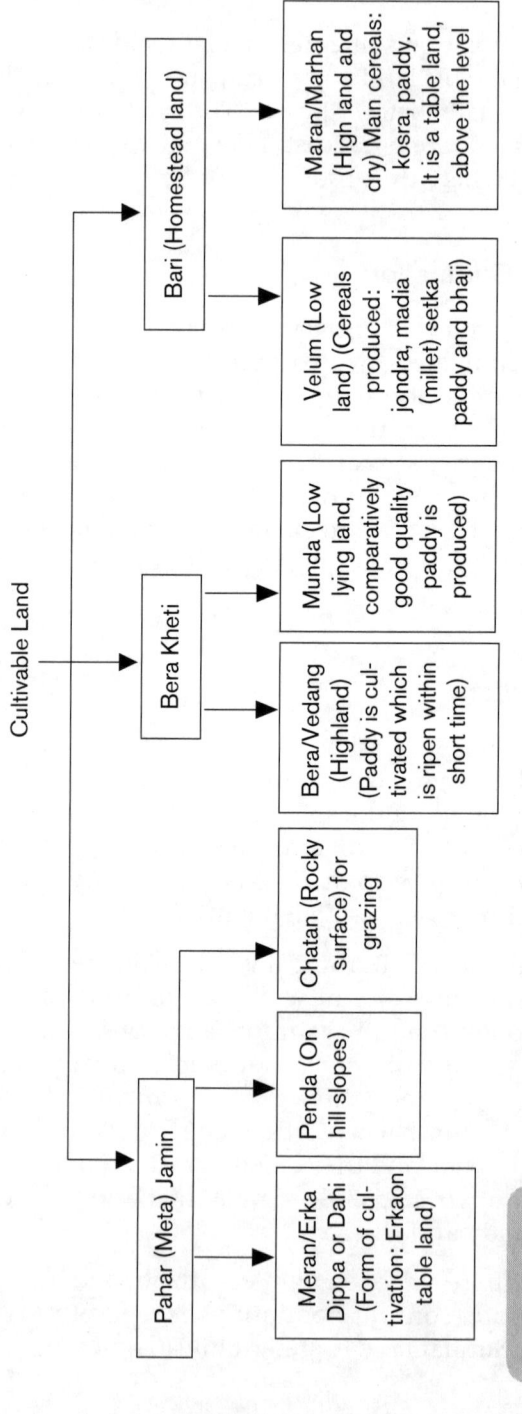

FIGURE 17.4 *Livelihood Practices—Role of Cultivable Land*

Source: Author's fieldwork data.

Classification of Cultivable Land as per Retention of Water Capacity

Supernatural Entities in Nature

Among the Dandami Maria every natural phenomenon is explained with activities of some spirits. Those supernatural beings have important roles to play in their life. The earth goddess, Bhum is worshipped at the tallin; at the onset of the new year they celebrate *mati-teohar* where Bhum deity is worshipped for good yield. Bhum is a female deity who looks after natural resources and creatures on the earth. Bhum gaita is the priest who presides over the ritual, which are much different from other clan and community rituals observed by the community.

Socio-cultural Practices Related to Food

Life and culture of Dandami Maria of Bastar is largely governed by the local environment. Relationship between humans, nature and supernatural entities is like a meshed fabric; their existence is linked with forest and land and the spirits residing therein, try to appease those spirits in various ways (Sarkar 2004; Sarkar and Choudhury 2013).

Dandami Maria, a sub-division of the generic group of Gond, are divided into a number of septs. Different septs belonging to a common group are known as *bhaiband or dadabhai* to each other; they are thought to be cousins and children of co-uterine brothers and marriage within same bhaiband group is prohibited. From the perspective of one such group, another group of septs would be known as *akomama* or *mamabhai* or *saga*; the term mamabhai stands for maternal uncle's son and akomama signifies having the same maternal grandfather. Marriage between a boy from the dadabhai group with a girl from mamabhai group is allowed. Again, the Dandami Maria are divided into two broad exogamous halves, each of which has some totemic classes or *phratry* and each class has number of *bas* or clans in it. Each bas possesses a *pen* deity of their own, who has dadabhai and akomama relations in their celestial world. The pen deities form a great family in which they are all related to one another; the Dandami Maria are aware of pen genealogies. Often a clan god would visit his or her relations in other villages. The bas or clan groups are usually totemic in nature, they have totems like *sodi* (tiger), *marvi* (goat), and *oymi* (tortoise).

The traditional belief system associates a clan god with territory in which members of that clan reside. Solidarity and unity among members of a clan is ensured through observance of annual festival for clan god. Individual members or groups of clan members depend on their clan god when in crisis. While suffering from some setback in life like diminishing livestock, relations falling ill or crops damaged, they seek help of clan god. Only the clan god can remove troubles, reasons for distress, which can be sorcery or witchcraft or breach of taboo.

Earth goddess Bhum, who resides at tallin, is believed to be the ultimate source of life; she is the mother who feeds and sustain her children. The priest Bhum gaita can communicate with her and solicit her help. It is Bhum who divides land into areas, one for each clan, and fixes the boundaries. To the original priest of every clan she has revealed the territory allotted to his clan. That information is handed down through succeeding generations.

Thus, religious beliefs and activities of Dandami Maria are intimately connected with their sustenance activities against the backdrop of a given ecological web. The fruits, flowers or any other forest produces they collect form the forest as food, are offered to the pen and bhum deities before those can be eaten. Same practice holds good for horticultural and agricultural products. They observe various rituals and festivals to seek help from benevolent spirits and to ward off the malevolent ones. The ritual and festival calendar of the community is closely linked with different food collection and production activities. *Korepandum* is observed in early February, that is the time for cutting trees on hill slopes for erka cultivation, *bhimulpandum* is observed in middle of February for good rain, *irpupandum* or *mahuapandum* is held sometimes in March before eating mahua flower, *markapandum* or *amakhani* happens in March, before eating mango, *wijapandum* is celebrated in March–April before initiating agricultural operations in field when village priest or *perma* performs rituals for Bhum at tallin. In addition, they perform *mati teohar* to appease Bhum, *haralipandum* in August–September to pray for good crop, *kurumpandum* or *kurmim-kortang* at the end of August, when new millet crop is eaten for first time. The last ritual is called *ikmapandum* or *nawa-khani*; before the performances of this ritual one is not allowed to consume even the vegetable grown in that season. *Korta pandum* or *punan-gkotang* is observed to mark first eating of the new crop of rice; *jata pandum* is observed before the new crop of beans and pulses are eaten. In fact, they do not take anything edible provided by nature prior to offering those to their deities and ancestors. It is believed that breach of such taboo may bring bad luck to the family as well as to the village.

The above description shows that the Dandami Maria of Bastar is one of those communities for whom food is not merely some substance used for satisfying corporal necessities, but is an extension of the universe constituted of humans; their natural surroundings that include their land, forest and water, and the supernatural entities are all bound together by certain cosmic laws. Any component of the scheme is damaged or is taken out; the rest would face the possibility of disintegration.

Impact of Developmental Programmes

Most of the development schemes in India are perceived as setting up of industries and producing goods for a market located primarily in cities. For the purpose, factories are set up in areas where huge land is available, mines are created where there are minerals, accompanied by laying of roads and creating other infrastructures to help the process of industrialization and urbanization. Urbanized and densely populated areas are generally avoided for the purpose, while mineral-rich hilly and forested terrains with low population density are much preferred for setting up large-scale industries. As a result, in post-independence India forest has been cleared and forest dwellers uprooted to make space for mines, factories and industrial townships. For the forest-dwelling small communities such activities mean displacement from the habitat they knew since ages, shrinkages of resource area from where most of their food and non-food necessities were collected for subsistence, and alienation from the abode of their ancestors, deities and spirits. Their socio-cultural values and practices which were deeply linked with the physical and metaphysical world are thrown into whirlwind.

Economic changes take place in an area where, till the other day, majority of the inhabitants were small communities having a subsistence economy. In that space, rapid and large-scale in-migration of urban, affluent, educated and skilled people take place jeopardizing the socio-cultural milieu. It widens the hiatus between people almost completely unknown to each other. While on one hand, there are powerful people firmly seated at the helm of political and economic power along with the upwardly mobile middle class who too are placed in relative affluence, on the other hand, the poor are left to plunge deeper into the shadow of poverty and hunger (Sarkar et al. 2014).

Studies of Orans (1965), Vidyarthi (1970), Dasgupta (1972, 1981), Singer (1972), Banerjee (1981) and Sarkar (1994) have noted that industrial set-up among the small and marginalized communities have changed their lifeways, and in the new economic arrangement, they have been compelled to adapt many cultural traits of the dominant sections of the larger society, metamorphosed into unskilled wage labour and maintain bi-cultural social life where their opinion is not counted much.

During the later part of the 1980s in Bastar, as per Government of India's instruction, work for building Indira Sarovar Hydro-electric Project, locally known as Bodghat Project, was stopped. After carrying out an empirical study, a committee of experts constituted with researchers from the Anthropological Survey of India and Department of Anthropology, Raipur University, recommended that the project work needed to be stopped. The committee found that 42 villages were destined to be submerged affecting 1,785 families and a total population of 8,775. In that population 70.9 per cent were Scheduled Tribe families from Muria, Dandami Maria, Dorla, Halba communities. The committee emphasized that the project would have caused huge displacement of Scheduled Tribe people as well as destroy a large area of forest; the combined effect of the two would be irreversible damage to the local eco-system on which society and culture of the displaced people are enmeshed (office copy of the report submitted to Government in 1987 available at Anthropological Survey of India, Jagdalpur Office for reference). On another occasion, plan to build a steel plant Maolibhata near Burumpal village was stopped due to agitation by the local people. It may be noted that this area is dominated by the Dandami Maria community. The industry lobby and their supporters were not so amenable always. On many occasions, they became aggressive and went ahead with their plans. Right now, NMDC is building a steel plant at about 10 km from Nagarnar village; this area is inhabited by Dandami Maria, Bhatra, Halba, Lohar and Panika communities and the site is very close to Tiriya-Machkot Reserve Forest. The ongoing construction work is going to expand further by engrossing a large part of the forest, which provides lots of resources to the local people for their sustenance. Obviously, destruction of resources will severely impact livelihood practices of the people as well as their social and cultural traditions.

One need not guess what will happen to the people once industries set foot in the area. We may consider the case of Padapur, where NMDC has started mining operation close to the village. In this village under Dantewada Block of undivided Bastar District, the Dandami Maria villagers used to practise plough cultivation. At present, they are engaged in wage earning from *goti khadan* or tin ore collection, and civil construction work. For ore collection they are paid ₹80 per kg. While 57 per cent of the working population of the village are engaged in cultivation either as primary or as subsidiary occupation, 45 per cent are wage earners from goti khadan and about 5 per cent are engaged in salaried jobs for NMDC. During peak agricultural season, most of them get involved in agricultural activities, but they find sustenance from agriculture rather difficult as yield from agriculture has gone down due to presence of mica in the soil.

Due to iron ore mining in the area, very often explosives are detonated for extraction of ore, restricting their movement in the mining area. Under such circumstances, hunting activities are not possible, huge area has been deforested affecting collection of minor forest produces. Moreover, the adjacent rivulet called Sankini, which is a tributary of River Indrabati, has also been turned reddish, as mined iron ore is washed in the flowing water before loading on train wagons. The water has become unsuitable for human consumption, aquatic life has also been affected, and adjacent land has been subjected to sedimentation of ore particles. It may be noted that iron ore extracted from Bacheli–Kirandul area is very rich; it contains about 85 per cent hematite. One can easily imagine what effect the ore can lead to if added to water and if the particles are deposited on land. This is only a glimpse of what is happening to the life of Dandami Maria people, their local ecosystem and their subsistence activities.

The food the Dandami Maria were eating for ages was required to sustain their lives, to say nothing about their cultural expressions related to food. Without any supplement from outside, the roots, tubers, mushroom, leafy vegetables, fruits and whatever animal protein they could cull, provided them a good diet. Depleting forest deprived them of those necessities. According to Rajyalakshmi (1991, 26) the tubers of *Dioscorea* species contain 0.6–6.3 g protein, 0.04–0.3 g fat, 0.2–106 g ash, 0.7–1.5 g fibre, 5.7–34.1 g carbohydrate and 27–131 kcal energy. The calcium content of wild roots ranged from 7 to 57 mg, and that of phosphorus between 5 to 275 mg. Dried bamboo shoots contain 302 kcal energy, 25.3 g protein, 9.5 g fibre, 42.8 g carbohydrate, 208 mg calcium, 569 mg phosphorus, 12.5 mg iron, 0.09 mg riboflavin and 3.8 mg niacin. It is also reported that mushroom is rich in 26.1 g protein, 6.9 g fibre; leafy vegetables collected from forest reveals that contain 1,708 kcal energy, 43 g protein, 1.2 g calcium and 62.7 mg iron. From this chemical analysis of edible minor forest produces clearly shows why those items were essential for a healthy living of the people of Bastar.

Political turmoil in the area as well as impact of industrialization left those small and marginal communities in distressed condition.

Whatever benefits were earmarked for them by the government were appropriated by a handful of elites from the community. Social relations of these pre-capital societies, which were nurtured through kinship and traditional social governance, cannot be changed into a new order where production, distribution and consumption of goods are dissociated from social relations based on reciprocity (Harris 1979). On the other hand, notional ownership of the community over common property resources like forest is not recognized by the industry lobby or the state and the people are seldom compensated for the loss (Mahapatra 2013).

Conclusion

The above discussion suggests that the environment limits the cultural expressions of the Dandami Maria. It can also be said that culture development among the Dandami Maria is dependent on environmental opportunities in which natural resources play a key role. Steward's view of 'culture core' (1955) can be used to assess the situation the Dandami Maria of Bastar are subjected to, especially of Burumpal and Padapur villages. There the Dandami Maria were wet cultivators, exploiting local resources with their traditional knowledge and also aided by certain 'non-traditional' knowledge and technologies. At Koduli, a forest village, the Dandami Maria practise penda cultivation after cleaning the forest thoroughly. In both cases, knowledge about the ecosystem and the resources available there, and the technology employed to derive the required material, are important, as important is the conservation ethics of the people. The variation in application of knowledge and technology shows their indigenous knowledge in exploiting their niche as well as conserving their activities with traditional wisdom where natural resources play a key role.

It is true that the economic and industrial development of a country involves large-scale deployment of resources. But by not paying attention to the lifeways of the affected people and by ignoring their aspirations, time and again, the profit-oriented system proves that there is a wide difference between the class that benefits from the development projects and those who pay the price (Mahapatra 2013).

Due to accumulation of too much of power in hands of the principal beneficiaries, they often occupy the articulation space when issues related to development are debated. The argument that the Dandami Maria have intricate and multi-layered relation with their immediate environment to maintain their sustainable lifeways and depletion of the resources they use may turn them into destitutes, does not travel beyond a limited articulation space. The question about 'development for whom' is drowned under the high-decibel sloganeering in favour of building a strong and powerful nation.

References

Banerjee, S. 1981. Impact of Industrialization on the tribal Population of Jharia-Ranigunge Coal Field Area. Calcutta: Anthropological Survey of India.

Buchman, U. K. 1992. *Mythen*. Geowissen: Hamburg.

Crookshank, H. 1963. 'Geology of Southern Bastar and Jeypore frol.87. om the Bailadila Range to the Eastern Ghats', Memoirs of Geological Survey of India, Vol. 87.

Dasgupta, P. K. 1972. Impact of Industrialization on a Tribe in South Bihar. Calcutta: Anthropological Survey of India.

——. 1981. 'Tribes in the Industrial Context of India'. *Man and Life* 7 (3–4): 95–104.

Gadgil, M., and V. D. Vartak. 1976. 'The Sacred Groves of Western Ghats in India'. *Economic Botany* 70: 152–160.

Geertz, Clifford. 1963. *Agricultural Involution: The Process of Ecological Change in Indonesia*. Berkeley, CA: University of California Press.

Hardesty, D. L. 1977. *Ecological Anthropology*, 289. New York, NY: John Wiley & Sons.

Harris, Marvin. 1979. *Cultural Materialism: The Struggle for a Science of Culture*. New York, NY: Vintage Books—A Division of Random House.

Mahapatra, L. K. 2013. *Development for Whom? Resettlement and Rehabilitation Policy in India*. New Delhi: Mittal Publications.

Orans, Martin. 1965. *The Santal: A Tribe in Search of a Great Tradition*. Detroit: Wayne state University Press.

Pranjpye. 1989. 'Deoral'. In *Deforestation and Drought*, edited by N. D. Jayal. New Delhi: INTACH.

Rajyalakshmi, P. 1991. *Tribal Food Habits*. New Delhi: Gian Publishing House.

Sarkar, Amitabha. 1994. Dhodia: Industrialisation and Change in a Primitive Community. New Delhi: Gyan Publishing House.

——. 2004. 'Bison-Horn Maria in the Midst of Forest Environment'. *Folklore Research Journal* 14.

Sarkar, Amitabha, and Piyush Choudhury. 2013. 'A Study of Traditional Wisdom among Bison Horn Maria of Bastar'. In *Traditional Wisdom and Sustainable Living (A Study on the Indian Tribal Societies)*, edited by Hrishikesh Mandal and Amitabha Sarkar. New Delhi: Anthropological Survey of India and Gyan Publishing House.

Sarkar, Amitabha, Samira Dasgupta, N. C. Sarkar, Niloy Bagchi, Samir Biswas, C. R. Mandal, and S. Panja. 2014. *The Fuming Forest: An Analytical Critique*. New Delhi: Mittal Publications.

Singer, Milton. 1972. *When a Great Tradition Modernises: An Anthropological Approach to Indian Civilization*. Delhi: Vikas Publishing House.

Singh, K. S. 1994. *People of India, Vol. III. The Scheduled Tribe*. Delhi: Oxford University Press and Anthropological Survey of India.

———. 1996. *People of India, National Series, Vol. VII. Identity, Ecology, Social Organisation, Economy, Linkages and Development Process: A Quantitative Profile*. Delhi: Oxford University Press and Anthropological Survey of India.

Steward, J. H. 1955. *The Theory of Culture Change*. Urbana: University of Illinois Press.

Vidyarthi, L. P. 1970. *Socio-Cultural implications of Industrialization in India: A Case Study of Tribal Bihar*. New Delhi: Delite Press.

18

The Idea of Food
A Discourse Encompassing Two Religious Faiths

Ratna Dhar

Introduction

One winter, sometime back in the beginning of the present millennium, I landed up in a desert village Barna, in Jaisalmer,[1] for conducting fieldwork among the Manganiyars, a musician community of the region.[2] By the time I reached the village from Jaisalmer with my team member, it was dinner time for the family of my host Gazi Khan. They had arranged our meal in a separate room of his house with two of his guests from the community. The dinner was sumptuous, and the food was placed on a *thali* (plate) on a *bajotha*[3] with a curry made from the locally available vegetables, a mutton preparation, wheat *roti* and *sheer*.[4] I was courteously asked if I have any problem in eating *halal*[5] mutton; I told them I have no such inhibition for any food.[6] I also noticed, Gazi Khan and his guests were having food from the same plate, but we were served food on separate plates. Later I came to know that eating food from the same plate even by non-related persons indicates a kind of amicable bonding between them. What surprised me most was that I could not get a glimpse of the womenfolk of the household for even a moment throughout the course of our dinner. Only on the next day,

I could meet my hostess inside the inner courtyard. Though members of the family were very helpful and had accepted my co-fieldworker warmly, but being a male, he was not permitted in the inner courtyard as it solely belonged to the womenfolk.[7] Gradually, I was getting intrigued to know more about the world of Manganiyars and their society.

My host Gazi Khan belonged to a community of hereditary musicians from the villages of Barmer, Jaisalmer, Jodhpur and parts of Bikaner districts of the state of Rajasthan and are believed to profess Islam as religion but work as traditional folk musicians for the Hindu patrons, mainly the Rajputs (Kothari 2001, 205). Gazi Khan himself is a khardtal[8] player par excellence. It is said that close interaction between the musicians and their patrons over the years has developed into a social norm of the area and the Manganiyars have gradually started following dual faith in their lifestyle.

Some studies reveal that several communities in India and particularly some from the western Indian states have segments among them who subscribe to different religious beliefs and practices drawn from Islam and Jainism in their daily life and share cultural space among them. Many of those communities and segments share several cultural traits such as language, naming pattern and ways of observing life cycle ceremonies with communities belonging to a different religion. It has also been observed, as part of their livelihood activities, many of those 'borderline communities' (Singh 1998, xxvii) behave in accordance with their occupational role in the larger society. While accommodating with the 'pressures' and 'demands', they identify themselves with the communities they interact with. Those relatively small and marginal groups thus start behaving in conformity with the culturally defined values, norms, attitudes and expectations of the dominant society where they live and whom they serve. Such adjustments are present even in 'low-caste' communities, though they may belong to the same religious aggregate.

Mckim Marriot (1968) tried to understand hierarchy among caste groups through transaction of food. He observed that in everyday life, rendering some service implies readiness to receive food, and giving food denotes an expectation that service will be rendered. He further observed that transfer of food also implies some values such as power and luxurious display of foods and 'any transfer of food always makes the giver higher, the receiver lower; suppose that and rendering of service always makes the master higher, the servant lower'(1968, 147).

In most cases, food plays a crucial part in defining family roles, rules and traditions and leads to understanding attitudes and practices surrounding social relations. Theoretically, food has been looked as a source of communication, a process through which one understands the world and is a non-verbal means of sharing meanings with others. Scholars have argued that food choices of different cultural groups are often connected with ethnic behaviours and religious beliefs and are reaffirmation of one's cultural identity (Scholliers 2001).

Scholars have also worked on how food is communicated and how food communicates and we communicate about food (Barthes 1964; Levi Strauss 1983; Stajcic 2013). On the other hand, Mary Douglas (1972) in her semiotic engagement with meal addressed food as a code that can express a pattern about social relationships. According to her, if food is a code, the messages it encodes will be expressed in patterns of social relationships in a society which again gives a direction to different degrees of hierarchy, inclusion and exclusion, boundaries and transactions across boundaries.

This chapter explores the community of Manganiyars, their musical journey among the neighbouring communities and how those mutual relationships negotiate and shape their identities and cultures. The chapter also strives to understand whether those relationships and the mutual journey are expressed through their cultural traits and in elements of life cycle ceremonies, including food-related practices and aspects. Further, the study has examined how food gets expressed in different kinds of relationships and plays a role in maintaining their livelihood process.

Social Situation

When we look at the marginal communities of Rajasthan, we find that the Manganiyars along with other musician groups of the region, such as Langha, Dholi, Bhopa, Charan or Bhat, have complex network of patronage largely with maintenance of genealogies of their patrons. Traditionally, along with providing musical and genealogical services to their Rajput patrons and their retainers, the Manganiyars are also obliged to serve the *jajman* (patrons) of their own village and to villages where their patrons have kinship relations. As per the norm of the region, they provide musical services in all important ceremonies at their patrons' homes relating to childbirth, marriage and death (Bharucha 2003, 224) based on the relationship between the jajman and *jachak* (service provider) (Kothari 2001, 206). Their mutual relations, such as consuming food in different situations and spaces are significant, as the interacting communities engage in common larger space to carry out their respective roles simultaneously. It may also be noted that discussion on people, identity, culture and food of a region also leads to the understanding of ethno-geographical categories of land and its people. Those categories are related to crop pattern, livestock, people's idea of common properties, ownership of land, sacred groves and staple food categories that often find place in their myth, songs and worldview.

Most of these small villages are situated within an approximate distance of 100 km from the Indo-Pak border and share the same cultural geography of Marwar with villages on either side of the border. Similar cultural habits and traditional ties are present between the villagers. They continued with their traditional practices for years irrespective of their caste and religion. Those villages are mostly multi-ethnic and dominated by Rajput landlords of various sub-groups.[9] It was therefore normal for a family of one village to take its *barat* (marriage procession) to another village on the other side of the border and bring the bride home. Thus, centuries of old ties and family links remained intact even after the partition of India.

The region is largely characterized by arid condition, extreme temperature and long periods of severe and unpredictable drought that destroy crops, fodder and water supplies (Henderson 2001) and have negligible rains even in rainy seasons. Adams (1889, 97), in his topographical accounts on the region, has shared a local adage which describes the tough nature of life in the arid region.

Bajri ki sogra mothan ki dar
Akre ki jhonpri phogan ki bar
Dekhi Raja Man Singh teri Marwar

(Bread of bajra[10] flour and dal of moth,[11] huts of aakado[12] and fences of phog[13]; O Raja Man Singh such is your Marwar)

Scarcity of water often forces the villagers to rely on whatever little they can collect for daily chores and as potable water. Over the period, the region has developed its *panihar* form of songs sung by the women who visit distant places to fetch water and talk about struggles in life, the wish for flowing water, the dream of splashing waves and rains and the adjustment and strategies adopted in such an environment. The only water course of semi-permanent nature of the region is the Luni River, which finds place again and again in the local musical repertoire. In a famous love ballad of the region, *Dhola Maru ra Duha*, the princess from Malwa, Malwani makes a critique of the region through her song. She says:

The land of Marwar or Maru is colourless where water is found so deep in wells that the people start fetching water at midnight. There are only shepherds, and there is either famine or an invasion of locusts, where grasses like *kareel*[14] and *untkatarao*[15] are regarded as trees, the only shadow to be found is that of phog and aakado and people have to eat seeds of *bhurat*[16] to lessen their hunger. (Swami 1995, 185–186)

In the past, people from many villages in Jaisalmer District used to travel frequently from one village to another; during famines colonies of people crossed the border to Sindh province in Pakistan. Similar situation is present in other districts also. The province of Sindh and town of Amarkot[17] was like an oasis in the midst of desert that people often visited for the availability of resources for their livelihood. This has entered in the folklore of the villagers who often talk of the wealth of these villages and their possessions among themselves.

Retelling the experiences of famines and scarcity of food was always part of the discussions I had with village elders; they often brought back stories of their tough life with scarce food and water. Story related to the establishment of many villages was often linked to migration in the wake of famine. In any agro-pastoral situation, collection of food and fodder are the most important activities. The elders of Barna village recalled with pride an incident related to Tejsi village and Barna and the younger persons enjoyed it too. About a hundred and thirty years back the original settlers of Barna village lived near Tejsi village and had their agricultural fields side by side. During the famines many of the villagers from both the villages lived in *gol*[18] situated in between the two villages with their cattle, camel, sheep and families. In course of time, a fierce fight broke out between residents of the two villages over right and ownership of the *oran*[19] land. The extant of bloody fight forced the then ruler, Jawahar Singh, to intervene and through bargain, the villagers of Tejsi had to leave the possession of oran land to the other group of villagers who had to form a new village Barna for their own on a small hillock nearby. It is obvious, in such a situation, the possession of oran land could sustain a village in times of crisis and scarcity.

In Barna village, the Rajputs possess most of the dwelling space and are centrally located with Brahmin and Bania, along with middle-ranking communities like Sunar, Darji and Khati. The marginal communities like Sansi, Khawas, Gwariya, Dishantri, Jatia, Jogi, Garuda, Babaswami, Manganiyar and the Bhil live in separate hamlets located on the periphery of the village. The area being under agro-pastoral economy, the agricultural fields surround the settlement on all sides where rain crops are grown if there is good rain. Almost all have large agricultural land,

a large part of which remain mostly fallow. The villagers are dependent on summer crops as agriculture is possible only for four months in
the rainy season. Many a time, the villagers solely depend on raising
cows, herds of sheep and goat, locally known as *chang*. The villagers
sell produces derived from livestock for their livelihood.

Rajput values, including that of honour, are prevalent in the entire
area. The idea about the honour of women is also closely linked to the
Rajput system of patriarchy. A woman can be held in high esteem if
she is the wife of the ruler, but she has no place in the administration
and in feudal politics. The value system prevalent among the ruling
classes demands that girls get married at an early age, they are subjected
to purdah and accept the ideology and practice of sati.[20] The ideal roles
of women are of daughter, wife, mother and mother-in-law, which are
defined in accordance to the patrilineal norms. All these traits have not
only contributed to the dominant idea of the Rajput as a community of
rulers and warriors, but also a referent group for the middle order and
lower castes in the villages. Therefore, it was observed, though the system
of *nata* (remarriage for a widow or divorced woman) is prevalent among
the lower-ranked castes, many communities, including the Manganiyars,
follow the footsteps of 'higher' Rajput ideals and do not go for a second
marriage. Once, a young girl from a Managaniyar familywas widowed
within seven days of her marriage. The bridegroom was from a well-
known musician family in a village near Jaisalmer town and worked in
para-military force; he was killed in a road accident in Jaisalmer. Among
Muslims it is not unusual that a young widow will get remarried, but
in this case, the girl did not remarry and kept good relationship with
her in-laws. Later, she adopted the child of her younger brother-in-law.
It was found that such incidents are not any aberration in this region.

Along with Rajput influence, the myths on clan or *jati* formation from
different caste groups prevalent among the Manganiyars also shed light
on their efforts to remain close to the Hindu groups. The Manganiyars
feel proud to inform their pre-conversion linkages with the Hindu caste
groups of the area. According to Bharucha (2003, 228), they were probably converted to Islam during the late medieval period but continued
to uphold Hindu social customs. This reveals a syncretic culture in which
both Hindu and Muslim elements have been accommodated.

The Patronage, the Reality and the Segregation

The Manganiyars claim that Rajputs are their patrons, but they serve
retainers of their patrons; they have Muslim patrons too. This part of
Rajasthan is known as Sodhan, where Soda Rajputs were the rulers. Few

generations back, a section of the Soda was converted to Islam. Most of those Rajput groups had their agricultural land spread in many parts of Jaisalmer that extended to the Sindh region. Thus, when a Rajput landlord shifted their family and property to another village, they moved with their retainers and subjects. For example, in Barna village, the original Soda ruler came from Sindh province along with their subjects, which included their musicians. It may be noted that in this region, a caste is only recognized as a caste when it has a genealogist and official musicians; a group without these services may exist, but it is in social limbo (Kothari 2001, 208).

In the villages a Manganiyar is not only a singer, he is part and parcel of his patron's life. He is attached not only to the entire line of his patron's family but also to patrons who reside in different villages and to those who have settled in distant places or different villages or cities for their livelihood. For instance, the Manganiyar who is living in Barna village is obliged to render services to the Baran Soda of Somesar and Awae village of Jodhpur, Bhaluri and Darba of Jaisalmer and Chatrori of Barmer District. They have a right to visit the villages of the married daughters of the patrons on festive occasions to earn his *bhati*.[21]

This relationship entails close association of a Manganiyar with families of his patrons for a certain period, when power relation between them becomes explicit, especially in relation with food. Usually, a Manganiyar would carry a small brass bowl and thali with him, in which he receives his food from his patron while paying any service or simply visiting them. The patron may serve any item of food excepting any mutton or chicken preparation. The Hindu patrons prefer *jhatka*[22] method of slaughtering; though the Manganiyars are non-vegetarian in their food habit, they abstain from eating any meat preparation which is not halal.

The patronage enjoyed by the Manganiyarsis a complex set of mutual relationships based on rights and obligations between the Soda patron and Manganiyar, the service provider. The patron, on the other hand, inherits his father's servers and the servers simultaneously inherit their father's patrons, whom they refer as *dhani*. The inheritance is on both sides based on division of any property. A patron would have several sons, so his sons would inherit all his servers following the rule of male equigeniture and the servers also inherit the jajmans in the same process. Patrons of the Manganiyars range from the royal houses of Jaisalmer and Barmer to Rajput *jagirdars* or feudal lords and common villagers.

There are few specific roles to be performed by a Manganiyar for his patrons. In case he is unable to attend to the services, his family members are bound to provide the services by tradition. Firstly, the services provided by a Manganiyar are in form of songs, *chhand* (poem) and recitation of genealogy of the patron's family. Secondly, he by tradition is obliged to attend all the festivals, rituals and ceremonies of the patron and pay respect to the patron and his family members, friends and relatives, irrespective of age by saying *khamaghani*.[23] Thirdly, he has specific roles in life cycle rituals of his patron; along with singing of songs he can be asked to entertain the guests with poems, *doha* or couplets and instrumental music at any time. Fourthly, whenever he attends his patron's house for some rituals or for any ceremonial gathering, he is supposed to address them by reciting the genealogy of his patron's ancestors, which is locally known as *subhraj*. It is through subhraj, one comes to know the family lineage of the patron and a Rajput recognizes his family of Manganiyar and the whole traditional system continues. Other than songs and doha, musical instruments of Manganiyars have an important role in a Rajput household. Dhol or *mangal dhol* (drum) and thali are played during life cycle events of birth and marriage in Rajput families and accompanied by songs related to each phase of the rituals. Other musical instruments like *kamaichaya*,[24] *surnai*,[25] *khardtal* and *dholki*[26] are played to entertain and are used while rendering traditional music or during musical programmes sponsored by non-traditional clients.

Though the Manganiyars and their patrons meet regularly, both maintain distinct segregation in relation to food. The Manganiyars on the one hand are followers of Islam, on the other they are accorded the lowest position in the caste society. They abide by following norms of the village community. As has been mentioned, the Manganiyars bring separate brass utensils to eat their food and while eating maintain some spatial distance from other caste groups. At such occasions they eat only vegetarian food at the jajman's house.

Maintenance of segregation was also felt by us in the village when after a few days we realized that though we were welcomed by the chief of the village, who was a Soda Rajput, and were generally allowed to take part in discussions about the village, we were never offered tea in any house. The guess was confirmed when a marriage took place in the village and the Manganiyars had their obligatory duties to tender. Though the whole village was invited for a feast, we were left out. That exclusion from the feast did not essentially mean that we were unacceptable, rather we were given ample opportunity to observe all the rituals of marriage ceremony from the front row. Later we came to know that they had a problem concerning our presence in the marriage feast. In those villages, maintenance of caste hierarchy is observed through the sitting arrangement in the feast. Our case was different, they were not sure where to define our place in the seating arrangement. One major hurdle for the village community was our regular mingling with the Manganiyars and partaking food with them. We could neither be placed with the Manganiyars or other marginal castes of the village, nor with the Rajputs and the middle-order castes.

Komal Kothari in one of his discussion with Rustom Bharucha (2003) made an interesting point. He noted, each of the musical instruments is 'linked to particular region', and says, 'each instrument has its own geography' but 'it is not the geography that determines the instrument, but the instruments that claim a particular geography'. He gives an example of the famous string musical instrument of the Manganiyars and said, if a person wants to identify the geographical features of the area where kamaicha is played, he would associate it with areas where *sevanghas* (a kind of local grass, *Lasiurus scindicus*) grows. The grass grows in areas with merely 3–4 inches of rainfall and grows so high that even camels can disappear in the grass. It provides good grazing grounds for non-stable-bound cows. The point made by Kothari is that specific musical instruments also contain information about specific geographical regions, people who live in those areas and their cultural adaptations.

Though certain food restrictions segregate the Mangniyars from their patrons, Manganiyar women and children are allowed into the *zenana*[27] of Rajput households for performing ceremonial rituals. On the birth of a boy in a Rajput household, the Manganiyar of the family brings with him a dhol, which is placed in the *otia* (a sitting place for the men just outside the main house) and thali, which are played for an hour to announce the birth of a son in the family. The occasion also includes offering of *akha* (wheat grain), *gur* (jaggery) and *neg* (ceremonial gifts) and putting a *tilak* (ritual mark on forehead) to the Manganiyar and the other villagers. *Gur* or jaggery is considered an auspicious food item in the region and any auspicious occasion is marked by the distribution of jaggery among the neighbours and villagers, irrespective of caste or religion.

During marriages in a patron's family, the Manganiyar and his family members are obliged to attend. The duties begin from the day of fixing up a marriage date when he plays the dhol in the courtyard of his patron. Three days before the marriage the Manganiyars of both the bride's and groom's families play dhol and sing marriage songs every morning and evening with or without an audience. The ritual is known as *sanjidena*. As a norm, women of the musician families visit the women's quarter of the patron's family where they sing marriage songs. The presence of dhol symbolizes the ceremonial character of the occasion; in their words, it is the mangal dhol.

The women's repertoire includes only the ceremonial songs, which include both *motageet* (songs with classical base) and *chhotageet* (songs based on light music). But the male performers generally do not distinguish between the categories as they often know some chhotageet. The truth is the women have more collection of ceremonial songs than the male. During my presence in the villages I realized, the women do not always sing at the patrons' house. But vestiges of the earlier tradition have survived, even if the women do not sing, on few ceremonial occasions their presence is a must. It was also observed that the women visiting patrons' house do not eat any food there, rather they bring the food home.

Influence of Rajput Ideal and Way of Life

As the Manganiyars mostly sing for Hindu patrons and feel attached to them, their repertoire of songs is related to Hindu customs, religious figures and themes. It has been discussed that there is a small group of Manganiyars who sing for Hindu as well as Muslim jajmans. There are few villages in Jaisalmer and Barmer where the Manganiyars live with Muslim patrons from communities like Janj, Gujju Soda and Gunga Soda. Here their behaviour and way of life is more inclined towards Islamic way of life. The visible similarity is found only in the women's dress; like their counterparts from Hindu villages, they follow the dress code of Hindu women. Depending on the situation where the Manganiyars find them placed, either Hindu or Muslim patrons, their behaviour oscillates. However, irrespective of whether they are performing for a Hindu or a Muslim patron, the context, content and structure of the songs remain alike to a large extent. Still, certain differences are created for respective groups of patrons; songs sung for Hindu Rajput groups mention rituals and gods related to Hindu tradition, while Muslim patrons ask them to sing different genres like *kafi, shehara,* and *kalam*. During *nikah* ceremony they sing kafi and shehara along with other songs reflecting Hindu traditions. Influence of Hindu traits in their daily lives is expressed in the naming pattern, marriage rituals and the observance of fasts and festivals. Absence of cross-cousin or parallel-cousin marriage among the Manganiyars demonstrates continuation of Hindu traits in their social life.

The dichotomous situation arose in the region mostly due to shifting of patrons' village or when a certain section of the patrons converted to another faith some generations back. For example, in remote areas of Sam in Jaisalmer district, the Manganiyars of Gujjuyon ki Basti sing for their Muslim jajman, whereas the Manganiyars of Khaltawala village have both Hindu and Muslim patrons. But two groups of Manganiyars can inter-marry among themselves. The difference between the two groups is only at the performance level. Traditionally, the kamaicha is played exclusively for the Hindu jajman whereas the *sarengi*[28] is played for the Muslims. In recent years most of the singers have switched over to harmonium as the accompanying ensemble instead of kamaicha, as many young performers have not learnt the art of playing kamaicha as the skill requires prolonged training.

It is almost difficult to distinguish a Manganiyar from any other villager of the area from the way they dress. The *potia* (headgear), *cholia* or *kameej* (shirt) preferably in white, *teota* (dhoti) and *juti* (shoes) are the traditional attire of males of the region, which they wear in musical sessions too. Few wear *gokhru*[29] or *murki*.[30] They, however, change to white lungi, kameej and *safa* (headgear) while attending a funeral in the community like any other Muslim. The women dress in *kachli* (blouse), *kurti* (long shirt), *lehenga* (frilled petticoat) and *ordhani* or *dupatta* (veil, which often are very colourful); *bichhia* (toe ring), *anguthia* (finger ring), *kada*, *chura* (white plastic bangles, 20 on each arm) and *nimboli* (necklace) are the symbols that they are married. However, the Manganiyars, who serve Muslim patrons, dress like Muslims, with lungi, kameej and safa when in a Muslim village. Otherwise, they wear the regular dress worn by others, but their women dress like other Manganiyar women of the area.

So, we find three different situations in these villages of Jaisalmer. Firstly, when Manganiyars have Hindu patrons exclusively; such cases are more in number. Here they maintain the Hindu way of living and this is reflected in their daily association with the Hindu patrons; their dress code, food pattern, the songs they sing, way of salutation, observance of Diwali and worship of folk goddess are part of such a way of living. The situation can be illustrated by citing the ritual behaviour of the villagers.

While travelling from Jaisalmer to Myajlar and across other villages located on the international border of Rajasthan, it was observed that each vehicle was stopped for a while at a particular spot for paying respect at the shrine of Malan Bai, a folk goddess of the region. The shrine was situated near a village called Sipla. On enquiry it was revealed that Dujra Dungar situated in Sipla village marks the beginning of the territory of

Malan Bai. Dujra Dungar is a small hillock and is an important land-mark in the myth of Malan Bai. The territory continues through the villages of Janra, Khuri, Dhaneli, Hatar, Bida, Tejsi and lastly, Barna. The shape of the territory is almost circular and is defined as *Malan bai ro raj*. The villagers believe that irrespective of caste and religion, villages falling in this territory are blessed with the divinity of the goddess; all villagers observe the prescriptions and prohibitions defined by Malan Bai and detailed in the myth. The belief system even impacted the collection of revenue in days of princely rule. Some villagers claimed, during those days even the king refrained from claiming taxes directly; it was always collected in the name of Malan Bai.

Barna village being a part of the sacred geography mentioned in the myth, it is believed that the blessings of Malan Bai have bounded the village and the people. They worship the goddess irrespective of their adherence to any religious tenet. The village has also several shrines dedicated to her and almost every house in the village has a small shrine of Malan Bai in their courtyard or some other place. The icon sometimes is a large oval stone or a trident on an earthen altar. Sometimes a sketch of the trident with altar is drawn on the wall. In a properly made shrine there is an iron *trishul* (trident) smeared with red dye. The tip of the trident is covered with red cloth, which symbolizes the presence of Malan as *shakti*, the female power.

As a mark of reverence to Malan, villagers of all castes and creed do not eat chicken and egg. Following her dictum, the women do not wear gold *bula* (a type of nose ring), anklets or jingles. Villagers are prohibited to wear any *guli* (blue-coloured cloth) and *ajrakh* like a Muslim. They do not own horse, put jingles on anklets of camel or build double-storied house. It is also believed that the gates of the house should not be locked; any visitor should not be denied entry. Another important prohibition is that the villagers refrain from cutting the *bordi* (species of Ziziphus) shrub as this is a sacred grove of Malan Bai. Bordi shrubs often grow in agricultural fields; the villagers may cut branches but not the stem.

As per the myth, villagers of Barna are brothers of the goddess; they have an exclusive right, irrespective of their caste or religion, to brand their cattle with trident mark so that the animals can be identified with the village. In most cases, the village shrine of Malan Bai is located inside Rajput settlements. The Manganiyars, however, build their sepa-rate shrine, as demanded by their low rank. This is also applicable for other marginal groups in the village; it is mandatory for a newly mar-ried couple among such communities to offer obeisance to the goddess.

The myth of Malan Bai has helped the Manganiyars to establish their belongingness to the land, their status prior to conversion status and their relationship with the Rajput landlords. Malan Bai also connects them with other caste groups of the region. The myth says, a Parmar Rajput named Berisal Singh, the father of Malan Bai, was a pastoralist by occupation. He lived in a village called Hariyar near Amarkot town. Later he shifted to Janra village (presently on the Indian side of the international boundary) with his wife and five sons Baran, Jaga, Barsiya, Netar and Baghmar. Presence of a similar narrative has been reported on the other side of the border in Sindh region, though with slight variation (Kalhoro 2015).

It is believed, years later, that an idol of Malan was found in Dujra Dungar; the deity used to drink milk of the cows of Barna and neighbouring villages that came to graze. The villagers consulted Bhopa,[31] who identified her as the daughter of Berisal Parmar and told the villagers of Barna that they are natural siblings of Malan Bai. Therefore, they must worship Malan and establish her shrine. By this time, her two uterine brothers, Jaga and Baran, started living separately. Jaga remained at Janra and Baran came to Barna village. The distance between the two villages is four *kos* (approximately 12 km). It is believed, Malan's blessing cured infertility and blindness in villages of Barna and Janra. She appeared in the dream of residents of those two villages and asked them to worship her and follow the prohibitions and prescriptions handed down by her. The other three brothers are known as Netar Brahman, Barsiya Charan and Baghmar Suthar; their descendants are fewer in number and settled in different villages. Presently, the Baghmar Suthars live in Jodhpur.

The way the myth of Malan Bai is held and practised in life in Barna and neighbouring villages is closely related to the Manganiyar claim for Rajput ancestry. The myth associates them with Baran Rajputs as their uterine brother. Going further, the myth associates them with the Hindus and reinforces their right of patronage from Rajputs and other Hindu groups of the area. After claiming themselves to be part of Rajput ancestry, the Manganiyars justify it by sticking to the prescriptions and prohibitions related to food. As Muslims, they could have overlooked the food restrictions, but they preferred not to do so for multiple reasons. It can be argued that their association with Sodha Rajputs has compelled them to abide by the restrictions, which they have made an integral part of their identity. They completely abstain from taking beef; pork is an obvious prohibition. At the same time, they have not completely been assimilated into the Hindu fold despite their long association with the latter. Likewise, their close contact with

Muslim communities also did not result in complete assimilation into that religious group.

It is true that the arid climate of the region has its influence on the food culture of all village communities. Normal food taken by the villagers is *bajra ka sogra* and *chanch* or *khato* (butter milk). Use of maize is also common among them. Locally produced vegetables are *kachra* (Cucumis callosus), *gwarfali* (cluster beans), *sangria* (Prosopis cineraria) and *kumbatia* (Acacia senegal), but the use of vegetables in daily diet is negligible among the people of the area. Watermelon is common, which again relates to aridity of the region and mainly consumed by the livestock. Local songs of the region also give an idea of the delicacies of the region, which are *shira, lapsi, bajre ki khinch, chawal ki khinch* and *ladu* that are prepared during marriage or *sunnat* (circumcision) of Muslim boys. Manganiyars, like their neighbours consume locally available cereals and pulses like *moong* (*Vigna radiata or gram*), *chana* (*Cicer arietinum* or chick pea), *urad* (*Vigna mungo*, black gram) and *moth* (*Vigna aconitifolia or Turkish Gram*). *Ghee* (clarified butter), *chanch* (buttermilk) and curd are consumed profusely. The socio-cultural practices have encouraged smoking of opium among a large section of people. Though *amal* (opium) is given an important place in their ceremonial life, it has become almost a daily routine. The use of *supari* (betel nut) and *paan* (betel leaves) often finds places during welcome of a visitor or a relative.

The only space the Manganiyars need as followers of Islam is for attending some Islamic rituals, which they prefer to confine within the community. They disassociate themselves from their Hindu neighbours while observing certain Islamic rites like circumcision, nikah or marriage and burial. On such occasions, they dress like their other Muslim neighbours and invite the maulvi to preside over the rites. So far food is concerned, they always insist that their mutton or chicken is halal.

Discussion

The descriptive account of the Manganiyar community presented here shows that they have adopted the dominant food tradition of the region and have made it part of their food habit. Though the marginal group has its own religion, which is different from that of the dominant group they serve, the compulsions of livelihood practices have forced them to adopt many cultural traits of the dominant groups of the region. It is to be noted that their livelihood practices are integrally linked with ritual practices of their patrons. The process of adaptation has not only influenced the dress pattern or ornaments they wear, but also the kind of food they eat, and participation in rituals and sharing the regional mythologies. Thapar suggests that myths often are 'connected with liminality and arise in transitional situation' and offer explanation to 'how things came to be what they are' (1978, 260). The myth of Malan Bai has allowed the Manganiyars to contextualize and rationalize their position in the larger society, thereby establishing them in the milieu of Rajput culture. This has even percolated to their culinary habits and caused change in their food habit.

The discourse also gives an idea of the formation of identity and how food develops into a cultural signifier. This also helps us to understand how food in a common household signifies and how its practices contribute towards shaping the identity of a community or of an individual. In the present case, the journey of the Manganiyars with the Rajputs has led us to understand different layers of their affiliation where religious beliefs, mythologies and rituals play significant roles; food is an essential part of that complex relationship.

Notes

1. A district town and tourist centre in the Indian state of Rajasthan.
2. This was my first encounter with the Manganiyar community; since then, I am in regular touch with them through visits and other forms of communication.
3. Bajotha is a small decorated dining table used to serve food to honoured guests.
4. A preparation of milk, rice and sugar garnished with dried fruits.
5. It is the prescribed method of slaughter for all kinds of meat, excluding fish and other sea-life, as per Islamic law. This method of slaughtering animals consists of using a sharp knife to make a swift, deep incision that cuts the throat, the carotid artery, trachea, and jugular veins.
6. I am often asked about such inhibition during my fieldwork, but my training in the discipline of anthropology and my upbringing have taught me to be more liberal towards acceptance of different kinds of food.
7. My male colleague could not enter the inner courtyard till the end of our fieldwork, but after a few days I was allowed entry even to the family kitchen.
8. Khardtal is a traditional percussion instrument or wooden clapper used by the Manganiyars; it is made from shesham or teakwood.
9. Major Rajput subgroups of the region are Gangdas Soda, Baran Soda, Sagrasi Soda, Kelan Soda, Bharmal Soda, Moolpasa Bhati and Solanki.
10. *Pennisetum glaucum*, a staple used as bread in desert Rajasthan.
11. *Vigna aconitifolia* is a drought-resistant legume, commonly grown in arid and semi-arid regions of India. It is known as mat bean, moth bean, matki, Turkish gram or dew bean.

12. *Calotropis procera*, a species of flowering plant.
13. *Calligonum polygonoides* is a very common shrub that grows on the sand dunes of the desert. During the months of February and March its buds, known as lasson, are used by the local population to garnish butter milk.
14. *Capparis decidua*, tender buds and fruits are used to make pickles while caper berries are used as vegetable. The plant has its wider utility in traditional medicine and is used as relief or cure from a variety of pains or aches like toothache, cough and asthma.
15. *Solanum virginianum*, wild dwarf brinjal or milk thistle.
16. *Cenchrus biflorus*, most widely grown grass of the desert that is collected in normal times, used as fodder for goats and camels. During famine this plant is used as emergency food in the area. Seeds that are enclosed in prickly husk are grounded and baked into thick sogra. It is considered as the most nutritious food in times of famine.
17. The city of Amarkot is in Umerkot District of Sindh province, Pakistan. Umerkot province was ruled by Hindu Sodha Rajput clan since medieval times until 1947, when India was partitioned. This region was fertile and people believe that in ancient times a river used to flow in this region, which was the source of water for Indus Valley Civilization.
18. *Gol* was a small space supported by the princely state during famines; groups of cattle herders could stay there safely as the king took the responsibility of the welfare of gol.
19. Oran is derived from the Sanskrit word *aranya*, meaning forest. An oran is a patch of jungle preserved in the name of local deities or saints and are usually located around a source of water on the edge of settlements. As sanctified space, an oran is often used as a venue for different kinds of local affairs related to politics, crops, livestock and the community. Grazing and loping trees for firewood or timber is forbidden, except in times of famine. Oran is a safety mechanism in arid and semi-arid regions; it evolved historically to protect livelihood of the economically vulnerable sections of pastoralists, that is, livestock-dependent rural communities by recognizing and securing their right to natural resources for subsistence and livelihood purposes. The orans provide vital grazing land for livestock, water, providing minor forest produce, medicinal plants and green cover for the villages they serve and play an important role in promoting a flourishing livestock-based economy and the growth of livestock rearing communities.
20. Sati is a historical practice found chiefly among Hindus in northern and eastern parts of India in which a widow sacrifices herself by sitting atop her deceased husband's funeral pyre. It was associated among Hindu Rajput clans in western India which did not allow widow remarriage.
21. After marriage of a daughter of patrons' family, the Manganiyar makes a visit to the home of the son-in-law of his patron, where he is paid a handsome amount in cash as well as in kind. It includes jewellery, dress, a camel or a horse.

22. Jhatka, or chatka, is meat from an animal which is slaughtered instantaneously by single strike of sword or axe tosever the head of the animal. The practice has been adapted from Sikh religious tradition and prevalent in most of the parts of North and North West India. In this case the animal must not be scared or shaken in any way before the slaughter.
23. An expression for greeting people.
24. Kamaicha is a string musical instrument with broad and round stem and mainly played as an accompaniment with the vocalist. The instrument is held vertically and played with a small bow. The music is very soft, delicate and melodious. It is used by the Manganiyar community for a Hindu Rajput audience.
25. It is a modified form of shehnai and used in ceremonial occasions.
26. A kind of drum that is played with hands and used in musical sessions, festivals and ceremonies.
27. Refers to the part of a house belonging to a Hindu or Muslim family in the Indian subcontinent which is reserved for the women of the household, especially among the Rajputs in Rajasthan. The *zenana* are the inner apartments of a house in which women of the family live, a concept or practice similar to that of a *harem* in Mughal palaces.
28. Sarengi is a bowed, short-necked string instrument used in Hindustani classical music; the instrument is of Persian origin. It is used by those Manganiyars who serve Muslim patrons only. It is the main musical instrument of another folk musician community of the region, the Langha.
29. An expensive earring with elaborate and intricate design. In princely times, this type of earring was used only by the Rajputs, but now this is worn by lower castes only.
30. This is a small earring mostly used by the commoners.
31. The word Bhopa in local connotation is the Shaman—an individual with supernatural powers. He is the medium between god and ordinary men and can belong to any caste. The villagers believe that these Bhopa, through their trance and magico-practices, can understand and convey the message of god to mortals and can heal many diseases of humans and animals.

References

Adams, Archibald. 1889. *The Western Rajputana States: A Medicotopographical and General Account of Marwar, Sirohi and Jaisalmir*. London: Junior Army & Navy Stores.
Barthes, Roland. 1964. *Elements of Semiology*. New York, NY: Hill and Wang.
Bharucha, Rustom. 2003. *Rajasthan-An Oral History: Conversation with Komal Kothari*. Delhi: Penguin.
Chaudhuri, Shubha. 2009. 'The Princess of the Musicians: Rani Bhatiyani and the Manganiars of Western Rajasthan'. In *Theorizing the Local: Music,*

Practice, and Experience in South Asia and beyond, edited by Richard Wolf, 97–111. Oxford: Oxford University Press.

Douglas, Mary. 1972. 'Deciphering a Meal'. *Daedalus* 101 (1, Myth, Symbol, and Culture): 61–81.

Henderson, Carol. 2001. 'Famines and Droughts in Western Rajasthan: Desert Cultivators and Periodic Resource Stress'. In *The Idea of Rajasthan*, edited by Karine Schomer. Vol. 2. New Delhi: Manohar & American Institute of Indian Studies.

Kalhoro, Zulfiqar. 2015. 'One Deity, Three Temples: A Typology of Sacred Spaces in Haryar Village, Tharparkar (Sindh)'. *Research Deliberation* 1 (2).

Kothari, Komal. 2001. Musician for the People: The Manganiyars of Western Rajasthan'. In *The Idea of Rajasthan*, edited by Karine Schomer. Vol. 1. New Delhi: Manohar & American Institute of Indian Studies.

Levi Strauss, Claude. 1983. *The Raw and the Cooked: Mythologiques*. Vol. 1. Chicago, IL: University of Chicago Press.

Marriott, Mckim. 1968. 'Caste Ranking and Food Transactions: A Matrics Analysis'. In *Structure and Change in Indian Society*, edited by Milton Singer and Bernard S. Cohen, 133–171. Chicago, IL: Aldige Publishing Company.

Scholliers, Peter.2001. *Food, Drink and Identity: Cooking, Eating and Drinking in Europe since the Middle Ages*. Oxford: Berg.

Singh, K. S. 1998. *Rajasthan. People of India Series*. Vol. 38, Part 2. Mumbai: Popular Prakashan.

Stajcic, Nevana. 2013. 'Understanding Culture: Food as a Means of Communication'. *Hemispheres* 28: 77–87.

Swami, Narottam Das, ed. 1995. *Dhola Maru ra Duha*. Jodhpur: Rajasthani Granthaghar.

Thapar, Romila. 1978. *Ancient Indian Social History: Some Interpretations*. Delhi: Orient BlackSwan.

19

Gender Politics and Food Practices in Urban West Bengal

Moumita Dey

Introduction

Indians not only abide by norms and rules of their society, they often celebrate ideologies justifying those rules through different practices.[1] Almost all aspects of their lifestyle[2] like dress, food, value, belief, and norm are affected by those ideas. In Indian society people consume different types of food based on their social rank, which is the sum of their ascribed status like gender, caste and religion as well as achieved status like educational qualification, occupational status and economic condition. Gender is one of the strongest among the assemblage as it cannot be easily modified or hidden from others. Since ancient ages to recent times, women have had to face gender politics in respective societies. Effects of such politics can be seen in their regular food practices. It starts from the process of food production and culminates at the selection of food and its consumption. It is an established fact that Indian women do not enjoy equal right for food and nutrition in comparison to their male counterparts. It is also true that certain movements claiming equal rights for women and some government initiatives have created some impact at a certain level. Gender role[3] is first learned inside the family as part of a socialization process. Gender inequality is taught to younger persons in Indian households by senior family members, the lessons are often passed through livelihood practices. Any opposition to gender inequality is incomplete without inclusion of the family in the process. Indian social scientists have amply discussed these issues in their studies.

While studying the trend of research on food and gender inequality in India, it has been seen that authors have mainly emphasized on issues like food security, malnutrition, deprivation of women from their rights to produce food. Several researches have also shown that gender ideology has played an effective role in creating deficiency of nutrients among Indian women (Agarwal 2012; Maharana and Ladusingh 2014; Rao, Pradhan and Roy 2017; Tiwari 2013). It has also been found in several studies that parents do not agree to provide basic food to their female children as they are biased towards their male progenies (Singh and Patel 2017). New-born babies, school-going girls, married women, aged widows—anyone can face this kind of problem inside their families due to these conventional ideologies of gender discrimination. Few studies have described a different scenario (Pradhan, Tayor, Agarwal, Prabhakaran and Ebrahim 2013). Some scholars have studied the role of women in food production, consumption and management inside the family (Agarwal 2011). Iyer and Wright (2016) have discussed about changing diet pattern of Central Himalayan people and how it has been experienced by the women.

Taking a break from the discourses mentioned above, this chapter has tried to explore the role of gender politics in 'well-educated' urban families of West Bengal in contemporary times. It has focused on the role played by gender ideology employed by family members to deprive the females among them from enjoying their basic right to select their foods and beverages. Bengali food and cuisine has been well investigated from different perspectives (Banerjee 1991, 2001; Donner 2008; Ray 2009; Roy and Das 2015; Sengupta 2010). Scholars have emphasized on changing food practices of Bengali people and highlighted connection between culture and food practices. In this chapter my intention is to identify different mechanisms of practising gender ideology through food practice by Bengali women at present time. This study is a collection of narratives of some of my childhood friends and respondents of my doctoral research work. I live in Madhyamgram since my childhood. It is an urban area[4] 20 km away from the main city centre of Kolkata. This locality was established largely by migrant Hindu families from East Pakistan in 1950. After Bengal was partitioned, many families from Faridpur, Khulna, Jessore and Dhaka migrated to this place.

Early settlers of Madhyamgram were primarily involved in agriculture, after arriving India and settling in a place close to a big city they had to look for new profession. Many of them joined salaried jobs in the government sector. My family settled here in 1960. I am now 30 years old. Since childhood I have listened to different stories of our ancestral village in Bangladesh from my family members and neighbours. This experience is common to all the children of our generation. Till now, people of this area consider themselves as 'Bangal'.[5] As the people stopped practising their caste-based ancestral occupations after migration, occupation-based caste structure[6] became weak and eventually non-existent in the society. The same people, however, enquire about caste identity at the time of negotiating marriages.[7] In recent times, people of lower castes are often identified and referred to by surnames. However, certificates issued by the state government to individuals belonging to Scheduled Caste communities bear their caste names.

In this locality individuals and families are generally known by their economic status; class-based discrimination is very common in this society, which is reflected in residential segregation.[8] In every neighbourhood, people of better economic condition maintain cordial relationship with those of same economic class[9] without paying much attention to their position in caste system. This class identity is also intertwined with the education level of the family members— occupational status of the earning members. In this society, women enjoy the same status as their male counterpart. They are participating in every political, social and cultural activities without any hesitation. New generation women are highly educated[10] but work participation rate is not at all satisfactory in this area.[11] It can be said the women of this area are facing the problem of absence of job opportunities. Women of this area are conscious about their class identity. This identity is the composition of several factors like her own education level, husband's education level, family income of their natal and marital family members. They give emphasis on maintaining family reputation. Sometimes their inclination towards practising family norms and culture forces them to practise gender politics inside their families even through regular food practice. I am well connected with my friends, thus they shared their experiences with me. I have a practice to note down those stories which touch my heart for their both positive and negative essence. Few case studies make up the collection of these stories. I have done my doctoral research work on the changing scenario of housewives. During my field work, I got an opportunity to explore some interesting stories regarding the food practice in the families of my area. My collection of narratives let me think about the existing gender politics in the food practice of the women. It may change its form, but it is not abolished from the mind of the people. All these narratives are documented between 2015 and 2018.

Discussion and Results

Most of the women interviewed for this study claimed they were not facing any discrimination in their respective families in matters of their selection of food; they could prepare dishes according to their wish. None of them has ever experienced a situation where they were given inadequate food. However, they had to follow certain rules and regulations regarding time of food consumption and the type of food they can or cannot consume. The general feeling was that they must follow those rules as they are women and it is part of the role assigned to them by society. All respondents were not in the same stage of life, so their experiences are varied; in a few cases though the respondents were not ready to be governed by gender politics in matters of regular food practices. The way majority of the respondents were thinking and acting can be described as a result of 'false consciousness'[12] which makes them to believe that existing food practices are just and ideal.

In the following paragraphs some of the interviews conducted in the course of the study have been presented to understand the range of experiences and views.

Societal Regulations Related to Various Stages of Life

Infancy

'Rice ceremony of a female child is not as important as that of a male child'.

A. Dey is a housewife, she was 28 years old when I interviewed her. She studied up to higher secondary level. Her husband has the same level of education and was employed as contractual worker in the local municipality. His annual income was about ₹96,000. The couple was living in an extended family where father of the husband was head of the household. Low income of the husband compelled him to be economically dependent on his father. Father-in-law of the respondent lady announced on the occasion of baby shower that if she gives birth to a male child, the family will celebrate his *annaprashan* or rice ceremony[13] with grandeur, but if it is a girl child, there will be no such celebration. His argument was that boys are bearers of heredity and family tradition while girls are not so important to the lineage. Rice ceremony is a ritual observed by the Hindus, it marks an infant's first intake of solid food.

I was present as an invitee on baby shower, when several members of the family were voicing their dislike for girl child in the presence of the guests. As determining sex of a foetus is illegal in India, the would-be mother did not know if it was a boy or girl she was carrying. From her look one could tell she was feeling tense, but she could not raise her voice against her in-laws. She also asked me to keep calm, as it could jeopardize her domestic peace. Later she gave birth to a male child and the family celebrated the rice ceremony with grandeur.

Though discriminated against occasionally, generally a girl child is not deprived of her basic needs. In such situations however, the children become victim of gender politics even before they are born.

Prior to Marriage

'Try to look slim otherwise we may lose your best chance in the marriage market'.
S. Das Chowdhury (age 24) was an unmarried working woman from an affluent family. She completed her university-level education before joining a private firm. Her father has been a retired government employee and her mother, a businesswoman dealing in clothes. The respondent often faced problem regarding her food habits; her mother always monitored what she was eating as she wanted her daughter to be slim. The mother claimed to believe in women empowerment, but she also felt that an obese woman might face difficulty in finding partner of her choice. She often expressed her anxiety to me. The respondent had to compromise with her selection of food to keep her mother happy. Eventually, the daughter subscribed to her mother's views and decided what to eat and how much to eat accordingly. It was noted that often other members of her family ate restaurant food, but she was often subjected to restrictions. At such times she was found to keep quiet to maintain peace, but she admitted that she was disheartened by her mother's attitude.

'You need to look slim and beautiful to be a perfect lover'.
J. Paul (age 29) is a working woman. She has completed her graduation from a premier college of Kolkata. Her family members are well educated and employed in different administrative posts of West Bengal Government. She used to be a food lover, but suddenly she started dieting. This respondent is my childhood friend, we often meet at friends' parties. In the last one year I have noticed that she has stopped taking

spicy food. I came to know through her best friend that she has changed her food habits to make herself slim and beautiful. She believes that her ex-boyfriend rejected her as she was not beautiful enough. To make herself sexually attractive she needs to control her food consumption. She received support of her mother in doing so. Now she was feeling good to see herself in this new slim look.

In both cases, respondents changed their food habit to enhance sexual attraction. The thought and the action were primarily targeted to increase chance of finding better match in marriage. Thus, under different influences the respondents accepted the gender ideology related to female body and marriage.

After Marriage Is Fixed

'Always think about our reputation'.
B. Aich (age 29) is a working woman. She was working as human resource manager in a multi-national company and her annual income was about one million rupees. She is my childhood friend and we share every incident of our life. At her office parties she often drinks alcohol. When her marriage was fixed, her would-be mother-in-law asked her not to post any picture of her office parties on social networking sites. If anyone from among their relatives find their daughter-in-law holding a glass of alcohol, it may jeopardize their reputation. It is interesting to note that her would-be mother-in-law also drinks occasionally. Her own son has posted pictures of booze parties he has attended, but his future wife is subjected to certain restrictions.

In this case, the would-be mother-in-law was objecting to bringing certain food (and beverage) practices to public domain and not to the actual practices. The respondent was initially shocked by the demand, but she eventually withdrew all pictures from social networking site that could portray her 'negatively'; she did not want to jeopardize her prospect of marriage in a reputed family and was ready to compromise her freedom to discuss her way of life with others.

'A daughter-in-law must help her mother-in-law in kitchen'.
A. Chowdhury (age 28) is a social activist working at a non-governmental organization. She too is my childhood friend and together we have organised several social awareness programmes in our community. She is in relationship with a boy who also is her childhood friend, the couple has decided to marry. Both the families have accepted their relationship. In a family function at her boyfriend's home, his mother

asked the girl to help her in kitchen. She was chatting with other friends and her boyfriend was present there. None of them was asked to help the lady in kitchen, the lady never asks her son for help. The girl was annoyed because she alone had to leave the company of her friends. However, she obeyed the instructions of the lady silently. The lady told her, 'You are going be my daughter-in-law, so you must help me in kitchen. It is your duty now.' The girl never felt her boyfriend's mother was being cruel to her, but she could see the lady was being partial. The would-be mother-in-law was making it clear that the girl must shoulder some duties from now on. It is again the issue of expected gender role. Later, my friend discussed the matter with her would-be mother-in-law, and she realized her mistake. As my friend was confident about her standpoint, she sorted out the issue rather easily. As the lady also is an educated employed woman, she gave priority to the viewpoints of my friend.

One inherent contradiction in patriarchal societies is, while the women are not considered important as bearers of heredity or of family tradition, even in their natal homes, they often are held responsible for protecting (and tarnishing) family status and prestige, especially at their in-law's place. When a woman has been selected by a man's family as a bride, she is supposed to respect this idea.

Early Days of Married Life

'Do not eat rice on Ashtami day'.

S. Roy (age 28) is a working woman who got married into a prosperous family. She was earning a monthly salary of ₹25,000. She became pregnant after two years of her marriage. During those days, she and her husband used to stay with her mother-in-law, who is a retired schoolteacher. Her mother-in-law forced her to eat *luchi*[14] instead of rice on *Asthami*[15] of Durga Puja. It was custom of the family that the women would abstain from eating rice on that day and her mother-in-law believed breaking the custom might cause some problem in the household. The pregnant woman was not willing to eat deep fried food and started vomiting after taking it. In the evening her mother-in-law and other family members broke the rule and ate *khichdi*, which was made of rice. On discovering that she felt utterly dismayed but preferred to keep quiet and avoid any complication.

In her pregnancy, the woman wanted to stick to her routine and comfort food, but her mother-in-law mentioned some religious custom to stop her from eating food of her choice. The elder woman possibly made use of the occasion to teach the newly married daughter-in-law some rules and regulations that she herself violated later in the day. It was also noticed younger women often keep quiet in face of discriminatory treatment. This respondent explained, such stance would help her to maintain whatever good relations she has developed with her mother-in-law.

'Wait until the male members eat their meal'.

G. Dey (age 60) is a housewife. She got married in an extended family. Her husband was employed in a central government office in Kolkata. She had to wake up early in the morning to prepare breakfast and lunch for the male members. Her husband left for office at 9 in the morning and the respondent could eat her breakfast after that. She had to work for about four hours without eating anything. Due to this routine she developed some health problems later, though she was not willing to give any importance to her health issues. She continues her routine of working empty stomach till this date. Despite all her sufferings, she argued she has done what a woman is supposed to do.

'You need to think about others before your own needs'.

Sengupta (age 45) is a housewife. She got married in an extended family. Her husband is employed in a contractual job in municipality. She has studied up to higher secondary level. At her natal home she used to eat spicy food. She got married in a family where spicy food was never cooked. She did not like the food she herself was cooking for all at her in-law's place. Her husband and other family members suggested her to prepare spicy food items for her separately. She did not do this for two reasons: cooking twice would require more of her time as there was nobody in the family to help her in the kitchen, and it would be a burden on the family coffers. She said, 'Being a woman I need to think about others first, then about me'.

The decision to eat food that she did not like was her own, it clearly was not imposed on her. Apparently, it was a rational choice on her part, but her decision of not preparing separate food for herself was largely influenced by gender ideology.

'Eat according to your financial ability'.

K. Das (age 43) is a housewife. Her husband was working in a private firm. She is the younger daughter-in-law in an extended family where contribution of her husband to family fund was less than another brother. She was often scolded for drinking tea several times a day, her sister-in-law said her habit might result in increase of monthly expenditure for sugar. Being a homemaker, she must think about family budget. The respondent did not give up. Within a few years of her marriage, she and her husband with their son got separated from the extended family to establish their nuclear family and shifted to a separate house. She said, 'Why should I compromise; I have the right to eat or drink according to my will'.

This respondent stood for her rights; while her sister-in-law tried to alter her behaviour using logic of economy and notion of gender ideology, for the respondent individual freedom was more valuable.

Few Years After Marriage

'Don't waste money on fast food as you have not contributed to family income'.

N. Dutta (age 42) is a housewife. Her husband is a wholesale vegetable trader at the local market. Both of them have middle school-level education. Respondent lives in a nuclear family with her husband and son. She prepared food for the family according to her will every day. She has never faced any discrimination regarding food consumption in her family. However, she likes to eat fast food purchased from local shops and her husband has serious problem with this. 'My husband never allows me to eat fast food because he feels that is waste of money,' she said. 'As I do not earn money and contribute to family income, I'm told by my husband not to indulge in these habits. Now my son has started to earn, I often eat those dishes. When I spend money earned by my son, my husband doesn't oppose me.'

In this instance, the woman is required to compromise with her choice of food because she is treated as a non-earner in the family, even though she was contributing her labour and time for the family. This lady had to depend on others to purchase food of her choice. Recently she has started to earn some money on her own by making handicraft items; at last this sum she can spend freely.

'Fasting is important to hold superior position in the family'.

J. Mitra (age 43) is a well-educated housewife; her husband is engaged in a salaried job. He was earning about ₹20,000 per month. The respondent was married in an extended family. After few years of her marriage her brother-in-law also got married. Her mother-in-law observed certain rites on some specific days of each Bengali calendar month.[16] None of the daughters-in-law observed those rites with their mother-in-law. After her mother-in-law passed way, the respondent started to observe those rituals. She used to fast on those days for well-being of all family members. Reportedly, she was never asked by her family members to observe those rites and rituals; still, she considered it as her duty. 'Nobody will tell me anything if I don't observe those rites, but as senior most woman of the house it is part of my duty', she said, 'and other members have some expectations from me'.

Such act can be interpreted as an attempt to maintain her superior position in the family. She was ready to compromise with her hitherto food preferences to gain and maintain the status of a dutiful woman.

After Separation/Divorce from Husband

'A woman dependent on others must control her lust for food'.
S. Dey (age 48) is a divorcee who was staying with her mother. After the demise of her mother she shifted to the in-laws' place of her sister. The respondent is a hardworking lady and she loves to eat, especially sweets and fast food. In the presence of others, she shows indifference towards food. However, members of that family have discovered that she eats foods of her choice taking out of the refrigerator surreptitiously. Though it has become an open secret, she never admits her habit. Conversing with her for long hours it was revealed, she believed that she must not make her desire for food public. As she considered her as a supplementary member of the family, she cannot do such things. She said, 'A woman should eat all the things which are available inside the house. I am thankful to god that he has provided me the opportunity to fill my stomach three times a day.'

The social environment has created this idea in her mind; a woman dependent on distant relatives cannot express her desire for food of her choice. This has been accentuated by the way she was treated by her relatives and neighbours after her divorce; she was always asked to adjust with the situation. She now believes, unless she compromises with her desires or hide them from public scrutiny, she may lose her shelter again. Clearly, her relatives and neighbours forced her to compromise with her personal choice related to food consumption.

'I am head of the household; you must follow my instructions'.
S. Dutta (Age 29) is a married woman who was living separately from her husband with a daughter at her natal house for four years. She is doing a job. She is my college friend; on her birthday she invited her friends, I was part of that group. She initially had a plan to prepare luchi

and curry, so she bought the ingredients. On that day she thought, it might take a long time to prepare the food for her friends, so it would be better to order something from restaurant. Her mother disapproved the plan of ordering food and instructed her to prepare food by herself. She followed her instructions rather unhappily. Later she said to me, 'My mother takes care of my child and I'm still a burden on her at this age. After all, she is head of the household, and how can I disobey her?' The respondent could not spend any time with us on her birthday, she was busy preparing food in the kitchen.

In this case, the respondent had to follow her mother's instructions on that day (and on other days as well) out of gratitude. A married woman staying with her mother instead of her husband's house has an element of shame in it. Despite economic empowerment, the respondent is engaged in a salaried job, she had to follow her mother's instructions, as her social position is vulnerable.

Widowhood

'A widow should be a vegetarian'.
S. Pain (age 74) is a widow. Her husband passed away four years before the interview was conducted. She liked to eat fish but now she does not touch it. She believes that a widow should be vegetarian. She knows that with ageing she has become physically weak and the doctor has advised her to take fish or meat everyday as she has developed signs of undernourishment. Her son and other family members also want her to eat meat and fish. But she is not ready to do that because she believes it is improper for a Hindu widow. Moreover, if she eats non-vegetarian food that may invite criticism from relatives and neighbours.

The respondent had prior ideas regarding the norms of widowhood. She was born in a village in Bangladesh and was married into another rural family. She shifted to an urban area when she was 50 years old. In this urban milieu too ideas common in rural Bangladesh about normative practices for Hindu widows are held by many. Under such circumstances, she herself decided what should be her diet for rest of the life, whatever be her health condition. She has seen other widows of her extended family and of the neighbourhood to stick to those norms. She feels, her 'exceptional' activity may tarnish her dignity among them.

'Don't eat oily and spicy dishes as you are a widow'.
R. Dey (age 65) is a widow. She was depending on her daughters for her sustenance after the demise of her husband as her husband could

not leave much for her maintenance. She had a taste for oily and spicy dishes and used to eat non-vegetarian food after the death of her husband. She said, her husband asked her not to change her food habit after his death. Her daughters and other family members never raised the issue at that time. Once she became economically dependent on her daughters, they started mentioning norms of ideal widowhood and virtues of austerity to her. More than once her daughters have told her, 'You are a widow; you need to control your desires. Why do you need to put so much of oil and spice in your food?' She sometimes secretly asked her neighbours to give her oily-spicy food items, if they were cooking any. She never told her daughters about the clandestine transactions fearing they might rebuke her for such behaviour.

Among high- and middle-caste Hindus, a widow was asked to control her appetite. A lot of restrictions were imposed on their lifeways and on food habits. In this case, the lady was asked to maintain those rules by her own daughters. Her daughters used traditional ideology as a tool to stop her from consuming food items of her choice.

The above discussion brings to the fore some noteworthy points. Inside the family women have often been deprived of their basic right of food selection, preparation and consumption of food of their own choice and of celebrating their food practice due to some gender role related ideologies that often are pre-conceived. It was not that those ideologies were always imposed on them by other family members; in most of the cases, it was present in their mind. They were found to carry those ideas within that they learnt in the course of their socialization process.

While discussing patriarchal ideas and ways, fingers are often pointed at the men for creating and propagating the system. In all the cases mentioned above, barring one, women were executioners of the norms and customs that deprive self or other women from enjoying the freedom of selecting, preparing and consuming food of their choice. In all these cases, women were never given less food in comparison to male members of their respective families, but that does not mean they have never faced the brunt of gender politics. Among the women, younger ones are frequently exploited by elder ones. The perpetrators always present some rationale, which apparently may sound logical, but on closer enquiry it is possible to discover subtle strategy of asserting their superiority.

It may not be very easy to find out sources of patriarchal ideologies, but one can discern with less effort how women contribute to keep the system operational. All the respondents mentioned in this chapter live in urban area and none of them hail from impoverished economic background. Rather, many of them are associated with several social organisations and work for betterment of the society. With time, they have changed their ideas regarding propriety of dress, food, and lifestyle. But seldom they can go beyond the barrier of 'gender role preference'. If the case studies discussed above are arranged according to the age of the respondents in descending order, it can be seen, previously a woman was deprived of her rights because another woman told her how to act. She was ordered to follow norms prevalent in the family or in the local society, sometimes for the sake of economic advantage and on some other times to become the 'ideal' homemaker. In later years, the younger women were not instructed by anybody; they were requested by the elder ones. If the rationale is discussed in two sets of cases, it remained the same except the economic one. Sometimes actions leading to deprivation are the result of self-imposed regulations on lifestyle. This conformation to socially valued practices is part of strategy to gain higher status by demonstrating dedication to familial or social norms and claiming a superior position in the family. The situation can be different in case of separated and divorcee women; they follow instructions of others out of their helplessness. Sometimes it is their parents who make them insecure.

Food is more than just a component of culture; it reflects the relations in a society. If gender politics regarding this issue is measured based on quantity of food taken by the women, then some important issues may be overlooked. Food practice at different stages of life can reveal nuances of relationship and is related to efforts made to gain social status. Sometime these practices reveal politics of power within the family. The constructed idea of gender always comes with prescribed virtues for each of the gender categories. Based on gender identity few roles are assigned to individuals and collectives. Adherence to those roles ensures their importance in the social system is maintained. There are few customs which must be obeyed by men and women to fit themselves in those roles. In Indian society where women are identified as the bearer of culture and tradition, they do not only follow those customs, but also pass it to the next generation. Female family members were found to execute customary practices related to food themselves and made others to do the same. It is true, working women enjoy more liberty in their life, but they also must pick up and stick to those customs at a certain stage of their life cycle. Situations discussed in preceding pages have amply shown that rank gained through education, urban living, and economic empowerment does not make much difference in gender status of women.

Conclusion

This study has revealed association between idea of role preference and gender politics in the context of an urban society. It cannot be denied that women are conspicuously unequal with their male counterparts in different spheres of life and are largely responsible for this condition. They are considerably influenced by traditional values and customs causing gender inequality and often place barriers for them asking for parity. Rather, quite a few of them were found to compete to achieve perfection for those gender-specific roles.

Food is the basic need of life, and nobody can stop any member of the society to get access to food. Empowerment is not an abstract idea; it can be objectively assessed by understanding the extent of gender inequality in daily and occasional food practices. Evaluating efficacy of norms and customs associated with food practices can be an effective tool to understand the inequality discussed here.

Notes

1. I have considered the idea of practice put forward by Stephen Turner (1994). He mentioned, 'The idea of "practice" and its cognates has this odd kind of promissory utility. They promise that they can be turned into something more precise. But the value of the concepts is destroyed when they are pushed in the direction of meeting their promise'.
2. The term lifestyle has been used here to mean the sets of act, symbol and behaviour that are assigned to a given status group of the society. This idea is put forward by Scheyes (1986).
3. Gender role ideology is defined as the attitude of the person regarding the role of men and women and how this role can be shaped by their sex (Somech & Zahabby 2016). Gender role ideology refers to the attitude of the person regarding the role, responsibility of men and women in the society (Kroska 2007).
4. Madhyamgram is a municipality area. The total population is 155,441 persons. According to the definition put forward by Census of India 2011 regarding classification of cities, this area comes under the category of class 1 town having 100,000 or more population.
5. People who migrated from Bangladesh after partition or who have their ancestral origin in Bangladesh are called Bangal.
6. In Madhyamgram, Brahmins are considered as higher and Kayasthas as intermediate caste while others are identified as lower caste. Brahmins are identified through their surname as Mukherjee, Banerjee, Chatterjee, Bhattacharya. Common Kayastha surnames are Das, Deyand Dutta. There is some confusion about surnames like

Saha, Roy and Biswas as those belong to both intermediate and lower castes.

7. Caste identity is almost always mentioned in matrimonial advertisements in newspapers or in matrimonial sites.

8. In Madhyamgram, people tend to move from their old residential areas to the newly built apartments along Sodepur Road and Jessore Road (these two roads are the main connectors between Madhyamgram and Kolkata City). I was told, they have done it to maintain or improve their status. Apartment dwelling is associated with higher status (better income and education level). They also enjoy better transport facilities.

9. I applied snowball sampling method for this work. During field survey, women of well-to-do families often referred me to families having similar economic condition, though they were not always next-door neighbours. Even few women expressed their disappointment in having poor families as neighbours. In this area, class is mainly identified through family income and occupation of male members of family. People who are employed in white-collar jobs and have monthly income level of more than ₹40,000 per month are considered to be of higher class. Families with monthly income of ₹15,000–40,000 are described as middle-class and those with less than ₹15,000 are lower-class families. Families engaged in trading activities are generally considered as middle-class, though some of them earn more than the salaried people.

10. Most of the women of age group of 18–40 have completed their college-level education. Few have post graduate degree.

11. In Madhyamgram, woman work participation rate is 11.27 per cent (Development and Planning Department Government of West Bengal, Government of West Bengal 2010).

12. Originally proposed by Marxist theoreticians and later adopted by the feminists, the concept of 'false consciousness' describes how oppressed people, through the process of socialization, are taught to justify acts of the oppressors. In this case, the women often falsely recognize their problems as they are socialized in such way to accept their subordinate position gracefully. Majority of the respondents described in this study do not realize their basic rights to food consumption and food selection is violated due to inequality in gender ideology.

13. Rice ceremony is a ritual observed by Hindus; it marks an infant's first intake of solid food.

14. Luchi is rolled and deep-fried wheat flour dough.

15. Ashtami is the third day of Durga Puja. Durga Puja is the main festival of Hindu Bengalis. In some families, people do not eat rice on that day.

16. During every Bengali calendar month ladies in some Hindu Bengali families observe certain rites and rituals, one of which is called *sashthibrata*. On this day, women, especially the mothers, observe certain food restrictions including fast until completion of the ritual.

References

Agarwal, B. 2011. 'Food Crises and Gender Inequality'. DESA Working Paper No. 107 (June). New York, NY: DESA.

———. 2012. 'Food Security, Productivity and Gender Inequality'. IEG Working Paper. New Delhi: IEG.

Banerjee, C. 1991. *Life and Food in Bengal*. London: Penguin.

———. 2001. *The in Hour of the Goddess: Memories of Women, Food and Ritual in Bengal*. Calcutta: Seagull.

———. 2010. *District Human Development Report, North 24 Parganas*. Kolkata: HDRCC.

Development and Planning Department Government of West Bengal, Government of West Bengal. 2010. *District Human Development Report, North 24 Parganas*. Kolkata: HDRCC.

Donner, H. 2008. 'New Vegetarianism: Food, Gender and Neo Liberal Regimes in Bengali Middle Class Families'. *Journal of South Asian Studies* 31 (1): 143–169.

Iyer, D., and W. Wright. 2016. 'Food Insecurity, Helplessness and Choice: Gender and Diet Change in the Central Himalaya'. *Journal of Gender, Agriculture and Food Security* 1 (3): 63–84.

Kroska, A. 2007. 'Gender Ideology and Gender Role Ideology'. In *The Blackwell Encyclopedia of Sociology*, edited by George Ritzer, 1867–1869. Malden, WA: Wiley-Blackwell.

Maharana, B., and L. Ladusingh. 2014. 'Gender Disparity in Health and Food Expenditure in India among Elderly'. *International Journal of Population Research* 13 (1): 1–8.

Pradhan, M., F. Tayor, S. Agarwal, D. Prabhakaran, and S. Ebrahim. 2013. 'Food Acquisition and Intra-household Consumption Patterns: A Study of Low and Middle Income Urban Households in Delhi, India'. *Indian Journal of Community Health* 25 (4): 391–402.

Rao, N., M. Pradhan, and D. Roy. 2017. 'Gender Justice and Food Security in India—A Review'. IFPRI Discussion Paper. Washington, DC: IFPRI.

Ray, U. 2009. 'Aestheticizing Labour: An Affective Discourse of Cooking in Colonial Bengal'. *South Asian History and Culture* 1 (1): 60–70.

Roy, S., and A. P. Das. 2015. 'Some Favourite Rajbanshi Cuisine from the Northern Part of West Bengal, India'. *Pleione* 9 (2): 471–485.

Scheyes, M. 1986. 'The Power of Life Style'. *Society and Leisure* 10 (2): 249–266.

Sengupta, J. 2010. 'Nation on a Platter: The Culture and Politics of Food and Cuisine in Colonial Bengal'. *Modern Asian Studies* 44 (1): 81–98.

Singh, A., and K. S. Patel. 2017. 'Gender Differentials in Feeding Practices, Health Care Utilization and Nutritional Status of Children in Northern India'. *International Journal of Human Rights in Healthcare* 10 (5): 323–331.

Somech, A., and A. D. Zahabby. 2016. 'Gender Role Ideology'. In N. A. Naples (ed.), *The Wiley Blackwell Encyclopedia of Gender and Sexuality Studies*. Hoboken, NJ: Wiley-Blackwell.

Tiwari, A. K. 2013. 'Gender Inequality in Terms of Health and Nutrition in India: Evidence from National Family Health Survey–3'. *Pacific Business Review International* 5 (12): 24–34.

Turner, S. P. 1994. *The Social Theory of Practice: Tradition, Tacit Knowledge and Presuppositions*. Chicago, IL: University of Chicago Press.

About the Editor and Contributors

Editor

Kanchan Mukhopadhyay is Tagore National Fellow, Anthropological Survey of India. He has obtained his master's degree in anthropology from University of Calcutta and doctoral degree from Vidyasagar University. He has worked for Anthropological Survey of India for most part of his career largely in eastern and north-eastern parts of India and in Andaman and Nicobar Islands. One major area of his research interest has remained construction and maintenance of identity among migrants and refugees; he has worked among such groups in West Bengal and Andaman Islands. He took part in the national ethnographic survey called People of India, especially in North-East India, which helped him to gain some insight into the multifaceted ethnic situation prevalent there. He has also taken interest in the study of relationship between small communities and nation-state and has written on paradigms of development and programmes for welfare of Scheduled Tribe communities. His other major work was study of impact of technological developments such as introduction of irrigation facilities, high-yielding varieties of seeds and chemical fertilisers on small-scale cultivators. He has also worked on methodological and ethical issues in social science research. Another area he has worked in is visual anthropology; he has supervised the 'Visual Anthropology Unit' of Anthropological Survey of India for many years and has made several films on various subjects like modes of cultural transmission, traditional knowledge system among artisanal fishermen and people's initiative for conservation of culture. A film on the last topic 'Tryst with Times' was screened at Kolkata International Film Festival in 2017.

His interest in ideas and practices related to food developed since early 1990s when he studied processes of food production, distribution and consumption among certain socially and economically weak communities. He has probed into dimensions of power relations as expressed through food behaviour, collective memory of availability or scarcity of food, and food as symbol of social status.

As a Tagore National Fellow, he is researching on changing food practices in rural India. He is passionate about food and travel and loves to indulge in adventures while eating and travelling.

Contributors

Ala Uddin has been teaching anthropology in the Department of Anthropology, University of Chittagong, Bangladesh, since 2003. He has been conducting research on diverse issues of the indigenous people in the Chittagong Hill Tracts. His major research dealt mainly with the survival strategies of the indigenous people—how they try to manage their survival affected by the outsiders (i.e., settler Bengalis). Among other issues, he worked on religious pluralism, street vending, health and diseases, refugees and diaspora, and forest management. He has written a book entitled *Theoretical Anthropology* (in Bengali) and several articles published in peer-reviewed national and international journals. His current research works look into the plight of the Rohingya refugees in Bangladesh and the urbanized lifeways of the indigenous migrants.

Amitabha Sarkar is a MSc, PhD (science) in anthropology from the University of Calcutta and specialized in advanced social-cultural anthropology. His remarkable empirical contribution in anthropological research arena is on impact of industrialization, tribal ethnography, culture ecology, ethno-science, religious belief system as integrative process, culture change, and management of environment with traditional knowledge. He has published approximately 19 books and more than 170 research papers in reputed journals. He possesses 35 years' research experience and carried out empirical study among tribal and weaker sections of Rajasthan, Gujarat, Jharkhand, Chhattisgarh, Odisha and West Bengal. He is the life member of Indian National Confederation and Academy of Anthropologists (INCAA), Indian Science Congress Association and Indian Anthropological Society. He was associated with Anthropological Survey of India from 1977 to 2012. He is also a consultant researcher and involved in collecting empirical data from tribal areas of Odisha.

B. Francis Kulirani was formerly Deputy Director (Cultural), Anthropological Survey of India, Kolkata. Kulirani obtained his MSc degree from the Pune University and Doctoral Degree from University of Calicut. He has written or edited 10 books and many articles in national and international journals. He was awarded Shastri Indo-Canadian Research Fellowship in 2006. Upon retirement from Anthropological Survey of India he was Course Director, Department of Tribal and Rural Sociology, Kannur University, Kerala, during 2015–2017 and visiting faculty during 2018. Currently, Kulirani is pursuing Tagore Research Scholar programme of Ministry of Culture (Government of India) and attached to the Indira Gandhi Rashtriya Manav Sangrahalaya, Bhopal. He is founder secretary of the Anthropological Association, Mysore, a life member of the Indian National Confederation and Academy of Anthropologists (INCAA), Kolkata, and the North East India Council of Social Science Research (NEICSSR), Shillong, Meghalaya.

Chhanda Mukhopadhyay obtained her master's degree in anthropology from University of Calcutta and doctoral degree from Vidyasagar University. She has worked in Anthropological Survey of India and has worked extensively on social inequality, cultural syncretism and urban studies in Andaman and Nicobar Islands, and eastern and north-eastern parts of India. Her major work was on sex-workers and their children in Kolkata city, where she tried to understand the process of socialization in a marginalized and socially outcast group.

Dharitri Narzary teaches history to undergraduate and post-graduate students at School of Liberal Studies, Dr. B. R. Ambedkar University Delhi (AUD). She specializes in Japanese studies and her interest areas include race and minority issues, marginality, multiculturalism, imperialism and colonialism, society and culture. She is also the founding convenor of the North East Forum (NEF, 2011–2017) at AUD and closely works with the University's Centre for Community Knowledge (CCK). She completed her BA and MA in history, MPhil from the Department of Chinese and Japanese Studies and PhD from the Department of East Asian Studies, University of Delhi.

Madhumita Mazumdar is associate professor at the Dhirubhai Ambani Institute of Information Communication Technology,

Gandhinagar, Gujarat. She has a specialized interest in the social history of science and technology and in colonial and post-colonial histories of the Andaman and Nicobar Islands. Apart from her publications on the disciplinary histories of science in Bengal, she has co-authored a book titled *New Histories of the Andaman Islands-Landscape, Place and Identity in the Bay of Bengal, 1790–2012* (2016).

Manish Chandi works in the Andaman and Nicobar Islands on the interface between communities and the natural environment. He has been working in the islands for past 25 years in association with the Andaman Nicobar Environmental Team (ANET). He completed his doctoral thesis in 2016 with the Oceans and Coasts programme of the Nature Conservation Foundation, Mysore, in which he explored the impact of the 2004 earthquake and tsunami on community sharing mechanisms in the Nicobar Islands. In the Andaman & Nicobar archipelago, Chandi began work as a volunteer restoring forest vegetation at the ANET base station at Wandoor village while also creating the water harvesting structures for the location. Since then, he has been involved in various projects related to primary research, collaborative projects, applied social-ecology projects in both the Andaman and Nicobar groups of islands with communities such as the Karen of Mayabunder, settlers in the Andamans and Nicobarese of Little Nicobar Island. His interests and work have ranged from surveys and research work on salt-water crocodiles, sea turtles, forest trees and indigenous communities particularly of the A&N archipelago. He has presented papers at international and national conferences while also giving speeches to interested groups and communities on his work and understandings at various fora. He is currently on sabbatical for one year, living with his wife and new-born child in Aldona village, Goa.

Moumita Dey is an assistant professor in Department of Geography, Amity University (Kolkata campus). She has done her doctoral research in feminist geography from Department of Geography, University of Calcutta. Her main areas of interest are gender, feminism, culture and society. She has deep interest in visual and qualitative methodologies. She has published papers in different national and international journals and has also worked as a reviewer in a peer-reviewed journal.

Nabakumar Duary has obtained master's degree from University of Calcutta and doctorate degree from Ranchi University. He has been working for Anthropological Survey of India since 1992. Duary has published several research papers in journals and edited books. He has edited two books and has authored one on education in tribal communities of West Bengal. He has also done significant research on folk painting, traditional knowledge, tribal education, tribal and folk culture and visual anthropology. He has remained involved in anthropological research and in making of several documentary films.

Om Gurung holds PhD in anthropology from Cornell University, Ithaca, New York. He is one of the founding faculty members at the Central Department of Sociology/Anthropology at Tribhuvan University, Nepal. He has been teaching anthropology to graduate students at Tribhuvan University for more than 37 years. In addition to teaching, he is heavily engaged in organizing national and international seminars and managing academic exchange programmes. He has completed a number of research projects on contemporary social, political and environmental issues in Nepal and published dozens of research articles in national and international scholarly journals. He is a co-author of several ethnographic profiles of indigenous peoples of Nepal. He is also a co-editor of ILO Convention 169 and Peace Building in Nepal (2005) published by NEFIN and ILO Nepal, Occasional Papers in Sociology and Anthropology of Nepal (2009–2011), Ethnicity and Federalization in Nepal (2012) and Social Inclusion Atlas and Ethnographic Profiles (2014) published by Tribhuvan University. He is also a Member of Editorial Board of *Asian Anthropology* (2006–207).

Dr Gurung has received many prestigious fellowships from various institutions. He received research fellowship from Norwegian University Committees for Development Education and Research (NUFU), Developing Country Training Fellowship from Wenner-Gren Foundation for anthropological research for his graduate studies at Cornell University, PhD Dissertation Research Fellowships from Social Science Research Council (SSRC), New York, Research Grants from National Geographic Society, and World Wildlife Fund, Washington DC. He also received several visiting fellowships to University of Wisconsin, Madison; Cornell University, Ithaca, New York; University of Bergen, Norway; Liverpool John Moores University, UK; and University of Lille, France.

During the 37 years of his teaching service at Tribhuvan University, Dr Gurung headed the Central Department of Sociology/Anthropology for more than 13 years. He also served as a chair of the Curricula Development Committee, executive member of the Center for Economic and Development Administration, research director of Social Inclusion Atlas and Ethnographic Profile and an executive member of Faculty Board of Humanities and Social Sciences at Tribhuvan University. Beside academic positions, he also holds various public as well as social positions in Nepal. He is the former general secretary of Nepal Federation of Indigenous Nationalities (NEFIN), adviser to Indigenous Peoples' CA Members' Caucus in the Constituent Assembly of Nepal, coordinator of High Level Task Force for the Revision of Official List of Indigenous Nationalities, member of National Development Council of National Planning Commission, member of Social Inclusion Program Monitoring Committee of National Planning Commission, board member of Poverty Alleviation Fund (PAF), coordinator of Dialogue Team of NEFIN to lead the dialogue with the Government of Nepal, member of the High Level Monitoring Commission on Code of Conduct of Ceasefire, and a member of High level Local Body Reform Advisory Committee.

Dr Gurung is an influencing intellectual and a prominent public leader. As an academic and a public leader, he has made substantial contributions both scholarly and socially to the understanding of social and political issues of Nepal. He is a promising intellectual leader of ethnic rights and politics of social inclusion in Nepal. He has played a critical role to raise social awareness among Indigenous peoples of Nepal and mobilize them for an assertion of their ethnic identity and cultural rights.

Ratna Dhar has completed her post-graduation in anthropology with specialization in socio-cultural anthropology from University of Calcutta. She earned her doctorate degree from Vidyasagar University, West Bengal. In her initial years of career, she worked among the Santal community in rural as well as in industrial areas of Birbhum District of West Bengal, in a research project in Visva-Bharati University. Presently she is attached with Anthropological Survey of India as a member of the research wing. Her major research concerns in early years have been the folk traditions of the Manganiyar musicians and Bhopa performers of Rajasthan. She has varied experience in working in the tribal regions of Sikkim, Jharkhand and Nagaland. In recent years, she looked into the problem areas of biosphere and has published a number of articles on development issues and conservation process in Sundarban Biosphere as well as in tribal areas in reputed journals. She has two books to her credit which include an interpretation of folk music and contents of songs practised by Manganiyars' folk singers within the socio-cultural matrix and another on impact of tourism on the heritage site of Chittorgarh fort. She is currently working on issues involving the problems of border communities, enclaves, identity and citizenship in Nagaland–Myanmar border and West Bengal–Bangladesh border.

Saradindu Biswas is an activist working for the cause of Dalit and Bahujan communities. He has researched intensively on sociological aspects of folklore and has collected vast body of material on folk-music, folk-theatre, rituals and fairytales from many communities. While investigating into origin of the Bengali-speaking people, he has searched for their roots in the language, arts and lifeways of the Santal, Munda, Oraon, Pahariya, Mal, Asur and other indigenous communities of Eastern India. He has written several articles in Bengali on ethno-history of indigenous communities, some of which have been highly appreciated.

Saw John Aung Thong is from the Andaman Islands, a second-generation Sgaw Karen from Webi village. Saw John has managed the Andaman Nicobar Environmental Team (ANET) research station at North Wandoor for past 25 years, playing multiple managerial roles in facilitating various research projects. His work has ranged from interfacing with local government offices, individual researchers, visitors and in construction as well as field research including much work which has contributed to this article. John's background managerial work has helped develop various facilities and infrastructure at ANET. Belonging to the small community of Karen in the Andaman Islands, much has been learnt by his co-authors from and through him. He has played a particularly critical position in leveraging many researchers into the islands especially into Middle and North Andaman by hosting them at his home. Over the last few years he has begun a homestay facility while also coordinating and facilitating the growth of a women's self-help group called the Andaman Karen Craft Society which was initiated by ANET as a small project towards becoming an entity in its own form. Through such engagement he has also seen the community he belongs to through dual lenses and works with others in facilitating positive change on various fronts.

Shiba Desor is a researcher and facilitator exploring the intersections of policy, culture and ecology. Her work experience ranges from studying forest governance issues at the national level with the environmental NGO Kalpavriksh to facilitating local action of women-based collectives with Maati Collective in Munsiari and Dakshin Foundation in Andaman. She is a co-author of 'Dhontang-Food in Ladakh' and 'Something to Chew On', publications that highlight multiple dimensions of food. She is presently a senior research associate with ATREE, working as part of a team studying the political ecology of the green economy. Desor is an avid believer in the healing power of art, *khichdi* and afternoon naps.

Shibani Roy, after obtaining PhD in anthropology from University of Delhi, conducted empirical research among tribes, castes and religious minorities of Northern, Western, North Western, Central, North Eastern regions of India and Iran. Based on the findings she has authored 24 books and contributed 135 research papers in national and international journals. Her seminal contribution in the field of women's role among inbred Muslim families has earned her a place of distinguished scholars of Indian anthropological studies on minorities. She has served Indian Council of Medical Research, New Delhi; National Institute of Health and Family Welfare, New Delhi; Anthropological Survey of India, Indira Gandhi National Centre for the Arts and Culture, New Delhi; and Office of Registrar General and Census Commissioner of India, New Delhi, in various capacities. She has been the recipient of Fellowship of ICSSR, New Delhi; CSIR, New Delhi. She was awarded senior fellowship of Ministry of Culture, Government of India. She has been the technical consultant, National Commission of Denotified Tribes, Nomads and Semi Nomadic communities, New Delhi; adviser, Vimarsh Solutions, Gurugram, Haryana. At present she is guest faculty at National Institute of Criminology and Forensic Science, Ministry of Home Affairs, Government of India. Her training and field experience have enabled her to contribute in understanding of human behaviour within the precincts of cultural matrix of Indian population groups.

Sreenathan M. is professor and dean, Faculty of Linguistics, Thunchathu Ezhuthachan Malayalam University, Kerala. He was formerly associated with the Central University of Kerala and Dravidian University as well as with the Anthropological Survey of India. His research experience in anthropological linguistics includes work on the Palaeolithic remnants of the Andaman and Nicobar Islands among tribal and caste population in mainland India. He is reputed far and wide as a productive member/leader of teams of anthropological or linguistic survey, an inspiring teacher-cum-researcher, a motivating head of academic or administrative departments, a persuasive director of research projects, a painstaking author/editor/compiler of academic books and reports of projects, capable of executing time-bound minor or mega programmes successfully. His publications consisting of numerous technical or popularizing papers and dozens of books and reports constitute an unparalleled contribution to various aspects of language and culture.

Sumit Mukherjee, MA (Geog.), PhD, formerly a field-based researcher in the Human Ecology section of Anthropological Survey. Currently he is engaged as guest teacher in the Department of Geography, University of Calcutta. His major research works in human ecology include several high altitude tribal communities in Himachal Pradesh, the Onges of Little

Andaman, the Khasi and Garo of Meghalaya, Social Impact Assessment (SIA) in six core villages of Achankmar Amarkantak Biosphere Reserve, Chhattisgarh, issues in man and environment relation in eight Biosphere Reserves of India. He has co-authored five books and several research articles in national and international journals including two atlases on Scheduled Tribes and Scheduled Castes of India.

Svetlana Ryzhakova is a leading research fellow in Institute of Ethnology and Anthropology, Russian Academy of Science, Moscow. She is PhD and Dr. habil. from Institute of Ethnology and Anthropology, Russian Academy of Science, Moscow, 1998 and 2011. She is also associated with Indian Anthropological Society, European Association of Social Anthropologists. Her major research interests include cultural anthropology, ethnology, mythology and folklore, symbols, regional culture and nationalism, religious practices and performing studies. She has carried out extensive fieldwork in India (West Bengal, Assam, Kerala, Karnataka and Rajasthan), Indonesia (Bali) and Baltic countries since 1998, exploring traditional culture and day-to-day life, local and ethnic identities, myth-making, invention of traditions, communities engaged in arts and crafts creation and transmission. Her writings include books and numerous articles published in scientific international journals: *Language of Ornament in Latvian Culture* (2002), *Cultural Anthropology* (with Dr S. Arutiunov, 2004), *Indian Dance, an Art of Transformation* (2004), *Historica Lettica* (2010); publications on neo-paganism (*dievturiba* and *Romuva*); various local traditions and communities of India. In 1996 she joined class of Guru Rajendra Kumar Gangani in *Kathak Kendra* (New Delhi), so she has both practical experience and theoretical knowledge in Kathak as well as some other forms of performance (kinesthetic and dance traditions of Bengal, Kerala and Karnataka, Manipur, Bali). She performs in India, Russia and European countries, representing both traditional Indian dance styles and her own artistic vision based on extensive research in comparative arts history and theory, philosophy, spirituality and ethnography.

Uddhav Rai completed MA in anthropology from Tribhuvan University (TU), Kathmandu, Nepal, and completed MA (Econ.) in applied social research at Manchester University, UK. Furthermore, he completed post-graduate diploma in universalizing social security for the poor from the Institute of Social Studies, The Hague, Netherlands. Dr Rai received PhD in anthropology from TU with a fellowship from Wenner-Gren foundation at Cornell University with the thesis entitled 'Food Security and Exclusion among the Chepangs of Nepal'. Dr Rai has taught anthropology in TU for 18 years and engaged in development research and provided consultancy services in agriculture and rural development projects of national and international organizations. He has published research papers and articles, and presented papers in national and international symposiums. He is a pioneer to the work on food security of indigenous people of Nepal. Dr Rai has interests in the work on policy issues of food security of marginalized communities of Nepal, South and East Asia.

Urmimala Sarkar Munsi, PhD in social anthropology (with specialization in dance studies), is an associate professor at the School of Arts and Aesthetics, Jawaharlal Nehru University, New Delhi, teaching dance studies and performance documentation methodology. Sarkar Munsi is a choreographer and scholar, and has published widely in national and international journals. Her edited books are *The Moving Space: Women in Dance,* co-edited with Aishika Chakraborty (2017), *Dance: Transcending Borders* and *Traversing Tradition: Celebrating Dance in India* (2010). She has co-authored *Engendering Performance: Indian Women Performers in Search of Identity* (2010) with Dr Bishnupriya Dutt.

Vishvajit Pandya is a professor of anthropology. He earned his doctorate in anthropology from The University of Chicago. He has been involved in ethnographic research in the Andaman Islands since 1983 and has published widely. He has held teaching positions in the United States, New Zealand and India.

Ziya Us Salam is a noted literary and social commentator. A student of history from the University of Delhi, he is engaged in building bridges of commonality between communities through recourse to the Quran and the Vedas. He has been associated with *The Hindu* for almost two decades and has been its features editor for North India editions for 16 years. At present, he is an associate editor, *Frontline*, and writes on sociocultural issues for the magazine besides doing book reviews. A prolific and an acclaimed author, in 2019, he published *Lynch Files*, a take on victims of hate violence, and *365 Tales from Islam*, a book that aims to introduce Islam to children. In the previous year, he had released *Of Saffron Flags and Skull Caps*, a take on the challenges to the idea of India, and *Till Talaq Do Us Part*, a study of various divorce options available in Islam. His book *Delhi 4 Shows*, a study of cinemas since the talkie era began, was released in 2016. His book *Women in Masjid: A Quest for Justice* has been released recently. Ziya was a jury member of the International Film Festival of India (non-feature film, 2011), Best Writing on Cinema (2008) and Vatavaran.

Index

Komal Kothari, 377
Kshatriya cluster, 129
Kuhl, 9
Kurinji, 55

Lahaul and Spiti district
    studied villages in map, 5
    traditional fermented foods, 24
lamb korma, 76
land and people, 93–96
laothai, 260
Lucknow cuisine, 71

Mahali and Dom
    artisan communities, 95
mahua, 96
Malan Bhai
    idol, 381
    myth, helped Manganiyars, 381
Manganiyars community, 369, 371
    doha, 376
    influence of Rajput ideal and
        way of life, 381–382
    khamaghani, 376
    maintenance of segregation, 376
    patronage, reality and
        segregation, 374–378
    scarcity of water, 372
    social situation, 371–374
    subhraj, 376
    weather conditions, 372
Manganiyars community
    Barna, 374
    Dhola Maru ra Duha, 372
    dichotomous situation, 379
marginalization, 203
marhan, 357
master-narrative, 66
meat sellers, 34
medieval period (AD1100–AD1800),
    128
memoir literature, 66
mere rice, 298
me-to-pi, 329
monatandunamey, 151
Mud village, 7

munda, 357
munneer, 55
Munshigunj
    adhia, 215
    Munni Begum, 219
    Papiya, 217
Munshigunj road, 210
    15 line-baris, 211
    multi-functional rooms, 211
musical traditions of India,
    Ethnographic classification, 65
musk melons, 33
Mutiny
    movement, 42
mwitha, 271
Myth of the Holy Cow, 40
mythological patrons of art, 66

Naduvazhis, 128
na gurnai, 256
Nambuthiri Brahmins, 127, 130
napham, 271
National Foundation for the
    Development of Indigenous
    Nationalities (NFDIN), 184
National Mineral Development
    Corporation Limited (NMDC),
    347
natural food, 148
Navodhanaprasthanam, 127
Navratras
    meat shops forcibly closure, 35
Nepal
    Chepangs community, 183
    conversation on food, 182
    food consumption, 182
    food, ritual hierarchy, 182
    people care for others through
        enquiring food, 182
    power of exchange and social
        relations, food, 183
    rice, staple food, 183
Nepal Chepang Association (NCA),
    184
Newari food
    Per Lodwin classification, 187